THOMAS O. LARKIN

A Life of Patriotism and Profit in Old California

THOMAS O. LARKIN

A Life of Patriotism and Profit in Old California

by Harlan Hague and David J. Langum

UNIVERSITY OF OKLAHOMA PRESS : NORMAN AND LONDON

Also by Harlan Hague

Road to California: The Search For a Southern Overland Route, 1540–1848 (Glendale, Calif., 1978)

Also by David J. Langum

(ed.) *Law in the West* (Manhattan, Kans., 1985)
Law and Community on the Mexican California Frontier: Anglo-American Expatriates and the Clash of Legal Traditions, 1821–1846 (Norman, 1987)

Publication of this book is made possible in part through the generous support of The John Randolph Haynes and Dora Haynes Foundation.

Library of Congress Cataloging-in-Publication Data

Hague, Harlan.
    Thomas O. Larkin : a life of patriotism and profit in old
California / by Harlan Hague and David J. Langum.
      p. cm.
    Includes bibliographical references.
    Includes index.
    ISBN 0-8061-2302-8
    1. Larkin, Thomas Oliver, 1802–1858. 2. Pioneers—California—
Biography. 3. Consuls—California—Biography. 4. California—
History—To 1846. 5. California—History—1846–1850. I. Langum,
David J., 1940– . II. Title.
F864.L32H34 1990
979.4'03'092—dc20
[B]   90-50234
                                            CIP

We dedicate this book to our children,
Cary Lynn Hague, Merrilee Catherine Hague,
and Jennifer Michelle Hague
Virginia Eileen Langum and John David Langum

CONTENTS

ILLUSTRATIONS

PREFACE

ALTHOUGH THOMAS O. LARKIN is a major figure in California's transition from Mexican rule to American, we have intended to write a biography and not a history of California. Therefore, we pared the abundantly rich historical materials to those which had a genuine impact on Larkin himself. Another thing we have trimmed is the use of *sic*. Larkin's writing could be described, charitably, as picturesque, as is that of many other nineteenth-century figures. As a result, we would be constantly using *sic*; it seemed simpler to avoid its use entirely except in a few instances where it seemed important to underscore accuracy. Notwithstanding any appearance, the quotations are exact.

Since this was a collaborative effort, we should give the reader some idea of the division of responsibility. Harlan Hague was entirely responsible for chapters 7, 8, 10, 11, and 12 (excepting the concluding paragraphs of chapter 12 which were joint). David J. Langum was entirely responsible for chapters 2, 3, 4, 5, and 9. Chapters 1 and 6 were divided in various ways. Of course we took counsel with one another continuously.

We each have our separate duties of acknowledgement but we share several. We must thank Doyce B. Nunis, Jr., who gave us the benefits of his thoughts on preliminary drafts of several chapters. We are indebted to the Bancroft Library, University of California, Berkeley, for their careful preservation of much of the Larkin materials, and the arrangement of them in a form that readily permits their use. The courtesy of the Bancroft personnel in answering questions and making photocopies was endless. We sincerely thank the John Randolph Haynes and Dora Haynes Foundation for its generous support.

Our chief acknowledgement must be to Larkin himself. Thomas Oliver Larkin was nothing short of a pack rat. He saved most incoming correspondence and had copies made of many outgoing letters. Moreover, he systematically saved such things as butcher bills, statements of account for his daughter's piano lessons, receipts for pew rent from his church, in short all the minutiae that give texture to life as it is actually lived. This is obviously of enormous benefit to the biographer. For example, if one wants to date a particular trip from New York to California, it is possible to pick up and hold in one's hands Larkin's dated receipt for the rental of a mule with which to cross the Isthmus of Panama. The biographer can feel quite connected across time with such a man.

Each of us has special acknowledgments. Harlan Hague wishes to thank the staff of the Huntington Library for everything they do on a regular basis to make research at the Huntington a joy. Special thanks go to Martin Ridge for his encouragement and to William P. Frank who showed me the uncatalogued papers now known as the Larkin Family Collection. Thanks also go to Charlene Gilbert of the California State Archives and the personnel of the California Historical Society Library in San Francisco and the California State Library in Sacramento for their assistance. I would like to acknowledge the encouragement of George P. Hammond in the early stages of my work on Larkin, and of Doyce B. Nunis, Jr., who had much to do with the beginning of the project.

I am grateful to the Huntington Library and to the Sourisseau Academy for research and travel grants. I hope they will find the product of their generosity acceptable, as I found their assistance crucial. I wish also to acknowledge the support of San Joaquin Delta College for a sabbatical which included work on Mexican California.

Finally, I want to express my appreciation to my wife and daughters for sharing our home for these many years, longer than we expected, with that other immigrant.

HARLAN HAGUE
Stockton, California

David J. Langum has special thanks to Barbara J. Burdick, formerly Curator of the Larkin House in Monterey, for permission to look closely at several items in the house, including family genealogies and photographs, many previously unpublished, found in Larkin's bedroom. She helpfully arranged the duplication of these genealogies and the numerous illustrations used in this book that are based on materials in the Larkin House. Thanks are also due to Jonathan F. Williams, Supervising Ranger of the Monterey State Historic Park, for his help with the photographs, their duplication and permissions.

I also wish to thank the Cumberland School of Law, Samford University, not only for its financial and institutional support, but more importantly for an institutional climate that encourages scholarly research. Edward Craig and Rebecca Hutto of the Cordell Hull Law Library, here at Cumberland, were very helpful in arranging considerable numbers of interlibrary loans. Burton Weaver, Administrator of Trinity Episcopal Church, San Francisco, and Jane Porter, Keeper of the Portsmouth Athenaeum, both were kind in answering special inquiries about Larkin.

Special thanks are due to my daughter, Virginia Eileen Langum, who was always enthusiastic and encouraging. I benefited greatly from the very close readings of the draft manuscript by Benjamin F. Gilbert and by Monte A. Horton. During my many research trips to the San Francisco

Bay Area I was sustained with the fine conversation and company, not to mention bed and board, of good friends Stanley and Joan Siddle.

Thomas Oliver Larkin was a man who overcame many obstacles and long odds by quiet persistence and hard work. Two young men of my close acquaintance have helped me to understand Larkin by their own examples. One is Dean James Puccini, my stepson from California days, who has demonstrated these characteristics in his successful educational endeavors. The other is my own son, John David Langum, who on a daily basis is still struggling persistently against severe physical disabilities. I am proud of them both.

DAVID J. LANGUM
Birmingham, Alabama

THOMAS O. LARKIN

A Life of Patriotism and Profit in Old California

CHAPTER 1

INTRODUCTION

LARKIN laid the paper on the desk in front of him. It was a message from James K. Polk, President of the United States. Written in Washington, D.C., October 17, 1845, exactly six months had passed before the dispatch reached Larkin on April 17, 1846, in Monterey, Upper California, Mexico. He selected a pen from a box and pondered his reply.

It was to be a thoughtful, deliberate response. Larkin had already requested Captain William Mervine, in command of the United States Sloop of War *Cyane* at anchor in Monterey harbor, to delay his scheduled departure for a day to allow Larkin to compose his response and for Mervine to carry it back to the United States. Doubtless, Larkin read and reread President Polk's message contained in the dispatch written by Secretary of State James Buchanan:

> . . . should California assert and maintain her independence, we shall render her all the kind offices in our power as a Sister Republic. . . . Whilst . . . this Government does not . . . intend to interfere between Mexico and California, they would vigorously interpose to prevent the latter from becoming a British or French Colony. . . . Whilst the President will make no effort and use no influence to induce California to become one of the free and independent States of this Union, yet if the People should desire to unite their destiny with ours, they would be received as brethren.[1]

Surely Larkin focused particularly on words outlining his functions:

> On all proper occasions, you should not fail prudently to warn the Government and people of California of the danger of such an interference to their peace and prosperity—to inspire them with a jealousy of European dominion and to arouse in their bosoms that love of liberty and independence so natural

3

to the American Continent. . . . In addition to your Consular functions, the President has thought proper to appoint you a Confidential Agent in California. . . . You will take care not to awaken the jealousy of the French and English Agents there. . . . You will not fail by every safe opportunity to keep the Department advised of the progress of events in California, and the disposition of the authorities and people toward the United States.[2]

Thomas Oliver Larkin—successful merchant, financier, confidant of California officials, and American consul to Mexican California—was now a secret agent of the President of the United States. Although he was a serious man, Larkin probably smiled ever so slightly. Larkin's appointment gave official sanction to do what he had been attempting for some time: to influence the Californians to separate from Mexico and to establish an independent republic. Because of the suspected machinations of other countries, chiefly Great Britain and France, Larkin had come to believe that an independent California must seek a close association with the United States. Only this would ensure California's safety and freedom from European domination.

Perhaps Larkin sought some night air. His second story porch was at hand. From it he could gaze over the rooftops and enclosed courtyards of Monterey. If it were the usual night he would see a crude Mexican cart, the *carreta*, drawn by oxen moving slowly down the unpaved street. A mounted *vaquero* might flash by the cart at full gallop, leaving a trail of billowing dust in his wake, while a richly dressed *ranchero* rode his mount with more dignity. The air would have been filled with the perfume of spring flowers.

Had he glanced toward the waterfront, he would have seen the customhouse that he had built for the government four years before, and beyond it, Monterey Bay. Just offshore the *Cyane* rocked at anchor. The warship had arrived only that day. Lieutenant Archibald H. Gillespie, United States Marines, was on board, traveling in disguise as a convalescing merchant. In reality he was an American courier, and he quickly summoned Consul Larkin on board to deliver the Secretary of State's letter.[3] Beyond the *Cyane*, to the north, a ring of green hills fronted by sandy beaches encircled the bay. Now calm, the bay had been the sometimes stormy arena around which much of the drama of Hispanic California had unfolded.

Spanish navigators had sighted Monterey Bay as early as the sixteenth century. But settlement in California was not made until the spring 1769 arrival of the expedition headed by Captain Gaspar de Portolá. The initial colonists consisted of six Franciscan missionaries and soldiers to protect them. Actual occupancy by Spaniards was thought necessary to thwart supposed British and Russian designs to the region, and the Portolá party came armed with a mandate to establish a permanent Spanish presence.

The Spanish had employed the mission for many years as their principal tool for civilizing frontier regions. Indians were encouraged to cluster around the missions, where the padres taught them the Catholic faith, trades, farming, and stock raising. Under their tutelage Indians were to learn the Spanish way of life.

The mission was never meant to be permanent, but simply a station for Indians on the road to the white man's ways. Once it had accomplished its civilizing objective, the mission would be secularized, reduced in status to a simple parish church. Mission properties were then to be distributed among the civilized Indians, who would take their places as equal members of the local Hispanic society. Royal regulations prescribed ten years for the process, but the system in fact never worked so efficiently. The California missions continued to serve their original purpose beyond the period of Spanish occupation, 1769–1821.

Some soldiers served as guards at the missions, but the Spanish quickly built forts at San Diego, Monterey, San Francisco, and Santa Barbara to quarter most of their forces. These *presidios* were woefully inadequate for defense; their troops were few in number, indifferently trained, poorly equipped, and often unpaid. As the provincial capital, the Monterey presidio enjoyed a relative superiority over the others.

Within a decade of the original occupation the Spanish authorities induced civilians, both male and female, to trek northward from Mexico to California and populate the small communities known as *pueblos*. These towns provided only minimum comforts and were squalid and dusty by today's standards. The population growth was agonizingly slow because abundant lands remained available much closer to the center of Mexico. In spite of inducements offered by the viceroyal government to colonize California, there were few takers. The civilian population had to be augmented by convicts and orphans, and soldiers induced to retire in the pueblos.

The beginnings of the missions were as inauspicious as those of the pueblos and presidios. In the early days the padres struggled simply to survive. However, the missionaries planned well and founded their missions at locations whose qualities had already been recognized by the presence of a substantial local Indian population. Eventually the missions began to succeed and then to thrive. Eventually, twenty-one were built in Alta California, the last in Sonoma in 1823 following the success of the Mexican revolution.

From the capital of Monterey, the Spanish governors presided over a pastoral California that was little influenced by the world beyond its shores. However, New Spain, like most of Spain's other American colonies, had rebelled during the turmoil of the mother country's preoccupation in the Napoleonic wars. After a decade of struggle, independent Mexico was born in 1821. Californians took almost no part in the revolution, but on the whole their sympathies were with Spain. Soldier, settler, or missionary, each had benefited in various ways from royal largess. Nevertheless, there was little resistance to the change, and California accepted her Mexican status quietly. The last Spanish governor simply stayed on as the first under the Mexican regime.

The missions reached the peak of their influence and prosperity in the early 1830s. The Indian population at the missions peaked in 1821 with about 21,000. However, livestock continued to climb. By the end of 1832, mission herds numbered 151,000 cattle, 138,000 sheep, and 60,000 horses.[4] The converted Indians, or neophytes, harvested thousands of bushels of wheat each year. Corn, beans, and other vegetable crops were grown as well. Mission industries varied as local need and commerce required. Skilled Indian labor produced wine and brandy, leather, soap, brick and tile, tobacco, cotton and linen cloth, wool, carts, saddles and bridles, sheepskins, and more. By the early 1830s, the missions had become almost entirely self-sufficient and the chief source of goods for trade.

The very success of the missions proved their undoing. Since almost all were older than the unrealistic ten years, the Mexican authorities concluded to convert them into parish churches and take their lands and herds from the control of the padres. This process of secularization, undertaken in California in the mid-1830s, in theory was meant to benefit the Indians. Each would receive a share of the mission's land and livestock and would thereby become self-reliant.

Notwithstanding the theory, secularization in fact was a disaster for the Indians, heartbreak for the missionaries, and a boon for the land grantees whose ranches were carved out from former mission lands. Indians were caught between two cultures. They had lost their primitive way of life, but had not yet absorbed the new. Instead of becoming independent owners of the soil, the Indian population became employees of the rancheros, hired to tend the stock and care for the crops.

Almost all of the great land-grant ranches originated during the Mexican administration. Less than twenty land titles were granted by Spain. However, after independence the local government offered huge grants to encourage economic development. The minimum size for *ranchos* was usually one league, or about 4,500 acres, and the maximum was eleven square leagues. Following secularization in 1834–1836, choice ranges of the missions became available and passed quickly into private hands. Between 1834 and 1846, private owners received more than 600 rancho grants, including garden plots.

Most grants were enormous, some stretching for miles, and their herds of cattle, sheep, and horses numbered in the thousands. Cattle provided beef, leather, and tallow. But of supreme importance, the cattle provided hides, the "California bank notes," that became both the primary medium of exchange in specie-short California and the principal export commodity.

By the 1840s, California's population of whites, half-bloods, and assimilated Indians numbered about 14,000. Of these, perhaps 60 percent lived on the ranchos. The remainder lived in the few towns. A well-to-do ranchero might have a house in town in addition to his ranch properties.

There was always time for play in this placid society. Gambling was a popular pastime, although officially disapproved. Californians bet on bull-and-bear fights, fighting cocks, horse races, and cards. They greatly enjoyed dancing and were always ready for an evening fiesta. The numerous Saints' Days provided opportunites for festive picnics outside the towns where dozens could feast on barbecued slabs of beef, turkeys, and chickens. When the meal was finished guitars were tuned and the *Californios* whiled away the afternoon with dancing and singing. Large weddings provided another source of community entertainment.

In the world of work, cattle raising was primary. It had been so even in the Spanish period. Cattle provided occupation, food, fiber, and fat. Beef was always the staple food of California and was eaten both fresh and dried. Rawhide was an essential ingredient in locally made saddles, harnesses, shoes, chairs, beds, mats, and rope. The Californios used cattle fat in cooking and in the manufacture of candles and soap. But the small California market was easily supplied. A few shipments of hides and tallow had been made to San Blas during the Spanish era, but the amounts were small. By the beginning of independent Mexico in 1821, the herds had grown so large that the supply far outstripped demand.

Foreigners saw opportunity in the excess. Cattle hide was useful in the industrial manufacture of many articles of clothing, especially shoes. Soapmakers employed the rendered fat or tallow. Mexico had just opened her ports to foreigners, and the first to seize upon these advantages was the English partnership of McCulloch and Hartnell, which negotiated a three-year monopoly in 1823 with most of the California missions. Even before the expiration of that agreement, American competitors arrived on the scene. Soon Boston companies dominated the market, bringing American manufactures to remote California to sell for hides and tallow. The hide and tallow trade dominated Mexican California's economy. It remained the most important business activity in California before the Gold Rush.

As the trade increased more Americans established residence in California. Some served as local managers of their firms' businesses; a few, including Thomas O. Larkin, carved out positions as independent merchants or middlemen, standing between the rancheros and the hide ships. Others saw different opportunities as ranchers or artisans. Typically, these early American settlers arrived by sea, although a few drifted overland from New Mexico.

These American immigrants of the 1820s thoroughly assimilated into Hispanic ways. They accepted baptism into the Catholic Church and naturalization as Mexican citizens; most married California women. Some married quite well and aligned themselves with Mexican California's most prestigious families. These Americans learned Spanish, adopted the local dress, and Hispanicized their names. This pattern contrasts sharply with the Americans who arrived by overland in the 1840s. As Mexican citizens this first group of American immigrants into California applied for and received many land grants. They accumulated great herds of cattle, held government posts, conducted most of California's business and financial affairs, raised large families, and contentedly prospered.

Thomas O. Larkin was one of these pioneer American residents. He was similar to the others, and yet was different in many respects. Arriving in 1832, he expected California to make him a rich man, and she did. But he did not convert to Catholicism, and he did not marry a local Hispanic woman. Instead, Larkin married an American widow in a Protestant ceremony. He steadfastly refused to become a Mexican citizen in spite of the economic and political advantages of such citizenship.

Larkin was entrepreneur par excellence. He owned a store, manufactured soap, supplied whaling ships and gold miners, cut and shipped lumber, speculated in land, operated ranchos, and introduced banking to California. Though he remained an alien, he was on the best of terms with California's Mexican leaders. Larkin's appointment in 1843 as United States consul was simple acknowledgment that he was California's foremost American.

Consul Larkin had to deal with a California government best known for its inconstancy. After independence California passed through a steady succession of tumult and revolt. Californios regularly overthrew and expelled governors sent from Mexico, and dissension among even the local politicos frequently led to conflict. By the early 1840s, the affairs of California government seemed bound in endless, agonizing chaos.

Wiser California leaders began to ponder the future. They wondered whether they should separate themselves from Mexico and associate California with a power that could ensure their stability and safety. If so, to which country should they turn for succor? France? Great Britain? The United States? As of April 1846, when Larkin was reading his letter from the Secretary of State, all were candidates.

The question was about to be settled for the Californians. Though both Great Britain and France had shown more than passing interest in California, their citizens had not responded by significant settlement. It was different with the Americans. Beginning in the early 1840s, California became a magnet to American overland migrants.

The first American overlanders were mountain men, trappers of beaver, such as Jedediah Smith in 1826 and 1827, James Ohio Pattie in 1828, Ewing Young in 1830, William Wolfskill in 1831, and Joseph R. Walker in 1833. The first Americans who crossed the Sierra Nevada as bona fide settlers came in 1841. The Bidwell-Bartleson party, a band of enthusiastic greenhorns, fortunately fell in with a Jesuit missionary group. At Soda Springs, Idaho, the party split. Travelers for Oregon continued northwestward with their guide, the redoubtable mountain man, Thomas Fitzpatrick. Those that remained bound for California bade farewell to their guides and turned southwestward. From that point these thirty-four pioneers broke a new trail, arriving in California at John Marsh's rancho at the foot of Mt. Diablo on November 4. Only days later the Workman-Rowland party from New Mexico reached southern California over the Old Spanish Trail. Another party brought three American familes south from Oregon to California in December 1841.

The emigrant trains thereafter located new paths, but also improved and stabilized existing routes. The year of 1843 saw significant explorations. A small group led by Joseph B. Chiles, who had been with the Bidwell-Bartleson party, returned east in 1842 and found a new, more direct route to California from Fort Boise along the Malheur and Pit rivers. Joseph R. Walker took a group through the Owens Valley and across the Sierra through Walker Pass. A band commanded by Lansford W. Hastings arrived in California from Oregon. Then in 1844 the Stevens-Murphy party followed the increasingly popular Platte-Humboldt route over the plains, pioneered the Truckee trail across the Sierra Nevada, and became the first party to bring wagons the entire journey.

The 1845 migration was the largest yet, including at least six groups. One party alone, the Grigsby-Ide band, coming by the Humboldt-Truckee route, counted over 100 members. Americans also continued to move south from Oregon to California. The McMahon-Clyman group from Oregon included 43 persons. Altogether over 250 Americans entered the Mexican department of California in 1845 alone. All lacked the legally required passports, yet all sought permanent homes.

These hopeful seekers were responding to a steady increase of California publicity. Americans read about the wonders of the distant paradise in newspapers and magazines and heard about it from returning travelers. In 1840, the year before he had joined the first pioneer overland party, John Bidwell had listened in awe to Antoine Robidoux's description of this fertile land where it was always spring, where everyone was happy and friendly, and where there was no fever. Official reports of the government exploring parties, those of Charles Wilkes in 1841 and John C. Frémont in 1843–1844, were published promptly and widely read. Lansford Hastings, an ambitious early traveler to California, was back in the United States in 1844, beating on the migration drum, and writing his influential travelers' guide.

But it was not just travelers and sojourners who aroused interest. Americans also read about California in the words of those who should know it best: expatriate countrymen who lived there. In addition to his regular correspondence with government officials, Consul Larkin wrote often to eastern newspapers, extolling California's virtues. John Marsh, an influential

American who lived near the slopes of Mt. Diablo not far from San Francisco, at Larkin's urging wrote similarly to editors. Newspapers throughout the United States picked up these letters and columns and reprinted them.

The shrill cry of Manifest Destiny swept the United States in the mid-1840s. Tinsel patriots from the Missouri frontier to the nation's capital urged American migrants on, to fulfill their divinely appointed task to expand and encompass all the lands of the North American continent that lay westward. The expansionists deemed any inquiry whether this might be stealing as irrelevant. Instead, the question they saw was whether to "extend the 'area of freedom' by the annexation of California?"[5] It was a foregone conclusion to Alfred Robinson, an 1828 American resident in early California who returned home in 1842 and published his recollections in the spring of 1846: ". . . it must come to pass, for the march of emigration is to the West, and naught will arrest its advance but the mighty ocean."[6] The overlanders were to be the cutting edge of American imperialism.

These new American immigrants into California were different from those who had entered before the 1840s and had become happily assimilated. The overlanders had no desire to assimilate. They neither applied for citizenship, learned Spanish, nor observed local mores. Most hated all things Mexican and established their farms in the interior where they were far from official control. They were far more agriculturally inclined than the earlier arrivals. These immigrants wanted land and were prepared to buy it if they could, and steal it if they must.

Whereas the earlier Americans were satisfied to live their lives in a Mexican department, the newer arrivals had brought their flag with them. They did not expect California to remain Mexican. The United States had long been interested in California and had more than once attempted to purchase it. The overlanders were embued with Manifest Destiny and convinced that it was only a matter of time until the Stars and Stripes waved over California. If they could assist the process, they stood ready. Once they learned that the empty lands on which they squatted were owned by other men, the trespassing Americans perceived that a revolution could be a means of regularizing their titles.

Settlers talked increasingly of a "Texas solution," remembering that American settlement during the 1820s in Mexican Texas was followed by a revolution, then independence, and eventual annexation to the United States in 1845. The Mexican government was aware of a similar pattern emerging in California. Officials had vainly attempted to forbid but had failed even to slow American immigration to California. There was even brave talk of expelling those who had entered illegally. But the Mexican officials, both in California and Mexico City, were powerless to stanch the flow of Americans.

Some California leaders openly welcomed closer ties with the United States. More feared domination by the expanionist, belligerent *norteameri-*

canos, but knew not what could be done. All leaders were worried about the growing possibility of violence. And throughout the spring of 1846 that possibility was increasing.

American visitors to Mexican California left undisguised their contempt for her owners. A visitor of 1840 wrote that "the Californians are an imbecile, pusillanimous race of men, and unfit to control the destinies of that beautiful country."[7] These Californians, other visitors added, were "a lazy, indolent and cowardly people . . . they are only a grade above the aborigines, and like them they will soon be compelled from the very nature of things, to yield to the swelling tide of Anglo-Saxon adventure."[8]

It was not just a matter of land. There were religious conflicts as well between the Catholic Californios and the American Protestants, whose heads spun with visions of God leading their march to the Pacific. Even such simple things as manners were in dispute. Many observers, Mexican, American, and European, commented over the rough, crude character of the majority of the American immigrants. They settled in a country where, in Bernard DeVoto's phrase, "the standard of living was far below the standard of manners."[9]

The contrast could not be more complete. Such a perceptive observer as Robert Louis Stevenson noted even later in an 1879 visit, speaking of the old-line Mexican Californian, that "it was a matter of perpetual surprise to find, in that world of absolutely mannerless Americans, a people full of deportment, solemnly courteous, and doing all things with grace and decorum."[10] In the later days of Mexican California the native Californians must have felt under siege by barbarians already within the gates.

Earlier in January of that eventful year of 1846, an armed military exploring party under Frémont had entered California without permission. As consul, Larkin had obtained consent for the Americans to winter in the department under condition that they would not enter the populated coastal regions. But in early March, Frémont had defied the California authorities by bringing his troops to Salinas, near Monterey. José Castro, the California military commander, then ordered them out of California. With a spasm of rodomontade, Frémont ensconced himself on top of the nearest mountain, Hawk's Peak, also known as Gavilan and Frémont, in the Gabilan Range overlooking the Salinas Valley. Castro brought his troops into line at the base of the mountain. Consul Larkin had worked desperately and narrowly averted bloodshed as Frémont slipped north for Sutter's Fort.

That had been only a month before the Secretary of State's letter arrived. Larkin must have pondered all these things as he read and reread the President's message. By the time of its receipt, April 17, 1846, the storm clouds of violence were building over California. That same day a young American, a paradigm for his entire nation, sat down in Sonoma, California, less than 200 miles from Larkin. He wrote a news-filled letter to his folks in Springfield, Illinois. This young man, William Todd, nephew of Mrs.

Abraham Lincoln, the future first lady, told his parents that "there will be a revolution before long and probably the country will be annexed to the United States. . . . I will take a hand in it." [11]

For several years Larkin had been patiently working for the peaceful Americanization of California. And now the Secretary's letter gave him official permission and approval. The hours were passing rapidly, and the *Cyane* had to sail. Larkin picked up his pen, dipped the tip in the inkwell, and wrote that he accepted "with unfeigned satisfaction the appointment now offered." [12] But would this man, Thomas Oliver Larkin, be able to succeed? Would he have time to accomplish his goal for the Californians themselves to agree upon an independent or American California? Was there time for a peaceful solution or would the rising tide of conflict and bloodshed overtake his purpose?

CHAPTER 2

YOUTH AND EARLY MANHOOD
MASSACHUSETTS AND
NORTH CAROLINA

WHO WAS THIS MAN, Thomas Oliver Larkin? What was his character, his merit, and how did he come to be a confidential agent of the President of the United States?

Larkin was a New Englander, born September 16, 1802, in Charlestown, Massachusetts, just across the Charles River from Boston.[1] On his father's side he came from ancient Yankee stock. One ancestor, Edward Larkin, had been a freeman of Charlestown in 1638. Through his paternal grandmother he was descended from Richard Warren, an immigrant on the *Mayflower*.[2]

Larkin's father was born too late, on July 11, 1769, to be more than a boy during the American Revolution. But Larkin's grandfather, Ebenezer Larkin, born on May 13, 1740,[3] had been active in the Boston tea controversy, and the horse ridden by Paul Revere on his famous ride of April 18, 1775 was owned by a relative.[4] Ebenezer and his brothers fought in the battle of Bunker Hill and family tradition has it, through an account from Larkin's son, that Ebenezer's house was "destroyed, burnt to the ground by hot shot from the fleet of Lord Howe during the bombardment of that town, while the battle of Bunker Hill was progressing."[5]

The background annals of Larkin's mother are simpler. Ann Rogers was born July 18, 1771, the daughter of an English sea captain, William Rogers, and his wife Martha. Ann was a native of Alderney Island, one of the English Channel Islands. Many of her relatives were shipmasters.[6]

In those years the life of a man or woman, while not necessarily "nasty, brutish, and short," often was indeed short. Ann Rogers was destined to know three husbands before her own death in April 1818 at age forty-seven, the first two unions having been dissolved not by divorce, but by death.

13

This accounts for Larkin's complicated family structure, with many half-brothers, stepbrothers, and cousins as well as full siblings.[7]

Ann's first marriage was to a ship's captain, Thomas Cooper, from Christchurch in Hampshire, England. This union produced one child, a son, whose birth was registered on Alderney, September 11, 1791. This boy, John Rogers Cooper, himself became a sea captain, settled in Mexican California in 1823, and was to be the immediate cause of the later move by Larkin, his younger half-brother, to the Pacific coast.

Ann's husband Thomas died at sea only a few years after the birth of their son. The widow and her son moved to Boston to join her sister, Martha. There she met Larkin's father, whom she married as her second husband, on November 29, 1801. There were five children of this marriage, including Thomas Oliver.

Young Thomas had the exact name of his father, Thomas Oliver Larkin, but almost never used a "junior" designation and was known as Oliver within the family. Perhaps the disuse of the junior was because his father died on April 18, 1808, in Charleston, Massachusetts, when the boy was less than six years old. Two of Larkin's siblings died as infants and one brother, William, with whom Thomas was close, at age seventeen. Only a sister, Ann Rogers Larkin, later married to Otis Wright, survived to adulthood. She was close to Larkin and, as a good correspondent, kept Larkin in touch with family news during his California days.

In 1813, the widow, Ann Rogers Cooper Larkin, moved with her family to Lynn, Massachusetts, a small town about ten miles north of Boston. In later years Larkin would regard Lynn as his hometown. The purpose of the move was for Ann to marry Amariah Childs on October 24, 1813. Thereby Larkin acquired not only a stepfather, but a new set of relatives. Ann's third marriage, like her first, occasioned only one child, George Edwin Childs, who became another half-brother to Larkin. However, Amariah was a widower with ten children from his first marriage.[8]

Not only did Larkin acquire ten new stepbrothers and stepsisters, but these new stepsiblings were also his cousins. This combination came about because Amariah's first wife was Ruth Larkin, a sister of Thomas Oliver Larkin's father. One of these new stepbrothers, simultaneously a cousin, was Ebenezer Larkin Childs.[9] He would become very close to Larkin and play a role in Larkin's life, in the move to California and the consular appointment, surpassing even that of half-brother Cooper.

Amariah Childs, Larkin's new stepfather, was a well-to-do banker with additional interests in leather manufacturing.[10] Apparently he treated young Thomas with tenderness and consideration. Amariah was very tight with his wealth and keenly interested in the making of money. Years later, in 1843, Ebenezer L. Childs, a close cousin, wrote Larkin in California that "father looks old, but is hearty & vigorous, still intent on the acquisition of money. He is said to be one of the richest men in town [i.e., Lynn, Mas-

Larkin's father, Thomas Oliver Larkin, Sr., died when Larkin was five years old. Photograph of damaged miniature portrait. Photographer, Chuck Bancroft. Courtesy State of California, Department of Parks and Recreation.

Larkin's sister, Ann Rogers Larkin Wright, with whom he maintained an extensive correspondence. From photograph in possession of State of California, Department of Parks and Recreation. Photographer, Chuck Bancroft. Courtesy Society of California Pioneers.

sachusetts] . . . . He has no charity for those who owe him & cannot or will not pay, & is as eager for money as he ever was."[11]

One of Thomas Oliver Larkin's lifelong traits was an eagerness for wealth, not for its enjoyment, although as he grew older he finally learned to enjoy wealth, but primarily for the joy of the process of making money. He was a classical capitalist. Larkin was but a boy of eleven when Amariah became his stepfather, and it is undoubtedly from him that he took on the acquisitive trait of character so pronounced throughout his life. At the same time it should be said that Amariah was not so tight that he refused to help Thomas, on at least one occasion, with a loan.

There is little that can be said with precision about Larkin's childhood and his upbringing. In personality, Larkin's sister described Larkin's eldest son, then just thirteen, as "presicely what you [i.e., Larkin] was at his age, ambitious, and fearless of danger." Another relative wrote that "Oliver [Larkin's son] resembles his Father. I mean when you was of his age though he is not quite so handsome. . . . you was thought a very beautiful boy from your birth and through your Childhood and youth."[12] In deportment, his stepbrother recalled, "You were a very nice & particular boy if I remember aright, but still I suspect you were not *always* in band-box order," while Larkin himself warned a relative in 1847, whom his son was visiting, that the lad was "of a speculative mind and may ask for a host of articles. At his age you remember I was just where he now is, and was a great trader for a boy."[13]

Larkin had some formal education, but was unpolished. He was sensitive to his deficiences and eager to compensate for them. Larkin's letters are replete with grammatical and spelling errors, and he was well aware of this. In May 1846, he insisted that the *New York Sun* carefully edit his letters describing California before the newspaper published them. He advised the publisher of the self-evident truth that "the letters I may send will require you carfull correctig in stile or grammer."[14] Another clue to his sensitivity is that letters Larkin personally regarded as important, particularly his official letters to the Secretary of State written as consul or to the President as confidential agent, are letter perfect.[15] Obviously Larkin sought editorial assistance in Monterey for his official correspondence.

Characteristic of many men lacking significant formal education, Larkin was an avid reader. As a young man he kept a travel diary during the years 1821–1826. He included many poetic quotations, particularly from Lord Byron. For several of the cities through which he passed, he made specific mention of libraries and bookstores. Under Camden, South Carolina, he wrote: "I saw no Book Store, or Auction here. A Southern City must be very large to support the former. They think they have no time to read." In contrast, for Lancaster, Massachusetts, he observed: "Literature is here Cultivated, the Literati are numerous. Their Bookstore and library are well encouraged."

These observations from 1824 and 1825 reflect a lingering professional interest in books since Larkin's first occupation, commenced in 1817, was the making of books, and his second was the selling of them. They also show the beginnings of his lifelong interest in reading.

As a youth Larkin obviously received some religious training. When a young man, he made only occasional scriptural allusions in his diary. He commented extensively on the style of service and size of congregation of several churches in Wilmington, North Carolina. He obviously had attended many of these churches on several occasions. He went to an entire series of sermons by the popular New England Universalist clergyman, Abner Kneeland. In traveling he mentioned the churches of the towns through which he passed. Once, in Charleston, South Carolina, he attended services at a synagogue.

Larkin's comments do not reveal which church he had attended as a child. One of his cousins became a Congregational pastor,[16] but it was probably the Anglican, Episcopal Church of his mother which he attended.[17] Later in life Larkin was a member of Trinity Episcopal Church in San Francisco, and he was buried from that church.[18] Larkin's uncle, Samuel, of Portsmouth, New Hampshire, was also an Episcopalian,[19] and one son of Ebenezer Childs, the stepbrother with whom Larkin was so close, became an Episcopalian clergyman.[20] In any event Larkin's childhood church was certainly Protestant and of New England simplicity. In Charleston, South Carolina, he observed the churches there were "unlike any I had seen before. They look more like those old churches I have read of in the old country, dark and gigantic, gloomy to the extreem, hung all round with large paintings, of the oldest dates, they look'd."

For a young man in his early twenties Larkin paid religion considerable attention, and this doubtless reflected an emphasis experienced as a child. Yet in 1826, in youthful rebellion, he wrote that "about the other world, I am not prepared to say. Its said in the multitude of counsellors there is safety, and in the multitude of ministers, there is confusion so I can not decide." Obviously Larkin knew his Bible well, as that easy, casual reference to Proverbs 11:14 suggests. The topic of religion would play a role in his California experiences.

In October 1817, just a few weeks after his fifteenth birthday, Larkin left Lynn for Boston "to learn the art of making books." While Larkin was living in Boston and learning that trade, his mother died, in April 1818, at age forty-seven. "There went the last of my peace and innocence," he wrote later, still deeply affected, "Peace be to her."

The making of books might be an art, but young Larkin quickly decided that it was a "poor business." There was more than money involved, however. Larkin refused to subject himself to training, to bow his head to authority, and instead he was, as he himself said, "stubbord." In 1819, he abandoned bookmaking and, staying in Boston, began working in a book and stationery store.[21] But he soon found he had "jumped from the pan into the coals." If bookmaking were a poor business, bookselling was too confining. "My collar began to chafe me," he wrote, "as I grew up saw the halter plainer, thought it might grow too strong."

On October 17, 1821, Larkin decided to leave Boston. Only three days later he sailed on the schooner *Maria*, bound for Wilmington, North Carolina. Wilmington was but a small rude port for the exportation of agricultural products, the importation of supplies for planters, and the amenities of life. Her free population in 1820 was a mere 1,098;[22] and the entire county in which the city was located counted only 4,921 whites and 341 free blacks in 1830.[23] Larkin estimated the city's 1821 population at 3,000, with half being slaves. It is unclear why Larkin chose this destination. He departed with a friend, Thomas G. Thurston, "to seak our fortunes, and rise or fall one with the other. . . . and share the humours and reverses of fortune in company." The two youthful New Englanders were off on an adventure.

The pair enjoyed a pleasant voyage and along with the ship's five other passengers landed in Wilmington on October 28. Here was a shock. The yellow fever was raging and most of the population had fled, leaving a town "without inhabitants enough to make a funirel." Larkin found himself without friends, without employment, and with little money. He "thought all day on the subject, and dreamt on the same at Night. Stood it out." Shortly the fever subsided and the Wilmington population returned.

Larkin found employment as a clerk within two weeks after arrival and began an investigation of the area's prospects. He was not favorably impressed; his initial reaction was that Wilmington would "never flourish to any great degree." Nevertheless, the two youthful adventurers confirmed their agreement to share their fates and entered into a written agreement in Wilmington dated November 11, 1821. In it they promised to "form a connection in business and share equally the expenses and profits to which may arise in all business done by us" for the period beginning October 20, 1821, and ending June 20, 1822. They further pledged that "if either of us should die in the above stated time the surviving one shall take . . . care of all clothes papers writings and effects of the deceased as far as lays in his power so to do and deliver the same to the relations or friends of the deceased."[24]

Perhaps the job was unsatisfactory or it was a matter of youthful impatience, but Larkin soon readied himself to leave Wilmington. He signed on as the cargo manager, or supercargo, on the ship *Susan* bound for Bermuda. Larkin was to be paid $20 per month and 2 1/2 percent of the cargo sales. From Bermuda Larkin intended to travel by himself to the Bahamas and to remain there for several years.

The *Susan* departed Wilmington, with Larkin on board, in February 1822. The voyage proved a disaster. The captain was frequently intoxicated and issued drunken threats to all. In Bermuda Larkin learned that business in the Bahamas was poor. Disappointed, he returned to Wilmington in April. Not only was Larkin not paid his wages and sales percentage, he was cheated of a small cargo he had shipped on his own account and lost the small sum he had advanced to furnish supplies for the ship.

After this miserable experience before the mast, Wilmington must have looked better. Larkin and Thurston opened a small store in June 1822. The two young men wrote to friends, and probably anyone they could think of, asking for financial assistance and capital. One of Larkin's correspondents replied that he did not believe there was an honest man south of Philadelphia. Since Larkin was now considerably further south, this erstwhile friend would lend him no money. Thurston had more success and received about $1,800 worth of goods to serve as an initial stock in trade.

The firm of Thurston and Larkin was primarily engaged in the retail sale of merchandise. Their partnership was renewed when the first agreement expired on June 20, 1822. This second partnership agreement established a broader agency and undertaking, essentially a more sophisticated version of their earlier agreement. It had an open time period and provided that "whatever laudable business either of the said parties may be concerned in whether in merchandise or other proffitable business the other party shall be equally concernd and connected as the contracting party."[25]

The two partners found their path "easy and Smooth." Nevertheless, they were merely making a living, not accumulating profits, and hardly moving towards wealth. In about two years they dissolved the partnership "with no profits, but considerable experience to go upon in future," as Larkin put it. Business failure or dissatisfaction was not the apparent cause for the winding up, but rather the desire of Larkin to take an extensive holiday in New England during the summer of 1824. Ostensibly the dissolution was amicable, but in fact Thurston held deep resentments which would surface later.

Just before his departure for the North in July 1824, Larkin traveled to a plantation some fifty miles northwest of Wilmington in Sampson County to settle some business. He rode the entire distance on horseback in one day. It was warm weather and he arrived at midnight, "completely wore down." For the next week he was in bed, desperately ill. He was so sick he thought he was dying, but at the end of the week Larkin made his way back to Wilmington and boarded a packet for New York. So severe had been the attack, probably of yellow fever, that after ten days at sea his condition was still so visible and pronounced that the "health Officer had a hard eye on my fever lips," before allowing Larkin to disembark.

The vacation in the north was enjoyable, although Larkin grew melancholy with the changes in sights and associations compared with his remembrance of years past. Few outside of immediate family seemed to remember him. His analysis of Boston was uncanny. The city had changed and improved considerably, he noted. But it was little compared to the energy of

New York. Soon, he predicted, New York City would eclipse Boston as a
harbor and the Massachusetts legislators, absorbed with trivia, "may walk
out of the house and find a branch of the Erie Canal runing between them
and their common. . . . N.Y. is the London of America and will one day
compare with old London herself."

In October 1824, Larkin sailed from Boston for Wilmington for the
second time in his life. This trip was in sharp contrast to his first voyage.
On the first trip he was but nineteen and had no experience in the South;
now he was twenty-two and had almost three years of residence. Before he
sailed to Wilmington without goods and with little money; now he sailed
with $5,000 worth of goods, on credit and not paid for to be sure, but we
can surmise handpicked by Larkin for profitable retail in the South. Most
important, in 1824, he set forth with a far more loyal ally than his former
partner Thurston. Returning to Wilmington, he took his younger brother
William, then a lad of sixteen. The passage went well, and they docked after
ten pleasant days.

Within the same month of October, Larkin opened another store in Wilmington. Now he was his own man, a sole proprietor, with the trusted
assistance of his brother. Business was good that winter, no doubt due to
Larkin's careful selection of merchandise in Boston. In March 1825, Larkin journeyed to Charleston, South Carolina, leaving his brother in charge
of the store. He left on missions both financial and personal. The business
purpose was to investigate the state of the wholesale market. He discovered
that the Charleston wholesalers imported directly from Europe, accepted at
no discount the paper currency retailers took in trade, and extended more
favorable credit terms than wholesalers in Boston or New York.

The second purpose of Larkin's trip was to seek a cure there for a chronic
illness which plagued him throughout his years in the South. Larkin was
very vague about this illness. We can rule out his attack of fever in Sampson
County just before his departure to the North on vacation. That was a sharp
and sudden illness, whereas the sickness of which he complained most was
chronic and more or less continual. Larkin traveled to Charleston by sea
and returned by stage through Camden, Cheraw, and Fayetteville. Enroute
to Charleston the ship struck a small sailboat and Larkin resuscitated a
drowning child, only to see him die later that evening. In Charleston he
enjoyed the local attractions, attended the theatre and circus, and visited a
museum and the public gardens.

A "professor" in Charleston treated him with "a large Electrician machine, cooperating with the Galvanic system. Both of them combined together was powerfull." To Larkin's credit he regarded the professor as
"rather foolish." But he was uncertain. "It may have been the wise man's
foolishness, for ought I Know." Larkin returned to Wilmington after a
few weeks of absence, $200 the worse for expense, and no better in his
complaint.

When he returned to Wilmington he found his business had gotten on well, but that there was a cancer spreading among his Boston creditors in the form of a rumor that was undermining his credit. In Larkin's absence, his old partner and "specious friend," as Larkin put it later, wrote to several Boston firms with whom Larkin had accounts. Thurston told these creditors that Larkin was neglecting his business and headed for failure. Thurston solicited the assignment to himself of Larkin's unpaid notes and accounts, so that he could sue on them in Wilmington and collect before it was too late. One evening while Larkin was absent in South Carolina he advised Larkin's brother William not to open the store the next morning since a local merchant was going to attach the trade stock. This closure would have confirmed his reports of failure. However, William knew that the financial condition of the enterprise was favorable and opened the store as usual in the morning.

Two of Larkin's creditors assigned their claims to Thurston in response to the false solicitation. Thurston's conduct now became even more devious as he began, in the words Larkin later used, "acting a double part, showing himself before our eyes, half in the light, the other half in the dark." He came to Larkin, who at the time did not know the source of the rumors, and showed him the assignments. Thurston assured Larkin that he would not proceed against him, that he, Thurston, saw no danger to Larkin's creditors. All this difficulty must be due, said Thurston, to the "secret Villiany" of someone. He implied that he had not solicited the assignments. For himself, Thurston "plead his long love, the support we had been to each other, the services I had been to him, the favors I had granted." No, Thurston would never sue his friend Larkin, and he would promptly write the creditors and assure them that there was no danger.

"Had I been told there was in days of yore, or in our days, such a Hypocrite, I could hardly believed it." But Thurston did write the creditors, the assignments and instructions to sue were recalled, and Larkin received apologies from the creditors. In subsequent investigation of the source of the rumors Thurston first blamed other local merchants, and after those leads proved false ultimately confessed his true role.

Larkin had been badly hurt in the entire affair. He was personally distressed by the breach of what he had thought was a "friendship of the strongest Kind." As for his business, "it was the cause of much uneasyness to me. I stood in a strange country away from home, without support, & without capital, and to have my character ruined. I thought I indeed must fall." Larkin stood his ground and saw this spring crisis through. But Thurston was not yet done.

Up to this point Thurston's conduct makes some sense viewed as an effort to curry favor with Larkin, to gain something Thurston wanted, by creating a crisis from which he would then save Larkin. That at least has a rational motive. But once the plot was uncovered, this "Hyena in mens cloths" be-

came irrationally vicious. Thurston returned to Massachusetts in that summer of 1825, following the spring credit crisis, and there spread rumors,
"by means of female conveyance," that Larkin was "not only ruined in
business, but in both body and soul." Young Larkin, Thurston reported,
was always at the theatre and frequented a gambling house seven nights a
week. There were overtones of even worse depravity.

What hurt most was that Larkin's relatives believed the rumors. "My
nearest Relations that should rose up against them, gave way, sunk under
the reports and believed them—they were easy of belief—and have my
thanks for the confidence they placed in my morals." Thurston's conduct
was the cause of "perpetual grief to me for months." We must remember
that we have only Larkin's account of these transactions.

There is a mystery here. It seems that some strange bond continued between these two erstwhile friends, which became apparent many years later
when Thurston renewed their contact. He showed up in California during
the Gold Rush and managed to borrow $500 from Larkin. Having done
that, he then asked for an additional $500 in a very peremptory manner that
suggested a certainty that Larkin would not refuse.[26]

In August 1825, Larkin did a curious thing. He quit his store in Wilmington, leaving his brother temporarily in charge, and opened another at
Rockfish, about forty miles north of Wilmington in Duplin County.[27] The
motives did not include a business purpose, nor did he enjoy country living.
To the contrary, Larkin enjoyed the cultural amenities of the city. Larkin
despised the country folk and called them a "miserble disapated lot."

The motive for moving into the countryside was a recrudescence, or fear
thereof, of his chronic illness, and in particular a sense of embarrassment
that his sickness caused him. He wrote:

"My old complaint render'd it necessary for me to leave a place of much
company, and settle in a Neighborhood, where every person would soon
know me, and where it would occation less distress to me than in town.
Thence the cause of my leaving a town that contain'd much to make life
agreeable, and retire to the country, where man is but half civilized or where
one half are in that situation.

Perhaps Larkin suffered from acute asthma produced by the pollen or mold
from the swamps surrounding Wilmington. The continual wheezing and
coughing of asthma would have caused Larkin far less distress if experienced among strangers rather than people who knew him.

Throughout the crises of 1825, first the financial rumors in the spring,
then the personal attacks of the summer and the recurrent illness, Larkin
had "one with whom I could commune" and who by his advice could "al-
leviate my distress." That was his brother William. But in the early fall of
that difficult year Larkin lost that consolation. William Larkin died in Wilmington on September 4, 1825.[28]

"If I never grieved before, I did now," Larkin recalled. "Thought I had had distress before and drank its dregs. At this time found I had never tasted of it before. Peace to the soul, and respect for ever for thy memory, my Brother." He had been close to William. Almost three decades later, in 1853, he made inquiries about the condition and marking of William's grave and about putting it into good condition.[29]

The hurt of spring and summer of 1825 seemingly dragged on forever. Just days after William was buried letters arrived from his sister and other relatives in the north with further remonstrances over Larkin's "infamous conduct." He wondered if he were going "forever to be a mark for sorrow to point her arrows." But time healed the wounds and after a month or two "a light heart" carried him through, and he laughed "at the idle and envious brain of others, who bore me any ill will, and dared them to the combat to again hurt my feelings in any point." Financially, the new store prospered enough for him to hire a clerk.[30] Larkin was far enough ahead in that year of 1825 to purchase a small plantation, complete with house, outhouses, stables, and 280 acres of land.

At the end of that year, the governor of North Carolina, with legislative consent, appointed Larkin Justice of the Peace and Justice of the Quarter Sessions for Duplin County. He took the oath of office on January 18, 1826. This caused quite a stir in the county, in part because of Larkin's young age, then just twenty-three, but more so because he was a Yankee.

As the commotion in the county died away, "retorts not cortious came thick from home on the Office." It is not clear why his relations objected. But for all the stir, in Duplin County and among his New England relatives, Larkin put far less importance on the position than others. He called it "rather an ungrateful office" and not "a post of much honour." He acknowledged that the Justice of the Peace had some importance because of the power attached to the office, but by his own account the judicial cases he handled were not of great moment. Probably the biggest job for this new justice was the stopping of fights, and in that regard Larkin felt the commission was most useful to prevent an attack on himself in that rural society "where a blow is the word for any thing."

Most important in Larkin's reckoning over his appointment as Justice of the Peace was that "the fees attached to it are nothing." In consequence his policy was that "the office of Justice I never let intrude on my other affairs. If a case should happen to come before me, it must be very urgent for me to neglect my own affairs to attend to it. When I am at leasure I attend to all cases with pleasure and patience."

There was a sickness during the summer of 1826 that caused many deaths, including those of Larkin's landlord and several of his customers, including one very heavily into Larkin's books. Still, Larkin kept busy with his store and judicial activities. To round out his time he received a commission in September 1826 to operate a post office. He operated the branch out of his store, and the postal duties were not demanding of his time. He anticipated the proceeds of this office would be very small, but felt the free postage given as an emolument of office might save him expense.

Herewith the chronology of Larkin's activities are brought to the end of September 1826 at which point his pen was laid down and the diary closed. He was storekeeper, postmaster, and magistrate. The three, he felt, would be enough to "Keep me in full business. If I attend to all, I shall hardly ever be idle."

Information on Larkin's life for the years 1821–1826 comes primarily from a document he prepared himself entitled "My Itinerary: U.S. America."[31] It is a curious work, loosely chronological in form, but hardly a daily account and with the chronology often interrupted by little essays on various aspects of southern living and commerce. Larkin compiled it in September 1826, but largely, as he said, from items he had written before. To complete the work he added several nicely executed drawings. It was dedicated to a "friend a thousand miles off," undoubtedly Ebenezer L. Childs, Larkin's stepbrother and cousin. Three years older than Larkin, Ebenezer was becoming a close confidant.

The style of this document, only forty-four pages in print, tells us a great deal about young Larkin's mind and thought. He was a product of the Romantic Age and his "Itinerary" clearly reflects that. Filled with youthful posturing, it shows the extent to which Larkin, by wide reading, had become imbued with the cultural motifs and literary conventions of his age.

One of the motifs of Romanticism was travel in the deliberate search for the strange and exotic. Larkin conceived of his move from Boston to the South as more than mere youthful adventure, more than just an attempt to test his fate elsewhere. It had overtones of this Romantic exoticism. Ten years later, still in the South but less interested in boyish search for adventure, he still described his youthful move to North Carolina in the following terms: "I left home at an early age, went to strange lands, and among stranger people."[32] It was the same search for the exotic that would soon be infused within such renowned travel books of the early nineteenth century as Dana's *Two Years before the Mast*, Melville's *Typee*, and Parkman's *The Oregon Trail*.

The quintessential Romantic poet was Lord Byron, and Larkin's "Itinerary" quotes him extensively and with approval. Larkin's writing frequently took on the characteristics, mysterious and lonely, melancholy yet defiant, of the Byronic hero. Never mind that he did not write as well as Byron; the Romantic influence was full upon this New England youth. In reflections upon his first five years in the South, written in 1826, he wondered why he had not been born with a fortune and had the necessity to work and struggle for a living. He quickly turned this to a Romantic pose: "Why then am I doom'd to lead the life I do. But it 'tis so, its fates unalter-

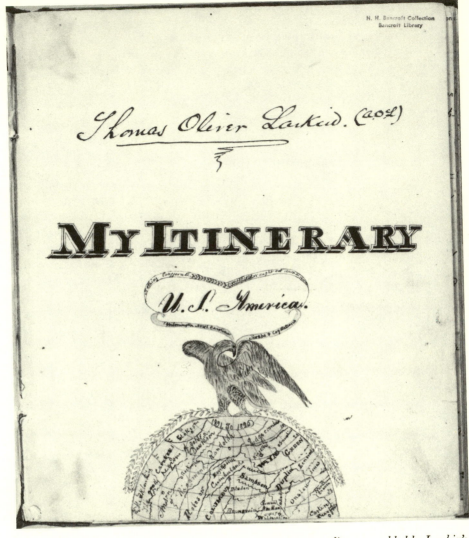

Cover of Larkin's travel diary, 1821–1826. The signature line was added by Larkin's son Alfred, identified by the initials "A. O. L." Courtesy The Bancroft Library.

able decree. 'tis gone forth and is established, and to my fate I must submit without a murmur."

Many of Larkin's observations, particularly of the South and southern society, have qualities of gentle satire and humorous cynicism. These styles are also found in much of Byron's writings, and Larkin's youthful writing bears a singular similarity to commentary on California he later sent to New York newspapers in the 1840s which he knew was destined for publication.

His diary lacks the grace and ease to qualify for good literature. But there is just enough artificiality, a reaching for literary style, that hints that Larkin had hopes for ultimate publication.

For example, Larkin described southern electioneering in some detail. One day there was a militia muster at which political candidates were invited to address the crowd. "Each one spoke in his turn, and I can safely say there was not a dry eye or face to be seen. But it was not the soft persuasive Eloquence of the candidates in labouring to convince their hearers of their own and countrys wrongs, but all this came by the still softer persuasion of a hot Sun ranging as warm 100." Later on the election day the polling place "was surrounded by men, women & Boys, a rather a promiscuous, and motley lot of constituents for any man to represent. But they were qualified for votors, and the Candidates for treating them, for Rum carried the day with many."

However, most of Larkin's observations about the South were straightforward and lacked literary pretense. He commented on the close chaperonage of unmarried young women, the shortness of southern courtships, and the length of the wedding parties. He noted the languid quality of southern living. "Everything goes on, as it did in the days of yore." As a young New Englander many of his observations are on regional differences.

Larkin missed the New England parlor diversions. "Those simple games played at the North can not be got up here often. . . . The men . . . consider them childish and foolish to the extream. Then their only alternative is to drink, and at the end quarrel." He was harshly critical of the southern country people. Those living outside the cities he considered "mostly low bred, brought up without any care, without Education, & without fear. . . . a miserble disapated lot."

Larkin's most detailed observations concern southern trade and commerce. He carefully noted the state of the soil, crops raised, their respective qualities, and other commercial activities of all the areas of the South through which he travelled or in which he lived. Of course, Larkin touched on the issue of slavery. Not a moralist, Larkin understood that the treatment of slaves varied vastly. Some classes of slaves were treated well and others fared miserably. The 1830 census reveals that Larkin himself owned six slaves, probably two couples with two children.[33] He treated his slaves so well that one of them remembered Larkin fondly and asked after him over thirty years later.[34]

The young Bostonian was neither a southern apologist nor a New England abolitionist. He did see clearly the economic necessity of slavery to the southern economy. "Only slaves," he wrote in his 1826 journal, "could live on a Rice plantation, two feet deep in the mud and water, and covered with every kind of insects whose stings would draw the blood from every vein." Larkin was concerned about the unfairness of the abolitionists' attacks, that they did not show both sides of the issue.

Notwithstanding his own neutrality, Larkin predicted slavery's ultimate abolition because of the increase in number of free states. He speculated that Northerners and Southerners would "feel a greater infinity [affinity] to each other" through increased travel and that there should be no difficulties between the states if "they would keep cool." However, he also feared the possibility, writing prophetically in the mid-1820s, that "at some future day they will rise on some subject, and come to dagger's end with each other, without considering the consequences, and whose at fault but that such a period may never happen should be the wish of every American."

Almost every manufactured item in Wilmington had to be imported from the North. But he noticed that many goods sent to the South on consignment by northern merchants were subsequently sold off at distress prices at great sacrifice. "Northern Merchants ship goods to the South without Knowing thing of the nature of the Market," he concluded. "Great care should be taking in every place to know what goods is wanted before they ship." It was a lesson not lost on this future importer of manufactured goods into Mexican California.

In his first five years in the South, 1821–1826, Larkin was growing in stature and experience with the world. If he was not making his fortune, he was gaining information and technique, and at the least he was enjoying himself. He wrote of the Southerners that "in spite of their faults, and what nation are free from them, their singularities oddities, & inconsistentency, I shall always remember their friendship & kindness. I have spent many a pleasant time with them. I always found a hearty welcome and always made myself at home among them."

Of what did this enjoyment consist during those early years in the South? The diary mentions cigars and wine a few times, but colorful descriptions of the effects of an overabundance of liquor leave no doubt that Larkin's use was very moderate. Occasionally he played cards for low stakes, although he assures us that one evening's loss of two dollars was his greatest ever. He attended the theatre in Wilmington, but there his enjoyment was marred by the distraction of tobacco. It seems "the proformers could not be prevented from spiting about as they were acting."

But his primary enjoyment was women. "Wilmington can produce more Beautiful Ladies," he boasted, "than any place of its size I ever saw, North or South." On his travels in the South, and on vacation in New England, young Larkin could not resist a comment or two on the pulchritude, and sometimes the lack thereof, of the women of each town through which he passed.

Larkin was meeting women at parties, at dinners, and at weddings. In March 1825, on his trip to Charleston, South Carolina, he discovered the waltz, that "Spanish dance" which allowed the shockingly close clasp of the female form. "It rub'd no qualms of conscince or attacted no point on my principles," he allowed. Still there was a drawback. "Was I paying my undivided attentions to some fair object of my heart, and was rapt all and all in her existence, I could not support the anguish of Soul to stand and View her in this same dance to see her claspd by another."

Larkin attended the theatre in Wilmington. Yet the play was not the only purpose. He frequently went with his erstwhile friend and partner, Thomas G. Thurston, in pursuit of women. "He boarded with and Actres, and so did I. We both saw them home, some nights after the proformance. He rode out and walk out with his." Deserved or not, thespians held a bad reputation in early nineteenth-century America. Associating with an actress was close to slumming. Perhaps that is why Larkin emphasizes that it was Thurston, and not he himself, who was willing to walk and ride, presumably in broad daylight, with a woman of such repute.

Larkin was not yet ready for marriage. In 1826, then only twenty-four years of age, he called it "an undertaken I am not qualified for." Still, he toyed with the prospect of marriage as a means of rapidly improving his mediocre fortune. The problem was that "the richest Lady of W [Wilmington] is not worth $5000 . . . . I would it were otherwise." He wrote himself a series of memoranda on the subject. "Mem. don't marry for property. Mem. again, who ever married for poverty. Mem. again what must one marry for, if not for property or poverty. Its not that every one can love. Some neither love, or have music in their Souls."

There was indeed a love building in Larkin's soul. But it was not for a woman but for mammon. "Why thought I, was I not born with a fortune." By 1826, Larkin had enjoyed only modest financial success. He was but holding his own and not accumulating. He wanted far more. But still young, Larkin was unwilling to sacrifice either honor or pleasure. "I'll not forswear myself of every pleasure, to make my purse outweigh my neighbors," he wrote. He was consoled by and resolved to gradualism. He made the point in a burst of grandiloquence. "Let me by a constant industry, and perseverance persist in a certain line of conduct, that shall lead on to those enjoyment, that I now pant for. To gain Wealth . . . . Shall I lay aside all thats noble in my nature, stoop to any means & measures to gain it, give up all that makes life agreeable, and pass my time solely in acquiring it. No!"

Over the next five years in the South, 1826–1831, and indeed over his entire lifetime, Larkin never abandoned his drive for wealth. But, by 1831, his viewpoint was radically changed. In 1831, his faith in "constant industry" was shattered; he was willing to give up "all that makes life agreeable," and because of his passion for money, he was becoming more willing to abandon gradualism and to "stoop to any means & measures to gain it." What happened to Larkin in the five years, 1826–1831, to account for this transformation?

At some time during the years 1827–1830 Larkin ceased his trade as storekeeper and embarked on an entirely new undertaking. It is probable that he sold the store, that is the operations only as the building was rented, to Dempsey Harrell, his former clerk, and Ebenezer Withington. Harrell continued to operate the store for a few years.[35]

After leaving the store Larkin entered the sawmill business,[36] operating a mill in Long Creek, North Carolina, about 20 miles north of Wilmington.[37] It is likely that the new business began in 1828 as in that year he was eager to borrow money, presumably as capital for his sawmill. By note of October 13, 1828, Larkin borrowed $34.72 from his stepbrother, cousin, and friend, Ebenezer L. Childs.[38]

The sawmill was a failure, and Larkin lost all his accumulated earnings.[39] A friend of Larkin from this period and with whom he had spent "many jovial and Happy hours," saw much that was sinister in the failure of Larkin's enterprise. A "Host of enemies," this friend wrote Larkin years later, "crowded on you and disposed you of all you owned and Left you penniless."[40] Notwithstanding, it was probably quite an ordinary business failure and the "Host of enemies" merely anxious creditors.

Whether simply commercial obligees or enemies, it is true that these creditors forced Larkin to assign his property to a receiver. A bond executed by this receiver, Ebenezer Withington, a friend with whom Larkin had done business before, tells the story.[41] It is dated March 27, 1830, and recites that Larkin on April 6, 1828, entered into a deed of trust to James Moore and Charles Henry secured by the sawmill.[42] Probably this was Larkin's initial financing, although the amount is not specified. These two men may have later become Larkin's partners, since they are not included in Larkin's 1831 list of debts. On March 27, 1830, Larkin, together with Moore and Henry, assigned the mills to Withington, but on the condition that if Withington were to make a profit of $1,000, beyond all costs, then he would pay Larkin $500.[43] The assignment effectively put Larkin as an individual out of business.

The bond does not state this but it was understood, or perhaps there is another document that is lost, that the receiver, or trustee, was also to collect assets and pay off Larkin's debts. Larkin estimated these at about $3,000[44] but felt "my creditors would willingly take one half. I give up certain property by their wish to this certain person [a reference to Withington] to do such & such things."[45] Typical of debtors in a similar situation, Larkin felt that the pressure by creditors for him to put the sawmill into receivership absolved him of moral responsibility to pay his obligations. If the trustee was unable to succeed in the operation of the mill and did not pay Larkin's debts, "the fault is there [theirs, i.e., his creditors'] as well as mine in his [the trustee's] having it. Therefore I shall think it no injustice to pay them but a part. And I may yet get off with less than a $1000."[46]

Many years later, when Larkin was wealthy, he made inquiries as to whether his trustee had paid any of his debts. The response from one North Carolina friend was, "I think I could safely say not the first copper. I heard no more about it after you were gone."[47] Ultimately, in 1854, Larkin sent funds to pay many of his debts owed to individuals, but apparently he never retired these commercial obligations.

In the spring of 1831, with the failure of his sawmill, Larkin was broke and deeply depressed. A young man of twenty-nine, driven to become wealthy, he had just seen the collapse of youthful ambitions. "My onset in life is overthrough," he wrote. "My first prospects are blasted, my warmest anticipations are given up, my youngest days gone by, and with them a thousand sweet thoughts, a thousand fond ideas, and all my young and fond expectations. All, all are gone, blasted, withered forever. All I have done is undone. All I have accumated has gone to the winds."[48] Moreover, Larkin's chronic illness continued to hound him.

The one bright light of Larkin's life, during the otherwise bleak period of 1830–1831, was his relations with women. "In fact [I] hear I am a Ladies man," he bragged in 1831.[49] Part of the reason for his success as he himself pointed out was that he was very eligible. There was hardly a man around of his age who was not married or divorced. "There may be 1 in 100," he estimated. Another factor was the "eloquence of my voice," as he immodestly claimed, and his tools of "more tongue, more flattery, more confidence . . . more brass & perseverence."

Another and very important part of Larkin's romantic success was that he genuinely enjoyed women. At this stage in his life he was far from the stern New England puritan whose image comes down to us from portraits and sketches during his later California years. In an amusing aside he acknowledged his enjoyment of women while also admitting, indirectly, his constant financial avarice. "I love the company of a fine girl above any or every thing. I would do more for them for the pleasure of it, than for any man for money—and thats saying a great deel for me."

In fact, his romantic powers were so persuasive, the youthful Larkin bragged, "a Lady told me . . . I could get any one." One of Larkin's more dangerous traits was that he refused to discriminate against young ladies already spoken for and was quite willing to bestow his ardent attentions upon married women. In early May 1831, for example, he attended a wedding, uninvited, where he pressed his attentions upon the bride. "I did not get introduced at all, but she knew my name and had for years, and all about me. We liked each others company. . . . And while she was up till 2 o clock or so, I had more of her Sweet company than the Groom. . . . She danced often with me, and told me she was sorry it was to be our last party together . . . . When we parted next morning . . . she looked so fair, her lips so tempting, and seem to ask for a Kiss. I could not refuse, & so parted. With a kiss and a press of the hand I left her." This was dangerous sport and foretokened the serious trouble that attentions to married women were soon to cause him.

Aside from passing fancies Larkin left behind in North Carolina broken hearts from serious relationships. One such was Susan Jane Jones, from a family with which Larkin was friendly.[50] Susan Jane did not find an easy path in life. She married Peyton Stringfield, an alcoholic husband with whom she had nine children. They were desperately poor, heavily in debt, and apparently had asked for assistance so often that friends and even her own father refused to help. In September 1855, she wrote to Larkin, referred to herself as "an old friend," and, in pitifully poignant language, poured out her heart. "I cannot discribe my feelings to you. neather could I tell you how I feel on this occation. There is no one on earth that cares for my wants and necessities but you . . . . I do not think of past times. I would have the blues sure enough, if I was to." She shared what little good news she had: her husband had recently reformed, they were holding their own, and in fact for the first time, "if nothing happens," they expected a good corn crop. She asked for nothing from Larkin except a letter and expressed the forlorn hope that she might "see you once more."[51]

A later letter of January 1856 revealed more clearly the nature of their relationship in the 1830s. She told Larkin that four years earlier she had named one of her children, Thomas Larkin Stringfield, in his honor. She then added "I would not name a child for you untill all our old enemies were dead or gone away. I have seen the time I would not mention you name I was so harshly accused some would say you told them ill of me but that I never believed but I am through with all that now and have a clear concience I know you always acted like a gentleman with me and also like a brother and to this day feels for me more than any one els [sic]."[52]

One senses that Susan Jane was protesting too much and that the actual relationship was quite different from that of siblings. This letter was jointly written with her husband, Peyton. Not only did her husband have opportunity to read her remarks there is internal evidence he did so.[53] It seems probable that Susan intended her husband to read her disclaimers of an intimate relationship while at the same time stating rumors of which he could not be unaware. Susan's statement, "some would say you told them ill of me," although only gossip, certainly does not speak well of Larkin's essentially amoral character.

By the spring of 1831, Larkin saw the logical relationship between his business failure and romantic success, logical at least for one so driven to fortune. The solution to his problems was marriage to a wealthy woman. However, he could not arrange that in the South. "I do not know a young Lady within fifty miles of W [Wilmington] worth $3000 and I know all the people more or less within that distance."[54] But he required more than merely money in a woman; he also insisted on some slight affection. He explained this in his incredibly candid letter to Ebenezer in May 1831.

> All love and no capital will never do for me. I could not live on it. Give me some of each, and I'll try the married life. . . . If I can make a fortune by marriage, I will do it providing I can find on being acquanted with the Lady any Small love for her. . . . You may say . . . that marriage is a fear full thing to tamper with, and according as a man's wife is, so will he enjoy life, and that he should marry no one but what he loved above all others, and should never marry for money. All this may be. In fact I do not doubt it and its also a fact that I want to marry and settle near home. This I can not do without the Lady is rich.[55]

This passage reveals not only Larkin's desperation but also that his preference was to live near his home, that is, near Boston. At another point in his May 1831 letter he wrote, "I would wish [to] marry that I might settle . . . near Boston." Actually, in May 1831, Larkin was considering three very different directions in which to take his life. The three alternatives, in order of his preference, were: to marry a wealthy cousin in Boston and settle nearby as a farmer; to obtain a postal appointment in Washington through the influence of his cousin Ebenezer; and finally, the least desirable, to move to Monterey, in Alta California, Mexico, to work for his half-brother John B. R. Cooper.

Larkin explained in May that he wished both to "settle near home" and to find "a girl well off that I think I can ejoy myself with thro' life. . . . And again to be candid with you it was on these thoughts that I enquired of you if our cousin was married." Larkin explained that he intended to return to Boston that summer and would call on the cousin to see if he could "be fond of her." In the meantime he asked Ebenezer for all information possible as to the lady, her disposition, and all past suitors. "I go for a happy partner, a convenience to all parties that will enable me to marry, take a house near Boston, cultavate a small farm, live well and happy, and within my income. This can be accomplished if the Lady would do her part. If it was otherwise the fault would be hers not mine."

Elsewhere Larkin explained that the lady's part would require she "study my disposition and adapt herself to it." If she did that "we Should be happy, otherwise we should be unhappy." Under the cousin alternative Larkin would have contented himself with a house and small farm, the most modest expression he ever made of his aspirations.

The second alternative for his future was a job in the Post Office. His cousin Ebenezer was personally stable and professionally secure. He was no longer in business, had worked in the postal bureaucracy for a number of years, and had been married since 1826. For some obscure political favors he had rendered, Ebenezer stood in hopes of imminent reward. Larkin thought Ebenezer might be able to land him a job in Washington. Yet loyalty to his friend and cousin made Larkin anxious that Ebenezer look to his own interest first. "Get me in if possible," Larkin wrote, "tho' dont push to much at first. When you at [are] purser cant I be clerk." Larkin counseled Ebenezer to "ask when you can, but dont sing too loud to hurt yourself. Dont keep in the back ground."

This alternative was not as desirable as marriage to the wealthy cousin. Larkin would not live near Boston, but in Washington; nor did government service offer any quick financial rewards. Still it was better than the third choice of Monterey. Larkin "had rather be under Uncle Sam than in Mexico."

Monterey, "the jumping off place of the world," as Larkin described it, was a mystery. He had found it impossible to get any information on the place from North Carolina. He knew that his older half-brother, John B. R.

Cooper, had become a sea captain and then settled in Monterey as long ago as 1823. He used California as a base for various overseas trading ventures. Within California he was engaged in such diverse enterprises as raising cattle, hunting sea otters, and selling merchandise. Cooper was not very well focused or concentrated. His books and accounts needed straightening, and his creditors and business associates frequently criticised his sloppiness and business practices.[56] Cooper needed an enterprising clerk and assistant, and he solicited one from his large extended family.

Cooper wrote to Samuel C. Childs, one of Larkin's many stepbrothers and cousins, and offered him the position. Samuel ultimately declined.[57] Apparently the offer was to be extended more generally to family members in the event Samuel declined, although Cooper had not thought Larkin a candidate and did not specifically offer him the job. Ebenezer Childs had sent a copy of Cooper's letter to Larkin.[58]

One aspect of the California alternative that doubtlessly interested Larkin was that his half-brother had become a Catholic and a naturalized Mexican and had married a daughter of the wealthy and influential Vallejo family. He was acquiring ranch lands and becoming wealthy, in large part due to his marital connection. Why this was Larkin's very strategy written large! Larkin assured Ebenezer that he was "too old to stand on trifles."[59] If it would aid his quest for wealth, "making myself inderpendent," as he put it, he would not himself hesitate to become a Catholic and marry a local daughter. "If I go to Monterey I shall do as the people do, if that will help me. And if I chose to marry there I should do it, providing I had any (say a little) love for the Lady, and the Lady had loot enough for me. A little of the former and much of the latter I'm a married man."

Although the prospect of emigrating to Mexico held some excitement, it was definitely the third choice out of three. For years Larkin had thought seriously of going to Mexico, even though the Mexicans were "a people that I always dispised and detested." He was disturbed that he would be required to "unlearn my native language, forget my Mother tongue," and learn to speak Spanish. "Think you I will not do much to avoid all this," he confided to Ebenezer in 1831. "Therefore give me a full account of our Cousin. . . . I will see her, and if I think I can love I will soon tell her, not that think I can but that I do, and that very soon."

These passages reveal Larkin's desperation. True, five years earlier he was already interested in wealth. But in 1826 he was unwilling to lay aside all that was noble, stoop to any means and measures to gain it, or give up all that made life agreeable. Now, in 1831, Larkin was willing to live among the Mexican people that he had always "dispised and detested"; he was eager to marry for wealth; and he was prepared to become a Catholic and overthrow his childhood Protestant heritage as a mere "trifle" in the path of his crusade for wealth. Larkin had become quite willing to sacrifice all principles for cash.

Captain Juan Bautista Rogers Cooper, half-brother to Larkin. Cooper's offer of employment brought Larkin to California. Courtesy Amilie Elkinton.

Although Monterey was the third choice of three, by May 1831 Larkin was resigned to that alternative. "I have nearly made up my mind on this subject," he wrote. As a fallback he intended to stand for election in June for the "Inspectors place" in Long Creek, the location of his former mill. Immediately thereafter he would return to Boston where he could find out more about California from sea captains and traders, while simultaneously inspecting the cousin. But he had already persuaded his stepfather, whom Larkin called "Par," and his uncle William to loan him $100 apiece for passage money to California and "my main thoughts are now on the M. trip."[60]

Larkin lost the election for inspector in Long Creek but with a campaign that was only half-hearted. He had already engaged his passage to Boston even before the election and he declined to spend any money in the nearly obligatory "treating" of the electorate with liquor.[61] We do not know why the wealthy cousin or bureaucratic appointment alternatives fell through, but they did. Probably the cousin turned him down,[62] and Larkin himself did not put much faith in the government job.

In the event, California was the final choice. He briefly returned to Boston and Lynn, exchanged farewells with relatives, and wrote affectionate letters to those whom he had no time to visit.[63] Larkin's sister wrote to their half-brother Cooper that she could not reconcile herself "to the idea of again parting with Oliver, it seems but a few days since we met after a long absense and now he is gone again. . . . I had indulged the hope that he would settle somewhere in Mass, that we might occassionally see him but how greatly am I disappointed."[64]

One further difficulty was that ships bound for Monterey were heavily laden with cargo and did not ordinarily carry passengers. Larkin found it difficult to book passage but eventually found space on the *Newcastle*, a brig bound for Oahu and thence for California. He would have preferred a different vessel, one that had "some passengers & many books," but her departure date was uncertain.[65]

Drawing on his background in retailing and what he had learned of the Pacific trade, Larkin thought it would be useful to carry a small amount of cargo on his own account for sale in Oahu or California. He could not afford to take much merchandise; the funds for his own personal passage were borrowed from relatives. The passage cost $300, $150 in cash, and the balance to be paid by Cooper when he arrived in California, with Par and Uncle William standing surety. The two relatives also lent Larkin $100 apiece, so that Larkin had a small cash surplus of $50 plus what few funds he himself brought out of North Carolina.[66]

He did scrape together sufficient funds to purchase a modest selection of goods for sale. Larkin's small cargo consisted of several pairs of boots, shoes, and trousers. A barrel of rice, six kegs of powder, one rifle, and several oars were included. The major items were one small boat and one wagon and harness.[67] On September 5, 1831,[68] thus accompanied by this sundry cargo, a record of business failure, and a steadfast ambition for wealth, Larkin quietly slipped out of the Boston harbor to begin his California career.

CHAPTER 3

ON TO CALIFORNIA
BUSINESS STARTS AND
PERSONAL LIFE

LET US EXAMINE more closely the young man standing on the deck of the *Newcastle*, looking backward at what he might rightfully believe was his final sight of his native land. Since it was a foreign country Larkin had chosen for his new home, the Massachusetts governor issued him a passport on September 2, 1831. It described Larkin as twenty-nine years of age, five feet, seven and one-half inches in height, with dark complexion, dark eyes, and black hair, and possessing a scar on his right wrist and another above his left knee.[1]

His health was not robust. Although he would not suffer in California the mysterious malady of his North Carolina days, his wife in 1846 would write to him while he was under particularly trying circumstances, "I think onley of your health and fear you my get Sick as your health is delicate."[2] There would be many illnesses during the California years. To complete his physical description, we must note that he was hard of hearing. This difficulty had appeared as early as his North Carolina days.[3] In 1843, a Monterey visitor would describe him as "dark and thin . . . with a slight stoop to his shoulders . . . . He appeared to be a little deaf, and held one of his hands back of his ear when he saw that you were disposed to speak to him."[4]

The voyage was long and apparently uneventful. Doubtless Larkin followed his original intention of studying Spanish much of the time. Also, contrary to his original understanding, there was another passenger on the *Newcastle*. That it was a young lady only made it the more pleasant for Larkin. She was Rachel Hobson Holmes, twenty-four years of age, from Ipswich, Massachusetts. She was traveling to California to join her husband, John A. C. Holmes, a sea captain sailing from west coast ports.

37

Finally, in February 1832, the vessel made a landfall in the Sandwich Islands, as Hawaii was then called.[5] The ship was in port for several weeks, and in March Larkin sold the cargo he had brought with him for $373.75.[6] He took time in Oahu to make the acquaintance of leading merchants and traders, many of whom had extensive commercial interests in California as well as Hawaii, all excellent contacts for his fledgling business activity in Monterey. The young affable Larkin made an enormously favorable impression on these traders, some of whom sent Cooper glowing praises. Alpheus B. Thompson, a merchant headquartered in Santa Barbara, wrote from Hawaii that "we are much pleased with him here, he will be of great service to you."[7]

It is ironic that Larkin, the recent bankrupt in North Carolina, made such favorable impressions in Honolulu. The slowness of news and the obscurity of his past certainly aided him. But Larkin's biggest help was the near desperation of these traders with John B. R. Cooper's erratic behavior and their hope that his half-brother might straighten out Cooper's tangled affairs. Another trader wrote Cooper that he would "recommend Mr Larkin to your most implicit confidence and hope you will listen to his advice."[8] A third trader, the American consul in Hawaii, John C. Jones, wrote Cooper that Larkin's "capability is well known. . . . I have no doubt but he will be of much service to you provided you follow his direction."[9]

Eventually the *Newcastle* was again underway. She entered the port of San Francisco in early April, but soon left for Monterey,[10] the capital city, where Larkin's employer and half-brother, John B. R. Cooper, made his home and business headquarters. Larkin arrived at his new home on April 13, 1832.[11]

Mrs. Holmes, Larkin's traveling companion, learned that her husband had sailed for Lima a short time previously and that she must wait for his return. There were no hotels in California at the time, so she was invited to stay with Captain Cooper's wife and family in their large home.[12] In all probability Larkin stayed there as well.[13]

Larkin went to work for Cooper as a clerk, straightening out his accounts and conducting his business correspondence. From late spring 1832 through the end of the year, Larkin's handwriting appears on many of Cooper's accounts, receipts, and invoices. Several business letters of Cooper dating from that fall were written by Larkin's hand.[14] However, Larkin was too much of an entrepreneur, too desirous of being his own man, to remain long as an employee. Accordingly, he began in business for himself in February 1833, at first operating without a store and solely on commissions, engaged in both sales and debt collection.[15]

The future importance of Rachel Holmes to Larkin warrants describing her with greater particulars. She was born Rachel Hobson in Ipswich, Massachusetts, April 30, 1807, the daughter of Daniel and Eliza Hobson.[16] In 1827, she married a sea captain, John Andrew Christian Holmes, a native

The buildings in the center were the home and office of Captain Cooper. Both Larkin and Rachel Holmes lived here immediately upon their arrival in California. Photograph of a card, the back of which was inscribed in 1875 by the former Californio leader Mariano Guadalupe Vallejo, "to my friend H H Bancroft, Esq.," the famous historian. Courtesy The Bancroft Library.

of Denmark. Shortly after their marriage, he sailed for the Pacific coast, leaving his wife temporarily with her father. Her husband later decided to stay on the west coast in the employ of Henry Virmond, a German merchant in Acapulco who owned many merchant vessels.[17] Holmes sent for Rachel, and she sailed on the *Newcastle* with Larkin. She would become the first American woman to settle in Alta California.

A biographical sketch, prepared while Rachel was alive and with her cooperation, states that "her early life was passed amid the hallowed retirement of home, and the quiet of domestic duties."[18] If this were a euphemistic statement that she lacked much formal education, it would be consistent with the general tenor of her few extant letters. However, Captain Holmes trusted her with business matters and directed that business receipts and funds, from the trading on his own account, be forwarded to his wife.[19]

During the spring of 1832 Larkin began an affair with Rachel Holmes. The romance may have begun even earlier on shipboard. By the end of April 1832, it was in full progress, as nine months later, on January 31, 1833, Rachel gave birth to Larkin's illegitimate daughter.[20] The pregnancy put both Rachel and Larkin in a serious situation. Rachel, married yet carrying another man's child, knew not what to expect from her husband. Larkin faced possible criminal charges or deportation. Rachel removed to Santa Barbara and remained there during her confinement, a guest in the home of Daniel Hill and his Californian wife.[21] It is not clear why Hill rendered such aid. A prominent American in his region, perhaps he was a friend of Cooper, since he arrived in California in 1823 on the ship Cooper then commanded.[22]

During her pregnancy, and perhaps to her relief, Rachel learned of her husband's death. His employer, Henry Virmond, informed her by letter that Holmes had died on March 8, 1832 enroute from Acapulco to South America. There were various trading accounts of her husband to settle, and Virmond offered his help with those as well as free transportation back to the United States.[23] It is unclear when Rachel received this letter, but it was dated July 16, 1832 and sent from Acapulco, so that she probably knew of her widowhood by October 1832.

The death of Rachel's husband, in turn, put new pressure on Larkin. Rachel was now free to marry. But what would this do to Larkin's carefully nurtured plans to marry a woman of means? He had schemed to do this for years, had developed skills and confidence through his womanizing in North Carolina, and had seen an excellent example in the case of his half-brother Cooper. Larkin's conditions for marriage in California, as he had explained to his stepbrother Ebenezer in 1831, were that "I had any (say a little) love for the Lady, and the Lady had loot enough for me."[24] Other attractive California women were available, of excellent families, and as a result of such a union Larkin could gain vast amounts of land and cattle, exactly as had Cooper. And of course Larkin's drive for wealth was by no means slaked. It had only deepened during his North Carolina sojourn.

Larkin must have pondered on these things. But his pondering did not produce a marriage. Thus, Larkin's first child was born illegitimate on January 31, 1833. The baptismal entry at Mission Santa Barbara dated the following day tells the story:

> Feb. 1, 1833. I solemnly baptized in the church of this Mission an infant born the previous day, illegitimate daughter of Rogers Laken and Rachel, married to Guillermo [William] Holmes, natives of the United States and Protestants, but the baptism took place with the consent of the mother. I named the said infant Isavel [Isabel] Ana; the godfather was Don David [Daniel] Hill, whom I apprised of his responsibilities. In testimony whereof I affix my signature.
>
> Fr. Antonio Jimeno[25]

Certainly by this date Rachel knew she was widowed. The recital that she was married to Holmes probably resulted from fear that she might be deported if the authorities knew she were single. Larkin was likely absent for the birth. He wrote a letter from Monterey, January 7, 1833, to Abel Stearns, a trading partner, that gives no hint he was leaving for Santa Barbara.[26]

Ultimately, Larkin did marry Rachel in June 1833 and by doing so legitimated their daughter. Even before June he had begun to divide his time between Monterey and Santa Barbara. Extant business letters written by Larkin in September and October 1832 and January 1833 indicate they were written in Monterey.[27] But later Larkin visited his daughter and her mother. Another business letter was datelined Santa Barbara, March 27, 1833, although he subsequently returned to Monterey. Later, in a June 2, 1833 letter, he stated he was about to sail for Santa Barbara on the *Volunteer*.[28]

Larkin and Rachel were married on the *Volunteer*, an American ship, while she lay in the roadstead of Santa Barbara, on June 10, 1833.[29] The ceremony was performed by Captain John C. Jones, who had brought the vessel to California on a trading venture. However, Jones was also the American consul in Hawaii. Larkin had the idea, he later explained, "that consuls can perform the ceremony of marriage between their countrymen in any port of the world if on board an American ship."[30] Twelve years and eight children later, Larkin learned from the State Department that he was wrong and that consuls, under then-existing law, had no authority to perform marriages.[31]

The wedding itself was a huge success. The trader William Heath Davis, Jr., noted enthusiastically that it was attended by the "elite of Santa Barbara." Both local wines and imported champagne were "freely used," the music and dancing lasted through the late evening, and "all had a very enjoyable time."[32] Larkin himself enjoyed the festivities, especially since Jones dressed himself in the full regalia of his consular office. "Ere this," he wrote Abel Stearns on June 26, while still in Santa Barbara, "you have I presume heard of my Wedding & all its Etc's. Mr Jones made a very fine display on board on the occasion."[33]

The interesting questions are why did Larkin marry Rachel, and why did he wait so long. Given that he married Rachel at all—and that decision in view of his history and ambitions seems very puzzling—why did he not do so before their child was born? There is a common answer that runs through the biographical sketches prepared during the lifetimes of the Larkins and written with their assistance, suggesting that they both, independently, were at pains to explain this. In the 1855 sketch of Larkin, the explanation is that "the bishop and padres of the pueblos and missions refused to perform the ceremony of marriage, as both the intending spouses were protestants, and they had objected to become Roman Catholics for the mere purpose of having the nuptial bonds tied by a priest."[34]

Mrs. Larkin's biographical sketch, prepared with her assistance but after the death of her husband, explained that "at this time, it should be remembered, the Romish Church was in power. It was 'church and state,' and the padres would not perform the marriage ceremony for 'heretics,' as they were pleased to call those who were not within the pale of the Romish Church."[35] This explanation implies that the couple had to wait until the availability of an American consul to perform the ceremony. The implicit suggestion is that they planned to be married as soon as Rachel learned she was widowed. However, their plans had to await John C. Jones's plans, birth of the child or not.

But this explanation is insufficient. Larkin's religious background, as we have seen, was Protestant. However, in his 1826 diary he had portrayed himself as somewhat skeptical, and this posture continued. Just before leaving for California in 1831 he had raised the issue of religion with his stepbrother Ebenezer. Larkin wrote that the other side of death is a "dark uncertainty." We think a lot of it, but know nothing. All we can do is prepare for a better hereafter as taught us by our forefathers. But as for sectarian creeds, their rites and rituals, he would "pass them by" and neither heed them nor scorn them. Larkin had discovered no reason to alter his opinion that "the Religious people are always selfish."[36]

In a slightly earlier May 11, 1831, letter to Ebenezer from North Carolina, he had discussed Cooper's joining the Catholic Church as a trifle, and in that specific context declared that he was "too old to stand on trifles that shall or should prevent my making myself inderpendent. If I go to Monterey I shall do as the people do, if that will help me."[37]

We do not know as much about Rachel's religious views. Undoubtedly she was also Protestant. Yet she was sufficiently liberal in her thinking that she permitted a Catholic priest to baptize Isabel. An important fact that must be added to this consideration of religion alone as an explanation of the delay in the marriage is that the Larkins later *did* briefly convert to Catholicism and were remarried as Catholics. It happened when Rachel was very ill and near death. Larkin yielded to the entreaties of friends that Catholic baptism was required for burial in the cemetery. Moreover, without Catholic marriage, their children were illegitimate and might be denied the right to inherit. Accordingly, Larkin "had the ceremony of baptism administered; after which the ceremony of marriage was performed by the padre according to the usage of the Romish Church."[38]

Unquestionably the desire for a Protestant wedding ceremony and his wish not to convert to Catholicism played some part in Larkin's delayed marriage. In light of his clearly expressed mercenary views, there were other relevant factors. One aspect, of equal importance and more clearly integrated into Larkin's character of self-seeking opportunism, was his discovery that the death of John A. C. Holmes had made Rachel a woman of financial means, something he had sought all along in his wife to be.

Since Rachel's marriage with Holmes was childless, she was her husband's sole heir.

Like most sea captains of the period, Holmes traded on his own account as well as navigating his employer's ship. In addition, he had joint investments with his employer in some specific ventures. The latter made accounting for profits and losses difficult, and in retrospect, renders it almost impossible to form a fully accurate appraisal of the sea captain's net worth that Rachel inherited. But there are clues from which an estimate can be made.

On Holmes's own accounts, there is one interesting insight. On December 13, 1831, just a few months before his death, he consigned a personally owned cargo of cattle hides to Thomas Shaw, a supercargo or ship's commercial agent. He asked Shaw to sell the cargo, 420 hides in good condition and 200 partially damaged, in Boston. This single transaction probably represented a gross of $1,560.[39] Most of this would be profit since Holmes would hardly have the expenses of a large trader. In analyzing the significance of the transaction, it must be remembered that the 1831 dollar was the equivalent of about thirteen 1990 dollars.[40]

There were probably many such individual accounts in Holmes's estate. He had adequate financing through a Massachusetts woman named Caroline Moore, who presumably supplied capital to purchase trading goods.[41] When Henry Virmond, Holmes's employer, wrote Rachel in July 1832, he offered to help collect from traders who owed her husband money. He mentioned four separate cities in Mexico plus unspecified places in California where merchants carried such debts.[42] Other accounts were also outstanding.[43]

In addition, Holmes's accounts with his employer's ships, the joint venture arrangements, had to be settled. Virmond mentioned these and offered $400 on account pending final settlement. The accounts due from Virmond ultimately were to Larkin's great advantage. In the early days of his retail operations, the fall of 1835, he received trade goods from one of Virmond's ships to the value of $950. By the end of 1835, they constituted Larkin's entire inventory of goods on hand for sale in his Monterey store, almost 40 percent of his net worth.[44] These goods were only on account, credited to the balance due from Virmond.[45]

Everything considered, Mrs. Larkin's inheritance from her first husband probably netted $3,000 to $4,000. Not a princely fortune, of course, but $3,000 was all the wealth he had required in a marriageable woman in 1831.[46] As Larkin well knew, he would have absolute control and disposition over his wife's funds. He could use them in his trade as he wished. That was the ordinary common-law rule of coverture for a married woman with financial means. All this, however, depended on one critical thing: he had to marry Rachel.

As the evidence came in concerning Rachel's inheritance, this must have made marriage seem increasingly attractive to Larkin. It is an oversimplification to believe that Larkin married Rachel *only* because of her money, or that he delayed the marriage until he was certain of the amount. There were other attractions. After all she was pregnant long before Larkin even knew of her husband's death, let alone his net worth. Then, too, the ability to marry and not convert to Catholicism probably really mattered to the couple. But the money factor, especially in light of Larkin's absolutely consistent drive for wealth and his willingness to sacrifice principle to opportunity, must have played an important role in his decision to marry. It is probably not stretching a point to note that Captain Holmes's money was the primary source of the funds used to build Larkin's initial trade and the Larkin House.

It should be added that after Larkin's marriage to Rachel, there is absolutely no evidence or even a hint of any further womanizing. The relationship was to prove neither idyllic nor crisis riddled. Theirs was a good marriage, with a normal allotment of problems and rewards.

One problem that would confront the couple almost immediately was the death of their daughter Isabel. Burial entry 308 of Mission Santa Barbara tells that:

> On July 9, 1833, in the cemetery of this Mission, I officiated at the burial of Isabel Ana, infant daughter of Raquel Laquen [Rachel Larkin] and Guillermo [William] Cuper, both foreigners. In testimony whereof I affix my signature.
>
> Fr. Antonio Jimeno[47]

The reference to William Cooper is puzzling. Hubert H. Bancroft's *Pioneer Index* does not list any William Cooper as being in California prior to 1845. Larkin's half-brother was John the Baptist Rogers Cooper, not William. This may have been a deliberate effort by the Larkins to disguise the fact that Larkin fathered the child in light of his then very recent marriage to Rachel.[48] The much later biographical sketches, prepared while the parties were alive, do not mention Isabel.

The couple stayed on in Santa Barbara, probably continuing to live with Daniel Hill and his wife. In the early fall of 1833 they returned to the Monterey area and began to live on one of Cooper's ranches, the Bolsa del Potrero y Moro Cojo, better known as Familia Sagrada, or Sacred Family.[49] Cooper had purchased the ranch in 1829,[50] and it lay between the Salinas River and Tembladera Slough, south of the present town of Castroville.[51] By Larkin's own estimation, it was about fifteen miles from Monterey.[52] The move was probably made at the end of August 1833 or the first days of September. Larkin's "Daybook" of accounts bears the entry "Salines Sept 5th 1833" on the inside cover, without explanation but near to the place where he entered "Arrived in Mont. April 13 1832." This book of accounts also records detailed entries dating from September 1833 through July 1834 under a separate section headed "SALINES."[53]

Photograph of portrait of Larkin's wife, Rachel Hobson Holmes Larkin. The oil portrait was executed in 1849 by Joseph Knapp. Photographer, Chuck Bancroft. Courtesy State of California, Department of Parks and Recreation.

Larkin was not merely trading from his country home. He was also in business in Monterey, as his daybook reveals Monterey accounts for October and November 1833, a time when he was certainly living on Cooper's ranch.[54] Also, in 1833 and early 1834, he built a wheat mill, probably in Monterey.[55]

Larkin was still doing a small commission business and was engaged in his early debt collection work, at first just for a very few customers, that would later blossom.[56] He showed an increasing interest in lumber and was shipping it to arid Los Angeles through Abel Stearns.[57] In 1833 and early 1834 Larkin simply purchased planks from independent loggers operating in the Santa Cruz Mountains. Between April and August 1834, he began to engage crews of sawyers as direct employees to cut redwood and finish it into planks.[58] Larkin prepared a chart entitled, "Wages paid Workmen from May 1833," which shows a significant increase in the number of employees beginning in September and October 1833, although it does not specify whether they worked on the wheat mill, the Cooper ranch, or in the mountains cutting timber.[59]

Larkin had a business interest in Cooper's ranch. He never acquired any equity in the property itself, but had some arrangement with his half-brother whereby he could profit from ranching activities.[60] Many months after he moved to Monterey he still maintained stock on the ranch. His holdings on November 12, 1834, included sixteen horses and mares, seven mules, twenty-four hogs, and twenty fowls.[61]

The Larkins moved into town in July 1834,[62] renting half of the Hartnell house,[63] which was probably made available because of that family's move to the country.[64] Larkin had planned it for some time. In April, he had told Stearns, "I shall this summer open store in town,"[65] and in his account book wrote, "opened store in Monterey Septeber 1834. Capital about Five hundred Dollars."[66] This was probably Larkin's first actual store, a fixed place for retail operations. Its spectacular success will be detailed in the following chapter.

Larkin soon thought of the construction of their own home. Perhaps it was due to the pressures of a growing family. His son, Thomas Oliver Larkin, Jr., was born on April 13, 1834,[67] and Rachel was already pregnant with their third child, a boy named William Rogers Larkin, who was born in 1835 but died in infancy.[68] Meanwhile there was a need even more pressing than a home: his accounts for October 14, 1834, show him indebted to his landlord, the English expatriate William Hartnell, in the amount of three pesos for "1 Bed for Mi & wife."[69]

Larkin constructed a house that unintentionally established an entire architectual style, known as the Monterey Style of adobe. It was the first two-story building in Monterey, and one of the earliest two-story structures in California. Larkin and his wife built what was essentially a New England Colonial style house, with two stories, traditional glass windows, center staircase, and an upstairs fireplace.[70] But adaptations were made to meet the materials available for local construction, specifically the use of adobe bricks.

Larkin did not like the use of adobe because of the measures necessary to protect against erosion from the heavy winter rains. The result, he noted, was that the Monterey "houses are much disfigured by having the south ends lumbered up with boards or brush to keep off the rain from the south."[71] Yet redwood planks were very expensive and the cost for an entire house in redwood probably prohibitive. Adobe was the local material.

Larkin thought he found a solution to the problem, although it turned out to be only a partial answer. However, through the attempt he created the distinctive look of the Monterey Style. Larkin deepened the eaves on one front to four feet, to keep off rain, but scaffolded another. This gave the traditional American hipped roof an exaggerated rake. A double veranda was added on two sides. The adobe bricks were then whitewashed, and the Monterey Style was complete.[72]

The appearance became popular, and soon the local Californios were building homes in this new manner. Juan Bautista Alvarado in Monterey, General Mariano Guadalupe Vallejo on his Petaluma ranch, Vicente Lugo in Los Angeles, these and others adopted the style.[73] The accompanying photograph of the Larkin house is dated 1901, although its appearance has changed considerably over time.[74]

Larkin began his construction in December 1834 with the assembly of various construction supplies, including adobe bricks.[75] On January 29, 1835, Larkin petitioned the *ayuntamiento* (town council) of Monterey for a grant of a vacant town lot thirty-four *varas* wide and fifty deep on which to build a commercial house and dwelling.[76] (A vara is just under a yard.) Larkin's accounts show expenses in April 1835 of about $16 fees paid to the municipality for processing the grant.

The difficult course of construction is reflected in a minutia of entries in Larkin's accounts from December 1834 through August 1836, then again for December 1836, and from August 1837 through January 1838. Almost all materials—glass, wallpaper, lead, furnishings—had to be imported at great cost and uncertain delivery. Craftsmen were largely exshipwrights and were unreliable. Laborers, mostly former Mission Indians, were careless or unproficient, as suggested by the numbers of entries relating to damage done to tools, molds, or the prepared adobes.

Larkin complained of both the expense and the intrusion of the project into his business concerns. On April 13, 1835, he wrote Stearns that he "had nine men at work on my house foundation. I had to leave the store to be with them."[77] A month later he complained that he was "now building—and am much in want of cash."[78] Larkin kept dual columns in his accounts of his estimated costs and the actual costs, and the actual costs generally exceeded the estimated. But the difficulties were not so great that

The Larkin house, Monterey, in 1901. Here Larkin maintained both his retail store, located on the ground floor, and his residence, where most of Larkin's lavish hospitality was extended. Courtesy The Bancroft Library.

he failed to treat his workers with rum in September 1835, in celebration of raising the roof, although even that happy expense was twice what Larkin had allowed in estimate.

The Larkins may have moved into the unfinished house in early June 1835 as a receipt for payment of a store license is dated June 10, 1835.[79] More probably, however, they moved in during 1836 as his year-end account for 1836, that is, as of January 1, 1837, stated: "On moving into the new House, I was without any funds having spent and invested every thing in Building—I remained therefore sometime without any Store, or having any trade."[80]

Larkin's store and a storeroom area occupied the first floor. A central staircase led to the family's living areas.[81] Their furnishings, as of January 1, 1836, consisted of a writing desk, two sideboards, twelve chairs, two looking glasses, and a bedstead.[82] Following his consular appointment, he ordered a considerable extent of additional American furniture including four sofas, four mirrors, two large dining tables, two round tables, and four dozen chairs,[83] the expense of which Larkin thought outrageous.[84]

In 1836, the Larkins wanted to add a garden and some adjacent buildings. Accordingly, Larkin petitioned the ayuntamiento for an additional grant on both sides of his lot. A committee of the town council investigated and approved one request but turned down the other because it would block the road. Later Larkin obtained a very small, two-vara encroachment onto this road, taking the precaution of obtaining his neighbor's approval in advance.[85]

Larkin's accounts show that the house cost $4,105 as of January 1, 1837. His accounts in later years showed a cost basis of the house in varying amounts, but are difficult to interpret as they probably included other nearby commercial buildings, for example, his bakery and warehouse. The original cost of the house itself and immediately adjacent outbuildings was probably very close to $5,000.[86]

It was a solid piece of construction. In 1843, Larkin described his house as having "walls lower story 33 inches thick, upper story 22 inches. Shingle roof. 3 chimbleys. Lenght of house about 60 Ft. by 40. Fourteen rooms. Land 85 yds in front by 30 yds back. Garden occupying about half the latter & the yard enclosed by stone wall 10 ft hide 2 ft thick." Unfortunately, the experiment on extra-length eaves to keep the rain off the adobe must not have been entirely successful. Notwithstanding Larkin's disapproval of the aesthetic qualities, he noted in 1843 that the south side of the house had "a scafford of boards to keep of the rain."[87]

No doubt Rachel appreciated having her own home, and a house in the New England style at that. She was kept busy with the maternal duties of an expanding family. The Larkins had lost a son, William Rogers, in infancy, but another son, Frederick Hobson, was born in 1836. Still another son, Henry Rogers, died while an infant in 1838, but two years later in 1840 yet another boy, Francis Rogers, came into the world. Up to this point all of the Larkins' children had been boys with the sole exception of little Isabel. But this streak was broken with the birth of a daughter, Carolina Ann, in 1842, and another daughter, Sophia Adeline, in 1843.

At the close of 1845 the Larkins had five living children, Thomas Oliver, Jr., born in 1834; Frederick Hobson, 1836; Francis Rogers, 1840; Carolina Ann, 1842; and Sophia Adeline, 1843. They would have one more child, Alfred Otis, in 1847.[88] Rachel obviously needed help with the raising of such a large family, and the Larkins had household servants as well as Larkin's business employees. As early as 1836, the *padron* (census) listed three household servants residing with the family.[89] At this date they were probably Indians who had been raised at one of the missions.

As more children arrived and as Larkin's entertaining became more pronounced, Rachel needed even more domestic help. By the early 1840s the supply of ex-Mission Indians became more limited. Many had died of disease, such as smallpox, or had become absorbed into the mainstream of ordinary ranch employment. Alternative sources of domestic servants had to be used. In 1842 Larkin attempted to procure servants from Hawaii, but apparently it was difficult to persuade husbands and wives to leave the Islands, although young boys were available.[90]

Toward the mid-1840s, Larkin, like many of the Californios, turned to orphan Indian boys and girls. These were not ex-Mission Indians. By the mid-1840s, the Indians of the central valleys had taken to raiding the settled areas to obtain horsemeat, for which they had developed a taste. Mexican troops and private groups raided their tribes in retaliation. In the process they captured young orphans after killing their parents. There was a market for these children and John A. Sutter conducted a business in their procurement and sale, under conditions very much approaching slavery.[91]

Although the California authorities approved of the Indian raids, they disapproved of the sale of Indian children, sometimes vigorously and sometimes not. Juan Bautista Alvarado, governor from 1836 to 1842, recalled that Larkin obtained Indian orphans from Sutter,[92] and several letters suggest Larkin engaged in that practice. One written in 1844 from a business associate advised, "I do not know if Mr Pico is at San Luis or not . . . I shell endeavour to find some person to take the girl you mention he has for Mr [i.e., Mrs.] L."[93] In a late 1846 letter Sutter mentions to Larkin that "the two little Girls are here. . . . I shall take care of them for you."[94]

In addition to the raising of the children and the supervision of the household servants, Rachel no doubt was at times almost overwhelmed by the volume of entertaining sponsored by her husband. There were frequently large dinner parties and dances, and it was not unusual for guests to stay weeks with the Larkins. The volume of entertainment increased with time, especially after Larkin's consular appointment.

Although there were periods of long separation, when Larkin was off on business trips of many months' duration, indications are that their relationship was warm and satisfactory. In 1852, Larkin wrote to a friend from his North Carolina days expressing his domestic happiness.[95] The advice he once gave to an American immigrant in 1844 suggests his own feelings: "I would advice you, as you value your peace of mind, your character, and future wealth and well being, to exert yourself in doing all you can to make your Wife's situation with you pleasant and happy, by which means you may both hereafter live in prosperity and contentment."[96]

During their years in Monterey Rachel remained in the background, but she still exercised influence and her own will. In 1846, as the crisis of war loomed over California, Larkin begged Rachel to take the family to Hawaii. She refused to leave. There was an earlier incident in December 1834 when Larkin had been threatened with imprisonment if he did not pay a trumped-up debt. He was told he could not put up security and could not even speak to the governor until he first paid the spurious debt. Apparently Larkin gave thought to defying the order and appealing to the governor before paying. Then, "as my Wife had been inform'd of it and was very uneasy, I pd it."[97]

Larkin's primary activities, above all else, were his business affairs. However, he was a man of broader interests. We have seen that Larkin was a reader, and to the extent possible in California, he indulged this interest. It was difficult. "There is no Books (excepting children first Books) for sale here," he wrote in 1845. Moreover, "but a few would purchase if there were."[98] Larkin's letters reflect a continuing interest in receiving newspapers and then passing them along. In 1840 and 1841, he showed considerable interest in obtaining California subscriptions for a fledgling Hawaii newspaper.[99] But the paper failed and Larkin's enthusiasm faded. By 1845, he wrote that there were "no Newspapers in California, for which I attribute Four reasons. Either one may suffice. First there is no printer. Second no printing press. Threee no Editor. Fourth there could no subscribers be obtained."[100]

His eastern correspondents occasionally sent whole crates of reading materials.[101] Then, too, Larkin could borrow books from visiting sea captains, as he did in July 1845, obtaining Farnham's *Travels in the Californias* from Captain Theophilus C. Everett.[102] Or he could borrow from the reasonably extensive private libraries of the leading Mexican citizens.[103]

Larkin was also a cheerful lender of books. He made a big impression on one young sailor, William H. Thomes: "He had in his library a complete set of Scott's works, and, it may not be believed I know, but still it is quite true, when he learned that I was fond of reading, lent me two or three of the works at one time, to peruse while we cruised up and down the coast, and continued to loan the books until I had read all."[104]

Obviously with his interest in reading, Larkin would be keenly concerned with the education of his own children. He took his first steps in this direction in late 1837, at a time when his eldest son, Oliver, was about three and a half, and Frederic less than a year. He asked his cousin, William M. Rogers, whether he might be able to board the children with his family while they obtained an education in New England. Unfortunately, the answer was no. "I suppose it is desirable that they should have a good New England education," Rogers acknowledged, but he could not help.[105]

Education in Mexican California was rudimentary and sporadic. Such as existed was conducted entirely in Spanish, and Larkin had no desire that his sons forget English. Earlier in 1834–1836, William Hartnell, an English expatriate, had conducted a private school in Salinas near Monterey. That effort failed for lack of students. However, there was a school in Honolulu, Hawaii, that enrolled foreign students as well as local children.

Andrew and Rebecca Johnstone, the teachers at the Oahu Charity School, were former missionaries, and Larkin held very negative views of the Protestant missionary efforts in Hawaii.[106] Nevertheless, by summer of 1840 Larkin decided to send his eldest son Oliver to Hawaii to board with the Johnstones. That five of his fellow expatriates in California, Americans and Englishmen, had already sent their children to the Hawaiian school helped Larkin make the decision. But the predominant factor was Larkin's fear that

Oliver was not learning English, and with that perhaps his American heritage. He wrote Andrew Johnstone that he thought Oliver was too "small to send so far. . . . I intended to keep him another year, but he has learnt so little english that I cannot talk with him as I would to do."[107]

Oliver sailed from Monterey on the ship *Alciope*, August 27, 1840. The vessel was to stop in Santa Barbara and then proceed on to Hawaii. Larkin's relationship with Oliver suggests a very concerned and caring father, hardly a stern and distant patriarch. To the teachers he expressed "my wish that you should treat him & school him . . . in the same manner as if he was your son, without saying or thinking what would his Father or Mother do in this or that case." Undoubtedly with great apprehension Larkin carefully noted the exact time at which Oliver's ship "went out of sight from the house" on a copy he kept of his letter.[108]

It was clear from Larkin's incoming correspondence that he had begged all his friends and acquaintances to send word immediately about Oliver's condition. Apparently he had asked these men to comment specifically on whether Oliver was lonesome, homesick, or seasick during the voyage, since they all wrote of this in reply. The first report came in from Alpheus B. Thompson with whose family Oliver stayed while in Santa Barbara. On September 12 Thompson wrote that during the voyage from Monterey the boy "was as much at home as when with you. He was sick for three Hours while beating out of the Bay but never complained." He added that Oliver's weight was 34 pounds.[109] Thereafter, a stream of correspondence arrived from acquaintances, fellow merchants, and sea captains, with their reassuring comments bespeaking Larkin's paternal anxiety.[110]

Oliver arrived in Hawaii on November 7, 1840, and thereafter a considerable correspondence ensued between the schoolteachers, Andrew or Rebecca Johnstone, and Larkin. It concerned the boy's expenses, for which Larkin volunteered generously; health and growth, generally good with minor maladies appropriate to the boy's age; academic progress, excellent; and amusements, which ranged from contented playing with toys to noise-filled parties given by the Hawaiian king.

Larkin sent frequent letters to his son, and eventually Oliver was able to write his parents. Following Larkin's appointment as consul, his son gleefully reported that he and his little friends had been invited to dinner aboard a visiting American man-of-war. An impressed nine-year-old Oliver asked his father to "let me know if they fire 7 gun when you go on board of a man of war."[111] But there was a touch of homesickness in Oliver's letters. He wrote his parents in June 1844, "do you know that once in a month an American man of war is coming here then going to Monterey. What a fine chance for the California boys to go home . . . . I cannot tell you how much I want to see you and my dear Mother and brothers and sisters. I think if I had wings like a berd I would fly there very quick."[112]

Actually Larkin had already thought of bringing Oliver back. On October 15, 1843, Larkin wrote his cousin to inquire into costs of private education in Boston for both Oliver and Frederic. Rogers reported the costs, but in response to Larkin's special inquiry warned that it "would be difficult if not impossible to find a school where they could retain their Spanish."[113] On August 12, 1844, Larkin advised the Johnstones that Oliver was to be sent to the East.

The plan was to send Oliver to Boston that year with the departure of the hide ship *Barnstable* from San Diego, and in a letter of November 17, 1844, Larkin asked James B. Hatch, one of the ship's managers, to accompany the boy. That was agreeable with Hatch, but he warned Larkin that the ship would probably be required to leave San Diego before Oliver arrived in San Diego from Hawaii.[114] In the event Oliver did just miss the connection. The *Barnstable* left San Diego on December 17, 1844,[115] and the Mexican bark *Clarita*, with Larkin's son on board, arrived in San Pedro by December 26. No other ships were scheduled to leave for Boston that season and soon Oliver sailed to Monterey with Captain Peter Petersen on the *Admittance*.[116]

There were changes in the Larkin household during his five years of absence. When Oliver left in 1840, there was only one brother, Frederic, but now he had two brothers and two sisters. There had been severe illness in the family. In the spring of 1844, when Larkin returned from a business trip in mainland Mexico, his ship brought back smallpox with it. Perhaps Larkin himself was the carrier. By April 1844, three of the children had the smallpox as well as four Indian household servants; even Larkin and his wife were affectly slightly by the disease.[117] The children recovered, but one of the daughters, Carolina, was severely marked by the pox.[118]

In the fall of 1844, Larkin busied himself in attempts to establish a private elementary school in Monterey for the benefit of the sons of the foreign expatriates and wealthier Californios. This was not to be for Oliver, as plans were already made to send him east, but Larkin may have contemplated such a school for the next boy, Frederic, and certainly must have thought it would suit Francis. Larkin circulated a subscription list among his friends and associates in California, and in September wrote his business associate and friend Alfred Robinson, a former California resident then residing in New York City.

Larkin asked his help to recruit a schoolmaster to come out to Monterey. In his organized manner Larkin sent Robinson an incredible mass of detail concerning salary, needed supplies, and prospective enrollment.[119] At first Robinson was excited about the project, but later entirely banked the fires of his enthusiasm.[120]

During that same fall of 1844, he wrote his stepbrother (and cousin) Isaac Childs to inquire about the housing and other costs of sending his entire family to Massachusetts.[121] Presumably this was an alternative plan for all of his children. But the idea never materialized, so that with the departure of Oliver and Frederic for the East, another son, Francis, and two daughters remained in Monterey. Larkin's interest in a good local school remained undiminished, but the fruition of his plans would have to wait until 1847, following the American conquest.

Throughout 1845 Larkin was peppered by queries from eastern relatives as to when at long last Oliver was finally going to be sent. His sister, Ann Rogers Larkin Wright, was especially persistent.[122] Larkin finally arranged passage in the fall of 1845 on the American hide-ship *California* under Captain James P. Arther. But the plan now was to send both Oliver and his brother Frederic for an eastern education.[123]

The boys left Monterey in very late 1845 and took the *Vandalia* to San Diego where they transferred to the *California*. Again friends and business associates were pressed into sending reports on the boys back to Monterey. From John C. Jones, the man who had married Larkin and Rachel in 1833, he heard by way of a January 24, 1846, letter from San Diego:

> I have seen your boys frequently; thy are in fine health and very contended. . . . little Frederick has become quite the man, nothing of the baby left about him. Tom is a real Coon, well calculated to fight his way thro' the world. He is an uncommon smart boy, has a great taste for drawing and displays quite a mecanical jenius. I shall not fail, as you request to visit them in the U Stats and will keep you advised of their situation &c."[124]

William D. M. Howard passed on the information from San Diego that the boys were happy, contented, and stout in letters of December 28, 1845, and January 25, 1846. They had been on shore several times in Santa Barbara. Oliver's chief interest was in building ship models and drawing vessels. Frederic had been a bit homesick, but now he had another boy about his age to play with who was also traveling to Boston. Howard predicted that the boys would pay close attention to their studies during the passage.[125] Doubtless, Larkin was gratified to read these reports.

The two children arrived in Boston on June 24, 1846. During the voyage they had had two very different kinds of experiences. On the one hand they apparently had studied well, or at least Frederic had, as the captain thought that he could now speak better English than Oliver. On the other hand, they were exposed to the talk of a fellow passenger, William Faxon, who had indulged himself, to the apparent eager interest of the boys, in "vulgar discourse & swearing, saying that he no lest seduce thirty marred women in Monterey during his stay there."[126] Hopefully, Larkin found it possible to smile at the interest of his sons in the seduction of married women.

Larkin received a fuller report from his sister Ann. The boys had spent a few days with them in Neponset, Massachusetts. By the beginning of July 1846, they were with Larkin's stepbrother Isaac Childs and his wife in Lynn, Larkin's own hometown. Ann gave her brother a good summary view of the boys' condition and their educational plans:

There is much in Oliver that reminds me of you when a boy. He is very social, amusing & intelligent. Though Fredric says less, he has as much thought, and knowledge according to his age as his Brother. He speaks english very well, having learnt it on the passage. Oliver is to attend the Accademy in Lynn. Fredric goes to a smaller school for a short time, untill he is prepared to go to the other.[127]

Such was Larkin's personal life for the period 1833 to the end of 1845, and just a bit beyond. In the meantime, he was very busy on other fronts as well. He was immersed in his business as a trader and merchant and was intensely interested in developing associations and networks of affiliates, both among the local Californios and the foreign residents.

CHAPTER 4

TRADER AND MERCHANT

WHILE WE CONCENTRATE on Larkin the individual, the special case, we should remember that the consequences of his mercantile activities transcend his individuality. Larkin is also the leading example of a type: the American merchant in Mexican California. These merchants did as much service in the Americanization of California, if not more, as the invaders of 1846.

Spanish California was a remote, isolated province of the Kingdom of New Spain, controlled economically by Franciscan missionaries and politically by governors appointed by the Crown. The Franciscans built an adamantine wall against the introduction of new ideas, while the governors strictly enforced the Spanish policies prohibiting entry of foreigners and disallowing commercial trade with other than the Spanish supply ships.

In such a culture, social and economic expectations were limited. A rough egalitarianism was imposed by rude frontier circumstances, but not by ideology. Few in Spanish California doubted that economic and social horizons were set, and properly so, by the status set by birth. Few aspired to wealth or had hopes of luxury. Men looked upwards to the authority of class and tradition. Opportunities for advancement were accordingly few. A governor, always assigned to California from the ranks of the Spanish born, might aspire through merit to be promoted and transferred elsewhere.

It would have been difficult to wrench the California of this milieu into the fold of rambunctious, industrial America, with its noisy, nervous capitalism. The government of post-revolutionary Mexico in combination with the American and British merchants of Mexican California supplied a transition. Mexican politicians created the opportunities for private wealth by the secularization of the missions and fostered economic freedom by opening California to foreign trade. But the actual availability of a steady flow of

merchandise, supplied by the merchants, played no small role in revolution-
izing social outlooks.

The catering by merchants to whim and latent interests in luxury changed
men's thinking. Social stratification was no longer a God-given constant.
Economic improvement was possible. Indeed it took place before men's
eyes. In Spanish California consumer products had been scarce. Now it was
possible to buy goods with wealth. Social modes need not remain rigidly
traditional. Innovation was possible; new fashions and changes in style and
technique for any activity could be seen at the merchant's store.

The ultimate Americanization of California was not to be smooth. But it
would have been far more difficult had not her people been prepared for the
intellectual and physical effect of change, had her people not been softened
by the prior peaceful invasion of the American merchant. In this sense the
leading merchant of Mexican California, Thomas O. Larkin, had for many
years been working as an agent for her Americanization, and, as it were, to
make California safe for capitalism.

Larkin's California career was meteoric. The fall of 1833 was a favorable
time for this ambitious thirty-one-year-old to open a general merchandise
store in the California capital of Monterey. He was personally prepared,
and the time and place were auspicious. The earlier business ventures in
North Carolina, although ending in failure, had taught Larkin much of the
ways of the commercial world. The treachery of his former partner only
added to Larkin's New England heritage of self-reliance.

Larkin had long been ambitious for wealth, but in a somewhat adolescent
and unfocused way. By September 1833, his earlier self-assured cockiness
had vanished. He had just married that June, and was settled and ready to
apply the energetic labor characteristic of his career. He would find long
hours and tenacity necessary to garner the desired fortune.

The year itself, 1833, was a propitious one for commencing business in
California. The missions still controlled the best lands, and their vast cattle
herds yielded the bulk of the cattle hides which constituted the chief
export commodity. But it was clear to all perceptive observers that the long-
threatened secularization was at hand. Within a few years the missions were
reduced to the status of parish churches and their lands distributed, through
numerous land grants, into private hands. This process of secularization
caused temporary chaos for all and permanent dislocation for the Mission
Indians.

By 1836, the purely economic aspects of secularization were stabilized
and had proven enormously successful. The private grantees of the mission
lands proved even more efficient than the padres in the production of cattle
hides and increasing production of shoes and other leather manufactures in
Massachusetts added to demand.

There was one critical difference between the older missionary production of hides and the new private ranchero's operations. The desires of the

missionaries and their Indian charges for manufactured goods had been relatively limited. However, the new owners of these valuable export commodities were individuals and their families. They were consumers and, after years of self-denial in isolated California, they were anxious to purchase the goods and trappings of nineteenth-century civilization. Desire had become coupled with buying power, and this stimulated an enormous increase in the effective California demand for manufactured goods of all classes. In the second half of the 1830s, California experienced an economic boom, and Larkin was there at the right moment.

Almost all manufactured goods in Mexican California were imported. Inexpensive wine and liquor, lumber, shingles, soap, and flour were among the few items processed locally. Consumer goods, from manufactured clothing to furniture, and trade goods, from nails to tools, all were imported by ship. Most came into California on the ships sent out by Boston merchants to trade these manufactures for cattle hides and, to a lesser extent, rendered cattle fat, or tallow.

The Boston ships, as they were called, put in at the capital of Monterey, paid duties, and thereafter coasted for a year or two up and down California, from San Francisco to San Diego, selling merchandise and collecting hides in payment. The companies sent agents throughout the countryside, selling by sample and receiving hides. But primary reliance was on shipside sales. After arrival at a port the ships were converted into retail stores, and ranchers and their families came into town from miles around. They met with their fellow ranchers, and their purchasing of goods became a festive social occasion.[1]

Although the shipside bazaars were colorful, the process was economically inefficient. There was a need for fixed independent merchants, middlemen between the hide shippers and the ranchers. Larkin's counterpart in southern California was another American, Abel Stearns, who also began business in 1833. As Larkin became the chief merchant in Monterey, so Stearns became the leading trader in what was becoming California's most populous town, Los Angeles.[2]

For the shippers the advantages of the fixed merchant had mostly to do with credit. The cattle were rounded up for slaughter over vast ranches. A California ranch of one league, or 4,438 acres, was considered small. Many were several times as large. The slaughter was conducted only once a year, and it was only then that the hides could be obtained. The result was that sales of merchandise to ranchers almost always had to be made on credit, pending the next slaughter, if a sale were to be made at all. Collections were often difficult for the shippers, in part because terms extended over such a long term. Larkin described the prevailing trade customs tersely in a letter of 1845: "Payment in full in California in 12 to 18 months is considered by us good, and we obtain no interest only on Cash lent."[3] The hide shippers began the appointment of resident agents in California to deal with the ranchers on a more continuous basis, but even so they could not develop the same feeling for a customer's creditworthiness as a local merchant.

A shipper who sold a substantial portion of his merchandise to a local merchant, even at a lower wholesale price, would accrue several advantages. He would no longer need to send drummers beating the countryside for hide collections and sales. If the shipper sold merchandise to Larkin for hides, and the California merchants usually paid in hides, there would be an additional efficiency in the service of the merchant as a year-round collection center. Even if the merchant demanded credit terms, as Larkin and Stearns often did, a few reliable American and British traders in a few towns along the coast made better credit risks than hundreds of Californio ranchers scattered throughout the countryside.

For the ranchers the fixed merchants also represented an advantage. The ranchers could bring in hides to pay their accounts whenever they were ready and the roads were passable; they no longer needed to coordinate with a ship's scheduled arrival at a particular port or off an isolated landing, at times which might be inconvenient for the rancher. Even more important, the merchant carried an inventory of merchandise, so that the baubles of fashion and the necessities of ranching were available on credit to the rancher and his family on a year-round basis. They would no longer be dependent on the uncertain arrival of a ship.

The method of shipboard sales continued throughout the Mexican period. Yet the convenience of the middleman's operations, resulting primarily from California's great distance from her major marketplace of Boston, insured the local merchant's success. While this trade did not alone produce Larkin's fortune, it certainly accounted for his initial profits.

Larkin sold a bewildering variety of items, from cloth, clothing, and furniture to china goods, crockery, farming implements, and even some foodstuffs, such as rice and sugar.[4] The goods had a tremendous markup in remote, frontier California. Retail goods whose origin was the United States generally sold at four or more times the equivalent retail price of Boston.

Larkin's customers were equally diverse. Most ranchers in northern California at one time or another bought something from him. They had credit accounts and their names were entered into Larkin's extensive set of ledgers. The foreign community likewise provided Larkin with a steady clientele. Of the expatriates, his books reveal primarily American and English patrons, but there are also French, Irish, Danish, Scottish, Italian, Portuguese, Chilean, and Greek customers.[5]

Cash was gladly accepted in Larkin's establishment, but specie was scarce in Mexican California. Most retail customers paid their accounts in cattle hides, the ubiquitous California currency, although Larkin regularly received such other local products as tallow, soap, lumber, dried beef, and produce. Larkin would then trade these at favorable rates with the Boston ships or in such foreign ports as Mazatlán or Honolulu.[6] Debts owed to

Larkin by businessmen or institutions—fellow merchants, Boston shipping concerns, and the Mexican or American governments—were often paid by credit instruments, such as bills of exchange or promissory notes, rather than goods.

Larkin's establishment changed its character over the years. Liquor led in Larkin's sales throughout his retail career.[7] But in the early days there was considerable on-premises consumption, and the store then had much more the character of a grog shop than a small department store.[8]

In addition to good supplies of liquor, Larkin maintained a small bowling alley and a billiard table for which he sold tickets for play. This bowling alley, over which customers undoubtedly wagered, accounted for a considerable volume of his early business. When he finally removed it in 1838, to devote the space to more upscaled commercial activities, he noted in his year-end accounts that "the profits of 1838 was less than of 1837 . . . in a great measure by my breaking up a Bowling Alley—which before gave large profits."[9] Space for larger inventory and increasing retail sales of merchandise would quickly make up for the bowling.

Larkin developed other outlets for his trade besides local ranchers and tradesmen. For example, the California coast was frequently visited by American whaling ships. They came into California ports to acquire meats, produce, and supplies, and for these purposes were permitted by the Mexican California government to trade a few hundred dollars of manufactured goods, carried for this trade from Boston, free of the normal tariff duties. Since the tariff approached 100% of value, this gave the whalers a great cost advantage which resulted in their charging lower prices for goods sold to the ranchers than could be charged by either the merchants or the hide ships.

Because of this price undercutting, most of the California merchants disliked the whalers. Larkin, however, saw advantage in their patronage and actually cultivated them as customers. He rendered personal assistance to facilitate their entry into the port, as well as simply selling them supplies. Larkin sent information concerning tariff regulations to newspapers in the whaling town of New Bedford, Massachusetts, and even dug water wells on the Monterey beach so that each whaling ship no longer had to dig her own.[10] He even advertised in newspapers for their patronage,[11] and had standing advertisements that ran regularly in the New Bedford (Massachusetts) *Shipping List* and the *New York Sun.*[12]

Larkin welcomed other ships as customers and some of his advertising was as much directed at the hide vessels as the whalers. In the late 1830s and 1840s, as American imperial ambitions increasingly aimed at neighboring Mexico's northern territories, the United States navy put in frequent appearances off the California coast. These warships generally came into the capital, Monterey, and even before Larkin was appointed the American consul, he was their chief supplier. Patriotism and profit combined in these sales, and that was much to Larkin's delight. However, his patriotic zeal did not prevent his provisioning the military vessels of nations other than his own.[13]

Selling to the American navy could carry some risk, as Larkin discovered in November 1842 when the frigate *United States* was suddenly ordered to Hawaii, leaving him holding about $1,000 worth of specially ordered produce.[14] Still, as Larkin confided to a friend in February 1843, "if our ships of war could be here a year or two as they have been of late, I could turned my property into cash. Supplying a Frigate is good business."[15] On one occasion in December 1844, which Larkin must have found memorable, a navy purser paid him $2,218.68 in silver coin for beef, vegetables, and soap.[16] That was an enormous amount of cash in Mexican California.

John A. Sutter was also a major customer. In the 1840s, he was busy developing an agricultural fiefdom in his large land grant centered around modern Sacramento. He had no need for many of the consumer products of Larkin's store, but had a steady correspondence ordering iron, saws, nails, and tools, and forever promising that payment would be forthcoming.[17]

The California departmental government proved to be a major source of sales. When the Californios prepared to revolt and expel a governor sent from Mexico, as they periodically did, Larkin found business in supplying local armies for their maneuverings and their marches back and forth from Monterey to Los Angeles. He wrote concerning the year of 1837 that "the Revolution of the California[ns] against the Mexicans, added to business."[18] Again, in March 1845, when the Californios deported Governor Manuel Micheltorena, Larkin sold provisions with which to feed the deposed governor and his soldiers on their voyage back to mainland Mexico.[19]

Larkin furnished goods and provisions to California administrations and military for many purposes and several sorts of emergencies. In 1840, when Governor Alvarado rounded up Isaac Graham and some forty other foreign ruffians, Larkin was asked to supply provisions for the prisoners.[20] Retail dealing with the California government was particularly good business as the government paid, not with the typical promises, but with a lien granted on custom duties to be paid by collections from the next foreign vessel to enter dutiable cargo. Because of his location at the capital, where ships were required to first call and pay duties before trading anywhere in California, Larkin was in a position to make sure his lien was honored.

In addition to simple retail sale of merchandise, Larkin engaged in the vending of other services and products. At times he ran a stable operation, renting his own horses and feeding those belonging to others. In February 1834, he build a flour mill in Monterey, enabling him to receive wheat in payment of goods, and then to retail finished flour. Later he built a bakery, a separate building in which he made bread for provisioning ships. In

1845, Larkin owned a blacksmith shop and a soap factory. He even acted as a contractor. In 1842, he was hired by the departmental government to make extensive additions to the customshouse.[21]

In the years 1834–1843, Larkin's primary dealings, aside from the wholesale buying and retail selling of goods, were in the lumber trade. In the mid-1830s, Larkin hired other foreigners, including Englishman William Garner, to cut lumber in the Santa Cruz mountains on a contract basis and to arrange for its transportation to the beach at Santa Cruz, at the head of the Monterey Bay opposite the town of Monterey. Larkin would then arrange for its transportation to customers, or sometimes would sell the lumber for his customers' own transportation from Santa Cruz. Larkin also contracted for the manufacture and sale of wooden shingles, a by-product of the lumber.[22]

Throughout the 1830s and the early 1840s, he sold a considerable quantity of lumber, hundreds of thousands of board feet, to such major customers as Alpheus B. Thompson in Santa Barbara, Abel Stearns in Los Angeles, and assorted merchants in Honolulu. In July 1841, he contracted for an Englishman and a Scotsman to cut even more timber, 100,000 feet.[23] Finally, in 1843, he opened a branch store in Santa Cruz, nearer the timber's source than Monterey, to facilitate the gathering of lumber products in exchange for merchandise.

Of course, Larkin needed to purchase the merchandise he sold. Most of the foreign merchants in California acquired their goods by wholesale purchase from the Boston hide ships. Stearns, for example, bought merchandise for his Los Angeles store primarily in that manner.

Larkin did buy from the hide ships, but unlike most merchants he relied primarily on purchases from wholesale merchants in foreign ports, such as John Parrott & Company in Mazatlán and the firm of Peirce & Brewer of Oahu in the Sandwich Islands, or Hawaii. Larkin personally traveled to Mazatlán on two occasions, the winter months of 1840–1841 and 1843–1844, during the former years going as far as Mexico City, to purchase goods for his operation.[24] On the first trip alone, he bought over $5,300 worth of merchandise at wholesale prices and on credit.[25] In 1842, he asked another trader to buy for him in Mazatlán more goods at a cost of $4,000.[26] In 1844, Larkin personally brought to California from Mazatlán goods with a wholesale cost of $18,500.[27]

Goods also arrived from Oahu, although Larkin often used Peirce and Brewer in Honolulu, not only as a supplier of merchandise, but also as an intermediary to pay his Mazatlán creditors. Peirce and Brewer were active wholesale merchants who had many accounts in Mazatlán. It was sometimes easier for Larkin to ship from Monterey to Hawaii, or to pay Peirce & Brewer agents in California, than to ship directly from Monterey to Mazatlán. Larkin might therefore ship hides, horses, soap, and timber to Peirce & Brewer, or pay them money or hides in California, and instruct them to apply the credit balance owing Larkin to his Mazatlán accounts, thereby satisfying Larkin's own obligations to the Mazatlán merchants.[28]

The California merchants were in frequent correspondence with each other. Their letters to one another were filled with political news of California and the United States, trade gossip concerning the financial condition and stability of fellow merchants, lists of current prices, and reports of what products were selling well or poorly at various ports. The traders bought and sold goods between themselves and also shipped goods back and forth on consignment for retail sale to their respective customers. Larkin was a leading participant in this correspondence.

Larkin employed many agents and employees in his retail operation, with the nonmanual labor always drawn from the foreign community. An American, Luther Cooper, worked for him in Monterey during the mid-1830s. James McKinley, a Scotsman, was Larkin's agent in Los Angeles in 1835. Early in 1842, Talbot H. Green, from Pennsylvania, began as Larkin's clerk. Green gained in Larkin's favor and, as we shall see, became a partner upon Larkin's retirement from active retail trade.[29]

Larkin often sent Green into the field as a troubleshooter to deal with difficult debtors. A second clerk was required, and George Allen, an Irishman, served in that capacity from 1842 onward until Larkin became consul. Thereafter he was the consular clerk. An American, William T. Faxon, took charge of Larkin's store for a time in 1841, presumably while Larkin was on a trip to Mexico.[30] In addition to these principal employees Larkin hired many others in a lesser and more manual capacity.

Larkin's trade was scattered through many ports. He bought from Mazatlán and Oahu, and he sold to other merchants in Los Angeles, Santa Barbara, San Diego, San Francisco, and Oahu. However, his direct retail sales to customers were all made out of his store in Monterey, with but two short-lived branch operations.

Larkin dispatched his employee, Talbot H. Green, to the coastal valley of Santa Clara in the summer of 1842. His primary mission was to keep a watch on some debtors. These debtors owed Larkin vast quantities of soap which they were engaged in manufacturing. The price of soap was rising and Larkin had a well-founded apprehension that the delinquents would sell their product to others rather than honor their obligation. Hence, the need for a resident agent was primarily to encourage contractual performance.[31]

Yet Larkin's ledgers reveal that Green also maintained a store on the ranch of the chief obligor of soap, John Gilroy, close to the present town of Gilroy. This branch operation opened for business on July 10, 1842 and was not closed until eighteen months later, in December 1843. The closure was probably coincident with Green's assumption of the full responsibilities for the main, Monterey store.

Although the Gilroy store was not as large as Larkin's other branch in Santa Cruz, the operation was not negligible. Larkin's books show that the

Santa Clara Valley operation received merchandise from Larkin's warehouse for the four months August–November 1842 to a value of $2,534.[32] These, however, were the primary months for sales as they overlapped the annual slaughter when the ranchers would be flush with cattle hides.

Larkin's major branch operation, which was in Santa Cruz, opened in February 1842. The idea was to encourage the sawyers in the Santa Cruz mountains to bring lumber, logs, and shingles to the beach in exchange for consumer items. Getting lumber to the beach over nearly impassable roads and, in the winter months, sending goods from Monterey to the mountains had both proved difficult tasks. Larkin hoped that a resident agent in Santa Cruz, equipped with his own inventory, would ease both burdens.

Larkin hired an energetic American, Josiah Belden, to manage the Santa Cruz branch, which operated in the old mission buildings.[33] Larkin furnished him with an extensive supply of goods. The initial inventory in February 1842 included varying quantities of eighty-seven separately described items, patterning the diversity of the Monterey store and valued at $2,188. In July, Larkin sent another shipment of goods worth $775. By year end of 1842, Larkin estimated the value of his goods and lumber at Santa Cruz at $8,500.[34]

Belden was no passive shopkeeper but was an active manager, traveling into the redwoods to take orders and exhort debtors. He sent Larkin a stream of detailed reports on timber conditions, sales, and shipments from his beach-side lumber depot. Larkin in turn dispatched lengthy instructions, and in these instructions he revealed insights into his own approach to the retail trade.

As to bookkeeping Larkin advised Belden, "soon as you get your Books posted . . . draw off from your lumber book and give each man credit for all he has deliverd to you. It will be a good plan to draw off this way once a month, checking the line in the lumber Book as you do it. You will find keeping your Books clear, & perfect as possible, the life of business." Credit was difficult for flinty Larkin to grant, yet it was essential to the life of California business. On that problematic subject Larkin counseled Belden to "hold in trusting as much as possible for the present. Collect all you can, under promise of trusting again by & by."[35]

Despite Belden's energy and Larkin's good advice, the Santa Cruz store ran into serious problems. There was some worrisome but never significant competition from Lawrence Carmichael, a Scottish fur trapper from New Mexico, now turned storekeeper, and later from a fellow American, Job Francis Dye, who had a small shop.[36]

A far more serious problem was theft. In May 1842, a California lumberman who was using an extensive amount of Larkin's tools—pit saws, crosscut saws, axes, and drawing knives—suddenly fled, but not before selling Larkin's property to others. Belden obtained the cooperation of the local judge and most of the property was recovered.[37] More significant in the early months of operation was the theft of goods valued at over $150 from the store itself. The padre then in charge of Santa Cruz was Antonio Suárez del Real, a man whose character may be described charitably as less spotless than that held by the vast majority of the California Franciscans.[38] Belden marshalled and transmitted to Larkin extensive circumstantial evidence pointing to Father Real, but apparently the loss was quietly absorbed.[39]

For these problems, however, the first year of operation at Santa Cruz was highly successful. In its first two months, the branch vended $1,250 worth of goods and took in exchange 11,500 feet of lumber, 4,000 shingles, and a few hundred dollars worth of hides and cash. In addition, Belden collected 40,000 feet of lumber already owed to Larkin from before the store's opening.[40]

By the spring of 1843 a large quantity of lumber had accumulated at the beach, more than Belden could dispose of conveniently at the moment. Accordingly, Belden suspended lumber purchases. Apparently this infuriated the sawyers, and on the evening of May 29, 1843 some of their number burned the lumber that had accumulated on the Santa Cruz beach. The point, according to Belden, was simply to make a new market for their labor.[41] If that were their motive, the tactic badly backfired.

Larkin was irate. The fire had burned $6,000 worth of his lumber.[42] Another American, Job F. Dye, suffered lesser but still considerable losses, and several other owners lost smaller lots of boards. Of all the lumber on the sands, half was destroyed. Larkin immediately offered a $100 reward. He also posted a public notice which declared that unless the culprits were discovered and severely punished, the fire "will cause an end to all trade in this article at Santa Cruz. . . . Confidence in the safety of lumber laying at the Beach will be lost, . . . and it is for the interest of . . . all deeling in lumber at Santa Cruz to use every exertion to find out who was concerned in this business."[43]

But precious little exertion had or would be applied. Larkin learned that Dye's storekeeper at Santa Cruz, Nicholas Dawson, had rushed to the beach just after the fire began, around 9 P.M. The priest at the former mission and several of the Indians still living there helped to fight the fire. However, Rafael Castro, the town's alcalde and the executive officer who should have taken action, did not sound an alarm or do anything else beyond sending his young son to help, who later demanded $100 for his trouble. During the entire night of the fire, no one from the town, not a single rancher in the area, came to help put out the fire, although some of the lumbermen did help.[44]

The timing of the fire was hardly accidental; the energetic Belden was in Monterey that evening. Dawson estimated that had the community been aroused to help, the effort could have saved up to half the loss. The locality's inactivity was exemplified by its alcalde. In the three weeks following the fire this official did nothing to investigate its cause.[45]

Disgusted by these events, Larkin closed the Santa Cruz store in November. A month later the smaller Gilroy operation was terminated.[46] The year of 1843, therefore, saw the end of Larkin's only branch operations. Because of the Santa Cruz fire, 1843 was also the only year since his arrival in California in which Larkin showed an actual loss.

Although Larkin never again had a branch store, he did have loose working arrangements with smaller, country retailers, and with such major dealers as Abel Stearns and Alpheus B. Thompson. Through these contacts Larkin could dispose of surplus goods, receive needed merchandise by purchase or on consignment, forward and receive mail, and exchange all kinds of political and business news.

The mercantile correspondence of Larkin and his fellow traders reveals conduct which was not always of an exemplary character. The traders constantly whined and complained about business conditions, more than justified by the facts. Also revealed in their letters are some rather sharp business practices and a resulting degree of anger and bitterness, vituperation almost, arising out of various disputes. With so much intermerchant trade and slow communications, it was inevitable that there would be misunderstandings and disputes. The vast majority concerned accounts, offsets, partial payments, and the like. The more interesting were grievances concerning the quality of goods sold, and of these Larkin received somewhat more than his proportionate share.

Eliab Grimes wrote Larkin in August 1844, "the lumber you sent last fall by Capt Paty is the most miserable trash ever taken from San cruz. Part of it is a gooddeal burnt and decayed." Larkin's shrewdness at times bordered on dishonesty. Many complaints were addressed to him concerning short weight and damaged goods. Marshall & Johnson of Honolulu wrote, "we are sorry to say that the Hides delivered us were very inferior . . . and 21 of them were damaged." They also charged a shortage in represented weight.[47]

Nicholas Den in Santa Barbara charged, "the last Soap which I got from you is very bad indeed. So much So that I will have to boil part of it over again." William Davis Howard in San Diego said he had "received likewse [*sic*] the Hides you sent only instead of 300 there were only 251." Stephen Reynolds in Oahu accused Larkin in January 1840 of shipping soap to customers that was inferior in quality and smaller in size than the samples by which Larkin had sold it. "Do as you would be done by," he counseled Larkin, "it is all can be asked."[48]

The charges must be put into perspective. Almost all the traders complained of each other. Their grievances were denied or adjusted, and without significant exception the men stayed in commercial communication with one another and remained on personally friendly terms. Cutting sharp ethical corners and the making and adjusting of resulting complaints was a somewhat puerile game played by the foreign merchants. Larkin *made* complaints as well as received them. Letters responding to Larkin complained that Larkin had been "heap[ing] upon me a torrent of invectives" (James A. Forbes) and "talking about me behind my back. You know very well that part of what you owed me in hides, you paid me off in old casks and other trash, which I was obliged to take, as I had no hopes of getting any thing els" (Henry D. Fitch).[49]

Although there was indeed much of a game to all this, still there was sometimes an especially acerbic quality to Larkin's dealings. Larkin knew how to take maximum advantage of economic pressures and geographic position. An example is the shipment of twenty-seven barrels of liquor to Larkin in 1839 by John Temple of Los Angeles. Temple asked a price of $60 per barrel, payable in hides. Larkin had previously indicated in writing that he would pay this price on any liquor he took on his own account, that is by wholesale purchase, as distinct from consignment. One problem arose when Larkin asked Temple to accept in payment flour he had already shipped to Los Angeles. Temple claimed he could not sell it at the price at which Larkin asked that it be credited because the current market for flour in Los Angeles was bad.

Other problems surfaced when Larkin claimed that only twenty-five barrels of liquor had been received, not twenty-seven, and insisted that he would only pay $50 per barrel. Larkin claimed that $50 per barrel was the current Monterey price, notwithstanding it was sharply below that originally specified. Apparently the price of liquor in Monterey had dropped because of the arrival of a ship from Boston. This brought to the Monterey market not only a greater supply, but a superior quality.

Temple protested, suggesting that Larkin inquire of the supercargo in charge of the ship that had transported the liquor concerning the shortage and where the two barrels might have gone. As for the price, Temple pointed out that he had a letter with Larkin's signature confirming the $60 figure. In gauging Larkin's response to these assertions, we must remember that he was already a major merchant, enjoying a far greater trade than Temple.

As for an inquiry of the shipping firm and the possibility of their making up the shortage, Larkin cavalierly wrote, "*I* shall not put myself to that trouble; if *you* wish for prove, I will enquire for you." Concerning the lower price for the liquor and Larkin's demand to pay through flour, he wrote, "you need not *repeat*, that you have my signature for payment of 60$ Etc. I also know you have. I thought you would be willing to take good flour at a fair price, in order to continue trade between us. . . . It seams not!"[50] It was a heavy-handed display of power.

Ultimately, with a few additional complications, the dispute was settled by economic and geographic pressures, although Temple and Larkin likely were simply weary with the conduct of the controversy through the medium of delayed mail. Larkin's flour was in a third party's warehouse in San Pedro near Los Angeles, hundreds of miles from his immediate control, and accumulating storage charges. Larkin decided to sell it to another person in Los Angeles. Temple's liquor was in Monterey, in Larkin's hands. Temple, reciting economic necessity, settled for the lower price and at the reduced number of barrels Larkin acknowledged having received. Later, the buyer of the flour complained to Larkin that the flour Larkin had catagorized to Temple as good was in fact full of boll weevils and could not be profitably sold.

A few of the traders disliked Larkin intensely. In August 1845, John Parrott wrote William A. Leidesdorff, the American vice consul in San Francisco who had been appointed by Larkin, "I have found . . . old Larkin to be precisely what you [i.e., Leidesdorff] told me he was, an infernal ass, full of little low dirty tricks."[51] This was hardly a balanced view, as Parrott was then under the stress of extreme economic loss from a shipwreck of his vessel near Monterey. He felt Larkin had garnered great and unfair salvage profits from his own misfortune. Larkin acknowledged that he had gained immensely from the shipwreck, although presumably he might have denied any unfairness.[52]

Much of the traders' criticism of Larkin was simple jealousy. As John C. Jones wrote Larkin from Santa Barbara, "All the fish appear to get into your net. You was born under a lucky star. I wish you would turn over to me a little of your good fortune."[53] The majority of all disputes, those relating to accounts and credits, can be assigned to a failure to keep adequate accounts. For all of Larkin's insistence to his Santa Cruz manager on good books being the life of business, neither he nor any of the California traders kept books adequate by today's standards, although Larkin's were far superior to most.

Still it is fair to conclude that Larkin's business ethics were not without blemish. Certainly his contemporaries never acknowledged a sterling character in his business life. But we must not make too much of this. In the early nineteenth century business practices were not expected to exhibit ethical standards much elevated above actionable deceit. Business was business. A man generally acknowleged as *good* could still be a sharpie in business. Probably the most balanced contemporary judgment on Larkin's business character was that given by a Scotsman, William G. Rae, the manager of the California operations of Hudson's Bay Company. In a letter dated September 2, 1844, he informed Larkin that "you have decidedly the most convenient memory for your own interest I have heard of for some time."[54] It is possible that Larkin viewed this as an unintended compliment.

It might be thought that the temperament of most traders, together with the large distances and poor communications, would have led to numerous commercial disputes difficult of resolution. In fact, there were many controversies between merchants, but they seldom proved intractable. The foreign merchants in Mexican California had a good working knowledge of the Common Law and the technical details of mercantile law. They often used that knowledge to resolve their disputes.

These expatriate tradesmen distrusted the local Mexican courts and seldom used them. When a disagreement amongst themselves became irreconcilable, the merchants often resorted to arbitration before a panel of other traders. Arbitration was an increasingly popular method of resolving commercial disputes in the nineteenth century and particularly advantageous to Anglo-American traders who developed disputes within their own communities in remote lands where the local courts were distrusted. Larkin engaged in several commercial arbitrations.[55]

The Anglo-American traders were frequently frustrated by changes in government regulations: tariff rates; the percent of the duties that could be paid with goods; rules for the coasting trade of hide ships after initial entry into California waters. All these could be quickly changed, thereby greatly affecting trade opportunities within California. Larkin in particular was annoyed at rules adopted in 1844 to curtail the rights of whaling ships to sell manufactured goods in exchange for provisions needed for their return voyages. He had invested much time and some money catering to the whaling ships' trade, and he worked energetically to block the offensive proposed regulations.[56] In his typically promotional style, Larkin wrote the editor of the whaling newspaper published in New Bedford, Massachusetts, enclosing a copy of the decree rescinding the proposed restriction and again praising the virtues of Monterey as a port for whalers.[57]

The frequent revolts and upheavals that punctuated California politics also caused concern. It was one thing for Larkin to profitably provision a rebel army marching from Monterey to Los Angeles, or a local army sent forth from Monterey to meet rebels from Los Angeles. The matter became quite different if the fighting lasted so long as to interfere with the annual cattle slaughter. Californios who were absent from their ranchos, marching and countermarching with enthusiastic bravado, could not produce the cattle hides essential for all California commerce. Larkin wrote Abel Stearns, his friend in Los Angeles, in November 1836: "By Garner you will hear of the Revolution this way. . . . This will for a long time cause unsettled times in C. [California] . . . It has broke up all work here for the present. I wish it was ended, for times to go Smooth again."[58]

Larkin and the Anglo-American merchants regarded the local alcalde courts as unable to collect debts. Notwithstanding, most of the trade, both among merchants and with consumers, was on credit. In fact, as we have seen, it was relatively long credit, up to eighteen months for timely payment. As a predicable result of this, all the traders experienced difficult problems of debt collection. Larkin himself was generally prompt in the payment of his debts. Although there were a few occasions on which he was

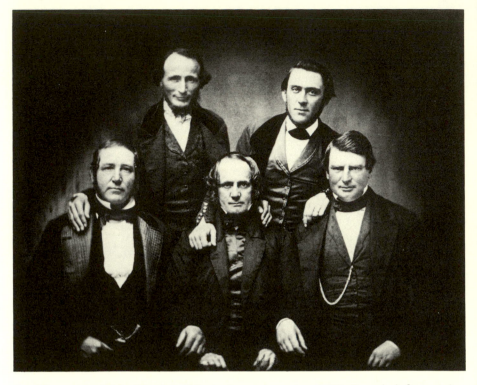

Larkin surrounded by friends and business associates, ca. 1850. Seated, left to right: *Jacob P. Leese, Larkin, and William D. M. Howard.* Standing, left to right: *Talbot H. Green (or perhaps Samuel J. Hensley), and Sam Brannan. Courtesy The Bancroft Library.*

hounded for debts,[59] they arose from complex situations in which Larkin probably genuinely believed no amount was due.

Larkin entered the California retail trade in February 1833, as we have seen, with a capital of $500. From the very first he was successful. We can trace his success rather precisely since he kept year-end summaries of his net worth.[60] On January 1, 1835, Larkin reckoned his net financial value at $2,650. That represented a profit of $2,150 on a venture of $500 in twenty-three months.

Two years later, on January 1, 1837, Larkin estimated his net worth at $5,626, although by his own notation most of that capital was invested in his new house. Thereafter his financial standing accelerated. We must remember there was no significant inflation during this period so that the dollar had a constant value, although worth thirteen times more than the 1990 dollar. By the end of 1837 Larkin's net worth was $11,013. In 1841, it increased from $21,493 to $37,958, and then again during 1842 to

Account of Stock. list of Debts. and other property
of Thomas O. Larkin. taken January 1. 1844

Dr.	Cr
Debts against	Debts due me
me this date — $6459 5	at this date — 32.513 6
	goods on hand — 3997 6
	Cash in the Store — 110
	House now worth 12000
	Chamberlain house 1300
	Marjares lot of land 150
	Lot of land at the Beach 150
	Cash. drafts and pro.
	duce taken to Mazatlan 4744
$6459 5	$ 52.965 4
	6459 5
	46.505 7

2641$ Lost from January 1. 1843. to January 1. 18

is for the Year lost 2641. 7. Amount Property $ 46.505 7

The Business of 1843. was not equal to that of 1842. as the
Sales on a credit in the town Store. were much reduced
to bring about a settlement of debts, a store this year was
carried on in Santa Cruz for lumber, on the month of
June 1843. some person or persons fired the lumber. do
up to the value of Six thousand dollars was burnt.
the actually gain in trade was this = 3359$ this year
by the loss of lumber, therefore. the yearly reduction of
property has been 2641$

46.505$ Forty Six thousand, Five hundred
and five dollars. and. Seven Cents.

Year ending Decr 31.
1843.

One of Larkin's annual summaries of his business operations, assets, and net
worth, this for the year ending December 31, 1843. In it he describes his loss
caused by the Santa Cruz fire. Courtesy The Bancroft Library.

$49,147. The year of 1843 showed a small net loss, reflecting the fire disaster at Santa Cruz and the closing of the branch operations there. But, by the beginning of 1845, Larkin rebounded to $60,175, and by the end of that year his net worth was $66,644.

The profits from 1844 onward reflect Larkin's operations as financier more than as retail merchant. The profits of his retail operation, through which his net worth increased in ten years from $500 to $49,000, gave Larkin the wherewithal to become a financier and then in the mid-1840s and later to purchase the real estate which ultimately would make his fortune.

To what can we attribute Larkin's commercial success? He was obviously at the right place, the California capital of Monterey, at the right time, just prior to secularization. But so were other men. There were other stores, other storekeepers in Monterey. More important was that Larkin was clever, energetic, and ambitious, and that he possessed these qualities more abundantly than his competitors.

Larkin's cleverness in retailing is seen in many of his trade techniques. He developed far broader markets for sales—the California government, the American government, and the whalers—than the other merchants sought. On the purchase side, Larkin was not content with buying at wholesale from the Boston ships but searched out even better sources of supply in Mazatlán and Oahu. He also was more careful than many of his contemporaries in the extension of credit.

His energy was reflected in hard work. A contemporary described Larkin as "active, nervous, quick-moving, busy."[61] This nervous energy produced voluminous commercial correspondence, carefully detailed ledgers, and the willingness to enter new retail ventures beyond a traditional store—flour mill, blacksmith shop, lumbering, soap factory, stable. Then, too, Larkin knew the art of cultivating friendships and associations, as is examined specifically in the following chapter. In the early years of his trade, Larkin was especially gracious and helpful in his commerical correspondence, particularly to traders in Oahu and Mazatlán and those California merchants, such as Abel Stearns in Los Angeles, whom Larkin sized up as having great potential.[62]

Larkin's ambition was a constant throughout his life. A drive for wealth animated almost everything he did. This may have been the wellspring from which his cleverness and energy derived, and it was undoubtedly a factor in Larkin's success. In February 1843, he had increased his initial capital about one hundred times over ten years, for an average increase in original capital of 1,000 percent annually for each of these ten years. At that point he wrote his friend Faxon Dean Atherton, mentioning the financial fortunes of many of their mutual friends. Some of their contemporaries had started to slacken their effort and to enjoy their accumulations with leisure. One friend, Larkin wrote, "lives easy & comfortable; don't hurry to trade."

Another "rose rapidly. I think his time is Setting. Being up, he now setts still or spends his time in the billiard table." None of that would do for Larkin, notwithstanding his hundredfold capital accumulation. "As I am not up high enough, I keep moving, trying to get up."[63] In addition to natural talents, luck, and location, Larkin succeeded primarily because he never fell victim to that social disease which claimed so many foreigners. He never caught the "California fever," as Richard Henry Dana called it.[64] That is to say, Larkin became wealthy because he never succumbed to laziness.

Talbot H. Green had been Larkin's clerk from early in 1842. Apparently Larkin was well satisfied with Green's services, for on May 16, 1843, Larkin entered into what can best be described as a management agreement with Green. It provided that Green would "take charge this day of the store and buisness in Monterey of said Larkin" for one year at the compensation of $400 plus 5 percent of the profits.[65] It would appear that Larkin made this agreement in contemplation of a voyage he was about to make to Mazatlán. Plans changed, however, as later in May 1843 Larkin sent Green on a business trip to Los Angeles,[66] and Larkin himself did not leave for Mazatlán until later. It is clear that when Larkin departed at the end of 1843, he left Green in charge of the Monterey store.

In late November 1843, just prior to his departure, Larkin gave Green a letter of instructions regarding the store's operations. This action suggests that Larkin still regarded Green's management as temporary. The management directions were explicit: "Do no buisness on credit either buying or selling. When you can purchace any sutible goods for the store with any produce on hand (Excepting hides) do so."[67] Moreover, while in Mazatlán Larkin purchased retail goods with a wholesale cost of $18,500, suggesting a probable interest in continuing personal involvement in the store.[68]

When Larkin returned to Monterey in March 1844, matters were quite different. He had learned in Mazatlán of his appointment as United States Consul for California and keenly felt the responsibilities and time the office would entail. Also, Larkin had increasingly turned his business interests to finance, the collection of commercial debts, and major trading voyages. These activities, together with the consulate, would be more than enough to occupy his time.

On May 16, 1844, one year from the date of the original management agreement, Larkin posted a public notice of his retirement from the retail trade, "for the present," as it was put, and the transfer of his stock to Talbot H. Green. Larkin thanked his customers and expressed hopes for their continued patronage of Green.[69] The details of their financial arrangements, or even management divisions, were not made public, and Larkin was still much more an owner of the store than the announcement implied. The public notice probably merely confirmed existing arrangements. Larkin had not been responsible for day-to-day management for some time, probably since his departure for Mazatlán, although he retained policy control and overriding management.

Green continued to do well and gradually sought a larger interest in the store. By agreement of January 1, 1846, Larkin transferred what were still described as "his Store and Warehouses" to Green under a partnership arrangement. In addition Larkin agreed to supply a stock of goods and provisions valued at $10,000. This compares with stock valued at $4,292 in May 1843 when Green originally took charge of daily operations. The 1846 agreement provided that the partnership would end in three years and the net profits, after first reimbursing Larkin for the original $10,000 stock, were to be divided two-thirds to Larkin and one-third to Green. Notwithstanding the lopsided distribution to Larkin, the business was to be conducted in Green's name, and there were no restrictions imposed on his management.[70]

Although Larkin retired from management, he maintained an interest in the retail trade all his life. He was actively involved in the wholesale provisioning of the American navy and army following the 1846 invasion. For a brief moment during the Gold Rush, Larkin even flirted with retailing mining supplies. However, these were exceptions. After firmly establishing the success of his retail operation, Larkin turned it over to other hands by stages, 1843–1846, in order to pursue other and larger endeavors.

In an April 1846 letter, he described his circumstances. He said he had given up completely his commerical business, yet continued on "in loans, advances, and money transacting."[71] Indeed, from 1844 onward, much of Larkin's time would would be concerned with his consular activities. However, the majority of his waking hours were still to be devoted to the garnering of money, but the arena largely shifted to matters of "loans, advances, and money transacting" and to the networks and associations Larkin had built to facilitate those transactions.

CHAPTER 5

HOSPITALITY AND ASSOCIATIONS
ASSOCIATES AND PROFITS

WHEN LARKIN first arrived in California, he was somewhat shocked by the scale of entertainment undertaken by his half-brother. In June 1833, while still living with Cooper and just before his marriage to Rachel, he wrote to Abel Stearns, "there is such a host of people the whole of this year makes our house their home. I believe men of any consideration think we have sufficient company."[1] There were no hotels in Mexican California and, until the very end of the period, no restaurants. Perforce commercial merchants entertained visiting traders and potential customers.

However, some merchants entertained with parsimony and others with open hands. Although Larkin was ever interested in the acquisition and keeping of money, in the realm of entertainment he was lavish. In 1833, he may have been skeptical of Cooper's open doors, but by 1847 a well-established American expatriate could remark quite accurately that Larkin's "unbounded hospitality is proverbial in California."[2] This hospitality consisted of the boarding and feeding of numerous houseguests and also the hosting of elaborate parties to which large numbers of Monterey's population were invited.

Numerous visiting merchants, government agents, ship captains, and American military men were entertained by Larkin during the period 1840–1846. Larkin gave bed and board to men such as merchants John Parrott from Mazatlán, whose business kept him at Larkin's house for several months,[3] Dugald McTavish, an agent of the Hudson's Bay Company,[4] and sea captains William D. Phelps of Boston[5] and John Paty of Honolulu.[6]

As American consul, Larkin naturally accommodated several American officials. The military explorer John C. Frémont stayed with Larkin for several days in the winter of early 1846,[7] as did the special government courier Lieutenant Archibald Gillespie in June of that fateful year.[8] But even before the days of his consulate, Larkin had entertained government officials. He hosted the special American commissioner Ethan Estabrook in 1840 and 1841,[9] and hospitality was extended in 1842 to a philologist attached to a government exploring expedition.[10]

Larkin's custom of holding parties and dances in honor of visiting American officials and naval officers was even more elaborate and expensive. These were no small affairs; typically all of the leading local citizens were invited and often the governor and his lady attended. For example, at one ball held in the fall of 1844 in honor of a visiting American warship, a naval officer, William M. Wood, recorded:

> According to previous invitation, we met at two o'clock in the afternoon at the house of our consul, and found there an assemblage of the citizens of the place, ladies and gentlemen, Mexican and Californian. General and la Señora Micheltoreno [sic, i.e., Governor Micheltorena], were of the party. . . . Dancing commenced immediately, and, in the various combinations of quadrilles, contradances, and waltzes, was kept up until nine o'clock at night. . . . We were not the only foreigners present; as Her British Majesty's ship Modeste, having just come into the port, we had the pleasure of their company.[11]

Most balls extended into the very late evening or early morning. The afternoon beginning of this particular party was unusual. Larkin's pace of this entertainment increased with his consular office,[12] but Larkin sometimes by himself and sometimes in cooperation with other American residents had given elaborate parties before his consulate.[13]

One particular occasion that was always festive was Larkin's traditional 4th of July party. The native Californios dearly loved parties and needed little excuse to attend a dance. By a happy coincidence the feast day of the patroness of the Bishopric of the Californias fell on the 4th of July. No one worked on this day and everyone had a good reason to celebrate,[14] excepting perhaps the resident British and French who did not begrudge the occasion in any event.

Many visitors commented on Larkin's 4th of July parties, which were famous or infamous depending on the observer, and perhaps the year. It was a great time according to Daniel Heustis, who attended in 1845:

> On the evening of the 4th of July, Mr. Larkin, the American Consul, gave a fandango, or ball, in honor of the day, at which the principal citizens of the place were in attendance. We had a fine dance, an excellent supper, and a gay and happy company. Every thing was conducted with propriety, and in good taste. The Spanish ladies made an elegant appearance, in form, dress, and manners.[15]

An account of the 1842 Independence Day ball presents quite a contrast. This was before the consulate was established, so perhaps Larkin was a bit less circumspect. Also the governor in 1842 was a heavy drinker, and the particular observer was William D. Phelps, a somber Boston teetotaler. The ball was sponsored by several Monterey merchants, including Larkin, and attended by all the principal residents, both native and foreign. The California government hall was decorated with American flags and portraits of appropriate patriots such as Washington and Lafayette. So far, all was fine for Phelps. In fact, he praised the excellent supper prepared by the cooks and stewards of American ships in port.

Nevertheless, according to Phelps, "a large quantity of liquors and wines disgraced the occasion and the Governor got drunk before midnight and most of the natives followed his example before morning." By four in the morning Phelps had had enough, but was dismayed to find soldiers guarding the door with orders from the governor to allow no one to leave. The governor explained that "the Americans invited him hither to celebrate the 4th of July and he should keep it up untill he was tired and no person should leave before he did." Phelps was not released until the dancing stopped at nine in the morning. He wanted to return to Boston. "My heart more than ever yearns for the land of steady liberty & cold water society," he concluded of the evening's entertainment.[16]

The entertainment undertaken by Larkin, both the room and board and also the parties, was expensive. In the early 1840s, many of the parties were sponsored collectively by several merchants, but by the mid-1840s most involving Larkin were on his own, separate account. In 1846, he groused that his entire consular fees would not pay for his annual 4th of July ball.[17]

In 1847, former Governor Juan Bautista Alvarado wrote Larkin that for many years he had observed that "your house is continually frequented by the most respectable strangers. . . . I doubt not but you must be at great expense & trouble."[18] One estimate is that during this time Larkin's table was frequently set for eight to ten guests and that his monthly grocery costs were $330, or around $4,000 per month in 1990.[19] Larkin himself in 1847 estimated that his household meals consumed half of his profits from the retail operation he had turned over to Green, and further, that in 1846 half (of Larkin's two-thirds interest in the profits) was $3,000.[20]

We have seen that Larkin was an energetic, serious man, eager to gather wealth. Surely this trait of acquisitiveness would not be suspended while he played the social butterfly with lavish entertainment. What advantage did he see, what return on these expenditures? In answer it will be useful first to consider what class of persons were *not* generally invited to sup at Larkin's table, to sleep in his rooms, or to dance at his parties—that is to say, who would *not* provide advantage.

That group was the lower class of Americans present in Mexican California, the deserters from ships, the fur trappers who strayed into California, and later, in the 1840s, the farmers arriving along the overland trail. There is considerable evidence of abrasiveness in Larkin's relationship with this

El Cuartel, a barracks and seat of the California departmental government, built in 1839. Some of the larger parties sponsored by Larkin were held here. Courtesy The Bancroft Library.

sort. In part the hostility of the lower class of Americans toward Larkin had to do with their respective status. Members of this class were frequently employees engaged in casual labor, and Larkin was often their employer. Then, too, one of Larkin's duties as American consul was to cooperate with local authorities in capturing deserting sailors and incarcerating them until they could be reclaimed by their captains. Beyond this, however, there is evidence that Larkin held a class consciousness, however justified by the circumstances, that must have infuriated the lower orders. Some of this may well have been derived from his years in the South.

In 1834, Hall Jackson Kelley, an American enthusiast for the settlement of Oregon, visited California. Larkin took an instant dislike to the man, probably because Kelley attempted to recruit Larkin's employees, even those who were in his debt, to leave for Oregon. Larkin and his bride were still living on Cooper's ranch on the Salinas River. He was busy with his plans and probably put up with Kelley only because of the half-hearted request of Ebenezer Childs, addressed to both Larkin and Cooper.[21]

Larkin showed Kelley around and took him to the Santa Cruz Mountains where his employees were cutting trees. Larkin left for a short time, knowing that Kelley was "stringing and wouping up" his pitch for Oregon. On his return Larkin found that six men had quit to go to Oregon. Worse yet was that "the men that Mr. K. had enticed from their work where [were]

4 in to heavily in debt, to people in M. They owed me some hundreds. . . . Mr. K tried to convince me that they could remit from the O. all they owed in a few months. I did not admire such tail leg for security."[22]

Larkin ultimately convinced his employees that Kelley was a fraud and they did not leave. However, Kelley also remained. When Larkin moved his family into town, he permitted Kelley to live on the ranch. There Kelley continued to proselytize Larkin's employees, this time the ranch hands. The way Larkin described Kelley's machinations reveals much about his own treatment of his American and British employees. Larkin's treatment, and the attitudes associated with it, may have generated some of the hostility that men of this class felt for Larkin:

> . . . during my absence he commenced coaxing and tampering with my foreign [i.e., American and British] servants altho I had told him previously that they were much in debt and could not go. he call'd into the house & request them to sit down men who never had that privilege before, Included some black ones. [sic]—gave them liquor & drank this liquor. This was for a week or two.[23]

Additional evidence is found in Larkin's treatment of his own menial employees, not his clerical employees or assistants at the store, but the men he hired to cut timber, the cooks who fed his crews, and the labor employed in the construction of his house. For the period May 1833 through April 1837, Larkin kept a careful record of the men he hired, the rate at which he paid them, and notations as to when and the circumstances under which they left his employ. The record included American and British employees, who comprised about half of all employees, as well as Indian and Californio workers.[24]

The first striking thing about this record is that almost all of the workers voluntarily quit their employment. There are 101 notations for the causes of termination and a very few others that have no specific notation as to termination. Of those 101, Larkin has written "ended" or "worked," or any other notation that might possibly suggest a layoff or firing, a total of eighteen times. In contrast there are eighty-three notations of "quit."

The second striking aspect to this record is the extremely short periods of employment of Larkin's employees before voluntarily quitting. Hardly anyone in a laboring position worked for Larkin more than two months, although many who quit were subsequently rehired. For almost everyone there are notations such as "quit in 2 weeks" or "quit in 2 months." But some are far shorter. In 1834, Henry Hicks "quit in two days," while Jack, no last name given, "quit in 3 days." The following year one Peter "quit in one day."

It has been suggested that the high turnover of employees was primarily due to the low wages which the penurious Larkin paid, especially for loggers, and the high markup on goods sold them on credit.[25] While that may be true, the large number of rehirings suggests that there may not have been many other opportunities to earn higher wages. Therefore, the quittings probably also reflect the workingmen's reaction to Larkin's attitudes and actions toward them. A clue to these attitudes are contained in some additional marginal notations Larkin made in regard to certain of the quittings. For one employee he noted, "worked two days then off to drink & gamble," and for another "run away in March." Still worse, from Larkin's point of view, was the notation for a cook in 1836: "quit 5 $2 in Debt."

The Graham Affair of 1840 furnishes another view of Larkin's relationship with the lower class of American and British residents in California. Isaac Graham was an American fur trapper who arrived in California in 1833. He operated a distillery and had become the leader, very loosely speaking, of a marginal group of British and American residents. Mostly deserted sailors and trappers, they were hardy and handy with guns and had helped Governor Alvarado overthrow his predecessor in 1836. As a group they were rough and violent and by 1840 they had become a nuisance to the Californio authorities. In 1840 Alvarado arrested a large number of these foreigners on somewhat specious charges. Many were released quickly but about forty, including Graham and his followers, were sent to mainland Mexico for trial. There they were acquitted promptly and most returned to California.

John Chamberlain, an Irish blacksmith who had deserted from a whaler, was arrested with Graham, but not expelled.[26] His opinion was that the government ordered the expulsion "in consequence of a plan concocted by Larkin" and others. When the boat carrying the men to Mexico had left Monterey, Chamberlain claimed he had "remarked to Larkin that I hoped the poor fellows would all come back safe & well—Mr Larkin replied he hoped not—that he was desirous that the few then in California should do well—but he wanted no more foreigners to come into the country."[27]

Perceptions are as important as reality in illustrating attitudes and relationships. Shortly after the expulsion Larkin travelled to Mexico on a business trip to purchase stock for his store. The expulsed foreigners saw only sinister intrigue in Larkin's movements and timing. Immediately after the foreigners' release and before their return to California, it was "the general opinion of the Foreigners in this place," one of those expelled wrote Larkin, "that you have gon [sic] on to Mexico on secret business, business against us that were of late prisoners in this place."[28]

Another of the imprisoned foreigners, Albert F. Morris, long afterward wrote that after the Americans had seized California Larkin published an article in which he claimed to have furnished food to Graham and his followers without charge. "Such are the phantoms of a guilty conscience," Morris charged. "I did partake of Mr. Larkins boasted hospitality but once. In the morning he sent me a breakfast."[29] The truth lies in between. Larkin did in fact provide food for the imprisoned foreigners. He also charged the California government for that food,[30] although there is no evidence Larkin ever claimed he gave it without charge.

Governor Juan Bautista Alvarado, the California official who ordered the expulsions, later recalled that Larkin had offered to provide bail for Graham and a few of his followers, and that after their return to California, Larkin had actually lodged and fed several of the principal exiles for months.[31] Whether that is true or not is difficult to say. Certainly Larkin's behavior in the Graham Affair was not the sinister conspiracy that many of the exiles believed; nor was it pure altruism.

What is important about it is the illustration of the relative antipathy between Larkin and the lower classes of foreigners. Some of them told the strangest stories about Larkin. John Chamberlain recalled that in Monterey in 1839 it was customary "whenever a vessel was in want of hands, for the Captain to apply to Mr Thomas O. Larkin, who would accompany him to the Govr.—by Mr Larkin's advice every foreign sailor in & about the place would then to put into the calaboose, and . . . the Captain would pick out the men he needed from the imprisoned crowd."[32] Albert Morris recalled that in 1836 several Americans who were owed money, riflemen of the lower sort, were "paid off in orders . . . negotiable at Mr. Larkins grog shop for half their value in aguardiente, or Spanish brandy."[33]

There is contrary evidence. William H. Thomes, a young common sailor, held a very favorable impression of Larkin. Not only did Larkin freely loan books to Thomes, but Larkin fed him and his crew, albeit in the kitchen. It was not just once. Thomes called Larkin "kind-hearted" and "a liberal, hospitable man," recalling that "many the glass of wine, plate of frijoles and tortillas did he give me, when I was sent to his store, or house, while we were in port."[34]

Larkin's sense of civic responsibilities certainly extended to all classes. An epidemic of smallpox raged in Monterey during the spring of 1844. Larkin may have felt some responsibility for the disease as it arrived with him from Mazatlán.[35] In any event his reaction was commendable. A traveling American with some slight medical training and a vaccine arrived during the epidemic, and immediately upon his arrival Larkin sought him out and offered to open his parlor if the visitor would "vaccinate the large numbers who were without the necessary means to pay." The following day upwards of 300 persons, young and old, were vaccinated in Larkin's house.[36] Apparently in the following month Larkin and William Hartnell personally vaccinated additional hundreds of persons, without distinction, in Larkin's house.[37]

Larkin was hardly an unconditional and enthusiastic friend of all Americans in California. Like most people he picked about for those he called his friends, and he can hardly be criticized for his hostility toward some elements in the expatriate community. The spirit of distance and remove between Larkin and Americans of the lower class extended to the Californio lower class as well. In June 1846 Larkin had occasion to stay overnight at an old, nearly ruined mission. At the sight of the ruins he grew eloquent and in his eloquence again revealed his attitudes toward the lower orders. "Tis a sad sight," he wrote, "to see the rooms formerly occupied by the good old pious Spanish Padres now used by Men who a quarter of a Centuy ago wher now [not] worthy of cleang the shoes of the Priests."[38]

Larkin's impressions and attitudes may have been well or poorly founded. It is enough that they existed, since they explain an important dimension in Larkin's character and even his actions. And it also explains the hostility toward Larkin that existed among many of the American community in Mexican California. A letter from Robert Semple to Larkin in May 1847 pulls these strands together. Semple was apologizing for some critical remarks he had once made of Larkin. His once critical opinions had changed because of discussions he had held with former government officals, merchants, and "other highly respectable gentlemen" in Monterey. His former poor regard for Larkin, Semple explained, had been formed through contact with certain Americans, "most of them sailors who had left their ships without leave of absence."[39]

It was probably true, as Albert Morris had charged, that his sole taste of Larkin's hospitality was that solitary breakfast. We can be quite confident that neither he nor his class was often invited to Larkin's frequent dinner parties and balls. He neither liked them particularly, nor were they useful for the business purposes of his entertainment. What then was frugal Larkin's purpose behind the seeming frivolity of dances and entertainments so expensive? Beyond question Larkin enjoyed being a host, and the boarding and lodging he provided to the government philologist, for example, had little utility to Larkin's financial ventures. Larkin simply enjoyed talking with interesting people. That, no doubt, explained his interest in the young sailor Thomes. It is also true that Larkin's pattern of entertainment served some very specific business purposes.

Larkin's entertainment of ships' officers was obviously useful in his retail business. The connection between the two was made explicit in an interesting letter of introduction given by the supply officer, or purser, of one American warship to his opposite number on another American vessel. A copy of this letter, dated July 4, 1840, found its way into Larkin's files. It tells how helpful Larkin had been in supplying bread and other provisions and suggests that his fellow officer will be "relieved from much trouble and vexation by employing him to procure your supplies." Then the officer writes, the "hospitality of Mr. Larkin's house only equals his attention to our interests."[40] The hundreds of ships that arrived in Monterey during the time Larkin ran his store suggest the importance of gracious entertaining for financial gain.

Other connections between entertainment and business arose out of the changed focus of Larkin's financial activities in the mid-1840s. Beginning with Larkin's management contract with Talbot Green in 1843, we have seen how Larkin began to withdraw from retail merchandizing activities. Financial services and debt collection replaced his earlier interest in retailing.[41] These had a direct connection to the development of a large network of associates and associations Larkin formed in California. It was to form and maintain this network that Larkin found hospitality so helpful. In turn it was those who would be most useful for that network's functioning that were most frequently invited to his entertainments. Larkin clearly saw this relationship of entertainment to business. In a much later letter to his cousin, Larkin explained how he had not been spending much time currying the favor of certain naval commanders. The way he put this is striking: "For a year I have paid but little attention to them personally, more than civility (not enough to gain favour)."[42]

Larkin's account books indicate that he undertook collection activities from his earliest days after leaving Cooper's employ in 1833. But his first collections were relatively small scale, intra-California matters. And Larkin continued to handle relatively small collections well into the mid-1840s. For example, he received an assignment for a debt as low as $25 in 1844.[43]

Over time, however, Larkin increased the scale of his collection activities, continuing to collect for Los Angeles and Santa Barbara creditors but also working for Honolulu and Mazatlán merchants. For example, in February 1845, the Mazatlán firm of Parrott & Company commissioned Larkin to collect a debt due from Alpheus B. Thompson of Santa Barbara in the amount of $5,371.59, about $70,000 in 1990 dollars. Another Mazatlán firm, Mott Talbot & Company, hired Larkin to collect a debt of $2,284.14 in May of the same year.[44]

Larkin attempted collections by cajolery of debtors, sometimes by creation of setoffs with other accounts, and rarely by litigation. The usual and most important method of collecting debts was the time-honored and traditional process of dunning, or as one American merchant, William H. Davis, put it, "persistent efforts and persuasion."[45]

At this Larkin was a master. In dunning letters to debtors, he usually appealed to pride rather than merely harassing or making fruitless threats. "This is the third person who has refused to take the word of D. Salvador Vallejo at his own request for a small debt," he wrote the same Salvador Vallejo in January 1843.[46] For an American debtor there was a different tack than the mere appeal to honor of name. He wrote to William S. Hinckley in October 1845:

I know . . . *you can* pay the debt if you choose. . . . It with pain I say it but . . . I can not believe all you have seen fit to write to me respectig my demands. . . . Your excuses have not only been too numerous, but so badly made out in one following the other. . . . 'Tis true you *may* "pay me before some of the Californians," but I do not expect so much from "some of them" nor do they promise so much as you do. . . . your necessities does not arise from want of talants or knowledge of business, both of which you possess far beyond the most of your Countrymn in California.[47]

He closed with an expression of expectation that he might receive partial payments, "by every Vessel a little flour, Wheat, Bean, Corn Etc." Larkin could do more than cajole. When necessary he could be quite forceful, as he was in December 1844 with Robert Ridley:

> When I lent you cash I told you candidly that my pay would be in promises and falsehoods. . . . You need not promise to pay any more Captains or Supercargoes, nor write again on the subject or expect to hear from me. If you want to pay the debt do so. If you can not, Say so, as you should have done at once, but make no more promises—or tell any more stories about it.[48]

The single most effective weapon he had was being at the pulse of a vast informational credit network which the foreign merchants maintained to check on the solvency of those with whom they dealt. For these purposes, Larkin's frequent entertaining and hospitality, extended to all classes of merchants, was extremely helpful. It gave Larkin access to information, the ability to spread information, and the feeling of gratitude on the part of many guests which facilitated an acquiescence toward his requests for the payment of debts.

Larkin did not collect every obligation referred to him, but he was generally successful and his clients were appreciative. For example, Mott Talbot & Company wrote in May 1846 that "we desire to loose no oppy to return you our thanks for your kind attention in the Collecting of Mr Thompson's debt."[49]

As Larkin collected debts, he generally held the funds, or more frequently cattle hides, a California cash equivalent, for the account of the creditor. The creditor was then allowed to draw against these funds on deposit by a bill of exchange drawn against Larkin. In this manner Larkin, in effect, operated as a bank for mercantile accounts.

Often military vessels arrived in California needing supplies but lacking coinage with which to pay. Frequently their commanders or pursers would write drafts, or bills of exchange, which were like checks drawn on home governments. Then, too, captains of hide ships or whalers might present drafts drawn on Boston firms. Larkin saw opportunity in these bills of exchange. Depending on the authority of the person writing the draft and the creditworthiness of the firm or government on which it was drawn, Larkin would accept these bills in payment for supplies, but always at a sharp discount. In this way Larkin gained profit not only through the sale itself, but also in the discount of the note from its face value. The drafts would then be sent to his eastern correspondent, his cousin William Rogers, and be collected at their face value.

Larkin often solicited drafts as an accommodation. In September 1841, he wrote the purchasing agent of an American warship for which he was obtaining supplies: "I want to purchase bills on home. Please inform me if you will have to sell Bills and at what discount." Again the connection with hospitality is explicit: "My house and myself is at your dispositio [sic] and of the officers of your three remaindig Vessels and I shall be happy to see you here."[50]

An additional way for Larkin to profit was to buy acceptable bills of exchange given to the other merchants. They were freely negotiable. For example, in April 1846, Larkin purchased from Captain Eliab Grimes a promissory note due from the San Francisco merchant William A. Leidesdorff in the amount of $726.59. Undoubtedly he purchased the note itself at a discount, so that by collecting the full amount from Leidesdorff he would turn a tidy profit. But Larkin wanted to extend his profit further. He suggested to Leidesdorff that "if you can send me good drafts on home at 20 pr. cent discount I should like to take them."[51] That is to say Larkin would credit them at a 20 percent discount against the full amount of the $726.59 note. The ultimate collection of such drafts at their full par value would thereby vastly increase Larkin's profit beyond the discount at which he bought the note itself.

Larkin's ability to engage in his many profitable arrangements with the California government depended, of course, on much more than mere entertainment of officials, although that itself was helpful. Larkin was also extremely helpful to the always financially embarrassed departmental government, but above all his attitude and demeanor towards the Californios, to whom courtesy held a high value, was critical.

It was the time of Manifest Destiny, and most Americans viewed the Mexicans with racial contempt. Not so Larkin. He once explained to his wife that he did "not look on the Mexicans so ill as many foreigners do—I have lived to longwith them not to have some good feelings for them, and belive they return that feeling towards me."[52] He expressed a note of tolerance, not very characteristic of most Americans of his time, to a merchant friend in 1842:

> I am remarkably well situated with this Government and its people; I never meddle seriously in their politics. I never speak against their laws, modes or religion. In my travels I have found almost all the people have some habits to be praised as well as to blame. They appear to be satisfied with me & why should not I be so with them.[53]

One way Larkin was helpful to the California government was by supplying every governor and military leader in the Department, from 1837 through 1845, "with most of their Merchandize and Provisions."[54] But more importantly he provided cash loans to most of the California administrations. Throughout his papers the reader finds evidence of these advances. For example, $3,700.00 was lent on November 21, 1844, and another $2,388.50 on February 5, 1845.[55] As of January 1, 1846, according to his own account, the departmental government owed Larkin $12,750.00, around $165,000.00 today, making him the second largest public creditor in California.[56]

Although there was considerable smuggling of goods into Mexican California, many large cargoes were entered legitimately and incurred payment of heavy import duties. Typically duties were paid in installments at 90, 130, and 180 days after entry, with the second installment generally in cash or cattle hides and the others in goods. The major commercial vessels, those coming from Boston in pursuit of the hide and tallow trade, for example, generally paid between $5,000 and $25,000 in duties.

After entry and settlement of duties, the government officials would then issue bills of exchange drawn on the vessel's cargo agent and against the cash duties of the second installment. These would be given to the government's creditors. The departmental government was chronically insolvent, and these infusions of cash from import duties was almost the sole method of paying creditors. If there were insufficient duties to pay all governmental creditors, the debts would be prorated.[57]

Larkin's position in Monterey near the customhouse was critical for monitoring this procedure and insuring that he received due payment for his cash advances, as also, of course, were his good relations with the California officialdom. As a result of close observation of customs procedures and good relations with all concerned, Larkin did well in his collection of government debts. In 1840, he observed that the California government had "done very well with me in respect to old debts."[58] Into the 1840s, with the arrival of the next governor, Manuel Micheltorena, in 1842, Larkin did even better. Larkin even found ways occasionally to circumvent the proration system and gain a preferred position in payment of government obligations—for example, buying government obligations to others at a heavy discount and then using that paper at par to pay duties on cargo he himself entered.[59]

At times Larkin virtually acted as a bank for the California government with collections and disbursements conducted from his house.[60] An agent of one vessel once asked Larkin: "Are you still the Baron Rothchild of California? Does the Govt of the time being use your purse as free as ever?"[61]

Larkin's reputation as a debt collector and a financier of government led to a third financial activity: the collection of private debts against the California government. Such obligations were frequently referred to Larkin for collection,[62] and he at times solicited the assignment of this sort of paper for credit on running accounts,[63] or offering to collect for cash on a 5 percent commission.[64] Arrears in salaries due to government employees other than those who worked in the customhouse were not generally included in the proration of receipts from the ships' duties. However in 1845 and 1846, when the governor's office was located in Los Angeles, Larkin offered to collect other governmental salaries from the Monterey customhouse, those due to the governor and his employees, at his customary 5 percent commission.[65]

The Monterey customhouse, the source of California's revenues and the key to Larkin's role as financier. As a contractor he rebuilt the structure in 1842. Photograph taken ca. 1875. Courtesy The Bancroft Library.

In one incident Larkin overextended himself in lending to the California government. This should be examined in some detail, as it is as much a comment on Larkin's character as on his business acumen. Specifically, it concerns Larkin's financial arrangements with General Manuel Micheltorena, governor of California from the fall of 1842 until the spring of 1845.

Micheltorena was sent from Mexico to assume the governorship in replacement of Juan Bautista Alvarado, a native Californio who had seized power in a 1836 revolt against the last governor who had been sent from Mexico. Micheltorena brought with him hundreds of soldiers, recently recruited from Mexico's prisons, who were forced to scavenge from the California ranchers and homeowners since Mexico failed to provide Micheltorena with funds to pay his troops. For this and other reasons the local Californios grew dissatisfied and began a revolt in the fall of 1844 that met with final success in the early spring of 1845, when Micheltorena surrendered and returned to Mexico.

Larkin's relationship with Micheltorena was as close to real friendship as he ever developed with a Californio official. He wrote to Alfred Robinson in April 1844 that Micheltorena "in his mode and manner is much of the Gentleman and is a man of talents." He was not without criticism, however, thinking that Micheltorena was "too lazy however and procrastinates" and

that he had "paid but little attention to the horse stealing."[66] When Micheltorena was forced to leave California, Larkin presented him with a drawing
of Monterey and wrote a very kind letter in which he would "regret the loss
of your society, after having (as a private person) received so many favours
at your hands as a Governor, a Gentleman and a Neighbour."[67] Larkin
ordered an elaborate cane for Micheltorena as a present, with an appropriate
inscription as governor. Unfortunately, it arrived after Micheltorena had
been expelled, yet Larkin still forwarded it on to him in Mexico, "as a
token of Friendship."[68]

More than mere friendship was involved in this relationship. Larkin was
heavily involved in the financing of Micheltorena's government. One
American resident of California recalled that Larkin "had a good deal of
influence there, because he acted as the financial advisor of Micheltoren[a],
and assisted him in getting supplies &c. They consulted him a good deal in
regard to the government, and placed a good deal of confidence in him."[69]
Not only did Larkin consistently loan money to Micheltorena's administration, he twice served briefly as a private bank from which Micheltorena
could draw funds.[70]

In the early stages of the revolt against Micheltorena, which began in
November 1844, Larkin loaned the governor massive amounts of money
with which to stave off the rebels. On December 12, he sent two drafts for
collection, for $10,000 apiece, to Parrott & Company in Mazatlán. They
were drawn by Micheltorena, one on a private trading firm in Mazatlán
and the other on the administrator of the Mazatlán customhouse.[71] $20,000
was an enormous sum for Larkin, almost half of his then net worth, and
about $260,000 in today's dollars.

There are many reasons to believe that the actual amount delivered to
Micheltorena, in money and goods, was a mere fraction of that amount.
First is the fact that Larkin had earlier accepted Micheltorena's draft on the
Mazatlán customhouse for $3,000. That draft had been refused, and Larkin was warned by John Parrott in April 1844, some eight months before
the $20,000 drafts, not to have anything to do with such paper.[72] Second is
Larkin's willingness, expressed *before* Micheltorena's defeat, to accept a
25 percent discount if the drafts could be sold.[73]

Only five days before the date he expressed willingness to discount the
existing $20,000 draft from Micheltorena, Larkin offered to loan him still
more money, this time on drafts drawn on the Monterey customhouse. Larkin was still speaking of big money, three or four orders of up to $5,000
each. The proposed transaction would be for "some certain amount to me,"
although unspecified. The concept came very close to corruption, and *possibly* may have been intended as such. Larkin offered to send the cash "to
any port to you you [*sic*] in your letter of intruction" indicate.[74]

At the time Micheltorena was in southern California engaged in an ultimately losing campaign with the rebels. The offer to send funds to "any

Governor Manuel Micheltorena (1842–1845) was the only Mexican official in California with whom Larkin was personally close. Courtesy The Bancroft Library.

port," with Santa Barbara mentioned specifically as a possibility, may have been merely to tailor the service to a shifting scene of battle engagement. However, it also smacks of the purely personal, as though Larkin is suggesting Micheltorena's personal use of these funds in "any port," rather than their application to governmental purposes. In any event, Micheltorena appears not to have accepted the offer. The suspiciousness of the entire affair is enhanced by Larkin's request to John Parrott, to whom he had sent the $20,000 for collection, not to speak of the matter to anyone: ". . . and should you have the money to Ship, have no one know it but the person who has it in charge." [75]

Although these activities of Larkin during the revolt against Micheltorena seem somewhat discreditable, there were others that were highly honorable. While the governor was off in the south in the campaign, his wife remained in the capital of Monterey. Rebels camped within a few miles of town and demanded its surrender. Señora Micheltorena was fearful of the loyalty of the convict-soldiers guarding her, thinking they might revolt and plunder the house. She went to Larkin for help, and he in turn asked another American, Josiah Belden, to "get a few Americans to act as a guard, with good arms." Belden recruited five or six Americans, while the governor's wife fitted out a room as an armory, and the small force organized at Larkin's request kept a watch there every night for four or five weeks. [76]

After Micheltorena's overthrow, Pío Pico, the new governor, ordered the Monterey customhouse not to pay any government debts until there had been an audit of accounts. Larkin protested that he was in desperate straits, out of goods for sale and actually owing cash because of the amount lent to Micheltorena. [77] He asked Abel Stearns to file a formal protest with Pico in Los Angeles, where the new governor was to maintain his office. [78] Stearns replied that he had heard a few individuals in Monterey had advanced Micheltorena as much as $50,000. "What surprises me most is, that you or any other merchant should loan to any officer of govt. so large a sum as you and others have done." [79]

Larkin was annoyed at this self-righteous tone. He pointed out that the Monterey credits to Micheltorena, mostly his, amounted only to some $12,000, but stressed that these were government obligations and not Micheltorena's personally. His letter omitted entirely any discussion of the two $10,000 drafts. He went on to express his understanding that the Los Angeles merchants had advanced to the new government—that is the successful rebels—nearly that amount. Larkin advised Stearns that his "supprise should not therefore be so great. Avarice I presume guided us all." [80]

Upon Micheltorena's departure for Mexico, certain governmental properties and personal goods of Micheltorena were left with Larkin for sale on consignment. [81] There is some indication that Pico later sent an agent to investigate Larkin's dealings with Micheltorena in an effort to force Larkin to surrender any surplus government funds in his hands, but that Larkin had so confused the accounts that this determination was impossible. [82] The general bar against the payment of government debts by the customhouse was gradually rescinded. Larkin was excepted, however, and Pico's ban on governmental payment to Larkin still stood as of July 1845. This angered Larkin, although he noted that the prohibitory order from the Los Angeles capital to the Monterey customhouse was "a dead letter from its reaching this place and hence forward will continue to be."[83]

Truly, it soon was a dead letter. The California government and the department's chief merchant quickly reestablished their customary symbiotic relationship, and California's public finances resumed their hectic and uneven course. Larkin was philosophical about these ups and downs, writing that "altho' once a Friend to Gen. M[icheltorena] he is now way from C[alifornia] and I am as much a Friend of the new powers."[84]

As a result of his financial activities, his favorable attitudes, and his entertaining, Larkin was on the best of terms with the California officials. In the spring of 1846, on the eve of the American invasion and the close of the Mexican era in California, he found many occasions to express this with pride. He told John C. Frémont that "for many years" he had found the California officials "well disposed to me."[85] To the American Secretary of State Larkin wrote that he had "the pleasure of saying that with every department of Office in this Country he is on the best terms of Friendship,"[86] and in a circular letter to a few fellow Americans in California he explained that he was "partial to the people [i.e., the Californios], and flatter myself they return my good will."[87]

Although Larkin may have held favorable attitudes toward individual Californios, he regarded their institutions and governmental practices quite differently and was very critical of the inefficient operations of Mexican California. Unlike other expatriates, however, he did not engage in shrill condemnation but viewed these foibles with mordant humor. His correspondence is filled with such expressions. In April 1835, the government was pressing men into a "voluntary" guard company. Larkin grumbled to Abel Stearns about losing employees, but added, "I hear they pay 2 rials in *rice* now. that is better than cash. the new Soldier can not get drunk on it."[88]

Some of Larkin's most witty and sardonic comments concerned the California criminal justice system. The following was addressed to a New York newspaper, and allowance must be made for literary reaching. It concerned the California practice of punishing minor miscreants by banishing them to another town:

> Some of the Monterey prisoners are banished to San Diego, those of the latter place to Monterey. Thats fair. If they commit a second offence they may be banished back, and find their own horses on the road, which are easy borrowed with a larzo [lasso]. So the owner of a Monterey Horse who may be stole once near home, and then at San Diego by another Explorer of the Country may see him again, minus some flesh & crooked legs, but then he gets his Horse by giving the man who says he found him at San D a dollar or two. That cheap for bringng a broken down horse 500 miles.[89]

No discussion of Larkin's associates during this period can be closed without mention of his voluminous correspondence with his eastern relatives.

Far more of their letters to Larkin are extant than are his to them. Yet we can be certain that Larkin contributed his share to the correspondence. The many letters from his sister, stepbrother, cousins, and other relatives frequently refer by date to letters of Larkin that no longer exist. Concerning his eastern relations one acquaintance wrote Larkin from Boston that "you must have kept them well advised of your family concerns, as they appear to know your children as well as I could tell them."[90] Larkin's principal family correspondents were his cousin, the minister William M. Rogers, his sister, Ann Wright, and his stepbrother and cousin, Ebenezer Childs.

With the Reverend Rogers, the correspondence primarily concerned business. Although Rogers did pass along family news occasionally, the great mass of the letters concerned the transmittal from California of eastern drafts for collection, Rogers's efforts in that regard, and the disbursement under Larkin's instructions of funds to business associates in the East. Rogers did other miscellaneous business for Larkin as well. For example, he arranged for the consular bonds when Larkin took up government office and was one of the signatories. Also, in 1844, he paid off Larkin's old notes to Ebenezer Childs for $75 and Amariah Childs, Larkin's stepfather, for $190.[91] These arose from funds borrowed years before, from his stepfather at the time when Larkin removed to California in 1832, and from his cousin in 1828.[92]

The funds in Rogers's hands gradually accumulated, and Larkin urged him to invest for him in real estate. Rogers demurred. "I am a clergyman," he wrote, "and this is out of my line of things . . . tho' I have more of a business tact, than ministerial in general."[93] A compromise was reached whereby Rogers would invest the surplus funds "in stocks in Boston, and no where else,"[94] and Rogers's letters were soon filled with details of Larkin's accumulating stock portfolio. Eventually Rogers loosened a bit and made much more far-flung investments for Larkin.

Curiously, given Rogers's status as a minister, there was less preaching in his correspondence than in that of his other relatives. At least once, however, Rogers did sound the theme of whether Larkin intended to return to his native land. "Your own affairs I understand," he wrote in 1840, "are attended with greater prosperity. But are you always to stay in Monterey. I sh. think you would wish to come back to the world again, and leave the Spainards to their superstitions and sluggishness, for the stirring world among the Yankees. The whole community is upon wheels or paddles here, and locomotives & steamboats are traveling land and sea."[95]

The numerous letters from his sister Ann Wright primarily brought family news. Larkin felt both close to and concerned about his sister. From a chance remark, probably from an 1838 letter of Rogers,[96] he acquired the notion that there was some serious and unspecified problem with his sister. Larkin demanded information, and reassurances streamed in from numer-

The Reverend William M. Rogers was Larkin's cousin and chief business agent in the eastern United States. Courtesy Society of California Pioneers and the University of California Press.

ous correspondents that Ann seemed fine. Eventually, in October 1840, his sister wrote that contrary to what he had heard all was well with her.[97] To satisfy Larkin further she wrote again, in July 1844, that while he was "still impressed with the idea that I am unhappy believe me Oliver, *it is not so,* far from it, neither have I cause to be."[98]

The most constant theme in Ann's correspondence, aside from steady news of kinfolk, was the desire that Larkin return to Massachusetts. Duty to children was invoked: "Most sincerely do I hope the time will come, when you will feel it a duty, to remove to Mass, and settle with your family, among your friends, and bring up your children in this 'land of steady habits.' "[99] Religion was also stressed: "I was surprised to hear . . . that no religion was tolerated among you but the Catholic. I feel on that account the more anxious that you should be . . . removing with your family, back to the land of your nativity, where you can enjoy the blessing of the Gospel, and be away from all popish idoletry."[100]

With very little subtlety, Ann suggested that Larkin had made enough money to retire and that kindness to his wife dictated he should. "Surely you have made enough to live among us, and enjoy the comforts of society, and civilization. I think it a duty you owe your family. . . . I know your Wife, must feel the need of the society of female acquintance, and refined associates."[101]

The letters from cousin Ebenezer Childs were filled with family news but largely reflected Ebenezer's anxieties, growing financial problems, and a sense of entrapment within a post office bureaucracy offering few opportunities for advancement. He often preached religion to Larkin: "Oliver, do you ever think of death & eternity, if not, begin *now*."[102] Larkin must have been drawn into a dialogue on these matters, for somewhat later came a strident rebuke. "Oliver," Childs wrote sternly, "are [you] yet so ignorant of the religion of Jesus Christ as to trust the safety of your soul on the efficacy of 'good will & good works' & a 'moral life'? . . . You have never spoken of Churches at M. [Monterey] . . . Have you any protestant instruction?"[103]

Throughout the correspondence with eastern relations there was much concern for Larkin's elderly stepfather, and this venerable gentleman finally died in February 1846. Beginning with the arrival of Larkin's children, Oliver and Frederic, in June 1846 their well being and education also became a primary topic.

Larkin's frequent promises to return to Massachusetts, coupled with his failure to do so, must have irritated his eastern relations. The promises began at least as early as 1841, for on July 16 of that year his sister wrote, "you say you may visit us, in 1842, and I shall be disappointed if you do not come."[104] Disappointed she may have been, but Larkin's expressions of interest in a return were undeterred. "We are very happy to hear," wrote his stepsister Ruth in September 1843, "you think of returning to America to settle after you have accumulated a certain amount of property."[105]

In the late fall of 1844, Larkin considered the much more serious prospect of sending his entire family, excepting himself, to Massachusetts for an unspecified period. Probably the thought was that his wife could establish the children in appropriate schools and visit her own relations. He even went so far as to make inquiries of his stepbrother Isaac as to the availability and costs of renting a house in Lynn, and estimates of other expenses, for the entire family.[106] Again hopes were raised. His stepsister Ruth wrote in March 1845 that she had "received your letter of 2d Nov. . . . We are all happy to hear that you purpose sending your family to Lynn. It would be gratifying to all the family to become acquainted with your wife and children and have them so near us, and we should certainly expect they would not be here long without you."[107]

But these hopes, as well as those of the earlier years, were to be dashed. Excepting his sons Oliver and Frederic, neither Larkin nor any of his family would see the East until 1850. It is difficult to understand why Larkin would raise these hopes in his family. There is no indication that he personally had a desire at that point in his life to either visit or live in the East. Possibly Rachel was applying pressure and the possibility of her moving with the children to the East was real. Possibly Larkin, under constant importuning from his eastern relations, wrote vague sentiments that were seized upon as expressions of intention. He did go so far as to inquire about costs in 1844. At least regarding his wife and children, he seems to have had some seriousness of purpose at that time.

CHAPTER 6

CONSUL AND PROPAGANDIST

HOWEVER LOYAL LARKIN was to his country, he went to California in 1832 with no unfurled flag, no patriotic mission. His purpose was much simpler. He had an empty pocketbook, and California seemed to offer opportunity to fill it. Like imperialists immemorial, he would bear his exile in a backward land among people he despised as long as the course led to fortune.

Prosper he did, and for years he was reasonably content with the political system under which he was gradually becoming a rich man. He groused about the ineffectiveness of California government and Mexico City's ignorance of and interference in California affairs, but he had no particular desire to influence a change in the system, nor to urge an association with the United States.

This is not to say that he became an acculturated Californian. Larkin adopted those features of Hispanic life that he admired, but he remained a proud Yankee in temperament, particularly in his energetic acquisitiveness. This loyalty to country and culture cost Larkin. There were inducements to assimilate completely, to do as most of his compatriots and accept Mexican citizenship.

Many immigrants married local women and became citizens. As citizens, they applied for and received land grants. Larkin's half-brother was given three. Land was the most certain form of wealth in Mexican California, and a grant of a ranch from the government was the easiest and least expensive path to ownership. As an alien, Larkin was not eligible for a grant and could only purchase land from private owners.

Larkin was also at a disadvantage in the political arena. Naturalized Mexicans could vote and hold political office, but Larkin, who was not a citizen, could take part only peripherally. Governors and other Californians repeatedly urged citizenship on him, but he consistently declined.[1] He was content that his residence in California was legalized by the *carta de seguridad* which he obtained in 1836 and renewed periodically thereafter. Larkin was ever interested in acquiring wealth, but he also loved his country—the United States—and his Yankee culture.

Larkin's consular appointment on May 1, 1843, was evidence of the growing American interest in California and Washington's recognition that Larkin was the leading American citizen there. His business ventures had made him a reasonably rich man, a requisite for a post of this sort which carried no compensation but many obligations. He had lived in California continuously since 1832. His location in Monterey, his mind and wit, led Americans and naturalized Californians throughout the province to ask him to represent them before the local government. He spoke Spanish fluently and was respected by California leaders. Governor Micheltorena was so pleased with the appointment that he gave Larkin permission to fly the United States flag at his house, a privilege that no other consul to Mexico enjoyed.[2]

Larkin was not the first consul appointed to represent the United States in California. Washington had been trying for ten years to establish a consulate there. Austin J. Raines of St. Louis, who described himself as a mariner and California trader, talked with President Andrew Jackson in early October 1833 about the need for official representation in California. Raines decided a few days later that he should be that official and applied for the post, explaining that he was departing soon for Monterey.[3]

Raines was issued a temporary appointment on October 17, 1833. The President sent his nomination for a permanent appointment to the Senate on January 20, 1834, but soon withdrew the nomination, possibly at the request of "Mr Benton," likely Senator Thomas Hart Benton of Missouri. Then Raines vanishes from the record. It seems that he intended to leave St. Louis April 1, 1834, for an overland journey to California—curious for a seaman. The story ends with an inquiry by a Virginia woman to the State Department in 1835, asking whether it had received any news of Raines, her nephew.[4]

Raines was but the first of a number of hopefuls. One "H. J. Kelley," probably Hall Jackson Kelley, better known for his belligerent demands for an American Oregon, applied in December 1834 for a consular commission at Monterey or any other place on Mexico's west coast.[5] It will be remembered that Kelley stayed with Larkin for a time, too long for Larkin's liking, during a visit to the town earlier in the year. Kelley wore out his welcome quickly. Larkin called him the "King of Beggers" and "sett him down as the greatest Bore I ever knew." When he finally left for Oregon with mountain man Ewing Young, Larkin breathed a great sigh of relief: "Thanks be given for his departure."[6] Nothing came of his application.

Charles Bent, of Bent's Fort fame, in 1835 urged his friend, William H. Ashley, fur-trade pioneer and influential Missourian, to recommend John Marsh for the consular appointment. Marsh, a merchant at Independence, Missouri, was planning a move to California and probably sought the post as a means of establishing himself on the coast.[7] The inquiry ended with the Assistant Secretary of State's reply to Ashley that "in consequence of the great distance, and the little direct intercourse between the United States and that Country, there is but little opportunity for any supervision, or control over the officers by the Department of State." The assistant secretary suggested rather coolly that since Ashley did not know Marsh personally, he should make further inquiries to decide whether Marsh had the qualities for the sensitive post.[8]

The next consul appointed to Monterey, after the elusive Raines, was Jonathan P. Gilliam. The commission, dated June 21, 1837, was delivered to Gilliam at Mazatlán. He acknowledged receipt in his letter of September 29, 1837. He never took up the position, death apparently intervening.[9] "J. T. Warren," almost surely Jonathan T. (Juan José) Warner, a California resident and merchant since 1831 and occasionally Larkin's agent, applied for a consular appointment in 1840. The application was referred to the Secretary of State, but its disposition is unknown.[10]

The Warner application is indicative of a growing interest within California in 1840 for a consulate. Larkin was prominent among those holding this opinion, and in the aftermath of the Graham Affair, he had a hint of the life of a consul. On July 1, 1840, "a number of respectable residents and transient citizens of the United States" met in Monterey, probably at Larkin's house, to talk about the incident. Larkin was named chairman and led the discussion. The group resolved to petition the United States to place a consul or other authority in Monterey for the purpose of protecting the interests of Americans on the coast. Captain French Forrest, commander of the United States warship, St. Louis, who came to Monterey in June 1840 to investigate the Graham incident and collect testimony, was requested by the group to assign an officer to perform the consular duties until Washington should act. Copies of the proceedings, signed by Larkin and Henry Paty, secretary, were sent to Forrest and, via the captain, to the President of the United States.[11]

Captain Forrest agreed to the need for an official American presence on the coast and appointed Ethan Estabrook temporary consular agent. Estabrook took up residence, but the California government did not recognize him, and his position was not legitimized by Washington. Estabrook and Larkin became friends and corresponded after Estabrook's departure in 1841.[12]

The State Department was not unmoved by the petition for a consulate and welcomed the next hopeful, New Yorker Thomas Carlile. Planning a voyage to the Pacific, Carlile sought an appointment "to secure a situation at some point on the Coast." He was aware of Washington's interest in establishing a consulate in California and believed that his knowledge of Spanish, gained during a three-year residence in Rio de Janeiro, would serve him well there. Carlile was granted a permanent commission as consul to San Francisco on March 10, 1842, but resigned on June 7, 1843, never having taken up the consular duties.[13]

If Carlile had assumed the post, he would soon have been tested in the "Monterey Affair," an ill-fated adventure that revealed in fact the need for an official American representation on the coast.[14] Commodore Thomas ap Catesby Jones, commander of the United States Pacific fleet and distant from any superior authority, seemed alone responsible for protecting American interests in the region. At Callao, Peru, Jones learned in early September 1842 that three British warships under Rear Admiral Thomas had sailed from Callao for an unknown destination. Almost simultaneously, he heard from John Parrott, United States consul at Mazatlán, that war between the United States and Mexico over the Texas question was likely. Mexico blamed the United States for the loss of Texas in 1836, and relations between the two countries had been deteriorating since then.

Jones had been stewing for weeks about the report that a French fleet had departed Valparaiso mysteriously the previous March. He was aware of the rumors of British and French designs for California, and he worried that one or both fleets could be bound there. There was risk in whatever course he chose, but he decided that the greater hazard was the possible loss of California. He sailed in haste from Callao on September 7.

Arriving in Monterey Bay on September 19, Jones demanded the capitulation of the town. Larkin and two California officers met Captain James Armstrong, commander of the flag ship, *United States*, at the landing. The party proceeded to Governor Alvarado's house, where Larkin left them. Alvarado's house was just across the street from Larkin's, and he watched people coming and going all evening, all considerably agitated.

Late in the evening, Larkin learned that Alvarado was sending a dispatch to the newly appointed Governor Micheltorena in southern California, who was even then marching toward Monterey with his troops. Larkin saw this as an opportunity to send a letter to his wife, who was visiting in Santa Barbara. It also was the excuse he needed to see what was happening at the governor's house. He had been wanting to get inside all evening, but had hesitated since he was an American.

His fears were for nothing. He was received as usual, as a *Montereño*, and he stayed to listen. Alvarado protested to those in the room that he had no authority, his successor already having been named, and that he wished to leave at once, but the others would not agree. Alvarado then appointed two commissioners to talk with the Americans. About 11:00 P.M., Larkin went home. Before he reached his bed, he was summoned to go on board the *United States* with the commissioners as interpreter.

The party was rowed out to the flag ship, where the commodore was awakened—he was not expecting the Mexican response until the next morning—and the treaty surrendering the town was negotiated amicably. Larkin was back in his bed before morning.

Before sunrise, the Monterey alcalde was at his house with an urgent message from the governor. In the letter Alvarado pleaded with Larkin to take charge of his property and interests since he had no other friends. Larkin went immediately to the governor's house. The family was gone, and the house was deserted but for one man who was there to turn it over to Larkin. Larkin and a sympathetic neighbor searched for Alvarado. They finally found him "at the billiard table, almost crazy, none the better or clearer for wine or brandy. He fairly raved." [15] He wanted desperately to leave the town, but agreed to stay for the time being if Larkin would try to get the commodore's permission for him to leave in peace and safety with his family and property.

Larkin returned to the flag ship with the commissioners early on September 20. Jones declined to grant Alvarado a special passport. The treaty was duly signed, and the *United States* and *Cyane* disembarked their landing forces. The town was occupied peacefully. A proclamation was read, declaring the pacific intention of the Americans and promising that civil liberties and property would be respected. There were no incidents, the troops having been given severe orders not to molest the inhabitants or their possessions. "There never was better order here," Larkin observed. [16]

But Larkin was baffled by the affair. During the previous night's visit with the officers of the *United States*, he had asked some hard questions. He wondered about the source of their information concerning the war. He asked which country had first declared war. He mentioned that Mexican newspapers dated as late as August 20 made no mention of war.

The next day the commodore saw late newspapers and private letters which convinced him that there was indeed no war. He also satisfied himself that a rumored scheme to cede California to Britain in settlement of a debt was equally false. By noon, Jones had signed a new treaty, restoring the town and authority to Governor Alvarado. The Stars and Stripes were lowered and the Mexican Eagle hoisted.

Some Americans expected repercussions. Commodore Jones had anticipated retaliation by inserting in the second treaty the condition that California authorities must take no action against foreigners or their property. Merchant John C. Jones in Santa Barbara expected the worst nevertheless: "I have drawn my head within my shell, and sneak about like a condemned criminal." Though he at first judged the commodore a madman for such an irrational act, he now hoped that he would keep the fleet on the coast and urged Larkin to try to persuade him to remain. [17] Nathan Spear, a San Francisco merchant, wrote Larkin that the people seemed to believe that the

Monterey in 1842. Photograph of lithograph by Charles Gildemeister, from an original drawing or painting by an unknown artist and commissioned by Larkin. Larkin's signature is in lower right with his distinctive Hispanic styled flourish beneath. Courtesy The Oakland Museum, gift of Mrs. Emil Hagstrom.

American flag's having floated briefly over the province somehow had canceled all debts.[18]

The affair ended not in repercussions, but in gaiety and harmony. On the afternoon of September 21, the American ships fired a salute in honor of the Mexican flag. An exchange of courtesy visits followed. The fleet remained in port, and during the weeks that followed the Americans walked and rode about the town and countryside in perfect safety and contentment. The officers, Larkin observed, "spent their leasure time ashore hunting wild Deer or dancing with tame Dear, both being plenty in and about Monterey." Both American and Californian officers attended "as many Balls as there was Sundays," dancing "Waltzes, Quadrilles, Hotas, Sons, Arabes, Bolero with the castanets Etc." to the music of the flag ship's fine band. "Some who never danced before," Larkin observed, "danced here."[19]

"The whole of this affair appeared at the time a dream," mused Larkin.[20] The Californians were perplexed by the incident. Most assumed that the action was planned from beginning to end, but to what purpose, they were not sure. Many suspected that there would eventually be a confrontation over California between France, Great Britain and the United States, and that the Americans expected that their flag having flown even briefly at Monterey would give them some sort of advantage. Commodore Jones had said that he sailed to Monterey with no hostile orders from Washington. Californians thought otherwise. Resident Americans worried about the effect of the affair on the treatment of foreigners in California, but Larkin believed that they were safer than they had been before. Commodore Jones had demonstrated how easy it would be for an American force to chastise a California government that mistreated foreigners.

In any event, Larkin expected no trouble, certainly not directed against himself. But the Monterey affair soon began to tell on him. When the fleet sailed away, he said later, "[a]gain do I feel the void they have left behind."[21] He began to ponder, more than he ever had in the past, a California with close American ties. He was convinced that Californians would welcome the change. Indeed, this conviction was widely held. This sentiment, and a growing apprehension about the future, heightened the call for an official American presence on the coast.

Larkin's distinction rests on his being the first—and only—person to actually serve as consul of the United States to Mexican California. He was clearly better qualified than the others who had applied for or were commissioned to the post. In appointing Larkin, official Washington undoubtedly was influenced indirectly by travelers and traders who had been helped in some fashion by Larkin or had enjoyed the famous Larkin hospitality in Monterey. Those who met Larkin almost without exception found him urbane, knowledgeable, competent, and attached to his country and her interests. When Ebenezer L. Childs, Larkin's stepbrother and a leading clerk in the Post Office at Washington, began a campaign to secure the consulate for him, he solicited support from a number of Americans with California connections. Stephen Smith, a ship master for over thirty years who traded regularly on the coast, replied to Childs that he knew Larkin well and was aware of "no man, more competent to fill the office than your brother . . . it would give me great pleasure to see him appointed to the Consulate of upper Calafornia [sic]." Assuming that Childs had some influence in Washington, Smith added that he would also like to see a new consul appointed for Valparaiso.[22]

Horatio E. Hale also wrote on Larkin's behalf. Young Hale, appointed philologist to Charles Wilkes's United States Exploring Expedition while still a student at Harvard, spent three weeks in Monterey in January 1842, staying a few days at Larkin's house. In his letter to Childs, Hale wrote of Larkin:

> He is a gentleman of property, much respected both by foreigners & natives, & bearing, so far as my knowledge extends, an irreproachable character. He is, beyond question, the principal American merchant resident at Monterey. He speaks the language fluently, & has, from the nature of his business, a general acquaintance with the commercial & political regulations of the province.

Hale added that he had heard talk in Monterey about the need for a consular establishment and that Larkin was frequently mentioned as the logical person for the office.[23]

Larkin received news of his temporary appointment as consul, dated May 1, 1843, in early 1844. Because Childs wished well for his stepbrother, and perhaps because he was trying to borrow money from him, he claimed credit for the assignment. In January 1843 he had persuaded the Postmaster General, his superior, to speak to Daniel Webster, the Secretary of State, about the appointment. At Webster's invitation, Childs submitted Larkin's name on January 25, 1843.[24] He notified Larkin in August 1843, "I wrote you last in May, & sent with your appointment as Consul at Monterey, which matter was attended to at the State Dept after much useless delay."[25] He was more emphatic the following December: "You owe your appointment more to my personal application & because your name is Larkin than to any other causes. Mr [Secretary of State Daniel] Webster & your uncle J. of P. were old friends." Childs mentioned in the same letter that Larkin's name as consul had been printed in the "Am. Almanack, Cong. Directory, Blue Book &c."[26]

Larkin was delighted, but still anxious. In April, he wrote to Alfred Robinson in the East, asking him to have a consular uniform made for him. He cautioned him to first verify with the Secretary of State that the Senate had indeed confirmed the appointment, "[a]s our Government in its wisdom often replaces their officers, before they have hardly began the duties of their respective office."[27] The permanent appointment, dated January 29, 1844, arrived in Monterey two months later, on June 24, 1844.

There was some confusion about the California consulate at one point, traceable to Washington's ignorance about California's political and commercial affairs. Albert M. Gilliam, brother of the previously-appointed Jonathan P. Gilliam, was named consul for San Francisco on January 29, 1844, also the date of Larkin's permanent appointment, but Gilliam never assumed the post. When Larkin learned of Gilliam's appointment, he explained to Secretary of State John C. Calhoun that San Francisco was not a port of entry, so there was no need for a consul there. Monterey, he said, was the only port of entry in California, so only one consul was required for the entire province, that one being Larkin himself.[28] Upon receipt of Larkin's letter, Richard K. Crallé, Acting Secretary of State, wrote to notify him that Gilliam had resigned and would not be replaced.[29]

Immediately on receiving his appointment, Larkin began a search for supplies, advice, and instructions to guide him in his official duties. He worried that "[a]t this place I have no councel, advise, referees or precedents to guide me, no books and barely instructions to draw from." Larkin hoped that he would acquire "knowledge before business."[30] He wrote to the Secretary of State on April 10, 1844, and again the following day, requesting a seal, stamp, flag, coat of arms, and "Books and instruction in full."[31] He also wrote for advice to the nearby American consuls of Mazatlán and Oahu.

Help was soon on the way. He received a long letter of advice from John Parrott, the consul in Mazatlán, dated May 22, 1844,[32] and from Vice Consul William Hooper at Oahu came information on consular forms.[33] Hooper also sent detailed advice, and the admonition that many shipmasters would now abuse Larkin, simply because he was consul, and would call him a "great rascal [that] . . . ought to be dismissed." As an offset, Hooper noted with the sort of sardonic humor that must have pleased Larkin, the new consul would have "all the honour (?) and, perhaps, fees enough to pay for your cigars."[34]

Eventually some general instructions arrived from Washington, although throughout his consulate Larkin constantly requested additional guidance. For example, on December 9, 1844, Larkin dispatched a very detailed letter requesting instructions on various questions relating to his maritime jurisdiction.[35] Another example was the vexing question of whether he had authority as consul to conduct marriage ceremonies for Americans desiring his services. Between 1844 and 1846, he wrote three letters requesting this information before finally receiving an answer.[36]

The problem was twofold. First was the considerable time required for a letter and reply to travel the large distances involved, with largely irregular service through Mexico. Second was the lack of an efficient modern bureaucracy in the federal government; most of Larkin's letters were answered by the Secretary of State personally. The result of this problem was that Larkin had considerable freedom of action. His activities as consul were guided by some general instructions and principles but with the specific applications to the California situation left to Larkin's own good sense.

An American consul in the 1840s had three primary duties: to advance American commercial interests, particularly maritime interests, in the territory in which he was stationed; to protect the interests of American seamen within his jurisdiction; and to protect the civil rights of all Americans within his area of duty. A consul received no salary as such, but was entitled to fees and commissions for many of his services. It was expected that his status as American consul would redound to his pecuniary advantage through his mercantile or other business. The system was antiquated for its time and was thoroughly overhauled and modernized in 1856.[37]

More specifically, Larkin was expected to: (1) take charge of the estates of American citizens who died without legal representatives; (2) provide relief to destitute American seamen and hospital and medical services for sick American seamen, and arrange for their transportation to the United States aboard an American vessel, for which he was to be paid his expenses and modest fees; (3) care for stranded vessels; (4) authenticate and register various maritime papers, protests, depositions, surveys, invoices, ships' papers, and the like, for which he could charge modest fees; and (5) generally protect the interests and rights of American citizens within the consular jurisdiction, which duty provided the most interesting and varied of his activities.[38]

Larkin discharged these duties well. In other chapters we have seen him aiding the whaling and Boston vessels, and his correspondence is full of advice to shipmasters regarding shipwrecks, insurance, problems with seamen, the deposit of papers, and the like. In his career as consul he furnished board, lodging, clothing, or medical help to at least eighteen sick or destitute American seamen.[39]

Larkin was energetic in working to protect the civil rights of Americans in Mexican California. He protested when Americans were held in jail for an excessive period without a hearing,[40] and when he heard of an American jailed without food.[41] When two Americans were assaulted and left for dead in San Francisco in October 1845, Larkin pressed for rapid prosecution of the suspects and even traveled to San Francisco to take depositions and urge the Mexican authorities to greater speed.[42] Although Larkin was indeed energetic, he was somewhat inclined to puffery and an overstatement of his importance in these regards. In July 1845, he wrote the Secretary of State:

> Our countrymen continue to receive, every assurance of safety and protection from the present Government. The different Alcaldies from San Diego to

San Francisco. . . . often send civil and criminal cases respecting Americans to me, for confirmation being willing for me to decide in many cases, which of course I cannot do. This causes me much trouble and personal expence.[43]

This statement is simply untrue. Neither Larkin's own correspondence nor the extant judicial records from the alcaldes support it. It is true, however, that there was no general principle of extra-territoriality in Mexican California, and that on the few occasions Larkin ventured a legal opinion, when pressed by Americans, he gave it simply as his own personal opinion and did not throw the mantle of his office around it.[44]

The most interesting part of Larkin's consular activities was his aid to immigrating American settlers. He gave them information and passports; he distributed avuncular advice to those with marital difficulties; and he urged dying Americans to write wills and notified their kinsmen in the East upon their demise.[45]

All of this was routine consular activity. Larkin went beyond the ordinary, however, in sending the Department of State a constant stream of reports on conditions in California. He reported on commercial conditions with changes of tariffs, regulations, methods of trade, statistics, number and nationality of vessels, and the like. But he also treated political conditions, other nations' consular activities, their representatives' expressed interests in the political future of California, and the revolts and constantly shifting alignments of Mexican politics within California. These political and economic reports, going far beyond normal consular activity, were sent regularly in the years of the Larkin consulate. They won the praise of the Department of State as early as October 1844,[46] and their sensitivity was undoubtedly a major factor in Larkin's appointment in 1845 as confidential agent to the President.

Both Larkin and James Buchanan, then Secretary of State, believed that the completion of the conquest of California terminated Larkin's consulate, although the secretary did honor Larkin's request to continue on as confidential agent.[47] As late as May 20, 1848, the American military governor, Colonel Richard B. Mason, asked Larkin to take charge of an estate in his consular capacity.[48] The official termination of both consular and confidential agent functions was as of May 30, 1848, the date of the exchange of ratifications of the peace treaty between Mexico and the United States. It was announced to Larkin in Secretary Buchanan's letter of June 23, 1848.[49]

Larkin's first full semiannual return, for the second half of 1844, shows expenses in caring for sick seamen of $724.22 and other disbursements of his office in the amount of $131.34.[50] Expenses increased enormously as the conquest neared. When appointed as confidential agent, he was offered compensation of $6.00 per day.[51] Almost immediately, Larkin asked for more compensation, $3,000 per annum, pointing to the value of the commercial business he was foregoing. He also argued that his expenses of "Office, Rent, Stationary, Clerk hire, Couriers . . . Purchase and Hire of horses . . . [made] the entire yearly expence of this Agency about five thousand dollars."[52] When the war came, these expenses sharply increased.

Yet, for the very small compensation—minimal in the case of the consulate—and for very large expenses, Larkin had an enormously difficult time in receiving payment from the federal government. He wrote drafts on the federal government which he sent to his cousin William Rogers in Boston for collection, and they were routinely dishonored. His first consular draft from 1844 was still unsettled as of the end of 1846.[53]

The slow payment was partly due to bureaucratic pettifoggery of the government auditors[54] and Larkin's lack of precise instructions as to the form of his accounts. And in part there was the turmoil of the war itself, and the necessity of Larkin's keeping many of his records on various naval vessels during the invasion and later insurrection.[55] "There has been no other consulate with so few emoluments, that has had the expense and trouble that has been attached to my office in 1845 & 46," Larkin concluded.[56]

Yet Larkin brought some of his problems down upon himself. He simply neglected to sign some large drafts that he sent east.[57] At other times, Larkin knowingly sent drafts on the government for collection without enclosing the required vouchers.[58] Ultimately, on September 1, 1847, Larkin transmitted his final consular accounts to the Secretary of State and asked that the unusual circumstances of the invasion be explained to the auditors.[59] At about the same time he wrote a long and detailed letter to the auditor directly, justifying his consular expenses for 1844, 1845, and 1846, and regretting "that such Vouchers, Receipts &c should not have been forwarded with my first returns . . . but the want of archives to refer to together with my having no definite instructions relative to the necessary forms of a/cs must be my excuse."[60] Larkin received a final accounting of his consular compensation and his compensation as confidential agent by letter dated June 23, 1848.[61]

The efforts that Larkin made as confidential agent will be followed in the next chapter, but this is the appropriate place to sum up his actions as consul. Larkin had widely diversified duties as consul, and his jurisdiction extended over a very large territory. Except for the brief service of William A. Leidesdorff as vice consul for Yerba Buena and the port of San Francisco, Larkin acted alone.[62] His employers expressed much satisfaction with the new consul. President Polk remarked in conversation that he considered Larkin a "very efficient and patriotic man."[63] On the consumer level we must use care, since most of the persons that had contact with Larkin, the consul, also dealt with Larkin, the merchant. Attitudes toward Larkin could be easily affected by considerations of commerce.

The destitute sailors whom Larkin helped did not write their memoirs, so their experiences are unclear. But at least one American citizen with no economic relationship to Larkin who dealt with him simply as consul wrote about his encounter. Daniel D. Heustis found himself in California unexpectedly, enroute to the East from an imprisonment by the British in Australia for his participation in the Canadian uprising in 1838. He and his companions had been released by a British ship in Hawaii. They made their way to California in May 1845 and "immediately called on the American Consul, Thomas O. Larkin, Esq., who received us in a very gentlemanly manner, and manifested a ready disposition to serve us."[64] The best summation of Larkin as consul was that of 1841 pioneer John Bidwell, who said that Larkin was an efficient consul and gave general satisfaction, possessing both shrewdness and tact.[65]

Larkin's correspondence to the East and his influence on national affairs extended beyond Washington officialdom. He wrote frequently to a number of eastern newspapers that published his letters, those about whaling under his name but many of the others anonymously.[66] The letters were a combination of bragging about his adopted home, warnings of British and French designs, recitations of the potential benefits of the region for the United States, and a repetition of his conviction that the only thing lacking to make the province paradise was a great number of Yankees. Larkin's objective was an American California, and in his letters he sought to sway both government leaders and the general public. If California followed the example of Texas, he hoped there would be no violence. Above all else, he favored a union with the United States initiated by the Californians themselves, a sentiment expressed to both officials and editors.

Larkin's public letter writing began innocently enough. He wrote in early 1843 to James Gordon Bennett, editor of the *New York Herald*, to enter a subscription, Larkin said. More likely, he wanted simply to tell Bennett and his readers something that they did not know. "I imagine you have never had a Correspondent from the 'Far West,'" he began. "In fact you have not found out as yet where the Far famed 'Far West' is. You now know, and so does Com Thomas ap C. Jones."[67] With this, he began a correspondence with eastern editors in a light-hearted prose that is not characteristic of his official and commercial letters. It is more reminiscent of the style of his 1821–1826 eastern travel diary.

Larkin often sent the same material to more than one editor. He told Moses Yale Beach, editor of the *New York Sun*, the *Herald*'s arch rival, about California's desire for "home rule," evidenced by the nullification of a Mexican tariff by the Monterey government, and a rising, the fourth in twelve years, that led to the ouster of General Micheltorena.[68] Under the pen name of "Paisano," he sent a more complete account of the revolt against Micheltorena to the *New York Herald*.[69]

Publishers, eager for any sort of printed materials about California, asked Larkin to send, along with his letters, any locally-produced publications. Larkin replied to such a request from Beach, explaining that though the Monterey government owned a printing press, it was of no use. Since no newspapers were published in California, Larkin instead sent copies of the *Friend* and the *Polynesian*, both printed in the Sandwich Islands. He added news of his own about the islands, particularly poking ridicule at the laws that governed most human activity there. California had its laws too, he said, mostly ignored. Mexico regularly sent its decrees to the province, but since "the paper is not very good to make paper Segars, the law Books are laid on the . . . shelf."[70] Californians were an independent-minded people and thought they should govern themselves with little interference from Mexico City.

Mexico was not alone in threatening California's tranquillity. A theme often repeated in Larkin's letters was the interest of France and Great Britain in California. Larkin expected that Britain would win the contest, unless the United States chose to intervene. Natives and foreigners alike were preparing for the change by being sure that their children learned English.[71] Some Californians, Larkin among them, sent their children to the Oahu English School to learn the language of the future.[72]

Larkin believed fate decreed and history proved that California would fall to Britain or the United States. He predicted that the Anglo-Saxon race, "their principles and their language must & will continually extend towards three quarters of the compass." He foresaw a country stretching from twenty-nine or thirty degrees latitude to a point far north of the Columbia River, containing millions of people, "under a happy Govt speaking the language we speak, under what flag I can not say nor when."[73] If that happy government were to be American, Larkin told his eastern correspondents, the United States must act before it was too late.

All of Larkin's letters included some sort of description of the attractions of California and the advantages of an American takeover. The bays were expansive, the rivers full of fish and the forests of game. California was a land where one could find happiness. Larkin was perhaps the first to pronounce succinctly what would become called in another century the "California Dream:" " 'Solomon, in all his glory,' " he told the readers of the *New York Herald*, " 'was not more happy than a Californian.' "[74] An American occupation, furthermore, would deny the province to a foreign power that could threaten the United States if it were to establish itself there. Larkin added another alternative for California. If the United States chose not to act, then California and Oregon must join and become a separate nation,[75] assuming that Oregon was not seized first by the British.

Larkin's letters were all of a sort. They described the country and told about recent events, but the underlying message was always clear: California was available; it would soon fall to a foreign power; the United States must act soon. Larkin became so enthusiastic that he urged like-minded acquaintances to write letters for publication. He was particularly insistent with John Marsh. Larkin called him to "shake off your apathy and idleness, come

forth into the field, and write for the Country you intend to live. . . .
Awake, slumber not forever." If he would but write, Larkin would arrange
for publication in eastern newspapers.[76] Marsh vacillated but, in January
1846, wrote a long letter to Lewis Cass, a personal friend, one-time Democratic nominee for the presidency and a United States Senator. In the letter
Marsh echoed the themes of Larkin's correspondence. Cass passed the
letter to the press and it was widely printed. Marsh sent a variation of
the letter to the *New Orleans Picayune*.[77]

As tensions rose between the United States and Mexico, eastern readers
searched for all sorts of news from California, Oregon, and the Sandwich
Islands. They devoured newspaper reports about ship sailings, markets, and
political developments. Larkin was the chief source for the news, and an
officer of the *Herald* wrote in October 1845 to urge him to keep the letters
coming.[78] A. E. Beach, an officer of the *Sun*, assured Larkin that his letters
were being read with great interest and were having a profound effect on
national events. The *Sun*, he said, was chiefly responsible for the annexation
of Texas. Now, the editors asked, " 'Why not California.' " Armed with
Larkin's reports about its land and harbors, the editors answered their own
question and were urging the purchase of California and the construction of
a transcontinental railroad with a terminus at Monterey. Beach asked Larkin
to continue sending letters for publication and to comment particularly on
the proposed railroad.[79] Larkin would have been deeply interested in the
latter, for in the 1850s he would become a chief advocate of the proposal
for a transcontinental railroad.

As late as mid-May 1846, Larkin still knew nothing of the influence of his
correspondence. He complained to Moses Yale Beach of "never havig seen
one of my letters printed nor know that you published them." He nevertheless assumed that they were being printed since he instructed Beach to publish only extracts rather than entire letters.[80] He finally received confirmation. He had been writing letters to James Gordon Bennett for two years,
supposing "that some of them might be worth publishing," and in May
received Bennett's letter verifying their publication and importance. Larkin
was so encouraged by the editor's letter that he tried, unsuccessfully as it
turned out, to engage a secretary to write for him.[81] He also learned that
some of his letters to individuals were being printed.[82]

By the spring of 1846, on the eve of the American conquest, Larkin and
other foreigners and immigrants in California awaited what they believed
by then to be inevitable. "The fate of California is one of the surest affairs
yet in the womb of time," he wrote to Beach in April. Signing the letter,
"Paisano," Larkin listed four alternative paths for an American acquisition,
in the order favored by the inhabitants of the province: (1) a sale to the
United States; (2) conquest, to end the suspense; (3) overland emigra-

tion, though foreign residents and Californians alike found the overlanders a disagreeable lot; (4) a migration of Mormons, which he labeled "the Worst." [83] Whatever the method, the result would be the displacement of the Californian by the Yankee. In a letter to Bennett, Larkin compared the two and concluded that even the Californians admired the Americans for their seeking and grasping. [84]

From the beginning of his correspondence with newspaper editors, Larkin expected that his letters would be published. The ending of his February 1843 letter to the editor of the *Herald*—"If its worth reading any one may read it withholding the name"—was lined out. [85] This might suggest that Larkin had second thoughts about implying to Bennett that he assumed the letter would be printed. A more plausible explanation is that Larkin *did* expect the letter to be published, and he lined out the sentence as unseemly false modesty. In another letter, this one to the editor of the *New York Journal of Commerce*, Larkin was more forthright: "These letter contans many facts well known to the writer and should be know to his Countrymen." He had read much about California in the pages of the *Journal of Commerce* and now sent his own information, unquestionably for printing, [86] not necessarily under his name.

Editors often asked Larkin what they could do for him, to show their appreciation for his correspondence. They volunteered to pay postage, send newspapers, place advertisements or some other service, at his request. Larkin usually accepted the offers for newspapers and postage but could think of no other tangible compensation. He asked Bennett simply "to keep this country (prehaps my hobby) continually before the public which I believe is already your aim. We must have it, others must not." As if in afterthought, he suggested that Bennett might yet be of some service to him. Writing in May 1846 and expecting momentous change for California, he saw an uncertain future: "In bringing about these events I may be brought into the whirlwind and political Vortex and rise or fall according to Curcumstances or what Nation gains the country, if my own, what party. In which case my character now fair, my name now unknown, my movments motives and prospects now blest, may be assailed." In that case, he told Bennett, he could serve him by wielding the power of the *Herald* on his behalf. [87] Larkin, indeed, would be attacked later in the decade by some who knew him and some who knew about him. There is no evidence that Bennett came to his defense.

Larkin continued after the spring of 1846 to write to eastern editors about the conquest, the gold discovery, and the rush to the mines. From the arrival of the United States fleet, Larkin no longer advanced the argument for an American California. Now he wrote of the opportunities in the new American possession.

CHAPTER 7

EDEN AT RISK

LARKIN REREAD a portion of Secretary Buchanan's letter of October 17, 1845:

> . . . the President has thought proper to appoint you a Confidential Agent in California: and you may consider the present Despatch as your authority for acting in this character. The confidence which he reposes in your patriotism and discretion is evinced by conferring upon you this delicate and important trust. [1]

He noted with satisfaction the secretary's comment that his correspondence had been favorably received in Washington. Larkin had a reputation for working hard, and often selflessly, but he needed to be appreciated.

If Larkin were sitting at his desk in his office as he read Buchanan's letter and had risen to pace, pondering the significance of the new assignment, his glance might have strayed to the recessed window and the patio. The yard was filled with stacked lumber and store merchandise, reminders of his commercial affairs. He had neglected his business lately.

The new appointment was the direct result of a letter that Larkin had sent the previous summer, July 10, 1845, to Buchanan. [2] Larkin had revealed in the letter the disturbing news that the new central government in Mexico City was assembling a military force at Acapulco for dispatch to California. Its apparent objective was to remove from office the native government of Pío Pico and José Castro, who had only recently ousted Governor Micheltorena.

That Mexico City should wish to reassert its authority in California was not unexpected, but Larkin added the alarming report that Great Britain was directly involved in Mexico's action. John C. Jones had written to Larkin in June 1845 from Santa Barbara that California was now "pledged to England" and that two rich British business houses in Mexico had promised to finance the expeditionary force for eighteen months. John Parrott, the American consul at Mazatlán, reportedly had $70,000 deposited with him to pay the troops.[3] Rumor held that Eustace Barron, the British consul at Tepic, also was involved in arrangements for paying and transporting the force to California. The size of the expedition was variously estimated to number from 700 to 1,800, either figure a formidable force. Shortly before writing his July 10 letter, Larkin had heard from Parrott, acknowledging that the Mexican government had in fact asked him to advance funds for the scheme, but he had refused.[4]

Larkin's July 10 letter to Buchanan continued. California leaders were aware of Mexico's plan. General Castro was preparing a defense, pressing young men into service and calling on the upper classes to send their sons into the service as officers. California leaders, Larkin told Buchanan, had repeatedly told him that they "will fight all troops Mexico may send here, to the *last* drop of their blood. . . . They wish to govern themselves." Failing that, they would "prefer to see the United States troops, to those from Mexico, to govern the country."[5] This last sentiment must have been equally intriguing to both Larkin and Buchanan.[6]

Larkin pointed out that the British interest in California was evident in the recent appointment of a salaried vice consul. James Alexander Forbes, a naturalized Mexican citizen, had established his residence forty or fifty miles from the coast and therefore could be of no service to British commerce in the province, had any existed. In fact, Larkin said, no English merchant ship had called in California for years, save the occasional ship of the Hudson's Bay Company. Clearly, said Larkin, the consul is "kept under pay for other purposes." Ominously, the British warship, *America*, fifty guns, was expected in Monterey within the week.[7]

The French, too, wrote Larkin, were showing considerable interest in California affairs. A French consul, Louis Gasquet, had been appointed, drawing an annual salary exceeding $4,000, "with no apparent business to do." A French man-of-war, the *Heroine*, of twenty-six guns, and a merchant ship were even then at Monterey.[8]

Larkin's July 10 letter had arrived in Washington in October 1845. Buchanan and President Polk would have discussed its contents in detail. Polk must have pondered the meaning of the situation in California. Mexico and the United States were moving closer to war over the annexation of Texas. He expected that California would be one of the spoils of that war, and he did not wish to see it slip away now.

The President's concern was heightened by another dispatch received the same day as Larkin's. William S. Parrott, Polk's special agent in Mexico and brother of John Parrott, American consul at Mazatlán, wrote that every scrap of news from California was causing great excitement in the English community there, but especially among those attached to the British legation. In earlier dispatches, Parrott had told of the scheme of Eugene Mac-Namara, an Irish priest, to establish a colony in California. He also described a strengthened British Pacific fleet with orders to seize California if war broke out between Mexico and the United States.[9]

Polk acted. Until now, he had been content to let matters take their course in California. The tide of emigration to the province seemed to ensure its Americanization and eventual absorption. The menace posed by Britain and France changed things. Direct American action, however delicate, was necessary.

On October 17, only a few days after receiving Larkin's July 10 letter, Buchanan replied to the consul.[10] In this significant document, the Secretary of State outlined the new United States policy toward California. Larkin's influence was obvious. Buchanan stated clearly that he was guided by the information contained in the consul's July 10 letter and often quoted verbatim from it.

The United States, Buchanan declared, would not interfere in the controversy between Mexico and California unless Mexico should initiate conflict with the United States. The United States, however, would not sit idly by and watch California be taken over by Great Britain or another European power. That event would benefit no one, particularly the monarchies. A European takeover would lead inevitably to war, since emigration of Americans to California would not permit the province to remain long in foreign hands. Larkin was instructed to warn Californios of the danger posed by interference from abroad. He was to "inspire them with a jealousy of European dominion and to arouse in their bosoms that love of liberty and independence so natural to the American Continent."[11]

Having established this ideological tie, Larkin was to explain to California leaders that "should California assert and maintain her independence, we shall render her all the kind offices in our power as a Sister Republic." Buchanan explained that the United States had no territorial ambitions in the matter and that President Polk:

> . . . will make no effort and use no influence to induce California to become one of the free and independent States of this Union, yet if the People should desire to unite their destiny with ours, they would be received as brethren.
> . . .

The end of this last sentence, "whenever this can be done, without affording Mexico just cause of complaint," seems a bit gratuitous following close on the Texas experience.[12]

Buchanan turned finally to the principal object of the letter: the appointment of Larkin as the President's confidential agent in California. The Secretary ended by urging him to double his efforts, to send information on the attitudes of California authorities and citizens toward the United States, sketches of principal government officials and influential citizens, composition of the population, location of American settlements, data on immigration, trade opportunities, and indeed "all the information respecting California which may be useful or important to the United States."[13]

Larkin's July 10 letter had an immediate effect on United States strategy abroad. On the same day that Buchanan replied to Larkin, the American position in California was strengthened. Secretary of War George Bancroft, who would have been briefed by the Secretary of State, sent new orders to Commodore John D. Sloat, commander of the United States fleet on the Mexican coast. He was instructed to avoid any hint of aggression, confer regularly with Larkin, nourish a friendly spirit among Californios for the United States, and to be prepared to blockade or seize California ports if hostilities began.[14]

That same October 17, Bancroft dispatched Commodore Robert F. Stockton to deliver the letters of the same date to Sloat and Larkin. In addition, Stockton was directed to learn all he could about local conditions and impress upon the Californios the depth of American good will. That done, he was to add his frigate, the U.S.S. *Congress*, to Sloat's squadron.[15] Buchanan would complete the instructions to the official American presence in California by sending to John C. Frémont, whose latest expedition had taken him to California, a copy of his October 17 letter addressed to Larkin.

Even before responding to Larkin, Buchanan had written to Louis McLane, the American ambassador in London, to alert him to the delicate situation in California. He paraphrased from Larkin's letter and included a number of verbatim passages. Buchanan emphasized the certain consequences if Britain should attempt to acquire California.[16] Americans would be outraged.

Secretary Buchanan also briefed John Slidell, President Polk's special emissary to Mexico, on the contents of Larkin's letter. Slidell, whose mission was to obtain Mexico's agreement on the Rio Grande boundary and settlement of the debt question, was instructed to try to learn whether Mexico intended to cede California to either Great Britain or France. He was to urge Mexico against a cession, impressing on the Mexican leaders that Washington would view the presence of France or Britain in California as a threat to American security. Buchanan invited Slidell to correspond with Larkin on the matter.[17]

There is nothing in Larkin's papers to indicate his state of mind on receiving Buchanan's letter the following spring. If his response were in character, he would have been enormously pleased. He now had official encouragement to do exactly what he had been doing for years: work for a close association between California and the United States. Until recently, Larkin had not anticipated annexation,[18] but now he was committed to a union with the United States. He still hoped that the process could be completed peacefully, without violence, at the initiation of the Californios themselves.

Secretary Buchanan's October 17 letter reached Larkin on April 17, 1846. A copy of the letter was brought by Lieutenant Archibald H. Gillespie of the United States Marine Corps and the President's secret agent. Gillespie had crossed Mexico, disguised as an invalid merchant traveling for health and business purposes. He was carrying documents, prepared at Buchanan's request, that showed him to be an associate in the Boston firm of William Appleton & Company which traded regularly on the California coast. Before landing at Vera Cruz, Gillespie had memorized Buchanan's letter to Larkin, then destroyed it. It would not do to have such compromising evidence if he should be questioned by Mexican authorities. He would rewrite the letter before reaching Monterey.

During his overland journey, Gillespie was stalled in Mexico City for a month by the revolution led by Mariano Paredes y Arrillaga against the government of President José Joaquín de Herrera. Arriving finally at Mazatlán, on February 22 he boarded the American warship *Cyane*, which sailed for Honolulu, thence to Monterey. Buchanan had assumed, correctly, that Gillespie would reach Monterey before Commodore Stockton, who carried the original of the Secretary's letter, completed his voyage around the Horn.

Almost immediately upon receipt of Buchanan's October 17 letter, Larkin sat down to respond. He accepted "with unfeigned satisfaction" the appointment as President Polk's confidential agent.[19] He promised to devote himself to the assigned task, adding that he was on the best of terms with leaders of California government. He made the rather cryptic comment that the leaders had no affection for Mexico and would take measures to separate California "if their salaries were secured to them, and they had reason to suppose they would not hereafter be thrown into the ranks of the comunality."[20] Larkin seems to be suggesting that the Californios would be open to overtures that would include assurances of place in an American California, thereby smoothing the path to a transfer of sovereignty.[21]

Larkin pointed out to Buchanan that the foreign threat was not as serious then as it had seemed in summer 1845. There was little communication at the moment between California government and the British and French consuls. The French official "lives very retired," and the authorities were irritated at him for his recent interference in a local dispute. The British vice consul, he added, "is not a man to exert himself in Government affairs."[22] Earlier in the day, before Gillespie's arrival, Larkin had commented in another letter to Buchanan about Britain's declining interest in California. He mentioned that Dugald McTavish, the new Hudson's Bay Company agent, had told him only the previous week that he had received orders to settle the company's affairs in San Francisco, sell their house, and return promptly to Oregon.[23]

Finally, the Americanization of California was assured, Larkin wrote, by the mounting tide of immigration. He expected the arrival of a thousand overlanders in October 1846. Anticipating that the trend would continue, Larkin predicted that "the destiny of this Department [California] in 1848, is decided."[24] Three days later, Larkin began composing the longest letter he would ever write. He responded to Buchanan's requests for information about the country and its citizens, its politics, politicians and leaders, its commerce, missions and towns. Though begun on April 20, 1846, it was probably not dispatched to the Secretary until July 20.[25]

Larkin believed in mid-April 1846 that affairs in California were taking an American turn. Perhaps there was still time for a peaceful, evolutionary transition from Mexican province to American possession. If so, there was work to be done, but quickly. Larkin could not have forgotten the military *junta* that had met in Monterey only days before. The junta had convened in late March at the call of General Castro, supposedly to discuss California's precarious situation, that is, the mounting fear of an American invasion brought on by Frémont's posturing and to plan for its defense. Governor Pico was invited to attend.[26] Suspecting that the junta would declare independence, Larkin had written to Abel Stearns, urgently requesting him to attend the meeting. Larkin offered accommodation in his home and $100 travel money. He had suggested that Stearns travel with Governor Pico, who he hoped would come, accompanied by two or three members of the legislature.[27] Larkin was disappointed, for no one from the south attended.

After some preliminary discussion at General Castro's home, the meeting moved to Larkin's house.[28] Castro's purpose in convening the junta was revealed when he made an opening address calling for the annexation of California by Catholic France. This surprised the others who thought Castro favored full independence with no foreign ties.[29] Other participants joined the debate. Henri Cambuston, a naturalized Mexican of French origins, supported Castro in urging union with France.[30] David Spence, a Scot, and William E. P. Hartnell, an Englishman, both Mexican citizens, spoke in favor of a British protectorate. Some native Californios favored unfettered independence. Captain Rafael Gonzalez called for a "California, libre, soberana, y independiente!"[31] Lieutenant-Colonel Victor Prudon, another French-Mexican, agreed, but feared European ambitions. "'I love France with the love of a son,'" he said, "'but I love California with all the fervent idolatry of a lover,'" and it was only the United States that could give California the protection it needed.[32] Other Californios also spoke for association with the United States.

The most eloquent among these last was General Vallejo. A California patriot, Vallejo was also pro-American. Larkin and Vallejo had been on friendly terms for years, and Larkin's influence on him was considerable. Vallejo called on his compatriots to look not abroad for protection, but to the United States. He urged Californios to welcome the American immigrants not as harbingers of American conquest, rather "as brothers, who come to share with us a common destiny." [33]

The junta members were not convinced. Vallejo sensed that the body was leaning toward a declaration in favor of England. To forestall a vote on the issue, he called for a recess, during which he and his friends left Monterey. The number remaining was less than a quorum, so there was no vote on the question. [34]

The pro-European views of some of the junta members foreshadowed another worry for Larkin. Attitudes toward Americans were changing. The change was long in coming, for Californios had been long-suffering. Contrary to the growing animosity in Mexico in 1845 for everything American, California authorities had been tolerant, indeed hospitable, to the overlanders who almost without exception entered California illegally. When the central government issued regulations that prohibited even legal entrance, California officials generally ignored them. [35] For example, when five Americans with passports issued by the American consul in Oahu were denied entrance under the new law, Larkin protested to General Castro. The *comandante* told Larkin that the five men could go anywhere they wished. [36]

Many American immigrants responded to this benign policy with contempt. They bristled at rumors that the "Spaniards" planned to prevent their entry to California, or that they might be driven from California. These American attitudes aggravated a growing resentment among Californios. Sub-Prefect Francisco Guerrero in San Francisco complained to Prefect Manuel Castro in Monterey: "'The idea of those gentlemen is that God made the world and them also; therefore, what there is in the world belongs to them as sons of God.'" [37] General Castro agreed with the prefect's sentiment when he said that "'these Americans are so contriving that some day they will build ladders to touch the sky, and once in the heavens they will change the whole face of the universe and even the color of the stars.'" [38]

By the summer of 1845, the number as well as the temperament of the new immigrants had increasingly worried California authorities. A rumor, probably started by John Sutter, circulated that a thousand overlanders would arrive by autumn. [39] Sutter, who was in the best position to comment on the overland migration, told Larkin that nothing could stop it. If any attempt were made by the authorities to oppose the well-armed newcomers, he said, "they would fight like Lyons." Because of the official attitude, Sutter believed that it was going to be difficult for the newcomers to obtain land, so he had persuaded some local landholders to give the immigrants some small pieces, "say a mile or 2 for a family." Sutter planned to set a good example and assumed that Larkin would do the same.[40]

The rumored thousand overlanders did not appear, but those who did struggle into Sutter's Fort during the summer and early autumn of 1845 were in desperate circumstances after their journey through the deserts and mountains. More serious, they felt threatened by the authorities who Sutter and the immigrants feared were planning to expel them from California. Sutter appealed to Larkin to do what he could to aid the newcomers. Realizing that Larkin was busy with consular affairs, he declared that if the consul or an American warship could not save the poor wretches, "*I will do it*. All are protected here and before I suffer an injustice done, to them, I die first."[41]

Sutter undoubtedly was reacting to Governor Pico's call in August to Californios to prepare to defend the province against the United States, and to a report that General Castro planned to visit the northern regions, probably to investigate the disposition of immigrants. Perhaps, said the rumor, Castro also was going to see whether Sutter was abiding by the recent order from Monterey which denied new grants to Americans and forbade Sutter from issuing passports to the newcomers.[42]

Larkin was indeed preoccupied at the moment in San Francisco with the Libby-Spear affair, involving an assault on two Americans, but he did take time to write a letter on November 12, 1845, addressed to the new immigrants camped on the Sacramento River. He suggested that the newcomers meet and elect four or five of their number to represent them. This committee should call on John Marsh at his ranch near Mount Diablo and ask him to travel with them to Monterey where Larkin would meet them at his house. The consul then would have the information he needed to talk with the authorities about the needs of the immigrants.[43] Larkin feared that the growing tensions between Californios and foreigners could erupt into violence at any moment. He would do all in his power to avoid a clash, but he expected an explosion nevertheless within one or two years.[44]

The anxiety was wasted. General Castro toured the northern frontier and called at Sutter's Fort, accompanied not by soldiers, but by Jacob P. Leese and Andrés Castillero. Castillero had just arrived from Mexico City with instructions to try to purchase the fort for the central government. The purpose was to eliminate the fort as an isolated gathering point for foreigners. Sutter was willing, but he rejected the terms: he was to be paid in drafts on Mexico, and he must leave the country.[45]

The negotiations broke down, but Castro made the best of it. He interviewed some immigrants and then declared in a decree dated November 6, 1845, "'conciliating my duty with the sentiment of hospitality which distinguishes the Mexicans,'" that the newcomers, consisting mostly of families and industrious people, could stay in the Department. The conditions, to which the immigrants agreed, required that they obey the law, settle near

Sonoma or New Helvetia, apply within three months for regular permits to settle, and leave California if the permits were not then granted.[46]

The immigrants were not persecuted, but they would not be pacified. They tilted at windmills, repeated the slogans of Manifest Destiny, and talked about a "Texas solution" for California.

Thus the California authorities politely and calmly assented to their fate. They were not ignorant of forces at work against their interests. Californios knew something, for example, of the ambitions of Lansford W. Hastings, whose *Emigrants' Guide to Oregon and California*, published in 1845, was designed to lure Americans to California. He touted California as a land of milk and honey, populated by barbarians, but soon to be displaced by a new democratic republic controlled by industrious Yankees.[47] Californios perhaps were not aware of the machinations of Thomas J. Farnham, another visionary who also anticipated a Republic of California which would bring "the blessings of Freedom over that delightful land."[48] Like Farnham, John Marsh counted on the rising tide of immigration to swell the American population sufficiently to force the issue in 1846. During the spring of 1845, Marsh and fellow conspirator, Charles M. Weber, had corresponded with Americans in northern California to begin organizing themselves for the inevitable coup.[49]

More than anything else, California leaders in the spring of 1846 were still angry and uneasy about the recent Gavilan affair and the continuing presence of John C. Frémont. Frémont was no stranger to California. This was the second time his explorations had brought him to the province, though he had not reached the coast previously. This latest visit began when the "Pathfinder" and his party of about sixty mountain men crossed the Sierra in December 1845, reaching Sutter's Fort the following month. From there, Frémont with eight men went to Monterey where he met Consul Larkin. The rest of the party remained camped in the central valley.

The prefect at Monterey, Manuel Castro, learned about the arrival of Frémont and asked the consul to explain the unauthorized presence of American troops in California. Larkin replied that Frémont, a brevet captain in the United States Army, was surveying the most practicable route from the United States to the Pacific. Most of his hired men—not army troops, Larkin assured the prefect—were left "on the frontiers of this Department" where men and animals were resting. Frémont had come to Monterey only to purchase supplies for the expedition. When that was finished, he would reassemble his party and depart for Oregon.[50] At General Castro's request, Frémont explained in the same terms directly to him, adding that the objectives of the expedition were both scientific and commercial.[51] When the comandante did not reply to the explanation, Frémont and Larkin assumed that he was satisfied.[52]

If Castro's silence indicated his assent, Frémont soon violated the agreement. After enjoying Larkin's hospitality for a few days, during which the consul advanced him $1,800 to purchase supplies, Frémont departed.[53] Collecting his men in the Central Valley, Frémont led the reunited expedition not to Oregon, but toward the coast north of Monterey.

It seems that Frémont had decided rather recently that he would like to make his home someday in California. He had been charmed by a number of locations, but these had lacked the sea. He decided that he must stand "by the open waves of the Pacific."[54] The Americans pitched camp near Santa Cruz in view of the ocean and enjoyed the luxury of inactivity for a few days. After this welcome respite, the expedition moved inland and encamped at Hartnell's rancho, east of Salinas.

Frémont did not notify California officials nor did he seek permission for the new itinerary. Indeed, by his actions, he virtually denied the authority of California tribunals over him. The affront was compounded when he rejected the claim of Sebastián Peralta, a Californio, that one of the expedition's horses was his own. When the San José alcalde, to whom Peralta had complained, ordered Frémont to deliver the animal, he replied that the claim was fraudulent and that the "'straggling vagabond'" was lucky to escape a good horsewhipping. Moreover, his duties left him no time to appear before the town magistrates.[55]

The California government's response to Frémont's unauthorized march and his belligerence was predictable. Fears of American interference had increased lately. Frémont and his party had arrived without the required passports. Yet the authorities had agreed to permit the Americans to remain in the province long enough to purchase supplies and to rest men and animals, under the condition that Frémont leave his men in the valley of the San Joaquin River, well away from settlements.[56] Frémont had broken that promise and violated the Californios' generosity.

Both Prefect Manuel Castro and the *comandante general*, José Castro, now ordered Frémont to leave the province immediately. Otherwise, said the prefect, "this office will take the necessary measures."[57] The letters were sent directly to Frémont, and copies of both were duly delivered to Consul Larkin.

Frémont was furious. He complained of General Castro's rudeness and "breach of good faith."[58] He felt that he had been personally insulted and that his country's honor was at stake. He peremptorily rejected the offensive order. Withdrawing his force to a small plateau in the nearby Gavilan Mountains, he threw up a log breastwork, hoisted the Stars and Stripes, and waited.

General Castro began military preparations to dislodge the intruders. Larkin was aghast, but his response was, as usual, calm and methodical. He sent a carefully worded message to Frémont: "It is not for me to point out to you your line of conduct. You have your Government Instructions." Still, Larkin wanted to be sure that Frémont had not misunderstood the letters from the authorities. "You are Officially ordered [by the California authorities] to leave the Country." To ensure that he understood his predicament, Larkin added that "in all probability they will attack you. The result either way may cause trouble hereafter to Resident Americans." Besides, said merchant Larkin, "the present state of affairs may cause an interruption to business." [59]

Then Larkin tried to help Frémont extricate himself from a situation that could only end badly. He knew that the Americans were heavily armed and determined. To oppose them, he estimated that General Castro already had gathered 200 men and could rouse the whole countryside, if necessary. Larkin believed that a clash could be avoided. He was on good terms with California officials and thought that they would not refuse a reasonable proposal. "Should it be impossible or inconvenient for you to leave California at present," Larkin wrote to Frémont, speculating that the captain's orders might not permit withdrawal, he could probably persuade the authorities to permit Frémont to move his camp farther from Monterey, thereby reducing the fears and hostility of Montereños. He volunteered to come immediately to the Gavilan camp if Frémont wished to talk with him. [60] Larkin dispatched two copies of the letter, one by a Californio, another by an American.

The next day, March 9, Larkin wrote an urgent message, addressed: "To the Commander of any American Ship of War, in San Blas, or Mazatlan." The letter recounted the events of the past few days, emphasizing that American residents in the region could be in danger, whatever the outcome of the Gavilan confrontation. He requested—as consul, he could not order—that a warship sail for Monterey at once. Prompt action was imperative since General Castro had told the consul that the American brig, *Hannah*, had just brought him clear orders from Mexico to drive Frémont from the province. Larkin enclosed his message in a letter to Consul Parrott at Mazatlán which repeated his "earnest desire" that a ship sail immediately. [61] Larkin's correspondence rarely betrays emotion, but there is much anxiety between the lines in these two letters.

Larkin's wisdom in sending two messengers to Frémont in his hilltop refuge was soon proven. The unnamed American was intercepted by Manuel Castro's forces and the letter seized. The prefect later sent the letter to Mexico as proof of the duplicity of both Frémont and Larkin. Larkin's Californio courier was given safe passage by the authorities and delivered his copy to Frémont on March 9. The Californio waited in the encampment while Frémont wrote a hasty, penciled note to Larkin. The courier was treated well, except by one American who pointed to a tree and said to him, "there's your life." Frémont could not have helped but be pleased by Larkin's comment later that the Californio had told him that 2,000 men could not force the Americans from their stronghold.[62]

Frémont's reply to Larkin's letter was filled with characteristic bravado. He had no intention of leaving his position, he said, nor any thought of negotiation. If attacked, he and his men would "fight to extremity and refuse quarter, trusting to our country to avenge our death." He had committed no wrong in California, he said, and "if we are hemmed in and assaulted here, we will die every man of us under the Flag of our country."[63]

With no cooperation from Frémont and no authority to compel him, Larkin found the role of peacemaker difficult. One longs for Larkin's personal assessment of the delicate situation and his comment on Frémont and his claims. He seems to have admired the captain and had praised him earlier in a letter to Secretary of State Buchanan,[64] but his patience appeared to be wearing a bit thin at this point.

Larkin's frustration with the affair shows in his correspondence. He explained to Manuel Díaz, alcalde of Monterey, that he had no control over the army officer. He could only offer his services to Frémont, just as he had already offered his services to the California government. He restated his understanding that Frémont intended to leave the country as soon as his horses were rested. This would be most difficult, however, surrounded as he was by a hostile force. To prevent a chance clash, indeed, he asked Díaz to propose to Castro that the latter request from Frémont a one-hour conversation before ordering any extreme measures. Otherwise, the consul predicted much bloodshed on both sides. He assured the alcalde that he "would with pleasure allay the present sensation [situation], if in my power," but the captain was not to be ordered by the consul.[65]

The affair ended abruptly. Before noon on March 10, General Castro's scouts brought him word that the American camp was deserted, abandoned the previous night. Victory was proclaimed, and the siege, entirely bloodless, ended. The Californios did not pursue the Americans.

Following his melodramatic response to Larkin's March 8 letter, Frémont had reflected on his situation. With his spyglass, he could see troops gathering and readying their cannon at Mission San Juan Bautista. The next day, a mounted body had advanced up the hill to within a few hundred yards of his position before turning back. An occasional cannonade was opened, apparently more for impression than effect.[66] Frémont *was*, after all, in sovereign Mexican territory, he *had* raised the American flag, and he had no orders from his superiors that warranted his action. To remain in a belligerent posture meant that he would eventually have to declare himself a filibuster, proclaim for independence, and call on resident Americans for assistance.[67] This, he knew, was out of the question. He recalled the objective of the United States to secure California and determined that he "would not let a proceeding which was mostly personal put obstacles in the way."[68]

The only alternative was to withdraw. When the flagpole fell down for no apparent reason, he took it as an omen that they should move camp. It seems that Frémont explained the retreat to his men, who undoubtedly were as disgruntled as he with the move, that the consul had ordered the withdrawal.[69] If, in fact, Frémont made this statement, the captain was deceitfully trying to shift the blame for an unpopular action, for he knew quite well that he was not responsible to Larkin.

Frémont felt so humiliated by the affair that he could not bring himself to tell his own wife the truth. In a letter to her, he complained that the "Spaniards" were rude and inhospitable and ordered him from the country, breaking their promise to let him winter there.[70] There was no mention of his broken promise to leave his men in the hinterlands and to march directly toward Oregon, nor his breach of California hospitality. "For my own part," he told his wife, "I have become disgusted with everything belonging to the Mexicans."[71] The memory likely festered until he found satisfaction in the Sonoma rising the following June.

General Castro issued a ringing proclamation on March 13, castigating the American "highwaymen" for their treachery and praising those who had rallied to the defense of the homeland. The proclamation called on the people to prepare themselves to defend their independence.[72] The comandante believed that Californios would yet have to deal with the Americans.

In his report of the affair to the Secretary of State, Larkin showed convenient hindsight. Though he had warned Frémont that Castro likely would assault him in his hilltop redoubt, he now informed Buchanan that he had not believed the general ever had wanted to attack. Indeed, said Larkin, he "was very confident that with all California he would not have attacked him."[73] It seems that most of those summoned by General Castro had no intention of actually appearing. They had made a show of responding, wrote Larkin, to give substance to the report that had to be sent to the supreme government of Mexico which had issued strict orders following Frémont's visit to California in 1844 that he must be driven out if he returned.[74]

Larkin's surmise was correct. General Castro later said that, while he had ample authority to attack Frémont, he had no intention of doing so. He admitted that he had exploited the affair to advance his reputation in Mexico.[75]

After leaving his hilltop redoubt, Frémont seemingly disappeared. Larkin was unsure of his location or his plans. In January, Larkin had informed Manuel Castro that Frémont would leave for Oregon as soon as he had rested and replenished his expedition. In February, Larkin understood that Frémont had changed his mind and now intended to return to the United States by way of the Colorado and Gila rivers. Accordingly, Larkin had sent a ship with provisions for the expedition to Santa Barbara.[76] On March 6, before the Gavilan affair, the consul reported to Buchanan that Frémont planned to go to Oregon after all and return to Monterey in May.[77]

Three weeks after Frémont's withdrawal from his Gavilan stronghold, Larkin still did not know his location. Indeed, Larkin appeared confused. On March 21, he guessed that he had gone to Santa Barbara.[78] Five days later, he reported to Stearns that Frémont "is queiteley presing his way to the Oregon or elsewhere according to his instructions from home."[79] The following week he notified Buchanan that Frémont had gone to Santa Barbara. "From there he proceeds on his journey according to his instructions from his Department in Washington."[80] What those instructions might be, Larkin did not know. Larkin had confided to Stearns: "From Captain Frémont's visit, I am under the idea, that great plans are meditated to be carried out by certain persons."[81] He could only speculate, for he knew no more. Larkin assumed that Frémont had his instructions, but he had not revealed them to the consul.

By mid-April, the excitement had subsided, and Larkin was confident that Frémont, without his party, could return in perfect safety to Monterey any time he wished.[82] For his own part, Larkin believed that the affair had done no injury to his relations with California leaders. He was confident that he was still on the best of terms with them.[83] The Stars and Stripes still flew at his house.[84]

Contrary to Larkin's speculation, Frémont was bound for neither Santa Barbara nor Monterey. The expedition moved northward in the great Central Valley toward Oregon, as originally planned, where the captain would join his survey with the line set during his 1843–1844 expedition.[85] That done, his explorations would be ended, Frémont thought, and he would return to the United States via the Missouri River.

Frémont and his party rode along the Sacramento River, enjoying the carpets of wildflowers. Running short of supplies, Frémont sent Theodore Talbot to Yerba Buena to secure a fresh stock. The expedition continued to Sutter's Fort,[86] then turned northward, stopping briefly in the vicinity of Lassen's rancho. From there, Frémont wrote to Leidesdorff to comment on supplies furnished him recently and to say goodby: "I shall start for the States in a few days."

Larkin finally received a letter from Frémont, sent from a camp sixty miles north of Sutter's Fort. The consul was irritated that Frémont said nothing about his itinerary or actions since leaving the Gavilan fort. The captain wrote only to ask for funds. Larkin nevertheless complied, sending gold back with Frémont's courier. Larkin soon reported the expedition's location, and a bit of his own pique, to Buchanan.[87]

On May 8, two men rode into Frémont's camp near the north end of Klamath Lake in Oregon. They were messengers from Lieutenant Gillespie, who was a two-days' ride behind. It was too late to ride that night, and Frémont ordered preparations for an early start the following morning. He lay awake for hours wondering what he would learn the next day. "How fate pursues a man!" he observed.[88]

At first light, Frémont and a small party set out on the back trail and met Gillespie and his three companions the next evening at the southern end of Klamath Lake.

Lieutenant Gillespie had been on Frémont's track since leaving Monterey on April 19. The air of crisis that had pervaded the capital during Frémont's belligerency had only just subsided when the *Cyane* carrying Gillespie arrived. Larkin, hospitable as ever, had celebrated with a party at his house in Gillespie's honor. One guest, easily seeing through Gillespie's disguise, thought it unlikely that an American warship's only mission to Monterey was to deliver a sick young man. Many Californios from the first guessed that he was a spy. Larkin also thought his disguise transparent.[89]

Gillespie found Monterey much as he expected:

> The town of Monterey is small, containing not over one hundred houses, built upon streets running back from the beach, but are in some cases far apart. Everything about the town has a primitive appearance, and nothing is to be met with, that will remind the traveller of the refinements of long settled countries.[90]

On the other hand, Gillespie was immediately impressed with the consul. In his report to the Secretary of the Navy that he wrote the day after his arrival, Gillespie praised Larkin's patriotism and his concern for his countrymen's interests. He found him worthy of confidence and was sorry to learn that he had contemplated resigning from his appointment because of the meager allowance for the post and the government's protesting his bills. He provided support for Larkin's claim of inadequate compensation by commenting in the letter that the expenses in California were much higher than he had expected.[91]

Local authorities were not fooled by Gillespie's disguise. The same ship that brought him also carried a letter from Mazatlán for David Spence. The letter charged Spence to watch the lieutenant closely; he was assumed to be carrying important official documents. Spence told General Castro about the message. A ball held at ex-governor Alvarado's house provided an opportunity. Castro plied Gillespie with wine and *pisco*, hoping that he would become drunk and divulge his mission. But Gillespie kept his head and secretly slipped away from the ball after midnight.[92] Larkin provided horses and a guide and sent him off for Yerba Buena. Gillespie carried letters of introduction from Larkin addressed to Leidesdorff and Nathan Spear at Yerba Buena, Jacob Lease at Sonoma, Charles M. Weber at San Jose, John Sutter, John Marsh, Peter Lassen at his rancho, and six other influential friends of the consul in northern California.[93]

In a letter to Leidesdorff, probably carried by Gillespie, Larkin did not confide the lieutenant's identity or his mission. He stated only that the gentleman was in poor health and wanted to travel through the country to enjoy the climate. "I beleive he has some personal aquantance with Captain Fremont," he added casually, "and may wish to see him if the trouble and expense is not too much." Larkin nevertheless instructed Leidesdorff to provide the ailing wanderer a boat, horses, or men, drawing on the consul if necessary.[94]

Before receiving any report of Gillespie's progress, Larkin sent a letter dated April 23 to him with the latest news of the growing crisis with Mexico. The *Portsmouth*, dispatched by Commodore Sloat from Mazatlán in response to Larkin's appeal of March 9 at the time of the Gavilan affair, had just arrived in Monterey. Captain John Montgomery reported that Mexican officials had abandoned Mazatlán, carrying away the archives. The whole Mexican nation seemed to be in chaos, northern states declaring against the Paredes government and for the United States. Sloat was preparing to blockade the port at Mazatlán and expected to receive in six or eight days a message containing an American declaration of war against Mexico. In that case, Larkin informed Gillespie, "we shall see him in a few days to take the Country."[95]

Larkin also informed Gillespie about an interesting exchange with some California officials. He had recently told Generals Castro and Vallejo that he expected the American flag to fly over Monterey in thirty days. This surprisingly frank statement is evidence of Larkin's friendship with the Californios. Castro, apparently exasperated by the uncertainty of recent months, replied that war was preferable to peace since affairs would finally be settled. Mindful of his confidential agency charge, Larkin suggested that Castro *could*, without the necessity of war, "secure to himself, and his freinds, fame, honour, permanent employ and pay."[96]

Castro did not respond to this overture. All of the officials seemed to be awaiting the arrival of the *Don Quixote*, expected on July 1, which should bring instructions from Mexico. This did not prevent the leaders from calling on the consul to ask for the latest news. Larkin believed that they were "fast prepareing themselves for the comeing events."[97] He predicted to Leidesdorff that "the pear is near ripe for falling."[98]

As storm clouds gathered, Californios could still put aside their troubles in favor of a good time. When the *Portsmouth*'s boats came ashore, there were some heated exchanges between the ship's officers and some California officials, but passions cooled quickly. The usual courtesies were exchanged, and General Castro and some of the leading Montereños invited Captain Montgomery and his staff to a picnic.

They gathered early in the morning at Larkin's house. Most of the ship's officers and, it seems, most of the townspeople were there. The chosen were soon in the saddle and rode in small groups to the picnic grounds, twelve to fourteen miles distant. They walked, then galloped, then walked again. There were about a hundred riders, with an escort of soldiers in front, banners whipping at the tips of their lances. Some women rode double with their men. They filed through the rolling green fields, past Mission San Carlos Borromeo at Carmel, to the picnic grounds where they spread a sumptuous lunch of veal, mutton, turkey, mussels, frijoles, dried fruits, and sweet cakes.[99] Frémont, wherever he was, was forgotten for the moment.

Gillespie received Larkin's letter, containing his prediction of war and an American California within thirty days, at Yerba Buena on April 25. He replied on the same day, thanking Larkin for the news, but said little more, perhaps for security reasons. He must have been deeply impressed, however, for he told Larkin his plans for setting out that very day, "it being now still more necessary for early information to reach Cap't Frémont."[100]

Gillespie might have been guarded in his reply to Larkin, but he undoubtedly shared the exciting news with Leidesdorff. The vice consul also wrote to Larkin on the 25th, and he was less restrained than his guest. "Glorious news for Capt Freemont. I thinck I se him smile." He added that California officials must have received similar news. The subprefect was busy, sending couriers into the countryside, apparently in the expectation of war.[101]

At the Klamath Lake rendezvous, Gillespie gave Frémont a sealed package from Senator Thomas Hart Benton, Frémont's influential father-in-law and an advocate of expansion. Gillespie would have told Frémont everything he knew of Washington's policies toward California and the deteriorating relations between the United States and Mexico. Following instructions, he showed Frémont a copy of Buchanan's letter of October 17, 1845, to Larkin, detailing the American position in California and appointing the consul confidential agent. Gillespie would have added his observations of war preparations in Mexico and Larkin's prediction that the Stars and Stripes would soon fly over California. This was heady talk for Frémont, a young, vain army officer, full of adventure and ambitious for himself and his country.

In some curious, tortured fashion, Frémont would explain years later that his actions following the dramatic meeting with Gillespie were based on his appointment as President Polk's confidential agent. He came to believe that Secretary Buchanan's letter of October 17 was directed to *him*, not Larkin. His wife supported her husband, claiming in an interview in 1884 with Josiah Royce, the philosopher and author, that she had never heard Larkin speak of such an appointment. Of course, Larkin would have told her, she said, since he was incapable of keeping a secret. General and Mrs. Frémont agreed that the government would not have entrusted this sensitive task to a man of so little education and experience, certainly not to Larkin.[102] Larkin, Jessie told Royce, was:

> . . . an ignorant and utterly tactless man. . . . He was deaf—very deaf. He talked therefore incessantly, being unable to listen. He spilled over with everything. He was prodigiously vain. Had he ever been Secret Agent, he

would have boasted of it endlessly.—Such a man for a delicate secret mission—absurd! Impossible![103]

Jessie Benton Frémont, thoughout her life, had a great capacity for protecting her husband.

Larkin's postwar silence on the matter is simple proof that he could keep
a secret. Part of Buchanan's letter containing Larkin's appointment would
remain classified for forty years.[104] In March 1848, responding to a business
inquiry from Charles V. Gillespie, Larkin said that he could not explain
his wartime connection with Charles' brother, Archibald.[105] The following
month, when Larkin submitted his final expense report for the confidential
agency, he told Buchanan that he had never told anyone about the appointment but Commodore Sloat. He guessed that Sloat had since forgotten about
it. He thought Lilburn W. Boggs, ex-governor of Missouri and then alcalde of Sonoma, might have gained some vague notion of the agency from
a Missouri member of the United States House of Representatives, but no
one else in California knew.[106] Hubert H. Bancroft noted in his history of
California, published in the late 1880s, that "the act [Larkin's appointment
as confidential agent] has never been made known to the public."[107] Bancroft learned about it from the Larkin letters that he collected.

Perhaps Larkin had been cautioned against discussing his wartime secret
assignment. If the appointment had been common knowledge after the war,
surely the contemporary record would have ample accounts of his service.
There are none. There is, however, one intriguing hint in the *Annals of San
Francisco*, published in 1855, which notes that in addition to his appointments as consul, navy agent, and naval storekeeper, Larkin "received from
President Polk another highly important" appointment in California.[108]
Surely General Frémont and Jessie read the *Annals* and wondered about the
mysterious post. The guarded comment in the *Annals* was indicative both of
Larkin's willingness to keep the assignment secret and his desire for recognition. The authors of the *Annals* could only have obtained the information
from Larkin, and the comment would have appeared in the book only with
Larkin's consent. Indeed, the authors in their preface credit Larkin for his
help with the publication.

Frémont's assertion that Buchanan's message was for himself, and not
Larkin, is disputed by later testimony given by Gillespie, who was Frémont's friend and, by then, no friend of Larkin.[109] It is further disputed by
Frémont himself. In May 1846, after receiving Benton's package from Gillespie, Frémont wrote to the senator complaining that Benton's letter "led
me to expect some communication from him [Buchanan], but I *received
nothing*."[110] To Commodore Sloat, who on July 19, 1846, asked on what
authority he and the other Americans had initiated hostilities against the
Californios, Frémont was more explicit. He replied that he "'had acted
solely on my own responsibility, and without any expressed authority from
the Government to justify hostilities.'"[111]

There is circumstantial evidence indeed that Gillespie's instruction to find Frémont, far from being central to his mission, was an afterthought. It seems that Buchanan originally planned to send Benton's package to Larkin through the regular—and, at the moment, uncertain—Mexican mails for forwarding to Frémont. Just before sending Gillespie off, the secretary decided that the lieutenant could carry the package to Frémont and inform him about the latest diplomatic developments.[112] According to this argument then, Gillespie's rendezvous with Frémont was a matter of convenience, not state.

The hard evidence shows that Frémont must have been aware that Larkin had been given confidential instructions, and he had not. His actions following his meeting with Gillespie at Klamath Lake had to be based on something other than instructions from Washington, for he had none.[113] For his own reasons, Frémont decided to return to California. There, he would await events and, if possible, give destiny a nudge toward an American conclusion.

In Monterey, Larkin was busy. Buchanan's letter and the new appointment did not really change Larkin's course. It did give him new authority, and he set to work at once. On the same date that he received the secretary's letter, April 17, 1846, he wrote to three American friends, Jacob P. Leese of Sonoma, Abel Stearns in Los Angeles, and Jonathan T. Warner, San Diego, to enlist their discreet assistance in intelligence gathering.[114] Larkin explained the President's policy toward California, but did not divulge his appointment as secret agent. He paraphrased from Buchanan's letter, particularly emphasizing that Californios must be persuaded that they would not be served by association with any European country. Nor could they continue happily as a province of Mexico, for that had meant only chaos for two decades. The Californio must look only to the United States for assistance, for only there would he "find a fellow feeling, with those who can participate in all his ideas, and hail him as a Republican and citizen of the land of Freedom." If war between the United States and Mexico should come, he predicted that the Stars and Stripes would fly over California by the fourth of July, "blessing those who see them and thier posterity after them."[115]

Larkin reminded his three compatriots that they had much at stake in approaching events and suggested that they could have a hand in shaping those events. He appealed to their ambition and sense of adventure and asked them to send to him from time to time by a safe conveyance any evidence that people in their regions might wish to change their condition. He volunteered to visit the north and south if warranted.[116] Larkin thereby attempted to enlist his three friends as *his* confidential agents.

A short passage in the letter seems, at first glance, to be out of context, contrary to the spirit of the message. After noting that the rancheros likely would benefit more than the merchants by a change of sovereignty, he added: "I myself as a trader prefer everything as it is. The times and the Country are good enough for me. I am partial to the people, and flatter myself they return my good will."[117] This wistful aside would have more meaning one day than its author suspected.

Having launched his undercover effort, Larkin devoted himself to writing a paper, remarkable in its content and purpose. The document summarizes his interpretation of United States policy concerning California. The United States would take no part in any conflict between Mexico and California, it read, unless Mexico shall initiate hostilities against the United States. If California should declare and maintain its independence, the United States would honor it as a sister republic. The United States "would not . . . view with indifference"—the meaning, by strong implication, is "would not permit"—the transfer or seizure of California by any European power, a measure which would not be in the interests of Californios and which could not last. If Californios should wish to unite with the United States, they would be welcomed, if the annexation could be accomplished without giving Mexico "just cause of complaint."[118]

Larkin translated the unsigned document into Spanish and showed it to California government officials. He was careful to point out to readers that the sentiments there were his personal opinions.[119] However, influential Californios would surely know that Larkin, whom most of them respected and counted as friend, would not advance a view that was alien to his government's position.

Larkin pondered whether his efforts to bring about a peaceful conquest might be too late. Perhaps the United States had already declared war on Mexico. The "great ones" in Monterey, he wrote Leidesdorff, were preparing for a change. With an eye always on the best chance, Larkin cautioned Leidesdorff not to sell any land at the moment; it might bring more in 1847.[120] Sure that events were moving toward an inevitable conclusion, he lectured the vice consul on his official duties and suggested what he should do in Yerba Buena if he expected to reap the considerable advantages of the rapidly approaching Americanization of California.[121]

Yet, he must persevere in his charge for peaceful change. Both Leese and Warner replied tardily to Larkin's call for assistance. Warner had hardly left his farm during the past year and had only infrequent contact with Californios. He volunteered his opinion that there was in the south a growing discontent with Mexico. He often heard the remark, "'would that the Americans would take this Country that we might be secure in our persons & property,'" but also "'would that any nation able would take possession of this Country.'" He nevertheless believed that, in case of war, the majority of southerners would favor the United States.[122] Leese wrote simply that his opinions were "the Same as G. Vallejo."[123] This terse reply did not necessarily mean that Leese was hostile to Larkin's position since Vallejo, though a patriot, and Leese's brother-in-law, also believed that California's future included association with the United States.

In contrast to the lukewarm reply of Warner and Leese, Stearns responded enthusiastically. Agreeing completely with Larkin's assessment of affairs, he said that Californios in the south strongly favored independence. He was personally opposed to a move toward separation, however, believing that it would fail for lack of the means to sustain it. Stearns added the startling note that British agents, weighing the situation—that is, the Californios' desire for independence, tempered by a fear of failure—had approached the California government. If the province would declare independence from Mexico and request Great Britain's protection, they said, the British would offer guarantees. "This I am certain of," Stearns added.[124]

Stearns did not think that southern Californios were interested in the British overture. Indeed, he told Larkin that a majority of the people in the south, including government officials, would support annexation by the United States if they could be assured that they would be protected by the Americans from being ravaged by Mexico. The dearth of news from Mexico seemed to indicate that war was not imminent, a turn, said Stearns, that did not please the Californios. "Ojala que toma esta los Americanos," they often said, expressing their wish that the Americans would come and take the province.[125]

Stearns also informed Larkin that the California assembly, supported by the governor, both headquartered in the south, had called a convention, with delegates from throughout the province, to deal with California's precarious political situation. Another objective of the promoters, as Stearns would later inform Larkin, was that the convocation, controlled by southerners, would "take into consideration the evil that has lately existed in Monterey of Squandering away in a most Scandalous manner the publick funds without any benifit to the publick and much to the injury of the people."[126] The governor undoubtedly was influenced by a delegation from Yerba Buena who had gone in person to Los Angeles in April to complain that "the Monterey Big Bugs" were spending all the customs duties on "Bailes y Meriendas," dances and merry making.[127]

Rumor held that the gathering would declare independence and request the protection of Great Britain or the United States. Further, said Stearns, if certain Mexican states try to separate from the Republic, one of many rumors flying about, California will ally with neither side. It "will look for friends in another quarter."[128] That is, it would seek protection during the turmoil from some source other than Mexico City.

Larkin had already heard about the proposed convention, and Stearns' letter simply added to his anxiety. It seems that the origin of the intended meeting can be traced at least partly to the quarrel between Governor Pico in the south and General Castro in the north. Each suspected the patriotism of the other, and each charged the other with dictatorial ambitions. A conference in the south presumably would offset the effect of the junta that met in Monterey in early April. [129]

The *Consejo General de Pueblos Unidos de California* was scheduled to meet on June 15 at Santa Barbara. The membership would include elected delegates from north and south and appointed members from the assembly, church, and army. Governor Pico would preside as president of the conference. [130]

Larkin was alarmed at Stearns's news that the British were interested in offering guarantees to California leaders. "I have never received so much startling information in so few words." Larkin asked him to send details concerning the British overture: times and dates, persons making the offer, persons receiving the offer, response if any, and "feeling expressed on the occation." Larkin added the conspiratorial note that the valuable information "will serve me and those who are unknown to you." [131] Larkin had already recognized in Stearns a valuable source of information in the south and had formally appointed him his confidential correspondent. He offered no compensation, but promised mysteriously that Stearns's interests "may be advanced at some future day, not far distant." [132]

The reason perhaps for Larkin's surprise at Stearns's news of British interest was his own belief, at least until then, that Britain was so exhausted with the Oregon question that it would not wish to become embroiled in a California question. He suspected, correctly, that vice consul Forbes had been chastised by London for involving himself in political affairs. [133]

Larkin nevertheless would take no chances. On May 21, he wrote to Stearns and Leese, both Mexican citizens, urging them to arrange to attend the Santa Barbara meeting as members. To Stearns, he expressed the hope that Juan Bandini, who had voiced views favorable to the American interest, also would be there. He asked Leese to persuade Mariano Guadalupe Vallejo, his brother-in-law and the commandant of the northern frontier, to attend the convention. [134] Larkin could have no official role in the convocation since he was not a citizen, but he made plans to be in the city on June 15, ostensibly to see Governor Pico about consular matters. [135]

In private conversations with certain unidentified persons, "those in power or of influence," Larkin suggested a strategy for the upcoming meeting: appeal to the supreme government in Mexico to improve, once and for all, the deplorable conditions in the province and protect its people; failing that, then respectfully request that California, for the sake of the inhabitants, be sold to a power that can protect them. Larkin was not naïve. He knew that the central government would not act on the suggestion, but at least the Californios could then say that they had tried everything to find a solution to their suffering before they took more drastic action. Those to whom Larkin proposed the scheme thought it unpatriotic and unworthy of consideration. Larkin believed that they might be more receptive later, when affairs had worsened. [136]

In spite of this rebuff, Larkin still thought that he could influence events. Reporting to Buchanan about the proposed Santa Barbara consejo, he reminded the secretary that he had withdrawn from his business pursuits and could go anywhere in California that required his presence. He volunteered to go to Mexico City and stay there some months if Buchanan wished. He knew some influential people in the national capital, including General Micheltorena, and could pretend to go on business, perhaps to collect debts owed to him by the California government.[137] While awaiting Buchanan's response, Larkin went to San Jose to see what influence he could bring to bear on California leaders, the "great guns and big bugs," he called them.[138]

As Larkin worried about the approaching Santa Barbara meeting, the British warship *Juno* arrived on June 7 from Mazatlán, bringing him another headache, Father Eugene MacNamara. MacNamara, an Irish Catholic priest who claimed to represent the London Emigration Society, had just come from Mexico where the government had given its assent to his plan to settle 10,000 Irish Catholics in California. President Paredes was somewhat reluctant, fearing that any immigrant whose native language was English would more likely ally with the United States than Mexico, but apparently he had been won over.[139]

Larkin was suspicious of MacNamara. The priest was too knowledgeable about government and politics to suit him.[140] Learning that MacNamara planned to go south, perhaps to call on the governor, Larkin wrote to Stearns to ask that he watch the Irishman and try to learn more about his intentions.[141] By this time, however, Larkin would have been less concerned about British intrigues than earlier. It was the Santa Barbara meeting that was on his mind.

The consejo never met. The reasons are not completely clear. Northerners feared that it would be dominated by the south and refused to participate. The assembly, which on June 3, 1846, cancelled the consejo, considered the Monterey junta's announced support for Paredes and against Herrera a contrary position to that of the assembly, virtually a declaration against the Pico government. They also believed that the supposed threat posed by Frémont, which persuaded Castro to declare martial law and call on the governor to assist in the defense, was but a clever stratagem to lure Pico north where he could be removed. At the June 3 meeting, the assembly in open session authorized Governor Pico to take whatever measures necessary to defend the province. In closed session they removed General Castro from office.[142]

Larkin learned about the cancellation from both Stearns and General Castro. Stearns believed that an opportunity had been lost. He thought that the consejo would have taken some dramatic step toward outright independence, or independence under another country's protection, perhaps England, more likely the United States.[143] At this point, Larkin would have discounted the danger of an English protectorate. Vice Consul Forbes had confided in him only days before that he had been instructed by his government not to meddle in California political affairs. A naturalized Mexican citizen and married to a California woman, Forbes had become convinced that it was inevitable that California must fall to the United States, by immigration if by no other means. He assured Larkin that if he were not employed by the British government, he would himself advocate that the Californios look to the United States for their salvation.[144]

Pico now assembled a military force and announced his intention to march northward in response to Castro's call to help save the country. His real purpose was to oust him. The comandante meanwhile was traveling between Monterey, Santa Clara, and Sonoma, trying to raise an army, whether to defend against foreign invasion or march southward against Pico is not certain. Larkin at least believed that he intended to go against the governor.[145] The province appeared to be on the verge of civil war.

The confrontation between the two California authorities never took place. General Castro at Santa Clara on June 15 and Governor Pico at Santa Barbara on June 23 were shocked by the news of the affair at Sonoma.[146]

Late in May, Larkin was becoming anxious for some word from Gillespie or Frémont. He instructed Leidesdorff to send assistance to Sutter so that any messages reaching the fort could be sent without delay to Monterey.[147] On the last day of May, Larkin at last received a letter from Frémont. The message told about the meeting with Gillespie and stated that the party had now turned southward. Larkin, still unaware of Frémont's intentions, reported to Buchanan on June 1 that "Captain Fremont now starts for the States."[148]

A week later, on June 7, Gillespie arrived in Yerba Buena and wrote to Larkin. Frémont had sent him there to get badly needed supplies. The captain did not come himself, Gillespie explained, because he did not wish to antagonize the California authorities. On receiving the supplies, Frémont would start for home.[149]

The officers were being less than candid with the consul. Both knew that Frémont by this time had no intention of leaving California.

CHAPTER 8

THE CONQUEST

IN LATE SPRING 1846, Larkin's plan for a peaceful, orderly transition from Mexican to American dominion in California began to unravel.

On June 14, Larkin first learned of the initial act of what would be called the Bear Flag Revolt. He heard that a Mexican patrol under Lieutenant Francisco Arce, traveling from Sonoma to Santa Clara, had been stopped on the road by a band of twelve Americans and Englishmen who had taken about 170 horses from them. Larkin promptly wrote to Prefect Manuel Castro and Comandante José Castro to offer his offices in recovering the animals.[1]

The action, which took place on June 10, resulted from a converging of two forces, one real and the other imaginary. Americans had heard a rumor that General Castro intended to rid the province of Americans. Armed Mexican horsemen, said the rumor, were riding toward the Sacramento Valley, burning and ravaging the countryside. In fact, Castro had visited Sonoma in early June to procure horses, probably for use against Pico. He then withdrew.

Frémont in the meantime had ridden down from the north and reached the Buttes, a circle of low hills near Marysville. At Frémont's call, foreigners had joined him at the Buttes. From this camp, the settlers set out to seize Castro's horses.[2] Frémont undoubtedly had encouraged the action. He certainly applauded its success and later would claim responsibility for it.[3] Indeed, according to William B. Ide, a principal in the Bear Flag movement, Frémont had decided earlier on a plan for a "neutral conquest" of California and had described the scheme on June 10 at the Buttes camp.[4] Following this initial provocative act, however, he was content to step back and watch events unfold.

136

Larkin was disturbed at the news of the horse theft; he was shocked by the capture of Sonoma. On June 17 or 18, he received word from Leidesdorff, notifying him that a body of foreigners had seized the town on June 14, carried off horses, and now held as prisoners, among others, General Vallejo and Jacob P. Leese,[5] unlikely hostages since they had openly favored an association of California with the United States.

Larkin did not know what to make of the affair. Was it a personal act of vengeance of some sort, or simple robbery? Or was this small band, rumored to include Americans, and anticipating the arrival of thousands of like-minded immigrants over the mountains, planning to overthrow the government? If the latter, Larkin mused, "I am two years behind the time in my supposition of affairs to come." What he expected in 1847 or 1848 was already happening.[6] Larkin clearly thought a change was coming. In a business letter written the same day that he pondered the meaning of the taking of Sonoma, he told an associate that he was unsure whether vessels visiting the California coast in 1847 would pay duties.[7] "If they have started the big Ball to roll," Larkin confided to Leidesdorff, "I can not stop it."[8]

Larkin did not at first agree with the Californios that Frémont and Gillespie, known to be in the vicinity of New Helvetia, were involved in the action.[9] Some Californios believed that Larkin himself was a part of the scheme and called for his arrest in retaliation for Vallejo's capture. Larkin denied any knowledge of the affair, indeed protested that he would "prehaps be the last person they [the Bear Flaggers] speak to on the subject."[10] "Prehaps" for once he was glad that Frémont kept him in the dark.

Frémont had not been directly involved in the attack on Sonoma, but he was soon assumed by some to be in command of the belligerents. To Vallejo's surprise, Frémont did not release the captives but sent them as hostages to Sutter's Fort for detention. Sutter, who was an officer in the Mexican Army, recognized an opportunity when he saw one. He resigned his commission and joined the Bear Flaggers.[11] Sutter's enthusiasm for the movement did not prevent his groaning that his "house is just like a great Hotel" since he had to board the "Gentlemen and comun prisoners" as well as the insurgents.[12]

The Bear Flag affair will forever remain an enigma. Perhaps the American settlers really believed that Castro threatened their homes and families. In April, Larkin had heard the comandante talk of taking a force of two or three hundred men to the Sacramento in July to oppose the expected immigration. Larkin doubted that he was serious.[13] There was in fact an order, which originated with the prefect of Monterey, that banned the purchase of land by foreigners who had not been naturalized and declared that the foreigners could be expelled "'whenever the government finds it convenient.'"[14] It is unlikely that Larkin worried about the decree, though it applied to himself as well as recent immigrants. In any event, it was never enforced.

Nevertheless, the idle comment and wishful thinking of the authorities could have bred rumor. One story held that 250 armed "Spaniards" rode toward the Sacramento Valley, their progress marked by flaming houses, ravaged crops and scattered herds.[15] Frémont claimed that Castro had incited the Indians to attack foreigners and burn their fields.[16]

It was all a fantasy. Castro had issued no proclamation against the settlers; he had taken no action to drive them away; he had gathered no troops to march against them. It was true that he was plotting, collecting a force, and preparing to march, but almost certainly against Governor Pico, not against the Americans.

If Frémont, to whom the belligerents looked for leadership, had wished to verify the truth of the rumors of imminent danger posed by the shadowy forces of Castro, he had only to send a messenger to Leidesdorff or Larkin. They would know Castro's intentions. Frémont in fact did send Gillespie to Yerba Buena, but for supplies, not information. While there, Gillespie talked with an American who soon reported the conversation in a letter. The letter betrays no alarm on Gillespie's part and no evidence of an impending Mexican attack on the American settlers.[17] Frémont did not seek confirmation of the threat because he did not sense a threat.

Certainly, Larkin was not aware of any danger to settlers or to Frémont's men. There was so little hint of trouble that Larkin, having learned that Frémont's party was back in the Sacramento Valley, wrote to Gillespie on June 1 to ask whether he would care to go to Santa Barbara with him. The consejo had not yet been cancelled, and though he held little hope for any success there, Larkin thought he should make the effort to go. He would not have thought of undertaking such a trip with little prospect, had he thought the settlers and Frémont were menaced by Castro. He did mention in the letter to Gillespie his impression that Castro had gone north— probably to raise a force to go against Pico.[18]

Larkin's hopes for a peaceful annexation of California to the United States ended. He had expected a change of sovereignty before 1847 was finished, and by action of the Californios themselves. Indeed, General Castro had only recently shown the consul, for his approval, a written plan for declaring California independent in 1847 or 1848, as soon as the number of immigrants was sufficient to guarantee success. Larkin agreed to the plan.[19] Visiting Sonoma just a few days before the attack, Castro had restated his desire for the United States to take possession of the province. Now, the Californios felt aggrieved and must defend their honor and country.

A saddened Larkin reported to Buchanan that he regretted "that a farther time could not be had to produce our flag in this country in another form." He blamed Frémont and Gillespie for the lost opportunity.[20] The Bear Flag

Revolt made war between Mexico and the United States almost a certainty, had it not already begun a few weeks before on the disputed Texas border.

The war in California was part of, but apart from, that other war. Never did war begin so peacefully. Commodore Sloat sailed his flagship, *Savannah*, into Monterey Bay on July 1 and anchored beside the American warships, *Cyane* and *Levant*. Following the usual practice when visiting a friendly port, the commodore prepared to salute the Mexican flag. The Mexican commander ashore politely declined the courtesy since he did not have the powder necessary for a response. Larkin was rowed out to the *Savannah* the next day for a visit and was honored with the customary consular salute of nine guns on his debarking. He was doubtless pleased. On the 4th of July, the American independence celebration, marked by dressed ships and booming guns, merged with the Mexican fiesta commemorating the patroness of the Bishopric of California.[21] Thus began the conquest.

The war with Mexico had commenced on the Texas-Mexican border on April 25, 1846. Mexico had never given up its claim on Texas, whose inhabitants had rebelled in 1836. When the United States finally yielded in 1845 to the application for admission by the self-proclaimed republic, war with Mexico was virtually assured. The newly-elected President Polk, who had campaigned on an expansionist platform, was determined to have not only Texas, but also New Mexico and California, peacefully if possible, but by war if necessary. Impatience and ambition decided that war would settle the issue.

At the end of 1845, the United States Pacific fleet lay at Mazatlán. Its commander, Commodore Sloat, had long-standing orders to seize San Francisco and other California ports in case war should begin between the United States and Mexico. On May 17, Sloat learned that hostilities had almost certainly begun with an action on the Rio Grande. The following day he dispatched a letter for Larkin in the *Cyane*. He told the consul the war news and confided to him what he had not revealed even to his own officers: he was preparing to sail immediately for California. His squadron would include seven men-of-war. He asked Larkin to be prepared to advise him on his arrival on what course he should take. In the meantime, Larkin should keep Sloat's communication strictly secret. If any word of the Rio Grande incident reached California, Larkin was to pass the action off as a "mere skirmish."[22]

Sloat, still unsure of his authority and having received no verification that war had begun, wavered. The commodore has been faulted for his timidity and vacillation, suggesting that a prompt departure for California in May would have avoided the counterproductive Bear Flag Revolt.[23] Sloat was not aware of that prospect; he was aware of the consequences of a premature seizure of California territory by a United States Navy officer. Whatever his reasons, he finally received decisive news on June 7 that the United States Navy had blockaded Vera Cruz. Sloat's squadron sailed that same day for Monterey.

Meanwhile, Larkin and other Montereños chafed for news. Larkin complained to Mott Talbot & Company in Mazatlán of "not even being able to say what country we belong to." [24] His anxiety was only heightened by the arrival of the *Cyane* on June 19, bringing Commodore Sloat's equivocal war report. Larkin wrote immediately and again the next day to John Montgomery, commander of the *Portsmouth*, then anchored in San Francisco Bay. He passed on Sloat's news, including the instruction to deny any rumor of hostilities on the Rio Grande, and asked Montgomery to remain where he was until he received further word. [25] The *Cyane* would stay at Monterey. Montgomery replied that he knew no more than the consul about the fleet's movements, though he expected its arrival at any moment. He assured Larkin that he was not involved in the Bear Flag affair. The captain resolved that he and Larkin must, for the time, remain "quiet spectators of passing events." [26]

As he waited impatiently for the arrival of the American fleet, Larkin took stock of his personal situation. He knew that many Californios still believed him a party to the Bear Flag affair. The presence of the *Portsmouth* and the *Cyane* added to the Californios' uneasiness. Larkin sensed a growing resentment against him, the leading American official in California. He had heard that some Californios wanted him seized and taken into the interior. He knew that he must stay at his post, "regardless of consequences to myself," but decided that he would protect his family by sending them to Hawaii where they would be under the care of the United States commissioner and the consul of the Sandwich Islands. [27] Larkin would soon find that Rachel had something to say about his plan.

Commodore Sloat's arrival on July 1 did not disturb the usual tranquillity of Monterey. The day after the *Savannah* dropped anchor without incident, the commodore conferred with Larkin about shore leave for his crew. Larkin sent him some books and a sample of quicksilver ore taken near San Jose and described a crude technique for processing it. Sloat sent his compliments to the consul and said that he would like to take a ride with him the next morning. Presumably they had their ride, but Larkin also found time that day to buy a house.

If there was a war, it was between the Bear Flaggers and the Californios. A party of Bear Flaggers had brazenly entered Yerba Buena at noon one day without opposition. A force under William Ide had taken San Rafael, and General Castro was collecting an army to attack him. Captain Montgomery warned Larkin that the insurgents were in control and "in less than fifteen days they will be in your Midst."[28]

"The Great Ball has been rolled. What can stop it?" Larkin wrote to his counterpart in the Sandwich Islands. Though the Californios outnumbered the Americans, Larkin believed the outcome certain as more immigrants inevitably would rally to the insurgent cause. Larkin indeed was "dreaming of trying to persuade the Californians to call on the Commodore for protection, hoist his Flag & be his Countryman, or the Bear may destroy them."[29] Even at the cutting edge of conquest, he was still trying to bring Californios peacefully into the American fold. There were limits to what he could do. To Governor Pío Pico, who had protested that the consul had not acted to end the Bear Flag affair, he explained that he had offered his services to the local authorities, who had rejected them. Beyond that, he explained, he had no powers; he certainly had no control over the Bear Flaggers.[30]

Larkin did have some influence on Commodore Sloat. Unsure of the war and his own orders, Sloat hesitated. On July 7, likely at Larkin's urging, Sloat finally and formally announced what the local inhabitants already knew. The United States and Mexico were at war, and California was forfeit. Sloat came not as an enemy of the Californios, but "as their best friend." Californios would, if they chose, become American citizens. Under the Stars and Stripes, there would be peace, order, and rapid advancement in all fields. Titles to real estate, held "under a colour of right," would be confirmed to the holders. Fair prices would be paid for private property seized and supplies provided to American forces.[31] Larkin had helped draft the proclamation, and his hand can be seen in these last two promises.[32] He would have frequent occasion later to recall them.

At dawn, Don Mariano Silva, the ranking Mexican officer in Monterey, was ordered to surrender the town and the country. He replied that he had nothing to surrender, no property, troops, or flag, nor any orders to direct him. At ten o'clock, American forces were landed, and the Stars and Stripes was raised.[33]

It was a busy day for the consul. Presumably he acted on the commodore's request to place men at strategic points around Monterey to warn of the approach of a hostile force.[34] He sent an urgent dispatch to Ide at Sonoma to notify him of Sloat's proclamation. He assumed that the change of government would end any further action by Ide and his followers against the Californios and recommended that Ide contact the commodore at once to explain his situation and plans.[35] The same day he wrote both to Frémont and Montgomery at San Francisco. At day's end Larkin and Sloat conferred aboard the *Savannah*.[36]

The next day Larkin assumed a new role, that of peacemaker. He wrote to two old friends, now officially enemies, to open communication between the two sides. To General José Castro he relayed Sloat's request for a meeting, "for the purpose of amicably regulating many things which are yet pending and for the accomplishing the tranquility of the Country."[37] Larkin assured their mutual friend, Juan Bautista Alvarado, that he had his best interests at heart, as always, and that he was sure Castro could reach an agreement with the commodore that Californios would support.[38] Both replied from Castro's headquarters at San Juan Bautista. Castro responded coolly that he had already written to Sloat, and Larkin should contact the commodore to learn the general's intentions. Alvarado was more openminded. He would like to accommodate Larkin, he said, but he was under military orders. He also claimed a certain patriotism and asked Larkin what he would do in similar circumstances.[39]

At the very outset of the conquest, Larkin urged on Sloat a policy of conciliation and continuity. Sloat had asked Larkin's advice on more than one occasion, and Larkin freely gave it. He suggested to the commander that he issue a new proclamation, promising that the families of those who chose to oppose the Americans would not be punished unless they gave actual aid to the belligerents, at the same time inviting Californios to "join his Standard." The appeal would encourage desertion from Castro's forces. In fact, desertion had already begun. Among fifty who had left their posts on one morning were the military commandant and the port commander of Monterey, both of whom, Larkin assured Sloat, would shortly contact the commodore.[40]

Larkin was anxious, but pleased. The conquest was proceeding in order. Monterey was quiet. He expected that American forces were about to be increased by 200 or 300 men under Frémont or Ide. He learned from Sloat that Castro had departed for the south to confer with Governor Pico. Larkin did not think that Pico would cooperate with Castro, whose troops, in any event, were melting away. Larkin was convinced that the people, if left alone by their leaders, would soon be content with the American takeover.[41]

"The fear, dread, and excitement have gone by," Larkin wrote to Stearns on July 10. Stearns, who had generally favored ties with the United States, was not so sure now that the future looked bright for his adopted California, and Larkin wanted to convince him that all was well. Larkin described the likely result if American forces were to withdraw. At "the moment the stars fell by suprem orders the Bear would take their place." Certainly, a reversion to the chaos of Mexican rule would be no solution. The best thing for California now, he said, would be a speedy end to hostility and uncertainty. Larkin urged Stearns and his compatriots in southern California to prevent the governor from issuing a bombastic proclamation and instead invite Sloat to San Pedro for the purpose of negotiating a treaty. Larkin would urge the commodore to accept. If Sloat were not able to meet with the governor, Larkin would come himself.[42] He was determined that nothing happen to prevent a happy conclusion to his efforts to make California American.

Indeed, he wanted to go immediately to Washington to advise and report personally to his superiors, but Sloat persuaded him that he needed him.[43]

The commodore employed Larkin as his advisor and assistant on both civil and military matters. Larkin helped Sloat with alcalde and justice of the peace appointments and acted as liaison with the Bear Flaggers. He also acted as buffer. At Sloat's request, he wrote to Frémont on July 7 to say that the commodore wanted Frémont's cooperation, and he urged the captain to contact the commander. He wrote again July 12, emphasizing that Sloat was anxious to see him, and requested that he come as quickly as possible with all the men he could muster. Sloat wanted to form them into a peace-keeping force for the interior. Still there was no reply.

Frémont finally arrived in Monterey on July 19 at the head of his rustic band of trappers and settlers, but Larkin saw little of him. Larkin wrote a third letter on the 24th, this one a bit stiff and formal—indicative of their relationship—complaining that Frémont had given him no official response to the other two. If he were offended, and it appears that he was, he would have been pleased now to notify Frémont that Sloat had decided he did not need his men after all, since he had decided to dispense with a cavalry and a police force for the interior.[44] Frémont was probably offended as well that Sloat had employed Larkin as a go-between.

The long-feared British challenge to American designs in California did not materialize. Rear Admiral Sir George Seymour, commander of the British Pacific squadron, had orders to try to counter American influence in California, but not to interfere in any concrete way. From Mazatlán in mid-May, he dispatched the *Juno* to Monterey to urge the Californios to keep themselves free of foreign domination.[45] Larkin was either ignorant or unconcerned about the *Juno*'s mission. He was considerably more interested in a passenger, Father Eugene MacNamara.

Soon after the *Juno*'s arrival on June 7, Larkin learned that the Irish priest had received permission from President José Herrera to settle an Irish colony in California, a project that MacNamara believed would be the salvation of thousands of starving Irishmen and could save California from "'the Methodist wolves.'"[46] President Mariano Paredes, Herrera's successor, objected to the plan, believing that the English-speaking Irish would soon join forces with the Americans, but apparently did not forbid its going forward. On June 17, MacNamara sailed from Monterey on the *Juno* for Santa Barbara to confer with the governor. Larkin wrote to Stearns to keep an eye on the Irishman.[47]

MacNamara was soon back in Monterey. He had seen the governor and assembly and secured a grant of 3,000 square leagues of land on the San Joaquin River where he would settle 10,000 Irish. MacNamara asked Larkin whether the United States government would confirm the grant, now that the American flag flew in California. Larkin told him that the grant was not even legal under Mexican law, since the governor had authority to grant a maximum of eleven leagues in a single deed. MacNamara had told Larkin that he was acting for a private London company, but Larkin believed the whole affair a scheme of the British government and so reported to Buchanan.[48]

If Larkin thought, incorrectly, that the British meant to have California by trickery, he learned soon enough that they did not intend to interfere at all. The H.M.S. *Collingwood* arrived in Monterey on July 16 to find the Americans in quiet possession. The British and American officers exchanged visits and news and agreed that there would be no confrontation. Larkin visited Seymour on the *Collingwood* on July 21. Upon leaving, the admiral "partly acknoweldge" the American flag ashore by explaining that he could not give Larkin the customary consular salute since Larkin was not now in office.[49] The *Collingwood* departed Monterey on July 23, with MacNamara aboard, ending American anxieties about British intentions and dashing any hope nurtured by Californios that the British might help them against the Yankees.[50]

The conquest, which was proceeding slowly and calmly, was about to accelerate. The *Congress*, Captain Robert F. Stockton commanding, dropped anchor in Monterey Bay on July 15. Stockton was carrying the original of Secretary Buchanan's letter of October 17, 1845, appointing Larkin the President's secret agent. Larkin had long since learned of the appointment in the copy brought by Gillespie. Since Stockton had orders to confer with Larkin, the two men undoubtedly talked soon after the arrival of the *Congress*. They would have discussed their similar orders to try to win the good favor of the Californios. Larkin would have told Stockton that he still hoped the change of sovereignty could be accomplished with the blessing of the Californios. Learning that Gillespie would be visiting Stockton on July 17, Larkin urged the commodore not to be taken in by the lieutenant's pugnacity.[51] Larkin's concern was prophetic.

On July 23, as the British threat in the form of the *Collingwood* disappeared over the horizon, Commodore Stockton took command of the conquest, replacing commodore Sloat, who had submitted his resignation. Larkin wrote to Stockton the next day to describe the state of affairs in California and to offer some advice. He urged the new commander to take immediate action, as Sloat had not done, to secure all of California, quickly and diplomatically. He advised him to go at once to Los Angeles, which, like the rest of southern California, still flew the Mexican flag, to determine whether General Castro and Governor Pico were in arms against the United States. If so, "you know the step to take against them." If not, he would be in a position to negotiate a peaceful transition.[52]

Having done his part to nudge a willing Stockton to action, Larkin that same day wrote an urgent letter to Cousin Rogers in the East. As soon as he could determine that California was to remain American, Rogers was to invest all Larkin's money held by him in a cargo for dispatch to the west coast.[53] An American California, without the high Mexican duties, promised high profits, and Larkin wanted to get the jump on his competitors in the trade. He saw no inconsistency in patriotism and profits.

Indeed, Larkin expected no war in California. He was convinced that the Californios would not take up arms against the invaders without outside help. That was not likely, since neither the British consul nor the British admiral had protested.[54] Salutes had been exchanged with the Americans, the British fleet had sailed, and now all was quiet. To James Gordon Bennett, Larkin wrote with considerable satisfaction that "I am in the U.S.A.—as well as yourself." Yet, in the back of his mind there was still an uneasiness, for he added that now the *Herald* "must come to the rescue."[55]

There was cause for uneasiness. On July 29, the same day that Larkin saw Commodore Sloat depart in the *Levant* for Panama, Commodore Stockton, now in clear command, issued an "Address to the people of California" that reflected more his own belligerent nature than the state of the conquest. He charged General Castro with "wicked intent" and violation of international law by his pursuit of Frémont. Castro and his men, aided by hostile Indians, he said, had committed "repeated hostilities and outrages . . . rapine, blood and murder," after which Castro and his officers "deserted, leaving the people in a state of anarchy and confusion." Since Mexico had never protected Californios from "wicked men," Stockton considered it his solemn duty to march on "these boasting and abusive chiefs" to bring order to "this beautiful country." That done, he would withdraw all his troops, leaving the people "to manage their own affairs in their own way."[56]

Larkin was dismayed at the tone and content of the proclamation. He regretted that Stockton, unlike Sloat, had not asked his assistance in drafting the statement. Immediately on receiving a copy, he sat down to write to Buchanan. With some restraint, he told the Secretary simply that he knew nothing about the address—he enclosed a copy—"not even knowing where Commodore Stockton obtained the statements it contains." The document revealed the influence of Frémont and Gillespie, who had no love for the Californios, and a broad hint of Stockton's strategy. Larkin knew that the proclamation would make his task of conciliating the Californios more difficult. He emphasized to Buchanan the importance of a prompt statement from Washington that the American flag was planted permanently in California. When native and foreign residents of California were thus convinced, said Larkin, they would return "with double energy" to their daily routines with no thought of Mexico.[57]

On that same chaotic day, Walter Colton, chaplain on the *Congress*, moved into Larkin's house. Stockton had just appointed him alcalde of

Monterey, and Larkin had invited him to stay with him.[58] Perhaps Colton, who was universally well liked, brought some calm to the household.

Whatever Larkin's state of mind, he would do his part. He had wanted to go to Washington with Sloat, but both commodores agreed that Larkin's place at the moment was with Stockton.[59] Vain and self-sufficient, Stockton relied nevertheless on Larkin for advice. On the same day as his severe proclamation, he issued orders on Larkin's suggestion for release of the Bear Flag captives.

On August 1, Larkin sailed with Stockton on the *Congress* for San Pedro. The *Cyane*, carrying Frémont and his men, who recently had been mustered into the United States army, had departed five days earlier for San Diego.[60] Upon arrival in San Pedro, Larkin dispatched two urgent letters to Abel Stearns. He called on his old friend to persuade the governor, general, and other authorities to come with him to San Pedro within twelve to fourteen hours to confer with Stockton about a peaceful settlement. Otherwise, the commodore would march in twenty-four hours. Larkin predicted that if leaders of the two sides did not meet promptly and agree to pacific measures, there would be much bloodshed. Now was the time for the authorities, under Stockton's protection, to declare California free and independent of Mexico.[61] The opportunity must not be missed. It would mean, finally, the success of Larkin's plans.

For reasons that are not entirely clear, Stearns was not enthusiastic about Larkin's proposal. A Mexican citizen and subprefect in Los Angeles, Stearns only days before had issued a call to the rancheros to come to the defense of their country and threatened fines for shirkers.[62] The capital, it seemed, was to be defended. Stearns replied to Larkin's letters, apparently after conferring with government authorities, that Stockton must address future correspondence to General Castro.

The evasion drained Stockton of his patience. Larkin wrote an immediate reply. He noted that Stearns's response to his letters "amounts to nothing" and regretted that he had not come himself to San Pedro. Stockton had done all that he could to avoid the shedding of blood, said Larkin, and would have no more correspondence on the subject. The commodore had wanted to look on California as apart from Mexico. Now he was left no choice but to consider California a part of the Republic of Mexico and proceed at once to hostilities. "The U.S & M are at war," wrote Larkin. He added that he himself had done his best "to prevent the visit of 800 Soldiers to your City and to advert the evils that must necessully attend a Campagn by such men."[63] So saying, Larkin dumped the responsibility for the mayhem to follow in the laps of Stearns and the other Mexican authorities.

Perhaps there would be no conflict. Apart from Larkin's letters to Stearns, Sloat had sent directly to Castro an invitation to confer. Though Castro initially had a superiority in numbers,[64] he responded to Sloat's invitation by sending two representatives on August 7 to San Pedro. The commodore appointed Larkin and Lieutenant James F. Schenck to meet them. In the exchange that followed, Castro agreed to negotiate, even perhaps to voluntarily raise the American flag, but Stockton refused. Even a favorable negotiation would leave the Mexican leadership in power. Stockton instead demanded that the price for peace was that Castro surrender unconditionally and hoist the American flag. Castro had little faith in the ability of his force to resist the invaders, but he nevertheless rejected the proposal as humiliating. He conferred with Governor Pico, after which the assembly met and was dissolved. On the night of August 10, the governor and the comandante quietly left the capital for Mexico, where their repeated petitions for help in recovering California failed.[65]

On August 11, Stockton began his march on Los Angeles. He sent Larkin and two others ahead under a flag of truce with a letter for Castro. Larkin met no resistance on the road to Los Angeles and entered the town where he and his companions took quiet possession of the abandoned Government House. By the time the army reached the town on August 13, its numbers swollen by Frémont's force, which had marched from San Diego on Stockton's order, Larkin had borrowed furniture from citizens and put the house in order.[66]

Commodore Stockton decreed in a new proclamation, dated August 17, 1846, that the conquest of California was finished. A local civil administration of elected officials would govern under military law. The people and their property would be protected, and they need no longer fear the tyranny of Mexico.[67]

Though he was not officially under Stockton's command, Larkin decided that he would stay with the commodore as long as he was needed. Larkin heartily approved the commodore's conduct and so reported to Buchanan that "[p]erhaps no officer in our Navy is better adapted for the capture, charge and care of California." Larkin also thought Stockton's appointment of Frémont as military commandant of California a wise choice. He applauded the commodore's plan for a provincial civil government, outlined in a draft of a constitution which Larkin termed "'The Organic Law of his Empire.'" He believed that the Californios at the moment could not adjust to more liberty than that provided by the document. "Our Flag now waives over all California," Larkin told Buchanan. All was going well. Angeleños were already submitting domestic disputes to the new tribunals. Larkin assured the secretary that Californios in general would soon realize they were better off under the Stars and Stripes and would prosper and be content.[68]

The conquest was complete, but there was still uncertainty about California's future. That question was in the hands of the Washington bureaucracy. While Larkin did not think the peace treaty would give up California, a prospect that he thought "impossible for anyone to entertain," he urged

Buchanan that in any event the province should be held until 1848. By then, enough American immigrants would have entered to assure that it would be American forever.[69]

With California now in American hands, Larkin assumed that his consular position was terminated, but he was not ready to end his government employ. During the turmoil of the past month, Larkin had told Leidesdorff that he had no plans to seek any new government post,[70] but now he wrote to the Secretary of State on August 27 to volunteer his services on any American commission that might be set up to work on a settlement with Mexico. Also, until California was secured to the United States by treaty he hoped that his appointment as confidential agent would remain active. On August 13, Stockton had appointed him navy agent for the California coast, and Larkin asked Buchanan's assistance in securing official confirmation of the post.[71] As we shall see, the agency promised both profits and headaches.

Southern California now seemingly pacified, the scene shifted northward. By August 26, Larkin, still in Los Angeles, was making plans to return to Monterey. He agreed to meet Stockton and Frémont at Yerba Buena in October to work with them on a set of laws for California.[72] Stockton meanwhile worked on an imaginative scheme to carry the conquest to Mexico's western shores. Definite news of the declaration of war against Mexico had arrived on August 17, and placid California could not encompass the commodore's enormous ambition. Frémont was sent northward to raise volunteers, supposedly to guard California towns but actually to take part in Stockton's design to invade Mexico's west coast.[73] The commodore divided California into three departments, with Frémont in overall command. Leaving Gillespie in charge of the southern department, Stockton departed San Pedro on September 3 in the *Congress*.[74] Larkin was aboard.

The *Congress* dropped anchor in Monterey Bay on September 15. Larkin was reunited with his family and found a multitude of affairs that required his attention. Anthony Ten Eyck, United States commissioner at Honolulu, had responded to Larkin's inquiry, saying that he would be delighted to look after Rachel and the children if Larkin should wish to send them to the islands. Larkin replied to the commissioner, thanking him for his kindness but saying that all was quiet in California now, and the family was safe. He did not tell him that Rachel had refused to consider the move in spite of her husband's beseeching.[76]

Larkin also found letters from Jacob Leese and Mariano Vallejo, verifying that they had been released from their detention at Sutter's Fort and thanking him for his help. Leese called Larkin "My Liberator" and declared that "Proven Friends is never to be Forgotten."[77] Vallejo said that he planned to come to Monterey to thank Larkin personally.[78] Larkin replied to Leese, thanking him for his kind words and blaming the delay in the captives' release on Gillespie, who Larkin suspected had persuaded Sloat against an early end of their imprisonment.[79]

After a few days respite, Larkin began preparing for the conference at Yerba Buena. He wrote to associates there to have the old Hudson's Bay Company house put in order for Commodore Stockton and to arrange for horses for his use. As an alternative, he suggested to Leidesdorff that he offer Stockton rooms in his City Hotel. Larkin himself planned to stay at the hotel during the conference. At the meetings Larkin would try to put his imprint on government. He had already strongly recommended to Governor Frémont that he appoint Mariano Vallejo and Juan Bandini legislators. "I am determined if possible to have those two Gentlemen in the new govermnt," he told Leese.[80]

Larkin had little to report to Buchanan, now that he was no longer the paramount American official on the coast: Commodore Stockton had dispatched his fleet "on a cruise;" Larkin had spent considerable sums on couriers; the commodore had ordered the election of town officers throughout California; Californios were reconciled to American rule; "the state of the Country is only in some excitement from the expectation of too many Mormons."[81] The war was receding as the new American possession settled into a routine. Larkin turned increasingly to business affairs. He might have agreed with Moses Y. Beach's comment that "[p]eople begin to think the Mexican War is great humbug."[82] This was about to change.

Larkin was shocked to learn in late September that the Californios under José María Flores had risen in Los Angeles and had laid siege to Gillespie's force at Government House. Stockton notified Larkin in haste on October 1 that he was dispatching the *Savannah* and the *Portsmouth* immediately and was preparing the *Congress* for sea.[83]

But Stockton did not sail. Instead he went to Yerba Buena, where the citizens regaled him on October 5 with a parade and patriotic speeches. The commodore was in his element. He announced that he would soundly chasten the insurrectionists. "The 'Sons of Liberty are on their way . . . but this is the time for fighting, not for making speeches—I am done.'" Perhaps he was done, but he did not leave. A reception followed and then a grand ball that continued far into the night. Days passed before the *Congress*, accompanied by Frémont and his band of 160 men in the merchant ship, *Sterling*, weighed anchor on October 14 for the south.[84]

Since the commodore planned war rather than diplomacy, Larkin stayed at home. He installed Rachel and the children at Yerba Buena, which he thought safer than Monterey. He made arrangements with associates to look out for them and sent Rachel two or three Indian girls, presumably as servants. That done, he devoted himself almost wholly to business, but the war caught up with him at Sonoma. During a visit with General Vallejo in mid-October, Lieutenant Joseph W. Revere, the commandant of the Sonoma garrison, disclosed to Larkin the contents of a dispatch that he had just received from Captain Montgomery in San Francisco. The message confirmed the startling news about the rising in the south. Larkin and Edwin Bryant, who was also visiting Vallejo, set out immediately for San Francisco, "riding at the usual California speed."[85]

There Larkin tried without success to learn more about affairs in the south. He also visited Rachel and the children in their spare lodgings. On October 22, Larkin and Bryant chartered a small sailboat for a voyage up the Sacramento River to New Helvetia.[86] Larkin always had business with Sutter, but the main reason for the excursion was to examine the upper San Francisco Bay and the Sacramento River.[87] Larkin had already begun to think about speculating in land near the mouth of the river.

Larkin was still at Sutter's Fort on October 28 when James Reed of the ill-fated Donner Party arrived to secure provisions and form a rescue party.[88] Unfortunately, Larkin made no comment about the affair in his letters. He would have seen the message that arrived that same day from Frémont, reporting that Los Angeles and Santa Barbara had fallen and that an American force under Captain William Mervine had been turned back at Los Angeles. Frémont was then in Monterey, recruiting troops before sailing southward.[89] His business completed at New Helvetia, it seems that Larkin returned to Sonoma to help Revere arrange a treaty of some sort,[90] probably with Indians.

Arriving in Monterey on November 9, Larkin was disappointed to find no letter from Stockton. He immediately wrote to Rachel and chided her gently for not dispatching two letters, including one for the commodore, that he had left with her during his brief visit. "I suppose they still lay where I put them." For weeks, he had heard only unverified reports about events in southern California. He had hoped that a reply from Stockton would clarify the situation and summon him to the south.[91] He was about to learn more of the war than he had hoped.

On November 15 Larkin received letters calling him to San Francisco. Commander Montgomery needed to talk with him about stores for the *Portsmouth*. More urgent, a letter from Rachel told of the illness of their daughter, Sophia Adeline. He set out for Yerba Buena that same afternoon, accompanied by William Matthews. He was not aware of any Californio forces near Monterey and made no attempt to conceal his departure. Sending Matthews six miles ahead to San Juan to ask a San Francisco-bound friend to wait for him, Larkin spent the night at Los Verjeles, the rancho of Joaquín Gómez, near Gavilan Peak. Before retiring, he prayed on his knees to God to spare Adeline and protect his family.[92] In bed he read Rachel's letter again "and cryed more than I supposed I could have done."[93]

In the middle of the night, Larkin was awakened by a party of Californios and carried away to a camp on the Salinas River. He was the prisoner of Manuel Castro, prefect of Monterey and an old acquaintance. When Castro had heard about the revolt in Los Angeles, he had pledged his service to Flores and been appointed commandant of the resistance in the north. Castro's charge was to raise a force to conduct guerrilla activities against the Americans. The insurgents had learned of Larkin's departure from Monterey and decided that such an important captive could be exceptionally useful later in an exchange of prisoners or negotiations for a truce, surrender, or amnesty from broken paroles.[94]

Larkin had long expected that he might be seized by the Californios. In the aftermath of the Bear Flag incident, he had learned that José Carrillo had wanted to take him prisoner but was dissuaded by Juan Bautista Alvarado and Manuel Jimeno. Another party wanted to seize him to provoke the Americans to invade at once and settle the California question once and for all. Larkin also had feared being taken as reprisal for the abduction of Vallejo by the Bear Flaggers.[95] In early July, he had almost expected to be kidnapped in Monterey by a party of Castro's men. He was saved, he decided, because "they did not think of it, although two days back they had it in contemplation."[96] Larkin accepted the prospect of imprisonment philosophically. "I do not care whether I am made Prisoner or not providing I sleap in a good Bed, under cover, and have tea or coffee before I start in the morning and during the day." He had put his business affairs in order, recorded his properties, and was ready for anything.[97]

Larkin's captivity was to prove a test of his nerve and his reputation among the Californios. Castro intended the day after Larkin's capture to attack a party of American volunteers who had converged, at Frémont's call, at San Juan Bautista. On reaching the Californios' camp, Larkin was ordered by Castro to write a letter to the American commander. He was to say that he was at a certain place, ministering to some destitute Californio families, and that the commander was to send twenty men to him so he could protect them. Whether the purpose of the letter was to reduce the American force at San Juan or lure the Americans into an ambush is unclear. Castro told Larkin that if he refused to write the letter, he could not protect him from the wrath of his men. Larkin, nevertheless, refused; he was asked again, and again refused, telling Castro that "my life is at your disposal, do as you like."[98] The scheme was dropped.

The next morning Larkin tried to persuade Castro to exchange him for captive California officials in Monterey, one of them Castro's own brother. Castro refused, saying that Larkin would not be exchanged for under 100 men. His value was later raised to ten men-of-war. With Larkin as a hostage, the fight for California was considered half finished.[99]

Castro marched his force northward toward San Juan Bautista. He planned a surprise night attack, but news of Larkin's capture had reached the Americans. They knew that a hostile force was in the vicinity and were ready. Outnumbered but better armed, the Americans advanced from their camp to meet the Californios near the rancho La Natividad, east of today's Santa Rita. A skirmish by advance parties began about three o'clock. The American patrol was quickly surrounded in a grove of oaks. During the fight, which lasted about an hour, Castro asked Larkin to persuade the Americans to surrender. Larkin consented on condition that they be guaranteed a safe withdrawal to San Juan or Monterey, but Castro refused. The two main forces converged for a furious battle of twenty to thirty minutes. Casualties were light, each side losing four or five men.[100] The result was inconclusive, but must be deemed an American victory since Manuel Castro thereafter abandoned his mission in the north.

Larkin was a spectator to the action, and he was troubled by it. On one side were his countrymen, and on the other, men who had been his friends and business associates since his arrival in California. Defeat by either side "appeard sad and disagreable to me," he wrote later to Rachel.[101] During the battle, Lorenzo Soto, on seeing his nephew shot down, rode furiously toward Larkin, with pointed pistol and clear intent to shoot him. Larkin kept his head. When Soto was but ten yards away, Larkin backed his horse behind one of his guards, and Soto turned aside. Thinking Larkin too well mounted in the midst of such chaos, his guards exchanged horses with him twice until he was riding, by his own reckoning, "a one dollar horse and two dollar saddle."[102]

The Californios hastily withdrew southward toward the capital. Castro led a force of about twenty-five or thirty. Larkin was closely escorted by a small party that traveled independently to Los Angeles. In charge of the guard was Francisco Rico, a Monterey acquaintance whom Larkin had known in 1845 as an honorable, straightforward man.[103]

Larkin was a prisoner of the Californios for almost two months. During the entire time, he was treated with the utmost respect and was made as comfortable as circumstances permitted. "In camp or in a house, the first & best was always presented to me," he told Secretary Buchanan later. "If there was but one bed or one piece of bread, it was mine." In spite of the care and politeness, Larkin throughout his captivity feared for his life. He was afraid that the friendly authorities would not always be able to control the drunken and lawless people, nor curb the Mexicans and Californios who fought among themselves.[104] During one of these anxious periods, he wrote a will which he later dispatched to Rachel. He was also bothered that he and those who visited him were forbidden to speak English; they could only converse in Spanish.[105]

En route to Los Angeles, Rico took the greatest care with Larkin, particularly watching to be sure that his horse did not stumble during night rides. In the course of the journey, several Californios, having second thoughts about the war, offered to escape at night with Larkin and return to the north. He declined. On another occasion, most of the escort had fallen behind, and only four others rode with Larkin and a leader, probably Rico. Larkin remarked to the leader that three of the men "will assist me to shoot you in the back, & it doubtful whether the other is for you or me." The leader admitted what he said, thanked him for the information and said that he would be more careful.[106]

The party stopped at Santa Barbara, arriving around November 21. Rico agreed to lodge Larkin with Dr. and Mrs. Nicholas A. Den, at their request and after they promised to feed the guard. A naturalized citizen of Irish origins, Den was a wealthy and influential stock raiser. The Dens were most hospitable, and Larkin was visited by every person of note, foreign and native, in the town. When Larkin left Santa Barbara with his guard, the Dens gave him clothing and provisions for the trip.[107]

With considerable relief, Larkin wrote to Rachel from Santa Barbara, telling her his story and assuring her that he was safe. She had long since heard about his capture,[108] but she would have known nothing beyond that. He told her that the Californios would take care that no harm should come to him. He was too valuable a property, and besides his captors were old friends. Larkin believed that they also feared retaliation if he were harmed while in their possession. He reassured her that he would be with her again, that is, if there were no accidents. If something should happen to him, she was to receive one-third of his property, two-thirds to the five children "and the child you may have within you."[109] Rachel undoubtedly had written to him before his departure from Monterey that she suspected she was pregnant. Adding to his worry about their sick Sophia Adeline, Larkin would have been concerned about Rachel's condition. Alfred Otis, their last child, was born in April 1847.

Larkin was moved on November 26 to Los Angeles. He was given the best room in the Government House. He could move about in front or back, but always under guard, even to the outhouse. Immediately on his arrival, José A. Carrillo, second in command, and other citizens called on him and sent meals and furniture. After two or three days, General Flores, who had been ill when Larkin arrived, and his wife visited. Thereafter, the commander and his wife were particularly solicitous, offering him furniture, bedding, food, clothing, and money. The commander apologized for not having the English books that Larkin requested. Señora Flores served him tea and bread four times a day, which must have made the captivity more bearable. Larkin liked his tea. He decided that some of the tales he had heard in the north about what was going on in the south were not true. "In fact," he wrote to Rachel, "both North & South have been prolific in falsehoods of late."[110]

Anyone but those known to oppose the resistance could visit Larkin. Few Americans called, fearing any association with the consul since many Californios blamed him, as the chief American official before the conquest, for their troubles. Those of other nationalities were not so bothered. Henry

Dalton, a naturalized Englishman and brother-in-law of General Flores, visited Larkin twice in December.[111] A naturalized Spaniard, Eulogio de Célis, longtime resident of Los Angeles and one of the grantees of the San Fernando rancho, often visited Larkin and other prisoners. Larkin was especially grateful for the friendship and assistance of Charles W. Flügge, a naturalized citizen of German origin who lived in Los Angeles and was an acquaintance of General Flores. Flügge secured Flores's consent for Larkin to write letters and brought pen and paper to him.[112] Whether from gratitude or opportunity or both, during their conversations Larkin bought a tract of land in northern California from Flügge. Larkin would not have let personal discomfort or war stand in the way of business.

Larkin was also visited by Californios. Several of them, saying they were deceived into supporting the war, asked him for safe passage so they could escape to Monterey or San Francisco. He refused. "I had a curious time with them," he later observed. "I held a place of half a captive and half master."[113]

At year's end, 1846, Larkin was despondent. In spite of the consideration of his jailers, his spirits over the past month had declined. The more he talked with local people, the more convinced he was that Gillespie and Stockton had bungled the conquest in the south. Stockton had not followed Larkin's advice to permit the Mexican officers to withdraw to Mexico. That mistake and the commodore's "cheap way of conducting," combined with Gillespie's harsh and arbitrary administration, "has brot the country to its present pass."[114] Everything that Larkin had worked for was crumbling.

In this dark mood, he pondered his personal condition. Worried almost to distraction about Rachel and the children, he slept little and his health worsened. He decided that the prospects of seeing his wife again were not good. On December 14, he wrote a long letter to Rachel, "who I value as my life," as if it were his last. He scolded her gently for his predicament, reminding her that he had begged her to go from Monterey to Hawaii. When she refused and went to San Francisco instead, it was her call to come there that had led to his capture. He softened his rebuke by admitting that she was right in the end, for if she had remained at Monterey, as she wished, he would now be with her and the children.[115]

Unknown to Larkin, Rachel was back in Monterey as he wrote. She and the children had left San Francisco on the *Euphemia* in early December. William Heath Davis, part owner of the brig, had tried to cheer her up, saying that the Californios surely would not harm him whom they had known so long, but she remained anxious and would not be consoled.[116]

Larkin's greatest fear at this point was that, because of uncertainty or an American attack, he might be moved and be witness to a battle which could lead to his death, whether from a chance bullet or an angry Californio. On December 3 or 4, Flores had made plans to transport fifteen or twenty prisoners, including Larkin, to Mexico. Larkin told his captors that "they must expect to pass Cape Horn if we was taken out of C.,"[117] presumably because of the American blockade of Mexico's west coast. The plan was abandoned.

Anticipating a clash and fearing that he might not survive it, Larkin described his will and the state of his business in minute detail in the December 14 letter to Rachel. He told her the names of men on whom she could rely for assistance. As soon as she accumulated enough funds, she was to return with the children to Massachusetts. "California is no place for you as a Widow." Wishing to leave no obligations unsettled, he requested that she send "a Ring of your best remembrances" to Mrs. Den and another to Señora Flores in gratitude for their thoughtfulness to him. Ending on a melancholy note, he sent his love to her and the children and expressed his hope that they might yet see each other again.[118]

With the coming of the new year, 1847, it appeared that the war was about to erupt again. Larkin knew about the arrival of the *Savannah* at San Pedro in early October and Captain Mervine's unsuccessful march on Los Angeles. He must have heard about the December 6 victory of the Californio lancers against the advance unit of General Stephen Watts Kearny's Army of the West near the Indian village of San Pasqual. Kearny's force had marched through the Southwest after a bloodless conquest of New Mexico. On January 3 or 4, 1847, Larkin heard that Frémont and his volunteers had passed Santa Barbara and were marching southward. Only days later he learned that a large column under Commodore Stockton was moving up the coast from the south.[119] All of the commanders—Mervine, Stockton, Kearny, Frémont—were poised for the march on Los Angeles.

The end of Mexican California came quickly. An American force of 600 men, led jointly by Commodore Stockton and General Kearny, marched from San Diego and met General Flores's troops at the San Gabriel River on January 8. This Battle of San Gabriel, more skirmish than battle, and the Battle of La Mesa the following day ended the opposition.

What Larkin feared most almost became a reality. At noon on January 9, General Flores, facing the advancing American troops on the outskirts of Los Angeles, sent for Larkin. Flores likely planned to employ him in negotiations. Larkin at the moment was staying at the home of Don Luis Vignes, a popular naturalized citizen of French origin, about a half mile from the pueblo. Larkin was not guarded, under his promise not to leave the premises. He had been moved there at the end of December because of his failing health.[120] Unaware of the reason for the summons, Larkin feared that he was to be sent to Mexico. He dallied in his preparations, complained of being ill, and walked his horse.

Larkin and his captors arrived on the field at 3:00 P.M. to find the battle over. Glancing about, Larkin and an idle Californio locked eyes. Larkin at that instant remembered that Monterey Alcalde Walter Colton had once jailed the man. The drunken trooper, apparently confusing Larkin with Colton, shouted, "here is the man who made a rope to hang me in M[onterey]," and rushed on him with pointed musket. Andrés Pico with some difficulty wrenched away the gun.[121]

Flores took Larkin aside, partly in response to Larkin's query, to justify his detention. The general said that he held him, a consul, prisoner on grounds that he had supported the American aggression, that he had appeared in fact "the most active of the enemies of Mexico."[122] He also gave Larkin "reasons and excuses why he was General." Flores was anticipating questions that must follow an American victory. The general then pondered the best way to set Larkin free. Mrs. Luisa Zamorano had dispatched a message to Flores, cautioning him to beware of what he did with Larkin and suggesting that he be sent back to the Vignes's home, where twenty families had taken refuge. Flores decided instead to simply free him to go where he chose. Larkin was agreeable, but only if he were protected from "the mad and drunken people" by an officer.[123]

Before leaving the field, several Californios asked him to assist their families after the American victory. Flores in the meantime organized an escort of five or six officers which he then led himself, probably to Vignes's home. That night, Larkin was free.[124]

One wonders in what state of mind he spent the night, amongst a defeated people, in a state of absolute anarchy. He would have breathed a great sigh of relief to watch the American troops march into the plaza at noon the next day, January 10.

The controversy over the title of supreme commander between General Kearny and Commodore Stockton during this campaign and after, and the role of Frémont, who supported Stockton, has been described elsewhere.[125] Larkin was not a principal party to the conflict between the commanders and did not interfere.

Larkin's deliverance was bittersweet. He rejoiced to be once again among countrymen who had worried about him and now greeted him warmly. He probably listened to the officers' accounts of the different campaigns and shared their camaraderie and satisfaction with a job well done. In this manner, he avoided for a full half hour asking what was uppermost in his mind, news of his wife and sick daughter. Then, without asking, Dr. Andrew Henderson of the *Portsmouth* rode over to Larkin and said that he assumed that he had heard about the death of his child. Larkin was struck dumb and could not reply to the questions that others continued to ask him. Henderson, realizing that Larkin had not before heard the sad news, told them to ask no more. Larkin backed his horse from the crowd and rode to Vignes's house, where he was staying. He dismounted, handed the reins to the first person he met, found his room and shut himself inside, where he "cryed and suffered like a child for hours."[126]

He still grieved the next day when he finally screwed up the courage to write to Rachel. "Since the death of my brother in twenty years ago I never suffered as I did then," he wrote, "and now I cry—I stop my writing. Oh Heaven could I but have been present to have consoled you, and gave Adeline my last kiss—but I can go no farther."[127] It was the lowest point in Larkin's life.

The Californios did not make their ceremonial surrender in Los Angeles to Kearny and Stockton, whom they knew too well. They capitulated instead to Frémont, from whom the Californios expected a larger measure of justice, at Cahuenga Pass overlooking the Los Angeles plain. Frémont's volunteer force had reached the San Fernando Valley, north of Los Angeles, on January 11. In the absence of General Flores, who had left for Mexico, Andrés Pico tendered the formal surrender. The terms of the Treaty of Cahuenga, signed by Frémont and Andrés Pico on January 13, 1847, were generous. The defeated Californios were required to give up their artillery, promise not to take up arms again, and go peacefully to their homes. The reconquest was complete. Frémont, who, on his own authority, had initiated military action against Mexican California, had ended it, again without authority.[128]

Larkin's liberators brought a letter from Rachel, written after she had received her husband's November 25, 1846, letter which told about his capture. With hostilities ended, he doubtless was relieved to read that she was once again in her own house, content as she could be after the loss of a daughter, and settled back in Monterey. Her concern for him is touching. She wished that she could visit him. She sent a box of clothing—"You must be in a miserable Condision without a Change unless Some kind friend has favoured you with a Change"—and some Sandwich Island newspapers, "for you to wile away the teagous [tedious] dayes of imprisonment." She wondered whether she should send tea and sugar and worried about his delicate health. She vowed that she would not be happy until he was liberated: "You are never out of my mind both by night and day." The children also missed him. "Francis feales vary much for you. Caroline frenquntley makes the remarks poor papa."[129] One cannot read Rachel's letter without seeing there evidence of a close, loving family.

The letter also brought back the agony. "It is with most painful fealings I now adrass you. . . . My Dear Husband I am pained to anounce the death of our dear little Adelaide." Rachel told how she had tried to reconcile herself to an uncertain life, God's will, and the promise of paradise, but she found it difficult to accept her loss, "as She was a sweete little Child."[130]

Larkin now had time to make a full report to the Secretary of State. His letter, dated January 14, 1847, included a description of the recent rising and an account of his imprisonment. Larkin also attempted to demonstrate that his perception of California affairs had been proven accurate by recent events. He restated his long-held desire to win over the Californios so they would look on the Americans as friends. He had come close to success, but American officials in California had not always been responsive to his advice. The Bear Flag affair and the harsh treatment by the American officers in charge of the occupation had ended his policy of conciliation. Larkin did not name the guilty parties, but in the case of Los Angeles, he meant Gillespie. Nor did he name Stockton, though he knew that Gillespie's view of the conquest and the occupation mirrored that of the commodore. The war was over, and it was time to look to the future. Indeed, Larkin told Buchanan, Stockton "has now sufficient knowledge of the Californians to regulate the new government . . . ,"[131] a tactful manner of suggesting that Stockton had learned a lesson.

"I shall require some days to be myself again," he told Buchanan, "and shall return to Monterey."[132] He had only to await transportation to his home to see what this new American world had in store for him.

CHAPTER 9

AFTER THE CONQUEST
BUSINESS AND POLITICS

DURING 1846, that important year of the American conquest, Larkin demonstrated ambivalent feelings about the effect of California's Americanization on trade and commerce. While the invasion was imminent, he wrote that he would "as a trader prefer everything as it is."[1] In the immediate aftermath of the invasion he believed that within a year prices would fall dramatically because of the American administration's removal of high tariffs.[2] Yet should the American administration become permanent and California be annexed to the United States, he foresaw that "business will increase astonishingly."[3]

The invasion certainly did nothing to decrease Larkin's own business. Even before the regular forces landed, he had furnished funds and supplies to Frémont in January 1846 to the extent of $3,600.[4] After the July 1846 invasion, he furnished goods and supplies to the American naval ships and to the battalion of volunteers organized by Frémont. The commodity he dealt in most heavily was hardtack, or ship bread, which he delivered to American warships in prodigious quantities. From September 1846 through April 1847, Larkin sold 50,000 pounds of hardtack to the American navy at 12 cents per pound, for a total sale of $6,000.[5]

Larkin contracted the actual making of the ship bread with another firm,[6] and much of it was sold through his old store, now run by Talbot H. Green. The records indicate some confusion as to whether it was Green who was nominally the seller or whether the sales were on a wholesale basis by Larkin. But that confusion is understandable. Although Green had management of the store, Larkin retained his two-thirds interest in its profits of the partnership until the firm was wound up, as previously agreed, on January

1, 1849.[7] In addition to the major sales of hardtack, Green sold daily supplies to the ships.[8] It was easy to do business with the military. As we shall see, the trick was getting paid.

In the fall of 1846, when the Californios went into revolt, Frémont organized a battalion of volunteers and scavenged the countryside for horses, cattle, and supplies of all description. Much was voluntarily given to the military; more was simply seized. In all cases, receipts were given and payment was expected. Merchants provided hardtack, provisions, and a large inventory of supplies to the naval vessels. The problems were, first, that the organization of the volunteer battalion was irregular, and second, that there was so much subsequent controversy as to which military officer should be the governor. In light of that dispute, the commodores and other military officials who arrived later were reluctant to honor the claims made against former commanders.

The result was that few persons were compensated for either their time or their property. Hardest hit were the newly arrived immigrants, who were described by one observer as "in a totally destitute condition."[9] But the merchants were equally hurt. Larkin and Green, and many other merchants, had not only sold goods to the government forces but also had obtained hardtack for cash outlays. Larkin figured that the government owed him $24,000 as of May 1847,[10] but the worst of it was that $8,000 of that figure was for cash he had borrowed and on which he was paying 2% interest per month.[11] When he was able to get some naval bills of exchange, they were offered only at par, and the discount rate in Yerba Buena was 15%–20%.[12]

As a result of this lack of liquidity, business in Monterey came to a standstill in the spring of 1847,[13] and the financing of Larkin's real-estate building projects became increasingly difficult as he was forced to buy supplies and services with goods and hides rather than nonexistent cash.[14] Naturally, Larkin wrote to numerous government officials in Washington and California seeking relief. He became somewhat bitter, writing to Leidesdorff that "the more one assists Government the less thanks they may receive,"[15] and to Stockton that while he was satisfied with the part he had played in the conquest, he had lost considerable earnings and now wished "to turn Merchant, and will prepare myself for business."[16]

Finally, in June 1847, Larkin and Talbot Green reached a settlement with the government for claims in a total of $31,044.29.[17] However, the settlement was not quite final. The claims for goods furnished to the battalion of volunteers under Frémont were not paid by the regular military authorities, and of this $31,044.29, almost one third, or $10,855.16, was represented merely by Frémont's certificate as to goods furnished. This certificate was passed to Larkin when the partnership was dissolved in January 1849 and sent by Larkin to his faithful cousin Rogers for collection.[18] It became part of the California Claims, which were not settled until special legislation of Congress and the report of a commission. The debt of the federal government, incurred in 1846 in the emergency of the Californios' revolt, was not paid until 1855.[19]

Larkin held two official roles in the financing and supplying of the American fleet off California. On August 13, 1846, Commodore Stockton appointed Larkin "Navy Agent for the Territory of California."[20] The navy agent held the responsibility of contracting with suppliers on behalf of the navy for the produce, goods, and other supplies needed in a particular port and which were not to be otherwise procured through the navy's own supply vessels. Doubtless, Larkin saw an opportunity to benefit himself as well as the navy by being in a position to patronize particular sources of supply. But his plans were temporarily thwarted when he was officially informed that Stockton had no authority to appoint an agent. Larkin, however, could continue as a supplier.[21]

This problem was rectified by a Presidental appointment confirmed by the Senate in early spring 1847.[22] Larkin heard of his official appointment in May 1847 and at once wrote the Secretary of the Navy indicating that, while he was entering into his duties immediately, he lacked official instructions as to the conduct of his office.[23] The lack of official instructions meant that Larkin could not know with certainty the proper limits of his official acts. If he overstepped his authority, the government might bring an action against his official bond or deny him compensation. It was a serious problem for Larkin, and his correspondence with the Secretary of the Navy repeatedly stressed his lack of official instructions.[24] He finally received them in late January 1849.[25]

Meanwhile Larkin had received an additional appointment, as navy storekeeper for the port of Monterey, from Commodore Shubrick in September 1847.[26] This post primarily involved the storage of naval property and the sale of condemned or defective goods. Larkin regarded the storekeeper position as one "of much trouble and responsibility," and took it under the express assumption that he would be compensated for it above and apart from the pay for navy agent. If the two posts could not be held by the same person, he made it clear that he preferred the navy agent position.[27]

Larkin's preference probably had much to do with the ability to use the navy agent position to steer lucrative business toward Green's store and toward business associates who would in some ways reciprocate. Then, too, the navy agent compensation was $2,000 per year whereas the storekeeper's pay was only $1,500.[28]

However, the financial aspects of the navy agency should not be overstated. It also offered more personal satisfaction. Larkin wrote his friend, Faxon Dean Atherton, that the appointment as navy agent "pleases me more than anything else. It proved to me my standing in Washington, and how any services of mine have been valued. I look on it as the highest gift of Government that I could receive in California."[29]

Larkin could have hardly been surprised to hear from the Secretary of the Navy that the same person could not hold both offices and, further, that one Charles T. Botts had already been appointed storekeeper and was en-route to California. But he may have been shocked to hear that no compensation could be paid him even for the temporary appointment, although his expenses, including his clerk salary, would be honored.[30] After Botts arrived in California, Larkin turned over the naval stores and sent his final returns as storekeeper in mid-June 1848.[31]

Larkin resigned from his position, formally designated as "Navy Agent for the North West Coast of America," on April 29, 1849, to be effective September 30, 1849. He stated that he desired to return to Massachusetts. However, even in his resignation he was thwarted by the government. He was shortly informed that the President had discontinued the agency as of June 30, 1849.[32]

The discontinuance may have been because of a specific desire on the part of the navy to remove Larkin from the office. Appended to one of Larkin's letters of complaint to the Secretary of the Navy, dated August 16, 1848, was the note, "Remove him. Wm. B. P. Done April 10, 1849."[33] On that very date, April 10, the then Secretary of the Navy, William Ballard Preston, wrote Larkin that the President was discontinuing the agency.[34] By then it could not have mattered much to Larkin. He wrote his friend Atherton in January 1849, "I am still Navy Agent in honor. I only hold it," and indicated that he devoted little time to the post.[35]

Larkin entered into his duties as navy agent on May 4, 1847 (excepting the earlier abortive appointment of Stockton), and as navy storekeeper on September 14, 1847.[36] Soon thereafter evidence appears of various naval goods being delivered to Larkin for storage and, occasionally, instructions to sell condemned products at auction.[37] These tasks would be assigned to Larkin in his capacity as storekeeper. Then, too, there was a steady stream of orders from carpenters, gunners, masters, pursers, and captains of naval vessels, seeking various goods and provisions of all possible descriptions, and asking Larkin as navy agent to arrange for their supply.[38]

Larkin was very busy with these duties piled on top of his own growing real-estate and financial empire. He was also experiencing the frustrations of dealing with the federal bureaucracy. In October 1847, he had rented one of his warehouses to the commander of the naval ship *Erie* for $50 per month; by June 1848, he had increased the storage place rented to the navy and was charging $100 per month. Later, by November, he even rented housing accommodations to a detachment of marines.[39] Larkin was some-how informed that either the navy regulations or statute prevented a naval agent from renting his own property, as this would entail a conflict of interest. Larkin wrote the Secretary of the Navy that he had rented his own warehouses to the government because "there are no other proper ones." The rainy season was beginning, and he would be compelled to use his own buildings. He advised that "there will be in this country constantly something to do . . . that must be done out of the regular way or government property will suffer a loss."[40] He also reiterated, pointedly, that he had not yet received official instructions.

Another snag with government regulations quickly developed. As navy agent, Larkin was obliged to expend considerable sums of money to purchase the goods needed by the navy. He needed to be certain of reimbursement and for a long period, as we have seen, was anxious for official instructions. When they finally arrived, in January 1849, he discovered that before he could write a bill of exchange on the Secretary of the Navy, he had to obtain the permission of the commodore, who was headquartered in San Francisco. That meant the expense of a courier. More important, the rate of interest on money was 2% a month, or 24% per annum, and the delay would be at considerable cost. Equally important, the local government officials in Monterey would not cash his bills drawn on the Secretary of the Navy. If Larkin had expended or was due (for example) $4,000, the only way he could collect would be to draw a bill for $4,000. To avoid the delay of up to a year by sending it to the East for collection, he would have to sell it locally at a heavy discount. "Cannot some available means be found of putting me in funds for the current expenses," he pleaded to the local commodore in February 1849. He even offered to defer his salary to "some future period." Specifically, he asked for immediate payment of expenses due from the past quarter and a prepayment of anticipated expenses through June 1849, all in the amount of $5,000.[41]

No answer was forthcoming. In March 1849, he wrote more pointedly, mentioning that he had already spent a "considerable amount of my own private funds with great inconvenience to myself for the necessary expences of this office." Doubtless he recalled the liquidity crisis of the spring of 1847. Larkin threatened that he could do no more and would be "compelled to suspend all further disbursements, until I am put in funds."[42] That triggered a solution, and within a week the navy had found a way to put $5,000 in gold into Larkin's hands.[43] Even with that gold and the June 30, 1849, termination of his agency, Larkin's entanglements with the federal government were far from over. Wrangles over his accounts continued on for over a year, with the "4th Auditor" reporting a balance owed by Larkin to the navy in the amount of $11,257.30 as late as August 1, 1850.[44]

Certainly most of Larkin's business affairs between the American invasion in July 1846 and his departure for the East in March 1850 concerned either real-estate speculation or mercantile affairs with the federal government's armed forces. In the earlier portion of those years, government affairs were clearly dominant. Larkin complained in October 1846 that it appeared "as if the circumstances of the country will never allow me to attend to my private business."[45] With the uprising in the south and his imprisonment, it only became worse.

In the following year, Larkin was frequently traveling in pursuit of his real-estate adventures. It is an interesting insight into his regard for his wife that Rachel held his cash while he was absent from Monterey.[46] Although he was preoccupied with government and real estate, Larkin still found it possible to conduct some of his other mercantile and financial business during these years. For example, while most of the lumber he acquired in 1847 was used in his own construction projects, Larkin did manage to offer some for wholesale sales.[47] While most of his leasing of buildings was for military use, occasionally there were leases to private individuals.[48] Furthermore, he still at times acted in the capacity of a bank,[49] and kept his hand in collections.[50] Hopefully, Larkin saw irony in his favorable reputation as a collector. Several claims against Frémont were submitted to Larkin for collection at the very time he could not collect his own debt.[51]

One unusual feature of Larkin's commercial experience dealt with wharves. He had built one in Monterey for the Mexican government, probably completing it in 1845.[52] It was not fully paid for at the time of the American invasion, and we shall see that Larkin had a most difficult time in collecting his unpaid compensation from the new American administrators. He formed grand plans to build a wharf for San Francisco. As early as October 1846, he organized a formal company with two partners to build and operate the structure.[53] Although the plans never reached fruition, probably because the military government felt it lacked authority to grant the land needed,[54] more than anything else the idea reflected Larkin's vision of San Francisco's future greatness. Even before the era of San Francisco lot speculation, and long before the Gold Rush, Larkin understood that Monterey was destined to remain a "gentle town," but that San Francisco "will be the busy, bustling uproar of places."[55]

Larkin's commercial activities continued throughout this period as multiple opportunities presented themselves. He noted in August 1847, before the tumult of the Gold Rush, that the commerce of California had trebled since the American takeover.[56] Summing up his commercial activities on the eve of his departure for the East, Larkin wrote out several lists of the current accounts, notes, and other obligations due him as of December 31, 1849. One list was of delinquent bills of exchange, most of them generated in commerce, with some few of them going as far back as 1840. These overdue accounts totalled $21,693.87 1/2.[57] On the other hand, his net worth, estimating real estate at then-current valuation, had risen to $106,732.88.[58] Another field to which Larkin turned, when he retired from the retail business in 1844 and 1845, was the engaging of entire ship cargoes for the California trade. His continued interest in merchandising turned increasingly to wholesale operations, freeing him from the drudgery of the daily routine of retailing.

The earliest of these ventures was a proposal made to a Boston merchant, Benjamin T. Reed, in late 1844 and repeated in 1845. Larkin offered to take a $10,000 interest in goods shipped in the next voyage of Reed's firm, sending around $5,000 in hides to Boston, drawing on funds in his cousin Rogers's hands, and requesting credit necessary for the balance. While this was not to be a full partnership, Larkin went on to suggest the possibilities for the following year of purchasing additional goods in Mexico. He even raised the possibilities of an annual voyage if, as was currently rumored, Appleton & Company retired from the hide and tallow trade.[59] By March 1846, Larkin had learned that Reed had backed out of the proposed voyage, and although Reed offered the hopes of voyages in the future, he became apprehensive because of the hostilities between Mexico and the United States. By October, Reed concluded that "in a state of war as at present it is impossible to say what we shall do."[60]

Larkin had imported large cargoes of merchandise before, but they had been from Mexico or the Sandwich Islands. He was now bargaining for Boston goods, better quality manufactures that would bring a much higher markup. Accordingly, he did not give up easily on the idea of a share of a Boston voyage.

At about the same time as the Reed negotiations, Larkin's cousin Rogers wrote to him of Alpheus Hardy, a "young Merchant of independent property," whom Rogers endorsed as "honest, capable, and competent to furnish the capital." Hardy had proposed that he and Larkin enter into an even more favorable arrangement than that Larkin had foreseen with Reed. Hardy suggested a true joint venture, with each man owning a half interest in two vessels and their cargoes.[61] Larkin responded favorably, agreeing to take a one-third interest in the voyage and offering all sorts of suggestions as to operations, the timing of the departures, a list of items to ship, and even the specific cargo agent who should be employed. The most interesting advice concerned how to drive a hard bargain with the Mexican customs officials. The ship's manifest, Larkin said, should indicate Oregon as the destination, and the ship should come into the Monterey harbor without laying anchor. "As there are many terms and mode of paying the duties, the best bargain is obtained by the authorities, supposing its a chance vessel . . . and therefore can enter or not, as the Supercargo sees fit."[62]

The American invasion had occurred during the time the voyage was under consideration. Larkin immediately suggested that the cargo must "fitt besides the Ranchor both the Emigration and the Squadron," and made detailed suggestions of changes in cargo.[63] He urged that Hardy call on the Secretaries of State, Navy, and Treasury to see if government freights could be procured,[64] and he himself wrote Secretary of State James Buchanan to solicit government shipments.[65] Larkin saw large profits in supplying the government troops and the large migration of 1846, and repeatedly urged speed. "Ask your freind to send out the Vessel you spoke off, and invest all my funds in it," he wrote Rogers in July. A month later he fretted that if

Hardy decided not to send the vessel, "it would be a great loss to me. . . . I want the business began soon as possible. . . . Have this vessel dispatched soon as possible."[66]

But Larkin was to be disappointed in this venture as much as in that proposed with Reed. Larkin's plans for multiple vessels were too ambitious for Hardy, and whereas Larkin saw the war as an opportunity to sell to the troops, Hardy saw it as an interruption. The hope was raised of a venture of reduced size and a single vessel, but apparently nothing came of it.[67] But in June 1846, an American bark from Salem, Massachusetts, that had been trading in Hawaii arrived in Monterey with a $10,000 cargo consisting of domestic goods, iron, soap, and sugar.[68] And it was for sale as a lot.

Larkin seized the opportunity and, in his words, "purchased the first cargo of goods ever sold at one time in California."[69] The credit arrangements showed Larkin at his financial best. The $10,000 purchase price was paid for by a $2,000 bill of exchange, a note for $4,000 to be paid the following year in Massachusetts, and $4,000 in value of Larkin's own lumber, shingles, and soap. Of course, this $4,000 would be at retail prices, including markup. Larkin purchased the lumber through retail sales to sawyers and soapmakers, with a separate markup and profit. Thus a double retail profit was built into the $4,000, and the true "cost" to Larkin of this was probably as low as $1,000 or $2,000. Then, of course, there were duties to be paid, $18,000 in all. But here, too, Larkin struck a remarkable deal with the military general, José Castro, perhaps because Castro was under the pressure of the opening phases of the Bear Flag Revolt. Larkin paid only $2,000 in cash, $8,000 in goods, and $8,000 in government paper, the last being only the cancellation of indebtedness owed him by the California government. This special treatment so outraged the regular administrator of customs that he refused to give his receipts and release for the cargo until he was pressured by General Castro.[70]

Larkin wrung still more savings out of the customs payment. Before buying the cargo, Larkin scouted about for obligations owing from the departmental government that he could buy from towns and individuals for 50% on the peso. He paid for these government notes by goods that also had a markup built into them.[71] In this way, Larkin's actual "cost" for the customs payment was far less than the stated $18,000.

During late 1846 and 1847, as the American occupation became firmer and more settled, Larkin laid numerous plans and received many offers for joint cargo ventures.[72] Larkin even thought of personally going to Boston and supervising an operation in which two vessels, at a cost of $20,000 apiece, would be purchased and outfitted with cargoes worth $35,000 each.[73] Although Larkin certainly succeeded in some modest ventures during this period,[74] he was unsuccessful in organizing any larger-scale joint cargo voyages in 1846 or 1847. His correspondence suggests two reasons for this. One was the inability of the naval commodores in California to commit for purchases because of ignorance of what their own supply ships would bring.[75] The other was the great difficulty Larkin had in obtaining his compensation from the navy, leaving him without funds with which to buy cargoes in foreign ports.[76] Probably the general uncertainty of wartime, particularly for Easterners unfamiliar with the realities of California conditions, added to the difficulties.

All this quickly changed with the coming of the Gold Rush in the summer of 1848, following closely on the heels of peace with Mexico. Larkin anticipated the influx of many persons into California as a result of the major gold discoveries, and their demands for clothing, food, and mining supplies. He sought to meet the demand as a wholesaler. On August 15, 1848, Larkin chartered the ship *Mary* at $500 per month, and later in the same month he and Job Dye agreed on a joint venture whereby they would each invest $4,000. Dye would accompany the ship to Mazatlán, buy goods, and return to San Francisco, where the cargo would be sold for cash.[77] Talbot Green then put in $5,000, making the total investment $13,000.

The returns were phenomenal. Larkin was able to sell a one-third interest in the cargo for $9,000 even before Dye had arrived in San Francisco and sold a second one-third shortly after his arrival. Dye sold the remaining one-third interest within days. By the end of December 1849, Larkin and his partners had realized $28,000 upon an investment of $13,000 made only four months earlier.[78] Larkin rushed to repeat this, sending Dye back to Mexico almost immediately, this time with a capital of $24,000, two-thirds of which was furnished by Larkin, and with an authorization to buy even more goods on credit (forbidden in the first contract), up to an additional $10,000.[79]

As a variation on these and other joint voyages of importation, Larkin also purchased entire cargoes after their arrival in California. In January 1849, he and Albert Packard jointly purchased the cargo of the Peruvian ship *Galga*, and agreed that Packard would earn $300 per month for selling the merchandise along the coastal communities of southern California.[80] Rates had increased with the fever of the Gold Rush. Larkin gave his promissory note for $19,281.57 for his half of the cargo, and the charter rate for the ship was now $500 *per week* (compared to $500 *per month* for the *Mary* in August), plus a freight rate on unsold cargo on the return from San Diego.[81]

Larkin's most wide-ranging venture came with the purchase of the ship *Eveline* and its dispatch to China to purchase goods for California. Characteristically, he operated with an active partner, Larkin remaining the financier and guiding spirit. Larkin and Jacob P. Leese purchased the ship in January 1849, each investing 1,500 "troy ounces of placer gold," or about $24,000 apiece, in the voyage. The unit of value, placer gold, reflects the Gold Rush times. Leese was to proceed to China, and was authorized to obtain additional goods on credit up to $30,000. For Leese's personal efforts, he received an additional $300 per month, but otherwise the two men were at equal risk and profit.[82]

Later the military governor of California, Richard B. Mason, speculated $8,000 on the voyage,[83] bringing the cargo investment up to around $53,000. Since Leese and Larkin had paid $15,000 for the vessel itself,[84] the total investment in the voyage was approximately $68,000, just short of a million 1990 dollars. Larkin soon found that there were risks in a venture of this scale. In June 1849, Talbot H. Green advised him from San Francisco that times there were "very dull . . . lots of goods but no buyers." More alarmingly, there were five ships in the harbor from China, with eight more on the way. Green could only suggest that Larkin send the *Eveline* to Monterey and further down the coast, "as this market [i.e., San Francisco] is completely overdone here in Canton goods for now and six months to come."[85] The voyage made only a very modest profit.[86]

It was a wildly profitable and exciting time, yet the risks and consequent pressures were immense. Larkin best described his own state of mind, his worries and concerns, in a January 1849 letter to his good friend Faxon Dean Atherton:

> My head whirls with speculation; my hair grows grey by the excessive working of my brain, and ambition. . . . One hundred and fifty cargoes will come here by 1850. Many will sell at a loss. Many will make. . . . Scores of traders will fall by fire and bad management. I do not except myself.[87]

It had been on January 24, 1848, that James W. Marshall had spotted the yellow flecks in the South Fork of the American River that were so soon to transform California. The original discoverers managed to keep their discovery a secret for a few months, but by May rumors were circulating throughout northern California. Larkin at first placed little faith in the reports, thinking they were true but exaggerated. Yet as early as 1846 he had declared that there was "no doubt in my mind but that gold . . . mines are to be found all over California,"[88] and in May 1848, he regarded it as "not at all un-natural" that gold should be found in moderate quantities in some parts of California.[89]

On May 24, 1848, Larkin set off from Monterey to San Francisco to settle the estate of William Leidesdorff, recently deceased. He then planned to visit his ranches in the Central Valley.[90] Enroute he passed through San Jose, and there encountered the full force of the Gold Rush. "Every body is in the greatest state of excitement," he reported to the military governor; "we can hear of nothing but Gold, Gold, Gold."[91] Larkin was still not a believer, and lamented the virtual depopulation of towns as workmen simply dropped their tools and struck off for the gold fields.

Larkin pushed on to San Francisco. There he encountered a reality that could no longer be denied: abandoned stores and offices, written accounts of men who had made thousands of dollars in mining, and runaway inflation.

In spirit ever the merchant, he carefully noted the fantastic prices being obtained for shovels and spades. Larkin wrote the Secretary of State on the first of June, detailing "one of the most astonishing excitements and state of affairs now existing in this country that perhaps has ever been brought to the notice of the Government," and promised that he would report further after visiting the mining areas.[92]

Larkin visited the gold country and, on June 28, 1848, he wrote that it was "all I had heard and much more than I anticipated." He personally saw men bring to their tents $50, $64, and $82 daily proceeds. Laborers in the East then earned around $1 to $2 per day. He estimated that one thousand men were then mining, but he predicted that soon California would be swamped with immigrants. And chaos was also coming to California. "Three fourths of the houses in . . . San Francisco are deserted. . . . Every blacksmith, carpenter and lawyer are leaving. Brick yards, sawmills and ranches are left perfectly alone. . . . A complete revolution in the ordinary state of affairs is taking place."[93]

In July, Larkin wrote the Secretary of State a third time, underscoring the tremendous implications. Gold was now being extracted at about $500,000 per month. Towns were empty, troops and sailors had deserted. "A few men who are working 30 or 40 Indians are laying up 1000 $ to 2000 $ a week. . . . None of these men had any property of consequence to commence with. . . . How it will end I know not. The future consequence or prospect is not pleasant nor moral."[94] By July 15, 1848, for lack of servants, the governor of California, the mayor of Monterey, and a commander of a man-of-war had come together in a single house and were reduced to cooking their own meals, "grinding coffee, toasting a herring, and pealing onions."[95]

The Gold Rush would have occurred, Larkin or no Larkin. Still, his letters from early and late June to eastern correspondents helped greatly to trigger the intense interest. Ebenezer Childs wrote Larkin on September 27 that "your letters & those of others have been running thro' the papers all over the country, creating wonder and amazement in every mind."[96]

The most immediate impact of the Gold Rush upon Larkin, individually, was that his employees quit to make their fortunes in the mines. It was a common enough experience in Gold Rush California, but Larkin handled it far differently than did most employers. He learned in May 1848 that John S. Williams, the foreman of his Children's Rancho in Colusa, was quitting,[97] and he lost his Monterey clerk, Charles B. Sterling, in June.[98] Larkin made the best of their desires to become rich by staking them with supplies and becoming their silent partner.

A company was first organized between Larkin, John S. Williams, and his brother James. In June, Sterling joined the company by a contract with Larkin whereby Larkin agreed to continue Sterling's salary at the annual rate of $500 for the next six months plus 6% of the gold recovered plus

10% of the gross sales of merchandise. The plan was that they would mine for gold, utilizing the Indians on Larkin's ranch, and that Larkin would furnish supplies and goods for their use and for sale to others.[99]

Larkin immediately ordered goods from Moses Schallenberger in Monterey for shipment to the Williams and Sterling party and for sale to the miners, white and Indian.[100] Schallenberger took merchandise to the Williams and Sterling group, but apparently he was also mining for Larkin. At the outset, therefore, there may have been two companies with which Larkin was involved.[101]

The early reports were very favorable, particularly on the mining side of the ventures. Williams and Sterling claimed they were averaging $500 per day in mid-August 1848, and had accumulated $10,000 according to the report of Schallenberger.[102] But Williams quickly disclaimed that the report was exaggerated. At one time, he wrote, they had mined $600 or $700 in gold daily, but by September they were barely making expenses.[103]

As the true state of affairs was revealed, it became apparent that just about everything that could go wrong had done so. With money to be made so quickly and easily, Schallenberger had foreseen that "our men will all leave us as soon as they arrive."[104] And as predicted, the partners of the companies steadily quit and reformed into different groupings with two additional men. In September, Larkin tried to hold his people together with a new agreement embracing everyone, including the newcomers, but apparently that was unsuccessful, and the Williams and Sterling group split into two groups.[105]

Illness was rampant and debilitating.[106] The Indians ran away,[107] and for a time the company members did the "killing work" alone. Sterling reported that they "worked like *horses* every one of us."[108] There was also squabbling among the remaining members of the company.[109] Larkin's loyal partner, Talbot H. Green, was dispatched to the gold regions to investigate. He reported to Larkin that he did not think "they are doing much. I dont think they pull well together but I suppose they will pay something."[110]

Green's supposition was quite accurate. By the end of November the mining had been abandoned for the season.[111] Soon thereafter Larkin settled with Williams and received as his share of the mining venture the sum of $5,000 plus a balance to come of under $500. But $3,333 was a return of capital, so that the actual profits were only around $2,200.[112] Additionally, there is indication that Larkin may have earlier received some small amount on account.[113] A total of (say) $3,200 was hardly close to the staggering sums made by some of the early miners. However, in his settlement with Williams, Larkin sold his livestock and leased his Colusa ranch for $10,000, half in cash.[114] The livestock and mining potential of the ranch had grown enormously. But Larkin's greatest profits from the Gold Rush were from his joint cargo ventures and the huge profits in San Francisco realty. His direct returns from mining were the mere "something" that Green had supposed.

By January 1849, Larkin had soured on the mining prospects. He thought of the thousands pouring into California, and who would be engaged in the gold diggings as soon as winter passed. "Hunger, sickness and misery," he predicted, "will be the fate of thousands of diggers."[115] This conclusion was not based solely on his experience with Williams and Sterling. On the two occasions he had himself visited the mines, he had taken ill.[116]

As the many business opportunities in the years 1846 to 1850 presented challenges to Larkin, so, too, did the twists and turns of politics. Shortly after the January 1847 suppression of the Californios' revolt, Commodore Stockton appointed a legislative council. Larkin was included among seven older residents, including four natives, for a two year term at a salary of $2,000 per year. Larkin accepted the post but planned to give up the position within a few months. His motive for serving was not financial. As Larkin explained to Mariano G. Vallejo in urging him to accept his own appointment, "if money was my object I would not act as one of the Legislature for $1000 per month as time is now very valuable to me."[117]

The council was scheduled to meet in March in Los Angeles, but it never did so due to the squabbles among the different American military officers as to who should be governor. Larkin did not even appear for the session, so convinced was he that it would not be recognized as valid. Some criticized him for this refusal to attend.[118] The planned meeting came while Larkin was experiencing the sharp liquidity crisis caused by the failure of the government to honor the obligations incurred by Frémont and the commanding officers of the original invasion. Probably at least part of his reluctance stemmed from the feeling he expressed in April that he was not "so much of a Govmt. man now as I was."[119] He was, however, commonly regarded as having influence in the early military governments, and he occasionally received letters seeking his patronage in appointments.[120]

Larkin was at his political best in the early phase of American occupation in matters of local concern. During the Mexican administration he had been a booster of local civic affairs and had regularly supported subscriptions to promote hospitals, schools, and newspapers. We have already seen Larkin's efforts to engage an eastern schoolteacher to come to Monterey. When those failed, he turned to John Bidwell in an unsuccesful effort to interest him in becoming Monterey's schoolmaster.[121] In the spring of 1846, just before the war, Larkin was still attempting to recruit local supporters for a school.[122]

Immediately after the American invasion, the *very next day*, Larkin attempted to induce Commodore Sloat to establish a school. He claimed that education was of such primary importance to California that the establishment of a Monterey school ought to be the first act of American administration. It would show "not only to the men of the Country, but even to the Mothers & children, that our Government seeks their welfare, and intend that even the youngest in the land shall immediately experience a benefit from the change of flags." He offered to raise private subscriptions for the schoolmaster's salary in the event that the commodore did not feel justified in the expenditure of public funds.[123]

All this activity was not undertaken without Larkin's own self-interest in mind, as he had young children at home in need of primary education. Nevertheless, the idea that the first political appointment of an American administration should be a schoolmaster was a good one. Although it was ignored, it would have been a noble gesture.

Larkin did not have to wait much longer. During the winter of 1846–47 an American overland emigrant, Mrs. Olive Isbell, had conducted some very informal classes for children in the Mission Santa Clara. The news of this spread, and when Mrs. Isbell and her husband traveled to Monterey to purchase oxen, she was met by Larkin and two other gentlemen. After much urging she agreed to conduct the first American school in California. Supported by private subscriptions, it was opened in a room in the custom house. Larkin not only subscribed, but provided books left by a vessel and also furnished paper and pencils without charge.[124]

As early as May 1846, Larkin had foreseen that with the "whilwind and political Vortex" caused by an Americanization of California, his own "character now fair, my name now unknown, my movments motives and prospects now blest, may be assailed by the firce partys of the day or demagoug of the times." He had asked his eastern newspaper correspondent, James Gordon Bennett of the *New York Herald*, for help if that came to pass.[125] As Larkin predicted, it did.

On September 13, 1846, the *St. Louis Daily Reveille* charged that there was but one opinion in California regarding Larkin, and that was one "declaring him a vagabond." It then reprinted a letter purportedly datelined New Helvetia, April 2, 1846, over the signature of John Armstrong. In sharply bitter tone Armstrong charged, among other things, that Larkin was chiefly responsible for the expulsion of foreigners in the Graham Affair in 1840 and that he forced Americans to buy passports from him. Armstrong continued with these remarkably false statements: "This man is bitter enemy to all Americans. How can he be otherwise, when he is and has been a Mexican citizen for years?"[126]

The letter was widely reprinted in midwestern and eastern newspapers. William Rogers sent Larkin a copy of the reprinted attack from the *Boston Post*, together with a retraction the editor later ran after an interview with Rogers.[127] Ebenezer Childs also sent clippings, and indicated that he had sent information in refutation to St. Louis. He also offered two consolations. The first was his own opinion that the article bore on its face such "bitter malignity & hate" that it wouldn't be believed. The second was more practical: he had checked with the State Department and it regarded the matter lightly. Newspaper complaints against American consuls were common, there were no complaints on file against Larkin, and the Department would not bother to retain a copy of the article.[128]

Larkin took all this seriously, however. "From all the long tongues and big tongues, I get it in every shape," he wrote. "I have seen a letter from Semple, in a home paper trying to prove I keep down all patriotism in California." This letter apparently appeared entirely independently of the *Reveille* story. Larkin noted that there were "other letters, printed and original, condemning me and my views in every way."[129]

He solicited and received letters of commendation from men who were in a position to—and did—specifically refute the charges: John Bidwell, a highly regarded emigrant from 1841, and Juan Bautista Alvarado, the former governor who had ordered the Graham expulsion.[130] He obtained a letter from a more recent immigrant, Lewis Dent, a lawyer in Monterey, who elaborated on the inquiries he had made about Larkin in California and the favorable reputation Larkin enjoyed.[131] Larkin sent published documentary evidence to Semple and asked for a retraction and also a comment on the *Reveille* letter. Semple retracted the letter, acknowleged his errors, and sent a testimonial.[132]

During the middle of this gathering of evidence, Larkin received a dispatch from the State Department containing words of praise. He rushed almost immediately to advise the Secretary that he was "extremely gratified" by his kind mention of Larkin's services. He wrote Buchanan that the St. Louis newspapers, which had also reprinted the Semple attack, had defamed him "in a higher degree than in general falls to the lot of one man to receive from one newspaper," and promised that he would soon send his cousin Childs "refutation of the whole."[133]

Larkin sent his letters of "refutation" to Childs on June 1; Childs then sent copies to Rogers in Boston, the *New York Herald*, and the *St. Louis Reveille*. But Childs and Rogers thought it best not to publish the evidence unless there were further attacks, as the original publication had caused no harm and by summer had been forgotten.[134]

It is an interesting question who made the attacks. Both Bidwell and Semple, in their letters of commendation, had mentioned that they had never heard of John Armstrong, the purported writer. Yet there was a John Armstrong who apparently arrived in California in 1840.[135] He had arrived just in time to be arrested, have his property seized, and be shipped to Mexico in the Graham Affair.[136] The letter published in the *Reveille* is much concerned with Larkin's role in this affair, and we have already seen that many of the lower classes who were involved in that matter were bitter towards Larkin. Undoubtedly, this was the same John Armstrong.

Some of the charges concerned events that occurred before Armstrong's arrival in California, and he must have picked those up from other sources. Some are twisted half truths. One of the most interesting accusations was that Larkin had seduced the wife of a "Capt. Combs" while on shipboard from Boston, and that Larkin was lucky her husband had died before they arrived. That, of course, is a distorted version of his affair in 1832 with Mrs. Holmes. It suggests that rumors of that affair must have been carried for a long time in the mind of someone who later told the story to Armstrong, who in fact arrived much later, in 1840.

On August 12, 1845, Henry Peirce, a merchant who had both a long-running dispute over accounts with Larkin and ties to California predating Larkin's arrival, demanded payment from Larkin in strident terms. He threatened that "a loss of your office is a consequence which ought to follow any refusal to comply with my just demand."[137] Subsequently, in 1846, someone sent a copy of the *Reveille* article to the State Department.[138] There is no specific evidence that it was Peirce, but it is interesting that the Armstrong letter demanded Larkin's ouster from office. Later, in 1848, John C. Frémont resigned from the army following his courtmartial and attempted to oust Larkin from his naval agency on grounds that probably had similarity to the Armstrong allegations. James Buchanan wrote Frémont that "the President does not think that any sufficient reason exists for the removal of Mr. Larkin as Navy Agent at Monterey. The allegations against him have not yet assumed any authentic form."[139] There is little question that Larkin had enemies.

By 1849, the war with Mexico was long over, yet Congress had failed to establish a territorial government for California because of an inability to resolve the issue of slavery in the new territory. Responding to overwhelming popular sentiment and pressures, the last military governor, Bennett Riley, issued a call for elections for delegates to a convention to determine a form of government for the province.

Several Americans whose presence in California predated the war sought to interest Larkin in running for political office in the new territory or state that the convention would form. "All the old settlers are anxious that their own people should represent them," wrote Jacob Snyder from Sacramento. "We have been talking of you. Will you accept of office. . . . It is necessary for us to be united."[140] But Larkin was much too busy with his trading and real-estate empires, and he had finally formulated some rather definite plans to return to the East. Perhaps, too, he recalled the bitterness of the criticism he had endured at the hands of the lower classes and had no taste for a repeat. In any event, he was not interested in elective office.

He was, however, elected as a delegate to what became a statehood constitutional convention; it opened its deliberations in September 1849 in Monterey. By then the historic Hispanic capital was a small town alongside the metropolis of San Francisco or even as compared with Sacramento or Los Angeles. This would be Monterey's last moment as a center of statewide government. Larkin's overt participation in the convention was slender. The official records demonstrate that he rarely spoke in the debates and that he voted with the majority.[141] Yet another delegate, Elisha O. Crosby, who recalled that Larkin had "a good deal of character and ability," remembered Larkin as "an honest man" who had made many suggestions on commercial matters.[142]

Larkin's influence at the convention was indirect and, as in the years before, he exercised it through hospitality. Crosby wrote that Larkin was very hospitable throughout the convention, which met from September to October. Every day he entertained delegates at lunch and dinner. He kept an open house and always set his table for eight or ten extra places.[143] In a real sense that was fitting. As the convention was the twilight of Monterey's dominance in California, so was it also the twilight of Larkin's own occupation of the Larkin House. Soon the capital would be changed, and Larkin would sell his house to another. Monterey would belong to the past, both for California and for Larkin.

CHAPTER 10

LAND SPECULATION AND RANCHING

By the late 1840s, the hide business was dying. The staple of California commerce, cowhides, had sold in Boston in 1843 for as much as thirteen cents per pound. At the end of 1848, they were quoted on the east coast as low as seven-and-a-half cents. There were few buyers.[1]

The fate of the hide and tallow trade is symbolic. As the Mexican government of California was replaced by an American government, the economy changed dramatically. The California economy, based on cattle, quickly gave way to farming and land speculation. It was the latter that increasingly occupied Larkin following the end of the war, and soon became his obsession.

The war between the United States and Mexico did not officially end until the signing of the Treaty of Guadalupe Hidalgo on February 2, 1848. California's separate war ended with the Treaty of Cahuenga, signed in January 1847. The changes wrought by the American victory began in California while the other war continued fitfully in Mexico. In Larkin's view, California was about to become "Yankefied."[2]

Awaiting transportation from Los Angeles to Monterey following the signing of the Treaty of Cahuenga, Larkin wrote to Rachel to tell her about his appointment to Stockton's legislative council and to reassure her that he was safe and his health was improving. In the letter he enclosed a present, a gold chain. He also had a dozen oranges, rare luxuries in Monterey, that he had wanted to send along for Caroline, Francis, and her—"Alas, poor Adeline," he wrote, remembering his dead child—but he decided that they might not reach them.[3] Before sailing, he wrote to Abel Stearns to ask

176

him to buy $10 or $12 worth of oranges for Rachel, and told him that he would likely see him in early March when he returned for the council meeting.[4] As we have seen, the council was in trouble from the start and never met.

When the *Cyane* dropped anchor in Monterey Bay on February 8, 1847, Larkin was welcomed warmly by Americans and Californios alike.[5] Kearny was a part of Larkin's homecoming, since the general moved immediately into his house and established his headquarters there. Larkin had undoubtedly offered his home; there were no other suitable quarters in Monterey. The general paid board, but Larkin would soon regret the arrangement.[6] Other officers, including Richard B. Mason, were also billeted on the grounds. A young lieutenant, William Tecumseh Sherman, lived in a small adobe behind Larkin's house. When Kearny left Monterey in May, Sherman occupied the general's office briefly.[7]

On February 10, just two days after his return to Monterey, Larkin wrote an open letter to the editors of the Monterey *Californian*, publicly expressing his thanks for kindnesses received during his captivity at Santa Barbara and Los Angeles. Among those specifically named were Nicholas A. Den, José Antonio Carrillo, José María Flores and his wife, Eulogio de Célis, Luisa Zamorano, Richard S. Den, and Jean Louis Vignes. The letter was published in the February 13, 1847, issue of the newspaper.[8]

Larkin recovered from his ordeal quickly. On February 16, the last night of carnival, he hosted a grand ball. The guests included Commodore William Shubrick, who had relieved Stockton on January 22, the French consul, about thirty army and navy officers, and most of the leading Californios. The correspondent for the *Californian*, Walter Colton, was especially impressed by the excellent supper and the large number of beautiful women.[9] There, he said, "I left the youth, the beauty, the wisdom, and worth of Monterey. There are more happy hearts there than I have met with in any other assemblage since I came to California. This is the sunshine that has followed the war-cloud."[10] Larkin would have been pleased with the tribute, for he loved a good party.

Larkin had been little involved in the controversy for supremacy among Kearny, Stockton, and Frémont. He observed later that "it appears as if there had been too many commanders among us. Give each a little praise and some blame, and you have our confused situation."[11] On occasion, he had expressed support for both Stockton and Frémont, but he still had his differences with Frémont: "He did refuse Gen. Kearney's orders, and for a long time, against orders kept in force the Battalion."[12] Larkin believed, nevertheless, that the policy of reconciliation advanced by Frémont and Stockton offered the best course for California.[13] With Commodore Shubrick's arrival, the controversy ended quietly. Kearny and a reluctant Frémont left Monterey on May 31 for an overland journey to the East. En route, the general placed Frémont under arrest. The "Pathfinder" would eventually be tried and convicted for mutiny and insubordination.

Larkin's official status did not end with the cessation of local hostilities. Buchanan notified him in January that he would remain the President's confidential agent until the signing of a peace treaty with Mexico. Larkin was relieved also to read the secretary's assurance, in response to Larkin's repeated entreaty, that the President had no intention of agreeing to any terms with Mexico that included the loss of California.[14]

Larkin now had time to think about his personal and commercial affairs. As we saw in the last chapter, he discovered at once that the government was not going to be eager to pay his claims for services and goods provided to Frémont, Sloat, Stockton, and the fleet in general. His attempt to collect compensation for government use of his wharf at Monterey is illustrative.

Larkin built the wharf in 1845 under contract with the Mexican administrator of the customhouse. It was commandeered the following year by American forces. Beginning in March 1847, Larkin sought either to sell the wharf to the government or to have it returned to his control, in which case he would bill the United States for its use.[15] For weeks he found no satisfaction, as officers of the army and navy pled a lack of need or authority. Commodore James Biddle, who succeeded Shubrick, suggested that he contact the army, which probably would need a wharf.[16]

Larkin must have cringed; it was General Kearny who had suggested that he see Biddle. The commodore was unmoved by Larkin's argument that his predecessors had promised that the navy would either purchase the wharf or pay for its use.[17] Larkin then sent his bill for wharfage to Commodore Stockton at San Diego.[18] No relief came from that quarter, and one can understand Larkin's lament to a friend that "Unkle Sam's Navy have taken possession of my wharf, and his Army my table and house."[19]

Larkin's claim was finally taken up by the army. Major Thomas Swords of the quartermaster's office in Monterey rejected Larkin's declared cost of $8,200.62 as excessive. Therefore, the army would not pay the claimed balance of $4,059. Swords declared that the army would have to determine the correct amount due; meanwhile, the wharf would be retained as public property.[20] Larkin must have been caught between rage and despair. He wrote a stern letter to Swords, reminding him that General Kearny had agreed to pay the amount claimed, and that Swords knew it. Larkin's even temperament and diplomatic nature apparently got the better of his temper. He reflected on the severe tone of the letter, and it appears that it was not sent.[21] An accommodation was eventually made, and the army agreed to Larkin's claim. Payment was to be made from fees paid for use of the wharf by all ships except United States warships. The agreement, which also obligated the army to maintain the wharf, was dated May 7, 1847.[22]

The agreement did not prevent Larkin from complaining later to the quartermaster that the wharf was in danger of falling to pieces from want of repair.[23] Ever the watchful businessman, Larkin was concerned that he might be forced someday to reclaim the property if the army did not complete the promised payment. Jacob P. Leese later bought Larkin's interest in the wharf and had the same trouble with government bureaucracy.[24]

The wharf imbroglio was one of many. Larkin's frustrations in collecting this and other claims that had arisen during the war increasingly distressed him. He reflected on the years when his prosperity was often tied to governments, first Mexican, now American, and concluded that he should divorce himself from bureaucratic entanglements. His growing resentment of a government and a public that did not acknowledge his contributions led him eventually to welcome the end of his official appointments. He had long complained of the losses he had sustained while in government service, and he knew what he would do. "I now return to what I came from—commerce." Resolved that President Polk himself could not persuade him otherwise,[25] he committed himself once again to the pursuit that brought him to California fifteen years before: becoming rich.

Larkin's principal means toward that end was to be land speculation. He was convinced that land was the path to riches in the new American California. By 1847, he was styling himself "a dealer in real estate,"[26] but his interest in California land was much older. In 1842, writing to Faxon Dean Atherton in the aftermath of Commodore Jones's brief occupation of Monterey, Larkin had speculated on the potential economic benefits of an American presence in California. He was most enthusiastic about the effect on real estate: "Farms now worth 1000$ might be worth from 20 to 100,000$."[27] Larkin's earliest real-estate ventures were in Monterey house lots, and he soon began buying and selling lots in San Francisco as well. By the spring of 1847, when his San Francisco speculation had increased to the point that he needed local representation, he appointed William A. Leidesdorff his agent.[28] In succeeding years, he bought and sold lots in Sacramento, Vallejo, Colusa, and Sonoma. He also erected buildings for sale or rent.

Like other speculators in California land during the transition from Mexican to American sovereignty, Larkin acquired some properties with clouded titles. The government of Pío Pico made a number of grants and sales in 1846 which would come under official American scrutiny later to determine the legality of the conveyances. The grant of Punta de Lobos, a two-league tract that encompassed the San Francisco presidio and Mission Dolores, to Benito Díaz, once collector of customs at Santa Barbara and San Francisco, on June 25, 1846, was one of these. Three months following the date of the grant, Larkin bought Punta de Lobos from Díaz for $1,000 and asked Leidesdorff to manage the property for him.[29]

Squatters and scavangers were a common problem for land claimants during the unsettled transition from Mexican to American rule, and Larkin's claim was no exception. Scavengers carried away fencing, tiles, and adobes from abandoned buildings. Others removed timber and collected ballast for their ships. Larkin instructed Leidesdorff and subsequent agents to secure payment for the materials.[30] The amount was of no importance. Any payment would be evidence of a recognition of Larkin's rights in the property. Looking forward to the inevitable battle over title confirmation, he clearly wanted to demonstrate ownership and control of the tract.

Larkin's claim was also challenged by the United States Army. Troops occupied the old presidio and began to repair buildings, using materials from other structures that they demolished. Larkin wrote a severe letter to Governor Mason, protesting the army's use of his property without paying him for the privilege,[31] but the army was not impressed. Larkin expected nothing less; he was not naïve and knew that his claim to the Punta de Lobos tract was questionable. He confided to a correspondent that the "Govt. of California one month before the flag was changed, granted this land (two leagues) to a Californian, who sold it to me. This may prove not right." Nevertheless, he would persevere: "If it's good, its value can not be named."[32] Larkin tended toward conservatism in his business affairs, but he was willing to gamble when the potential benefit was great and the risk bearable.

Another property whose title was tangled in controversy was the orchard of the old Mission Santa Clara, near present-day San José. Larkin purchased the orchard early in 1847 for $1,000 from Benito Díaz, the same who had sold him Punta de Lobos, and Juan Castañeda. The two, with Luis Arenas, had paid Governor Pío Pico $1,200 for it the year before.[33]

Padre José María Real, who was in charge of the mission, protested Larkin's claim as an abuse of the Indians' interest in the property. This was not Larkin's first brush with the padre. He had had some sort of trade with Real at Mission Santa Clara as early as 1844 that was not entirely amicable.[34] As sparks continued to fly, Larkin was forced to press his case with the American authorities who had given Real custody of the mission. Real was the winner. The original sale to Díaz, Castañeda, and Arenas was declared fraudulent, and Larkin was denied possession.[35]

In addition to his purchase of the Mission Santa Clara orchard, Larkin bought the orchard of the ex-Mission San José de Guadalupe, located about fifteen miles northeast of the pueblo of San José, for which he paid Díaz and Castañeda $1,000.[36] Real, who was also the custodian of Mission San José, did not immediately try to prevent Larkin's taking possession, but he promised to dispute his right to the property.[37]

The Mission San José de Guadalupe figures mysteriously in the relations between Larkin and Frémont. Edward M. Kern, one of Frémont's lieutenants, visited the mission on a February day in 1846[38] and would have told Frémont about its rich lands when the two met that same day. Frémont visited the mission in September and wrote from there to Larkin, telling him that he had "examined carefully the business of which we were speaking, approve your intentions, and enter into the agreement with you accordingly."[39] The subject of this cryptic comment is not known. Had Larkin specifically offered to buy Mission San Jose lands for Frémont?

Frémont certainly was impressed with the property: "This is a pretty place, this mission." He commented on the "gardens or orchards" and the rich land surrounding the mission.[40] Larkin later did purchase land for Frémont, and though the desired property was not identified, it was not what Frémont had requested. That the anticipated land was the Mission San José orchard is supported by Jessie Benton Frémont's anger on learning that Larkin had a claim on it.[41]

To further cloud the Larkin-Frémont arrangement, one might consider the letter written by Frémont in October 1847 to Pierson B. Reading, asking him to buy property for him. "*Las Pulgas* on the [western shore of San Francisco] bay, between Sanchez' rancho, & Santa Clara was for sale at two thousand dollars. I wanted Larkin to get it for me but for some reason he did not."[42] It is likely that Frémont had asked Larkin to purchase more than one property for him, a mission property and a rancho.

Larkin, in fact, made only one purchase for Frémont, Las Mariposas near Yosemite, in early 1847. Originally granted to Juan B. Alvarado, the property was a "floating grant" with no fixed boundaries. Larkin paid the ex-governor $3,000 for the ten-league property and charged Frémont 7 1/2 percent commission.[43] The Frémonts were perplexed and angry at Larkin for substituting the apparently worthless foothill grant for another property that they had requested. They were pacified the following year when gold was discovered on the tract.

In June 1847, Larkin leased the Mission San Jose property to James F. Reed. Larkin likely had met him at Sutter's Fort the previous October when Reed stumbled in to beg supplies for the Donner party. The lease required no payment from Reed other than his attention to repairing the buildings and walls and the cutting and pruning necessary to put the vineyard and orchard in good condition.[44] Larkin's object was to show occupation, or perhaps to get the place ready for sale. Reed had things in order shortly, for in October Sutter inquired whether he might get some saplings and vines from Larkin's mission garden.[45]

The disposition of the San Jose orchard is uncertain. Though his title to the property was at best questionable, it seems that Larkin eventually sold it to Andrés Pico, who wanted it to complement other holdings in the vicinity.[46]

Larkin's arrangement with his mission tenant was typical of the techniques he employed in his land business. He was neither orchardist nor a viticulturist. For the most part, he was not a farmer or rancher, though he would conduct some farming and stock-raising operations. He customarily settled reliable people on his properties to show occupation, put them in good order, and discourage squatters. He knew that the Mexican land laws of 1824 and 1828 required that land grants be occupied and improved, and further, that land titles would be scrutinized by the courts following the conquest. Larkin's arrangements with his lessees, usually favorable to them, were also designed to make the properties more attractive to prospective buyers.

When occupation or sale was not soon contemplated, Larkin still looked to the future. His instruction to an agent who had notified him that men were encroaching on his land was typical: " [If] any brickmakers wish to make brick on my land, I wish you would make a written contract with them in my name, obtaining as near five per cent for clay and firewood as you can. The chief object is to hold my right."[47] This attitude set the tone for his land speculations.

Larkin acquired his first large rancho before the conquest. Unlike many of his expatriate friends, he could not apply for a land grant since he was not a Mexican citizen. While he had shunned a change of allegiance, he was not so unyielding for his children. Born in California, they were baptized into the Catholic faith in Monterey within days of their births and were eligible for citizenship.[48] In 1844, Larkin applied to Governor Micheltorena for the naturalization of Carolina, Sophia, and Francis, and a land grant in their names. Micheltorena, then heavily in debt to Larkin, complied. Naturalization decrees were issued on December 13, 1844,[49] and just two days later, the governor granted to the three new Mexican citizens a princely tract of ten square leagues, 44,364 acres.[50] Variously called Children's Rancho, Larkin's Rancho, and Upper Farm, the property was on the west bank of the Sacramento River, a few miles above today's town of Colusa. Larkin knew exactly what he was getting. At his request, John Bidwell had selected and mapped the property the previous July.[51]

The grant was rejected by the assembly two years later, "on account of the law not authorizing the naturalizing *minors*," according to Abel Stearns, who had tried to push the measure through.[52] Larkin was not surprised. He was himself unsure of the rights of naturalized minors, and he had heard the rumor that none of the ranchos granted by Micheltorena to foreigners would be approved by the assembly.[53] He was not overly concerned. By June 1846, when Stearns wrote, the conquest had begun and Larkin knew that action by the assembly would be of no effect.

By the end of 1846, Larkin had contracted with John S. Williams to settle on the Children's Rancho for three years. Larkin promised to purchase supplies, cattle, sheep and hogs, erect ranch buildings, and "commence a trading store," while Williams was to receive half the increase of animals and produce.[54] Williams arrived on the grounds in January and pronounced it "one of the most beautiful countrys that I have ever seen, and is admirably adapted both for cultivation and the raising of stock."[55] Within a few months, he was growing wheat, building fences and corrals, and tending hogs and hundreds of horses and cattle that Larkin sent to him. A large flock of sheep and some geese were added. Larkin asked his tenant to purchase some turkeys. Local Indians were hostile at first, but Williams soon pacified them and eventually hired many to work on the farm. He was a faithful correspondent, writing long, detailed letters about the operation of the farm, and repeatedly asked Larkin to visit the place.

Williams made adobe bricks on the ranch for construction of a house, as required by terms of the grant, and a flour mill. He and Larkin pondered purchasing a launch and adding a saw to the mill. Plans were made for a survey of the ranch by William Ide, and Larkin and Williams discussed where to settle immigrants on the property.[56] It is unclear at this point whether Larkin intended to sell or give land to the immigrants. Either alternative would have gained allies against squatters and support for Larkin's title.

Larkin was pleased with Williams's industry and reliability. He commissioned him in October to oversee the operation of another property, the Rancho Jimeno.[57] Sometimes called the Lower Ranch, the property was a ribbon of land adjoining the Children's Rancho. Twenty-five miles long and one mile wide, it ran along the west bank of the Sacramento River from today's Colusa south to Knight's Landing. Larkin bought the eleven-league tract, 48,854 acres, in 1845 for $1,000[58] from Manuel Jimeno Casarín, who had acquired it by grant in 1844 from Micheltorena. Larkin soon sold half interest in the property to Lieutenant John S. Missroon, a United States Navy officer on the *Portsmouth*, for $1,500.[59] He would later regret the sale, but at the time he had no choice. He was being pressed by creditors and needed cash.[60]

The partners agreed that the land should be occupied so that it would warn off squatters and show occupation at the signing of the peace treaty with Mexico. They invested $550 each to purchase cattle and tools for a tenant who would receive as compensation one-half the animal increase. When Larkin could find no one who would go on the place for the outfit offered, he wrote to Missroon that they would have to invest an additional $300 each, later raised to $400 or $500. The figure was still low, Larkin told Missroon, compared with his investment of $4,620 on the adjacent Children's Rancho.[61]

Without waiting for Missroon's reply, Larkin contracted with Dolores Féliz and John Armstrong to settle on the rancho and begin improvements.[62] He instructed Williams to help the two men build a house and get the farm underway. Larkin knew that he risked by committing more of his own money to the venture before hearing from his partner, but he saw no other way. To Missroon he wrote, "I have made rather a blind bargain."[63]

Sparks flew between the partners. Missroon refused to increase his investment, claiming neither the means nor the will. He thought the original investment adequate and charged Larkin with having broken the contract.

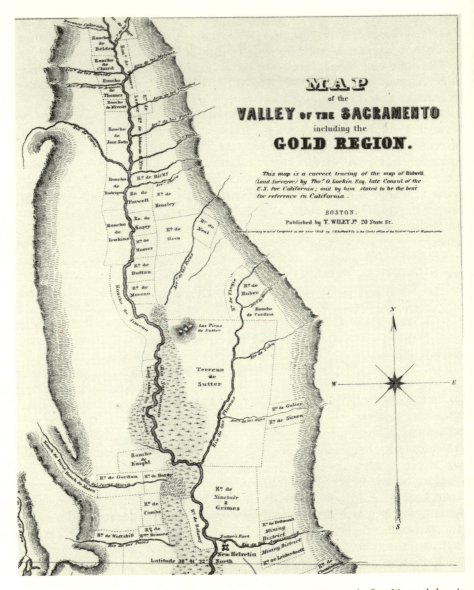

Map of the Sacramento Valley and gold country, prepared in part by Larkin and showing many of his ranches. Courtesy The Bancroft Library.

He halfheartedly offered alternative solutions. Expecting nothing but trouble from the partnership, Missroon asked Larkin to authorize him to sell the property in the east. As for Larkin's lament that he was forced to act alone, without assurance of success, Missroon was not impressed. He knew Larkin too well. If you have made a blind bargain, he wrote, "it is the first & only one of your life."[64] Larkin concluded that Missroon did not know much about California economic and political affairs, but he promised to consider giving him a power of attorney to sell the tract.[65]

The same year that he acquired the Jimeno property, Larkin added another valuable tract. On September 26, 1846, he purchased Rancho Cotate in Sonoma County, paying $1,500[66] to Juan Castañeda, who had received it by grant in 1844. The tract of four square leagues, 17,239 acres, lay between Petaluma and Santa Rosa. Larkin had the property surveyed by Jasper O'Farrell into twenty sections, which he promptly offered for sale.

Larkin had no doubts about the validity of the Cotate title. "I consider my rights perfect," he told an associate.[67] Castañeda's grant had been approved by both Governor Micheltorena and the legislature, and Castañeda had promptly built a house, as required, and brought in stock. Larkin decided nevertheless to make additional improvements and to build his own house.[68]

The structure was to be a grand two-story adobe with a vineyard and orchard worth $4,000 to $6,000. Larkin gave an advance of $800 to his builder, William M. West, on the contract price of $2,000, but protected himself by stipulating that the amount would have to be returned if West did not actually build.[69] The scale and detail of the instructions to West suggest that Larkin was going beyond simply protecting his title to the rancho. This was no tenant's house that Larkin was building.

Larkin might have considered his rights to the Cotate property perfect, and began to sell pieces almost immediately, but he nevertheless protected himself and his heirs by giving only quitclaim deeds. That is, he conveyed to a purchaser only the interest which he, Larkin, held in the property. Therefore, the purchaser would be compelled to support Larkin's original title in the entire tract, including any portion remaining in Larkin's possession.[70] If he gave a warranty deed instead, and title later proved defective, Larkin or his heirs would be liable for money damages amounting to the purchase price or more. Another technique Larkin employed to accomplish the same result was to sell an undivided share of his own interest in a property. Both practices are evidence of his considerable legal sophistication.

By August 1847, Larkin was thinking seriously about a move, perhaps to withdraw to a slower-paced existence. He was subject to moodiness, and it seems that the world was changing too fast for him. "I cannot cope with the many hundreds of new Yankees who are daily making their appearance in California," he wrote to a friend. The mood passed, and he added: "I however am content with my lot and station in life."[71]

Mariano Vallejo had written recently, lauding Sonoma as a pleasant place for a family home. He was sure that the town was destined to be the most comfortable in California because of its happy blend of climate, water, production, and contact with the bay.[72] Larkin was impressed. He replied that he expected to be living at Sonoma, or somewhere in the vicinity, within two years and asked Vallejo to sell him a certain house. He appeared to be quite serious, stating the terms he wished and asking for a deed, signed by the general and his wife, witnessed by the alcalde, to be sent forthwith. Larkin added that he would "see about the having an orchard &c &c on it."[73]

Larkin's enthusiasm soon faded. His house on the Cotate property was to have been finished by summer 1847, but it was hardly begun in May 1848. West, the builder, complained of a scarcity of labor and a sore hand. Besides, there was little water on the place. He suggested that Larkin make the best of a bad deal by trying to find a buyer the following spring when the land would show grass and water. Larkin suspected that West simply wanted to break the contract.[74] Nor did Vallejo produce the property that Larkin wanted. Larkin gave up any plans that he might have had for living on the property. "If I had the least idea of ever farming," he told a friend, " [I] should keep it, but I have not."[75]

Larkin decided that he would use the Rancho Cotate as payment, piece by piece, for building houses elsewhere.[76] One of Larkin's house builders, Samuel Brown, liked the rancho so much that he offered to operate the place for Larkin if he would buy the livestock.[77] Larkin declined the offer.

Larkin purchased other substantial properties in 1847. He bought two farms at Carmel. He paid William R. Garner $575 for a tract of one square league; the other, two thousand varas square, he acquired from José María Escobar for $300.[78] From Charles W. Flügge, he bought the Rancho de Boga on January 21, 1847, for $2,800.[79] Flügge had received the grant in 1844.[80] As we have seen, the transaction was negotiated while Larkin was a prisoner of the Californios in Los Angeles.

The isolated Flügge property of five square leagues, 22,185 acres, would prove Larkin's best chance for fabulous wealth. The tract, often called the Boga Grant or Flügge's Rancho, occasionally the Feather River Rancho, ran for about fifteen leagues along the west bank of the Feather River, just south of today's Oroville. The town's name, "Gold Town," suggests the reason for Larkin's later hopes for the property, though he knew nothing of the possibility of gold mines when he acquired the wild tract. The year after he bought it, he asked $4,000 for the whole, in cash or goods. He would eventually ask $1,000,000.

The southern boundary of Rancho de Boga adjoined Sutter's land. Taking advantage of the proximity, Larkin asked Sutter in August 1847 to have a simple house built on the land and rented at a nominal rate to anyone.[81] The house would prove occupancy. The builder was to receive a piece of the rancho land in payment, with the proviso that the land chosen must not include the large Indian rancherias. It was during a visit to their villages that Larkin had first been attracted to the rancho. In 1848, when the scurrying about for gold began, he would remember that he had observed during the visit that the Indians were peaceful and willing to work.[82]

For some reason, Sutter did not have the house built. Larkin then asked Williams, his Children's Rancho tenant, to build it. When Williams delayed, Larkin turned to John Bidwell, who agreed. Construction was well underway in early 1848 when gold fever made it impossible to hold workers. The house was left unfinished.[83]

One of Larkin's speculative interests, at the same time the most imaginative and the riskiest, has not been mentioned. This was the promotion of new towns. Larkin's most notable venture originated in his friendship with Mariano Guadalupe Vallejo. The general was grateful for Larkin's concern for him and his family while he was a prisoner of the Bear Flaggers at Sutter's Fort. On his release, Vallejo returned home to Sonoma to find his cattle and horses scattered, his houses looted, and his wheat crop lost. In despair, he sought out Larkin in September 1846: "I have a great desire to see you and speak about every thing."[84]

Vallejo saw an uncertain future for himself in this new American world and was drawn to associate himself with his old compatriot. He suggested a real-estate joint venture in Yerba Buena.[85] Larkin thought the tiny, windswept settlement had possibilities and had discussed them with Vallejo. There was another possibility. Vallejo reminded Larkin that when they were last together in Monterey, Larkin had prophesied that a great city would rise someday on the Carquinez Strait, a wide stretch of the Sacramento River near its mouth. Vallejo's Rancho Suscol ran for miles on the north side of the strait. He had received the tract as a grant in 1843 and followed up in 1844 by purchasing it from the government for $5,000.[86] Vallejo offered Larkin a house lot on the rancho to show his gratitude to his old *paisano*.[87]

Larkin was intrigued. On October 23, 1846, sailing up the Sacramento River from San Francisco to New Helvetia, he stopped and closely examined a likely townsite on the rancho.[88] He liked what he saw. In mid-November, he told a friend that he was "trying to screw myself up to *building a Town*, thirty or forty miles up the Sacramento (the straits of Kaukins). I have views and plans sufficient to amass a dozen fortunes. Time will tell. If I do nothing else I will make a bustle."[89]

Robert B. Semple had the same vision for a grand town on the strait and discussed it with Vallejo during the fall. Semple had arrived in California in 1845 with Lansford W. Hastings. He farmed a short while in the Sacramento River valley, then worked for Sutter. Semple first met Vallejo while he was a leader of the Bear Flaggers. He settled in Monterey, where he and his partner, Walter Colton, founded the first newspaper in California, the *Californian*. Now agreeing to a joint enterprise, Vallejo deeded an undivided half of a five-square-mile tract of Suscol to Semple for the establishment of a town.

Vallejo was less interested personally in the town than in increasing the value of the remainder of his rancho, so he was quite willing to relinquish his half share when he learned that Larkin wanted to acquire it. Larkin had written to Vallejo in January 1847 from Los Angeles, while awaiting transportation after his release, to remind Vallejo of his interest.[90] Semple was agreeable to the new arrangement, and on May 18, 1847, deeded back to Vallejo his half interest in the townsite.[91] The following day, Vallejo deeded the same five square miles jointly to Larkin and Semple.[92] The partners were required to name the town "Francisca" or "Benicia," both names belonging to Vallejo's wife, and to arrange for a municipal government and set up a ferry boat service, the proceeds of which were to finance the establishment of public schools.[93]

Larkin and Semple agreed between themselves to donate four squares of land to the new town for public purposes—such as promenades, town buildings, and gardens—two lots of land for the ferry landing, and four per cent of all building lots to the town to benefit public education. All remaining even-numbered lots, as surveyed by Jasper O'Farrell, were to belong to Larkin, and odd-numbered lots to Semple, and each could sell lots independently. The partners decided to name their town, "Benicia."[94] Irate citizens of San Francisco, the new name for Yerba Buena, had objected to the name, "Francisca," fearing that outsiders would confuse the upstart with their own town. Larkin and Semple also were concerned about the possible confusion of names.[95]

During the early summer of 1847, Semple from San Francisco and Larkin from Monterey oversaw the birth of Benicia, the first town in California founded by promoters rather than settlers. Semple was the more openly enthusiastic of the two, for he quickly began devoting virtually his whole attention to the enterprise while Larkin continued to have other interests. By July, Semple had moved to Benicia, where he acted as Larkin's general agent, and put the required ferry in operation. The original ferry was simply a ship's boat fitted with a lateen sail.[96] Semple, single-minded in his promotion of the town, soon became exasperated and insistent, even indignant, at what he considered Larkin's lack of zeal for the enterprise. Larkin did not appear overly concerned by Semple's badgering. Though the two partners were equals by contract, Larkin held the upper hand in experience and capital.

John Sutter was aware of Larkin's land speculations and wrote him in June 1847 to try to interest him in his own attempt at town building. He had begun construction on Sutterville, located on the Sacramento River three miles from the fort, in early 1846.[97] Sutter told Larkin that mutual acquaintances, Lansford Hastings and John Bidwell, were interested in the town and assured him that it would improve considerably faster than Benicia.[98]

Larkin likely investigated. He was not one to pass up an opportunity, particularly where speculation in land was involved. If so, he was not moved by Sutterville's prospects. Or, perhaps Sutter's involvement in the project dissuaded him. Larkin was not impressed with Sutter's business acumen. The visionary Swiss was perpetually in debt to him.

Larkin was not distracted from Benicia and in July 1847 began planning to build there. He bought lumber from Bodega,[99] the Napa Valley and Sonoma,[100] and Santa Cruz, but the supply never seemed to be sufficient. He paid for materials with cash, soap, hides, and Rancho Cotate land, and customarily compensated builders with half cash, half Cotate land. To Samuel Brown for building two houses, for example, he paid $600 in cash and two leagues of the rancho.[101] One mile and $50 bought 100,000 shingles.

Larkin's investment in Benicia grew so rapidly during the summer that he ran out of cash. He instructed his construction agent, Henry A. Green, to make no more house-building contracts that required cash,[102] but soon relented, realizing that the builders needed some money. He then offered one-quarter cash and three-quarters Cotate land.[103] He also had to pay cash for extensive landscaping, fencing, and planting and caring for one hundred locust trees.[104] Even Semple was impressed with the landscaping.[105]

Larkin showed considerable imagination in promoting Benicia. He offered town lots to any captain who would take his ship into the strait to the town's anchorage, thereby proving the passage safe. The first visit of the brig, *Francisca*, carrying lumber for Larkin, had shown that the river was navigable, but this was a shallow draft vessel. When Commodore Shubrick sailed the U.S.S. *Julia* in August to Benicia, Larkin deeded a lot to the commander and one each to seven other ship's officers. Larkin further honored the commodore by naming "Shubrick Square" in Benicia.[106] Larkin urged Semple to reserve lots of his own to reward officers of other warships, noting that commerce and settlement would be stimulated by their visits. Larkin was convinced that nine-tenths of Benicia's early settlers would be rich men, the other tenth remaining poor by their nature.[107] His children also would have a share of the fledgling metropolis; Larkin planned to deed an entire block to them and then build on it.[108]

The partners often differed on how best to promote their town. Semple customarily sold lots, believing that a man who had spent money for property would be most likely to build. Larkin gave away many lots, with the condition that building commence within one year, thus leaving the recipients the necessary capital to improve the property. A promise to build was not always a condition of the gift. Among Larkin's Benicia deeds is a document which, "in the consideration of the love and affection which I have towards my dearly belove Wife Rachel Larkin," transferred twenty lots to her which she could use and benefit from during her lifetime, but could not sell. On her death, the lots would pass to their children.[109]

By the end of October, Semple's obsession for Benicia was matched only by his irritation at what he considered Larkin's lack of enthusiasm. He scolded his partner for puttering with his few lots in Monterey and San Francisco and neglecting his "thousands" in Benicia.[110] Semple perpetually badgered Larkin to visit their town, and Larkin as often was too busy.

Larkin was hardly unaware of the opportunity in Benicia. He simply could not ignore opportunity elsewhere. Monterey was experiencing rapid growth. By mid-November 1847, there were sixteen houses in Benicia and others going up. In Monterey, during the past summer alone, thirty houses, almost all two storied, were built. Building was so brisk that the price of adobes climbed steadily, and Larkin had trouble finding carts to haul his lumber and shingles, if indeed he could find the materials to buy.[111] Nevertheless, he continued to build in the town, including the construction of two houses in February 1848 on Larkin Street.[112]

But the real boom was in San Francisco. The city, according to Larkin was "going ahead like a house afire."[113] He estimated that 200 houses would be built in 1847. Josiah Belden, his San Francisco agent, told him that he rose each morning to see a new house, as if it had sprung up overnight. Lots were in great demand and were selling fast, including some that were covered by six feet of water and ten feet of mud. "We are fast advancing to meet the times," Larkin told Flügge.[114] In 1847, Larkin began to shift the emphasis of his speculation in lots from Monterey to San Francisco. The shift would prove permanent.

Larkin continued to promote Benicia from a distance. Relations were so strained between the partners, however, that they agreed Larkin should find a new general agent. At Semple's suggestion, Larkin appointed Edward H. von Pfister, who had kept a store in the town since his arrival from Hawaii in 1847. With less stake than Semple in Benicia, von Pfister could be more forthright in his assessment of the town's progress. In March 1848, he reported that progress was slow indeed,[115] but Larkin remained optimistic and continued to build. By April, he had invested approximately $7,500 in Benicia. He had two small houses, two "common" two-storied houses, and two "handsome" two-storied houses under construction, and he planned to build others. By mid-summer, he expected to have 50,000 adobes and 30,000 feet of lumber available for sale to builders. Benicia would go ahead, he assured the carping Semple, and he would be a part of it. But he would not move to the town, as Semple urged.[116]

By May 1848, Benicia was almost deserted. Gold fever had carried away the town's small population to the diggings. Von Pfister left his Benicia store, which was losing money, to rush to the foothills to open a store. He turned over his affairs to Stephen Cooper, who had worked in Benicia for Larkin.[117] Apparently Cooper headed for the mines instead, for Semple soon reported to Larkin that there were but *two* men in the town other than himself, and that he would do the best he could with Larkin's interests. The perpetually optimistic Semple was not discouraged. Every boat that passed Benicia from the Sierra carried gold dust. He was convinced that any merchant with goods would want to locate as close to the mines as possible, and Benicia was that place. "Benicia will be no small business, in a short time," he wrote. He urged Larkin, once more, to come see the town,[118] Larkin did visit Benicia on occasion—but not often enough or long enough to satisfy his partner.

Larkin was too busy. His speculative nature had led him into yet another, altogether new venture. He was a leading spirit in a quicksilver mine, located adjacent to the New Almaden mine, south of San Jose. In 1846, he had sent ore samples to learned societies in the East and to government officials, including Secretary Buchanan. More samples were sent to Mott Talbot & Company in Mazatlán for testing. The instructions accompanying the ore show that Larkin had a clear understanding of the properties of quicksilver and the techniques for smelting it.[119]

The Santa Clara Mining Company was in operation by late 1847. In addition to Larkin, who served as secretary, the partners were John Ricord, Henry F. Pitts, William Blackburn, Jacob R. Snyder, John G. Christie, Josiah Belden, Grove C. Cook, and José Abrego, president. San Jose Alcalde James Weeks visited the mine in mid-December and judged that the ore would yield 35 percent metal. Alexander Forbes, the British owner of the New Almaden mine, complained to Governor Mason that the mine was located on his property. Mason, accompanied by Lieutenant Sherman, visited the site and investigated the charge, but did not intervene.[120]

The mine had hardly been opened when the partners made plans to sell it. They were speculators, not miners. Christie was given a power of attorney by each of the other partners to proceed to the East to sell their shares.[121] Contrary to his usual inclination to buy and sell on speculation, Larkin would rather have worked the mine, but he reluctantly agreed to the scheme.[122] Probably he wanted to prove the mine's richness before offering it for sale.

In early 1848, Larkin's enthusiasm for the quicksilver operation turned sour. Living in Monterey, he had to rely on others to keep him informed about operations, and visitors repeatedly reported that they saw no sign of quicksilver on the site. In April, Larkin pondered withdrawing from the venture. Before deciding, he sent an employee to make a personal inspection of the works.[123] The survey verified that good quicksilver ore had indeed been uncovered at the claim. His evaluation was supported by the rather ominous news that another company only 300 yards away was working a rich vein.[124]

In spite of this promising report, the prospects for the mine continued gloomy. Ricord offered to give his share of ownership to Walter Colton as a present. The other company working nearby, that of Anthony Suñol, a San Jose farmer and merchant who had once owned the land, brought suit to secure a tract of twenty to thirty acres. Larkin once again became discouraged and regretted that he had ever joined the venture, vowing that he would "give all I spent in the company and something more if I was not a member and very much if I was not its secretary."[125] He instructed Christie not to offer shares for sale unless prospective buyers were told about the lawsuit against the claim. He hoped that Christie would find no buyers as long as the title and prospects were in doubt. "In fact my friend," he wrote, "I am afraid we have engaged in an uncertain business if not a failure."[126]

With such a dismal prospect, Larkin would have been doubly pleased when the mine sold for $63,000. Christie concluded the sale to John B. Gray of Virginia on December 22, 1848.[127] Gray did not make a blind purchase. Larkin had met him earlier in the year when he came to California to search out likely investments. Gray had spent some time investigating quicksilver prospects in the vicinity of the Santa Clara Mining Company operation.[128] Larkin was satisfied that Gray knew what he was doing.[129]

Meanwhile, Larkin continued in early 1848 to pursue other investments. His zeal for the mining venture, or any other momentary obsession, did not force other interests from his mind. He thrived on diversity. He continued to build houses in Monterey[130] and, though almost the entire population of Benicia had gone to the gold fields, he looked to the future and continued his improvements there. His ranchos were firmly established now. Féliz and Armstrong had settled in sufficiently on the Rancho Jimeno that he sent horses and a starter herd of one hundred young heifers and ten or fifteen bulls.[131] John Williams reported from the Children's Rancho that all was going well there and that he was branding calves and marking colts.

The gold discovery, however, would prove near fatal for Larkin's ranching operation. As we have seen, by mid-summer Williams was part of a gold-mining venture that was financed by Larkin. When Sam Chase, Williams's successor, fled to the placers, Larkin moved Dolores Féliz from the Jimeno to Children's Rancho and combined the stock of the two properties.[132] But Larkin was not satisfied with the arrangement. In January 1849, he sold the stock to Williams, who had left mining for good, and agreed to rent the rancho to him for two years at no further cost.[133] Larkin trusted Williams and knew that he would maintain the property in good order.

Unfortunately, Williams died the following May. Charles B. Sterling, who had worked for Larkin in Monterey until June 1848, was named executor. Larkin sent his condolences to Mrs. Williams and advised Sterling to sell the stock to pay the deceased's debts, including a note of $5,000 to Larkin. He also instructed Sterling to return the deeds to two Benicia lots that Larkin had offered gratis to the deceased. Williams had decided shortly before his death that he did not want them. The following October, Sterling settled on the Children's Rancho, once more in Larkin's employ.[134]

Anyone who knew Larkin in the late 1840s might think him a very rich man, and he was, but rich in real property only. He groaned to Ebenezer Childs in December 1848 that he was "miserably poor." Childs did not believe a word of it.[135] Always ready to launch a new speculation, Larkin was often simply short of cash. The cattle sale to Williams, in fact, was largely traceable to his need of capital for his Benicia investments.

Because of this cash-flow problem, Larkin sometimes tried to invest property rather than cash in speculations. His use of Cotate land and Benicia lots as compensation for services rendered has already been mentioned. In December 1848, Larkin entered a joint venture in San Francisco with Bethuel Phelps that required no cash from Larkin. He transferred ten water lots valued at $30,000 to Phelps. For his part, Phelps agreed to construct buildings worth $30,000 on the lots and then manage the properties. Rents were to be shared equally by the partners.[136] Larkin had done well: his actual investment in the joint $60,000 venture was the $2,200 he had paid for the ten lots.[137]

When Semple heard about the plan, he was beside himself. For months, his impatience with Larkin had been growing thin. "When I exchanged Gen. Vallejo for you [in the Benicia venture]," he had written in July, "I thought I was swaping for a Yankee who at least knew *his own interest* if he had no other quality to recommend him, but I was sadly disappointed." He felt that Larkin had not supported his attempts to get a customhouse at Benicia, or at least permission for ships to unload there. He chided Larkin to stir himself and throw off his "California Fever" and complained that Larkin dawdled while he had sacrificed all for their town. He had pondered giving it all up and going to the mines.[138]

The San Francisco venture with Phelps was the last straw for Semple. Nothing would destroy confidence faster in Benicia, he wrote Larkin in December 1848, than the prospect of one of its owners building elsewhere. Once and for all, Semple implored, support the town or sell out. He offered then and there to pay Larkin $15,000 in gold for all his unsold lots.[139] Finally, he would be rid of his sluggish partner. But Larkin, placid and content, did not respond. One yearns for a glimpse of Larkin as he reads one of Semple's blistering epistles. If he were in character, he would have smiled thinly, shaken his head, gently set the letter aside, and turned to other business.

Larkin, in fact, was working hard for Benicia. He notified Semple that he had given ten lots and assistance in building a house to an English doctor who planned to build a hospital in the town. This would accommodate the sick miners who were expected to desert the placers with the coming of winter. Larkin also gave Semple the electrifying news that an associate was interested in acquiring one-third of Larkin's interest in Benicia, after which he would invest heavily in the town. Now it was Larkin's turn to criticize. He complained that Semple had not replied to his three attempts in the last two months to outline a plan of action. "If our town dont begin to rise in '49—some other town will," he said. "You may be as sanguine as you like, but I assure you the town needs starting."[140]

It appeared for a time that Benicia would get the boost it needed. The unnamed friend turned out to be Bethuel Phelps, and Semple must have regretted his harsh words about Larkin's relationship with the San Franciscan. In January 1849, Phelps agreed under separate contracts with Larkin and Semple to build a lumberyard in Benicia, spend $75,000 a year for the next two years on construction, and survey the unsurveyed part of the Benicia tract. In return, the two partners would deed one-third of all Benicia to him.[141] Semple for once was delighted. Now he would have an active cobooster of their town. Though this promising turn was Larkin's doing, Semple could not resist another jab at him, declaring:

> . . . if we put our own shoulders to the wheel and throw our whole energies into the thing we can make a mammoth fortune and the largest city west of the mountain, but if one pull one way and the other another way we shall have great difficulty to make anything.[142]

Semple told Larkin that he had such great confidence in Phelps' judgment—"and he will be here with me"—that he would in the future look to Phelps for guidance.[143] Larkin must have breathed a great sigh of relief at this news.

Prospects for Benicia brightened during the spring of 1849. The United States storeship, *Southampton*, with Commodore Thomas ap Catesby Jones aboard, called at the town.[144] This visit by a major, deep-draft United States naval vessel proved the bay navigable and the harbor safe. As promised, Larkin gave a town lot to each of the ship's officers. Jones purchased a number of lots for himself. Both he and General Persifor F. Smith, newly arrived military commander in California, preferred the Benicia area over San Francisco as a site for military and naval installations and a customhouse.[145] Smith would have heard a great deal about Benicia while he lived at Larkin's Monterey house.[146] The general bought lots for himself and announced his intention to establish his headquarters in Benicia. Other ships called, including the *Ohio*, flagship of the Pacific fleet.

Hopeful entrepreneurs inquired about lots suitable for a blacksmith's shop, a hotel, and a wharf. Larkin heard that Alfred Robinson, recently appointed agent for the California steamers of Howland & Aspinwall, was considering Benicia as the likely site for the company's depot.[147] Plans were announced for the establishment of a boarding school.[148]

Semple took all this in and appealed to Larkin to recognize once and for all that Benicia was going to be *the* city. He repeated his call to Larkin to sell his properties in San Francisco, which had neither port nor prospects, and come to Benicia. The same sort of advice, with a like objective, came from Talbot Green, who told Larkin about a new town being laid out on

"Martinez farm," across the Carquinez Strait from Benicia. Lots were selling fast, and Green urged Larkin to liquidate his interests in *Benicia* because the new town of Martinez would prove a formidable rival.[149]

As usual, Larkin kept his own counsel. He continued selling, buying, building, and leasing out in Benicia, but at the same he looked after his investments in San Francisco, where speculative mania was driving prices upward. For example, in September 1848 he sold a fifty-vara lot for $10,000, which he had bought two years earlier for $600 or $700.[150] He worked on plans to construct ten first-class brick buildings in San Francisco for use in wholesale and retail business.[151] During a visit to the city in April 1849, he and Phelps talked about General Smith's official request for a grant of land at Benicia to be used for an army supply depot and other government purposes. They were both enthusiastic about the prospect.[152] The land eventually was granted, and the army began construction of a warehouse and barracks.

Along with economic growth, Benicia's cultural prospects appeared bright. In April 1849, the three partners granted thirty-two lots to the Board of Education of the Presbyterian Church for the purpose of establishing a university. The deed required that construction begin by January 1, 1850 and that students be admitted without religious discrimination.[153] Larkin was "exceedingly well disposed" to the plan.[154] Though he had little formal education himself, he was a strong supporter of schools. When it became obvious later that the groundbreaking deadline was not going to be met, a new contract was drafted between the partnership and a new group, not associated with the Presbyterian Church, which would constitute a Board of Education of Benicia. The new indenture was similar to the previous document, with the additional obligation to build an observatory.[155] Whether the draft eventually became a legal document is not clear.

In spite of all of the positive signs, Larkin eventually acknowledged to himself, if not to Semple, that Benicia was at best an uncertain investment. During 1849, he increasingly compared Benicia's prospects with those of San Francisco. The comparison proved that he was correct in his investment strategy, which increasingly emphasized San Francisco at the expense of both Benicia and Monterey.

Larkin's speculation in San Francisco became more ambitious and more lucrative. He sold a lot for $10,000 that he had bought in 1846 for $500.[156] He sold the two-league Punta de Lobos grant to Phelps, who was obligated by the contract to lay out a town on the tract. The price was $20,000 and fifty lots of the town.[157] Larkin paid Phelps $75,000 for his interest in the joint building venture initiated the previous December in San Francisco, shortly before their association in Benicia.[158] In a general sale of San Francisco water lots, he and associate Talbot Green paid $80,000 for lots.[159] Larkin committed himself to an investment of $100,000 in a partnership with Henry A. Breed. The firm planned to carry on a real-estate and commission business, particularly dealing in building materials.[160]

Larkin concluded the biggest land deal of his life in December 1849. He sold eight San Francisco water lots between Clay and Washington streets, and a ninth on the corner of Washington and Montgomery, to Charles L. Ross, a friend and leading San Francisco property owner and merchant, for $300,000. The land and improvements at the time of the sale were leased out for a total of $4,001 per month.[161]

Larkin did not neglect his land business in the interior. He sold what remained of the Rancho Cotate for $16,000 to Joseph S. Ruckle.[162] He purchased an undivided half of 163 lots in Sacramento from William D. M. Howard[163] and the Rancho de los Sotos.[164] In February 1850, he paid Jacob P. Leese $40,000 for half of his Rancho Huichica, a grant of five-and-a-half leagues in Napa and Sonoma counties that he had received in 1844. Nor was Larkin through with town building. In 1849, Leese had founded the town of St. Louis on the Huichica. On the same date that Larkin bought half interest in the rancho, Leese and Larkin deeded one-third of the town to William M. Steuart, for which Steuart agreed to survey and lay out the town.[165]

Larkin's partnership with Missroon was not so congenial. His joint ventures were generally successful because he chose his associates with care, but the Jimeno was an exception. Missroon had brought nothing to the partnership but money, and, as it turned out, too little of that. By 1849, Larkin was willing to sell the ranch for less than its speculative value, just to end the annoying relationship. He offered to refund the $600 advanced by Missroon for operating expenses, plus interest, and urged him to sell the place if he could get at least $11,000 for it. Larkin had been offered that amount but would not sell it since he had authorized Missroon to find a buyer in the East.[166]

The frenzy of business in 1849 began to take its toll on Larkin. During one of his many extended visits to San Francisco to look after his interests there, he wrote to his friend Faxon Dean Atherton in Valparaiso, describing in detail his investments. The letter, filled with tales of profits and dreams of profits, was also laced with hints of stress: "My head whirls with speculation; my hair grows grey by the excessive working of my brain, and ambition. . . . I leave this next week for my Monterey home and would give 500 ounces of gold to chase out of my brain for a year or two every idea of trade or speculation."[167]

He found peace in Monterey. "Affairs go on in our quiet town as usual," he wrote to Talbot Green. "I have not felt or had an unpleasant day since my arrival." Yet, in the same short letter, he told about a controversy over a rental fee and the sale of a lot and purchase of gold by another party, mentioned an inquiry about one of his lots, offered a cargo for sale, and commented about a note outstanding.[168] Larkin could no more put business aside than he could put aside breathing.

Monterey nevertheless was increasingly a refuge for him. Others had the same opinion of the town. In San Francisco again, Larkin received a letter from a Monterey compatriot, datelined "Land of Quietness." The correspondent asked for the latest news and added:

> No news from here. Your family are well. School goes on as usual. One or two men are now & then seen walking the streets. . . . Your premises, office &c. look solitary enough. The garden flourishes. People get up in the morning, eat the requisite & customary number of times during the day, & go to bed. That is all of any public importance that I know of.[169]

Rachel wrote to ask about carpeting for the house, told about Alfred's recent illness and visits to new families, and ended: "Everything goes on well about the house; nothing new; vary dull; no buisness."[170] While Larkin sometimes yearned for the tranquillity of Monterey, Rachel's last comment explained succinctly why he could never be completely content there.

Larkin had loved Monterey well enough. "May California be the best country in the world and Monterey the best part of California, is my prayer," he had once written to Jacob Leese.[171] Ironically, after Larkin advertised his house for sale in November 1849,[172] it was Leese who responded. In January 1850, Leese, one of San Francisco's first settlers, traded properties in San Francisco, probably including his house, for Larkin's home and other properties in Monterey. Larkin likely got the better deal, since property values were going down in Monterey and rising sharply in San Francisco.

Larkin's reason for disposing of his house is not completely clear. The advertisement in the *Alta California* states that he was "preparing to leave California."[173] He was indeed planning a trip to the east coast. If he meant to make a permanent move, then he would not need a house in Monterey. On the other hand, he had talked lately about the glowing prospects in San Francisco. Perhaps he planned to move to the city, either before or after an extended visit to the East. Following the end of his imprisonment, Larkin's trips to San Francisco to look after his properties had grown in frequency and duration. He had never considered living in Benicia, and Monterey had remained a provincial Hispanic town in comparison with the vibrant American San Francisco. Before the end of 1849, he had decided that San Francisco was the city with a future. The only thing certain about the decision to sell his house is that Larkin planned to move permanently from Monterey.

If not Monterey, then where? Relatives and friends had worried about his imprisonment during the war and repeatedly urged him to come back to

Massachusetts. Others who knew something of his prosperity tried to convince him that his fortune was sufficient to provide independence in the East among friends and civilization. Was that not his intent, after all, when he went to that barbaric country so long ago? As early as 1840, Rogers had urged him to "come back to the world again, and leave the Spainards to their superstitions and sluggishness, for the stirring world of the Yankees."[174] Perhaps it was time now to go home.

There were good reasons for going. He was known in the East, and he was rich. He had investments there. In April 1847, he owned $6,360 in railroad and bank stocks and had instructed Rogers, who held $2,640 of his money, on strategy for buying stocks and real estate for him. He was interested in owning a house and some land in Lynn, Massachusetts, his boyhood home.[175] He was concerned about Oliver and Frederic in their eastern schools. He was determined that his boys would have the sort of education that he had not had and which was not available in California. And they needed their parents' care.

The trip was a long time germinating. In 1842, he planned a voyage to the East. In 1846, he thought about an overland journey.[176] For the next four years, he announced periodically to paisanos and anxious relatives alike that he would leave soon. Finally, in 1849, he decided. All his official posts had terminated, and he appointed agents in Monterey and San Francisco to oversee his business and land interests. To friend Atherton in Valparaiso, he reported that he was preparing to "steam it to New York" and, he added, "*am done trading.*"[177] Contrary to earlier plans to visit the East for a few months only, particularly when he had thought of traveling alone, he now anticipated a longer residence. In February 1850, he gave five notes maturing at six-month intervals to Mellus, Howard & Company, his general agents in San Franciso, instructing them to collect payments and send the proceeds to him in New York.[178] In the same month he backed out of a partnership arrangement that he had himself proposed only the month before. The disappointed associate wrote to a friend that Larkin "says he dont want to make any more property in California." He decided that Larkin was homesick.[179]

CHAPTER 11

CALIFORNIA PAISANO OR
NEW YORK NABOB?

THOMAS O. LARKIN, with Rachel and their children, Francis, Caroline, and Alfred, and his brother John B. R. Cooper, left San Francisco by steamer on March 1, 1850. Crossing the Isthmus at Panama, they arrived the following month in New York, where they were welcomed at a festive "Calafornia Jubilee."[1] The costly affair, hosted by old California friends, was reported in the *New York Herald* as "the most choice, recherché, elegant, refined, tasty affair that had ever been got up in New York."[2] Larkin would have been pleased to see his arrival announced in the newspapers.

This was a particularly happy moment for the Larkins. It was the first time the entire family had ever been together. Alfred and his two older brothers met for the first time.[3] Alfred had been born after Oliver's and Frederick's departure from Monterey for their eastern school.

The Larkins rented a comfortable three-bedroom suite at the fashionable Irving House, a popular gathering place for Californians. "Oh what a place!" Larkin wrote to Jacob Leese. "Everything *en grande*. . . . My whole time is occupied by continual calls."[4] Here the family lived well and entertained lavishly. When relatives visited the Larkins at the Irving House, Larkin paid their expenses. His bills were enormous, $2,708.12 for twenty-four days in May 1850, $2,451.38 for the following November,[5] about $35,200 and $31,850 respectively in 1990 dollars.

Within two months of his arrival in the East, Larkin was enjoying himself so much, he announced to Pablo de la Guerra in Monterey that he planned to buy a house in New York[6] and thought seriously of making it his permanent home. Rachel's influence might be seen here.[7] Yet, the same letter includes a hint of the uneasiness that would distress Larkin for the next three years. After telling about the excitement of New York, he turned to beg his friend Pablo for California news: "No doubt business will next year take me back to the land of adoption. The place of my name & fame and fortune will also call me back to see old Frinds."[8] Three months after leaving California, Larkin was homesick.

In time, the East appeared more hospitable. Larkin visited old California friends. He would have been especially pleased to see his old paisano and dear friend, Faxon Dean Atherton, who had come east from Valparaiso.[9] Older friends from North Carolina wrote to express a desire to see him, and he saw at least one in New York. Relatives from Tennessee, Kentucky, New Hampshire, and Massachusetts wrote about family affairs and pleaded with him to visit them. A few asked for assistance. Larkin frequently responded with funds or offers of employment. His invitation to Sophia Larkin, a distant relative who came to live with the family, was a boon both to Sophia and the Larkins. She would be a companion to Rachel and a governess-companion to the children.

During the first six months after their arrival in the East, the Larkins traveled often, visiting Baltimore, Boston, Philadelphia, and Washington. Their accommodations were always comfortable and costly. Bar bills at these and at the Irving House were always large, particularly revealing Larkin's fondness for brandy and entertaining.

Eager to "set up housekeeping" and settle down, the Larkins in November purchased a house at 101 Tenth Street, between Broadway and University Place in New York. Rachel had much to say about the purchase, and the property was recorded in her name.[10] It was only recently that a woman could own property in her own name, thereby protecting family possessions from a husband's creditors. New York's married women's property statute was enacted in 1848. The comparable California act was passed on April 17, 1850. Larkin would have known something of the debate on the bill before the family's departure for the East on March 1. Shortly after passage, he had an inventory drawn of Rachel's separate property in San Francisco.[11] His attention to the new law was typical of his legal proficiency.

The Larkins were pleased with their new home. "The house is in a very good Street," Larkin wrote to his sons at their school near Boston, "with trees both sides of the Street." The four-story, stone-fronted building had eighteen rooms, with the fourth floor devoted entirely to servants. The house and furniture cost around $25,500, a not inconsiderable sum in 1850. Larkin would spend an additional $1,000 per year improving the property.[12] Rachel had the house repaired and painted throughout, all "work to be done with the best materials and in the best manner."[13] John C. Jones called the house "a Palacia, in the fashionable quarter of the City," where "Mrs. L. presides with queenly dignity."[14] The house suggested permanency. So did Larkin's decision to join the local historical society, the New York Athenaeum, and the Union Club, paying twenty years' dues.[15]

Larkin's "Palacia," like his Monterey home, was a gathering place of old California friends and New York acquaintances. Orders for food and spirits at times were huge, suggesting large parties and many house guests. During eight days in January 1851, purchases of beef and mutton totaled 146 1/2 pounds.[16] This was shortly before Larkin's first trip back to California, and perhaps he was saying goodbys at his table. His return in November of the same year was also celebrated. On December 8, 1851, family accounts include a single order for a basket of champagne, a dozen bottles of pale sherry, a dozen port wine, one case of claret, and three dozen scotch ale. During the month of December, the thirsty family and guests also consumed 126 quarts of milk.[17]

Now settled comfortably, Larkin began looking at business opportunities, particularly comparing prospects in California and New York. Deciding in favor of New York, he encouraged Cooper in January 1851 to sell some of his own California properties because of squatter problems and the uncertainties of California land bills then before Congress. He urged Cooper to invest $40,000 as soon as possible, half in his wife's name and half in his own, in New York or Boston real estate. Larkin had decided to sell half of his own California holdings. Transferring the assets to the East would provide for his family and for the children's education in case of his death. His business strategy often was influenced by worry over his chronic health problems.

The Larkins were a close, loving family, and Thomas and Rachel were distressed at the separation from the boys away at their schools. Until late 1848, Oliver and Frederic had lived with Larkin's stepbrother Isaac Childs and his wife Sarah at Lynn, Massachusetts. When their parents arrived in 1850, the boys were with Ann and Otis Wright at Neponset, near Boston. The following year, Oliver was moved to Bristol, north of Newport, where he attended a drawing school. In 1852, he was enrolled in a school twelve miles from New York. Later in the year, he lived briefly with his parents in New York before moving—eagerly, according to Larkin—to a boarding house in the city.[18] For a few months in the spring of 1853, Oliver worked in a surveyor's office in New York, then in April moved to a school at Cambridge, Massachusetts.

Oliver did not enjoy school and did not do well. He enjoyed play more, especially horses, guns, boats, and sledding. He had a special affection for Tiger, the large family dog, that he wanted so much to have with him at school.[19] Letters to his brothers were often signed with a good imitation of his father's embellished signature. He realized that he was not getting the education that his father repeatedly told him was necessary, and he feared that he would have to go to sea, having no other prospect. He thought he might rather work on a farm. Oliver was distraught when his father decided to move him from Newport to New York, for he loved Newport and its harbor. He knew that his mother wanted to cure him of his bashfulness, but he did not like parties and company and dancing school. He did not like New York, sure that he would learn nothing there but dissipation. He was not a "dashy young man," he told Frederic and Francis, but "a fine common young fellow."[20]

Frederic performed better in school than Oliver, but Francis proved to be the family scholar. Francis joined Oliver and Frederic at Neponset shortly after the family's arrival in the East. When Oliver went to Bristol, the other two brothers moved to New York, where they and Caroline went to a local school. They lived at home but took their meals with their schoolmaster and mistress.[21] Late in 1852, Frederic and Francis were placed with Ebenezer and Sarah Childs in Washington, where they attended Rugby Academy.

Larkin's letters to the boys were filled with family news and repeated encouragement to study hard, not simply for enlightenment, but as a preparation for making money. "Those who expect to be rich require the most learning," he instructed them.[22] More than once, particularly after one of his frequent illnesses, he warned them that the day would come when they must stand alone. He urged them to write often, particularly to tell him when they were ill and whether he should come to them.[23] He sent them newspapers and magazines and urged them to study and practice their Spanish, which he was afraid they would lose. In California, he had favored speaking Spanish in their home, believing it would benefit them all, but Rachel would not cooperate. She insisted on speaking English, and it annoyed Larkin.[24] Nevertheless, when the the boys first came east, they spoke better Spanish than English. Ironically, Larkin made no attempt to retain his own Spanish. He wrote in English to Californio friends, who in turn wrote to him in Spanish and complained that they could not read English well.[25]

Rachel occasionally wrote to her absent sons, but she had little to do with their schooling and was less enthusiastic than Larkin about it. Her comment to her husband, following her outing to Niagara Falls with the children, that "Oliver is Stupid and Slow" and "Francis is to smart"[26] says more about Rachel than about her sons.

Childs was a faithful correspondent, reporting regularly on Frederic's and Francis's progress and lamenting regularly that they did not appreciate the opportunity they had for a first-class education. Childs also thought Larkin much too indulgent. "They shall dress in velvet if you say so," he wrote, "but if left to me they shall always be neat & clean, and not extravagant." He did his best to provide the boys a home and the opportunity to grow intellectually and socially. In February 1853, he introduced them to President Millard Fillmore, who said that "'he remembered their father well, & was very happy to see the young gentlemen.'" The following month, they called on President Franklin Pierce a few days after his inauguration.[27]

Frederic was a bit of a grumbler, but for the most part the boys were obedient and polite. They worked hard, though not always with enthusiasm, and laughed easily. Both enjoyed play and read novels, much to Childs's dismay. He suggested that they should go to Sunday school; they preferred to go to dancing school.[28] Childs rarely forced his will on them, and they usually had their way. Dancing lessons commenced, and they attended balls, dressed sometimes as California dons.

Satisfied that his sons were provided for, and generally content with his situation, Larkin slowed his pace and enjoyed the luxuries of leisure and other benefits that his fortune made possible. He was a voracious reader. During the early 1850s, he subscribed, perhaps not simultaneously, to the *Alta California, San Francisco Evening Journal, Daily California Times, Monterey Sentinel, La Crónica*, a Spanish-language newpaper, *California Farmer, San Diego Herald, Weekly Pacific, Golden Era*, even the *New Orleans Picayune*.[29] He was deeply impressed with his first train ride from Boston to New York, amazed that one could read or sleep while speeding along at fifty miles an hour, and send and receive a message by telegraph between the same two points in less than an hour.[30]

Larkin enjoyed luxury, but he could not be happy long just spending money. Since the end of the war, he had become so obsessed with land speculation that it was pastime as much as livelihood. Besides concern for the family, this was another reason for Larkin's plan to transfer California assets to the East. He needed the capital for his New York land speculation.

With Fernando Wood, a prominent New York shipping merchant and politician, Larkin negotiated a $100,000 exchange of San Francisco property on the corner of Washington and Montgomery streets for eighteen apartment buildings, all but one of which were three- or four-story brick, in New York and Brooklyn, and thirty-six vacant lots in New York.[31] With these and other properties, Larkin was once again in his element, buying and selling on speculation.[32]

Some of the new properties were in Rachel's name, and she sometimes took a hand in their management, particularly when Larkin was absent. On one occasion, in September 1852, she discussed a particular investment possibility with George Baldwin, an agent, and approved his suggestion to offer some houses for sale. Baldwin wrote to Larkin, then away from the city, to explain the sale, adding: "Of course any proposition will be subject to your approval."[33] There was a limit to Rachel's authority.

Conveniently located in New York, Larkin now had the opportunity to press his and California's interests in Washington.[34] He had access to government officials and, on at least one occasion and probably more, talked with President Fillmore.[35] For the most part, his claims were handled by his Washington agents, Andrew Wylie, Charles De Selding, and Ebenezer

Childs, aided occasionally by William M. Rogers. As we have seen, the United States government was cautious, reluctant on occasion, but eventually paid most of Larkin's claims.

His claims for compensation as navy agent and naval storekeeper were tangled. A reluctant Navy Department in December 1852 paid a $350 navy agent claim, but the Secretary of the Navy the following month balked on the storekeeper claim on grounds that it had been acted on by his predecessor.[36] The denial was particularly galling since the chief clerk of the Navy Department had virtually assured Larkin in December that he would receive at least $1,500 per year for his storekeeper tenure.[37]

While looking after his own affairs, Larkin did not neglect to lobby for California's interests, particularly where his and the state's fortunes were intertwined. He pressed for the naming of Benicia and Monterey as ports of entry. Larkin traveled to Washington to watch the progress of California bills before Congress, especially those bills concerning land titles. He also attempted to accelerate California's admission to statehood, notably by the gift of a watch chain made of California placer gold to Henry Clay. Clay assured him that all was going well.[38]

In January 1851, Larkin, "[w]ishing to be of service," applied for and was appointed California agent for the program to construct a monument in memory of George Washington in the nation's capital.[39] Begun in 1848, the marble shaft had reached a height of 102 feet by 1851. For the next three years or more, Larkin distributed prints, pamphlets, certificates, and books, appointed subagents and was dunned regularly by the Washington National Monument Society to send collections. While Larkin himself was not always prompt in meeting obligations that did not include monetary penalties, part of the problem in this case was with his subagents.[40]

Larkin was known in the East in certain circles, and his counsel and support were often sought. For example, R. R. Gatton, a newly appointed consul to Mazatlán, called on him for advice on consular duties at a Mexican post.[41] Larkin would have been flattered. Though there is no record of what followed the handshakes and polite introductions, there must have been hours of lively conversation during which Larkin might have paused to stare absently through the panes of a closed window.

Larkin's earlier pessimism about California land, traceable to the uncertainty of land titles and troubles with squatters, began to change soon after his move to the East. He was drawn increasingly to his California affairs, working mostly through agents in California, but also in person. As we shall see, he made two trips to California during his eastern residence.

After a hiatus resulting from the gold rush, Benicia's prospects brightened. In 1850, the city was granted a charter by the state legislature and was named the seat of Solano County. The Pacific Mail Steamship Company made the port its depot and constructed warehouses, docks, and shops. The following year, the War Department established the Benicia Barracks and Benecia Arsenal, and the *Gazette* began publication. A Russian company appointed an agent at Benicia to manage its trade between Alaska and California. Other shipping companies and businessmen planned to establish themselves there, provided that it be named a port of entry.[42]

The port-of-entry proposal before Congress had influential friends, and Larkin cultivated them. He solicited the support of General James Wilson, a member of the United States Land Commission for California.[43] Larkin and Bethuel Phelps agreed to give Thomas B. King, San Francisco Collector of Customs, ten lots in Benicia for his assistance, on condition that it win designation during the current session of Congress.[44] Larkin was behind memorials sent to Congress by eastern businessmen who would profit by Benicia's success. To certain government officials and to associates he sent maps of Benicia as well as two views of Monterey with explanatory keys.

Larkin's investment in Benicia grew. He constructed a wharf, costing $8,000, and leased it for $500 per month.[45] He continued to deal in lots. He pondered the establishment of a local newspaper and planned to open a "Reading Room." He subscribed to thirty-seven newspapers from twenty-one states and the District of Columbia to be sent to Benicia. His purpose in this is unclear, but it seems that he planned to advertise Benicia in the newspapers.[46] To advance education, he subscribed to the new Benicia Female Seminary[47] and deeded two lots to Charles M. Blake's Collegiate Institute, founded in 1852. Larkin sometimes kept strings on property donated for educational purposes. The deed to Blake required that a substantial building be erected on the property within one year, or Blake must pay Larkin $1,000 for the lots.[48]

Larkin was among the most influential persons in bringing the state government to Benicia. Acting for him, agent William J. Eames, a relative by marriage who came to California with Larkin in 1851, agreed to pay Major James D. Graham $2,500 in early 1853 to get a bill through the legislature.[49] This was a coup since Graham had been supporting Vallejo as the site for the capital and had secured a pledge of support from a majority of the legislators. Eames also authorized Graham to distribute twenty-five Benicia lots to legislators. Eames assured Larkin that the lots were of little value. The tactic worked, and the legislature passed a bill in February naming Benicia the permanent capital. The legislature moved into the recently finished handsome brick "City Hall," which, in fact, had been built for use as a state house. Sacramentans had spent $13,000 in vain, trying to woo members in food and drink aboard a large steamer moored at Vallejo for four days.[50] Legislators would not forget their generosity.

An era ended in Benicia when Larkin and Semple in 1851 terminated their partnership. Semple decided to withdraw, saying, "Your last letter satisfies me that you will never be convinced that I have an ordinary degree of common sense." He demanded a friendly division of their common property. Failing that, he would bring suit to accomplish that purpose.[51] Finally an exchange was made, Semple's Benicia interests for an undivided two thirds of the northern two leagues of Larkin's Rancho Jimeno.[52]

Semple moved to his new property and took up ranching and farming, joining his brother, Charles D. Semple, who had a long-standing claim on the land.[53] After the arrival of his brother, Charles became more belligerent, vowing to break Larkin's titles to both the Children's and Jimeno ranchos. He passed the word around the countryside that Larkin "had failed & was not worth a dollar." Charles invited immigrants to select farms and pay him a bonus, for which he would guarantee titles.[54] It was not all bluster. A tract of 8,876 acres of the original two-league grant was eventually patented to Charles in 1869.[55] Robert Baylor Semple and Larkin were never reconciled. Semple died in 1854 when he fell from his horse.

Larkin's California land holdings, like those of other landowners, became increasingly embroiled during the early 1850s. Since the conquest, titles to land had been contested between those who owned grants from the Mexican California government and Americans who claimed that same land under the Pre-Emption Act of 1841. The Treaty of Guadalupe Hidalgo guaranteed the property rights of those resident in California at the signing of the treaty, but questions remained. Were the grants valid, particularly those made in 1845 and 1846 when an American takeover seemed imminent? Where were the boundaries? Should these few grantees be permitted to own such huge tracts?

As relations worsened between grantees, also called "claimants," and squatters, or "settlers" as they called themselves, the United States government stepped in. Two surveys, one in 1849 and another in 1850, reached conflicting conclusions.[56] To settle the question, Congress passed the Land Act of 1851, which favored the settlers. Burden of proof of title fell on the claimants, most of whom spoke little English and had little cash to finance lengthy court battles. To raise money, they could sell their unconfirmed land, but only at a fraction of its potential value. The law was prosettler, but even the settlers were often reluctant to invest much in land that they might lose if the claimant's title were confirmed.[57]

Larkin plunged into the fight for title confirmation with more confidence than most claimants, but he had no illusions about the shaky legal foundations of California land titles. He believed that if the government viewed titles by the letter of the law, many claimants would be injured.[58] For that reason, he had taken care early to document and map his properties. In the 1850s, he had his claims formally surveyed. He also secured from Mexico documentation to prove that his three children, Francis, Carolina, and Sophia, grantees of the Children's Rancho, were properly naturalized.[59] From Monterey, he received a clerical certification of their Catholic baptisms.[60]

He asked friends up and down the state to come to San Francisco at his expense to testify in his behalf before the Land Commission, which had been set up to examine claims. He made plans to go himself to Los Angeles to gather evidence and to ask Pío Pico to appear before the commission there.[61] John C. Jones wondered whether the confirmation process might be accelerated with a little "greeseing," generously applied. "Will not gold oz's blind the Honl. Gentlemen."[62] There is no evidence that Larkin acted on this perhaps light-hearted suggestion.

In August 1851, Larkin leased the Children's Rancho to Charles Sterling and a partner, A. C. St. John. Planning to make substantial improvements to the property, and with some vague ambition to build a town, Sterling and St. John decided that they should have a local post office, which they intended to name "Larkin." Professing to be Whigs, they asked Larkin, also a Whig, to use his influence with the California postal agent to set up the post office and appoint the partners jointly as postmaster. Larkin was indeed interested, and Sterling and St. John, anticipating speedy approval, began to include the name in the dateline of their letters. Nothing came of it, and there was no post office, nor yet a town, named after Larkin.[63]

Larkin still had hopes for the Jimeno property, but no buyers appeared. Relations between the two owners in early 1852 were delicate. Missroon was not as financially secure as Larkin, and he was fearful of the costs of defending their title and fighting squatters. With no income but his navy pay, he urged Larkin to sell at least his, Missroon's, share of the remaining nine leagues[64] at almost any price. Larkin told him that he hoped to sell it for $18,000, but Missroon, now also living on the east coast, became anxious and negotiated a sale himself in April 1852. For his half interest in the rancho, he received $4,500. Two months later, Larkin sold his own undivided half to Adolphus C. Whitcomb for $12,000.[65]

The prospects for St. Louis, on the Rancho Huichica, also looked bright, so bright that Larkin on July 8, 1852, bought Leese's half of the Huichica grant. He had bought the other half earlier from Leese. For this second portion, he paid $15,000 and promised to pay an additional $9,000 upon confirmation of the original grant.[66] The following month, Larkin was selling Huichica land at $10 per acre.[67] A number of the pieces sold were on a tract claimed by the town of Sonoma. The deeds for these properties contained a clause providing that Larkin would refund the purchase money if Sonoma were to prove its claim.[68]

Not all of the controversy of the 1850s over land titles was between claimants and squatters. In 1850 Larkin, with Milton Little, Jacob P. Leese, and James Gleason, purchased from José Abrego the Rancho Punta de Piños, a two-league tract near Monterey. Abrego claimed ownership by purchase in 1844 from the original grantee and a regrant to himself by Governor Micheltorena. The heirs of the original grantee later brought suit to recover the property, claiming that the sale was never made to Abrego. The Mon-

terey district court decided in favor of the heirs, but Larkin and his associates pressed their case before the Land Commission. In the meantime, they
ran cattle on the ranch and pondered buying the claim of the heirs. Instead,
they eventually forced Abrego to pay them $15,000 as compensation for
having sold them a doubtful title.[69] Larkin sold his interest in the property
in 1852 to Jacob Leese for $3,000.[70]

Already a wealthy man, Larkin had visions of becoming much richer.
Following Frémont's example, he offered his Rancho Boga, thought to contain valuable gold deposits, for sale in London. Larkin's price: $1,000,000.[71]
His New York attorneys, Henry G. Stebbins and George E. Baldwin, urged
secrecy, particularly when an English company sent an agent to California
to investigate.[72]

In the meantime, Nicholas Gray surveyed the grant for Larkin and found
considerable evidence of placer gold and quartz deposits. With appropriate
works, Gray said, the property would yield profitably for at least a century.[73]
As if to verify Gray's assessment, J. Howard Wainwright, the London agent
of Stebbins and Baldwin, returned to New York in October with the stag-
gering news that he had sold Boga for $1,000,000. The buyer was Thomas
D. Sargent, who had been involved in the abortive purchase of Las Mariposas. Baldwin wrote an urgent letter to Larkin, who was in California at
the time, to return at once to New York, bringing all the papers relating to
the property. "Freemont & party," said Wainwright, "were very hostile."[74]

The celebrating was premature. The prospective buyer was concerned
about the clouded title, and the sale collapsed. In January 1853, another
offer from London, not completely clear, appears to have tendered Larkin
$700,000 if he would relinquish any further claim on the property.[75] That
sale also was not consummated.

The following month, Larkin and his agents, now Stebbins and Wainwright, switched strategies. They set up the Feather River Land & Gold
Mining Company and prepared to offer shares on the London market. Larkin pondered going to London himself but decided against the trip when
Wainwright wrote from London that the market was not favorable. He
advised Larkin to let it rest for six months until his title was settled and a
quartz crushing operations proved the presence of gold.[76]

The squatter problem would not go away. Reasonably sure that Boga and
his other titles would be confirmed, Larkin, through his agents, carried on
with business as usual and dealt leniently with squatters, a tactic designed to
secure their acknowledgment of his ownership. This was a critical factor
when negotiations in London on the Boga sale had reached a delicate point.
"Mr. Larkin must get a written agreement from the Squatters to pay a
royalty," Wainwright wrote, "*never mind how small*. If only a dollar a year,
it would be very valuable here."[77] On the Children's Rancho, Sterling had
to deal repeatedly with squatters. "I suppose if I have explained once," he

commented, "I have explained 500 times the nature of this grant."[78] He gave quick consent to those who asked permission to settle. Some of these soon bought the land, and some took generous leases, from three to five years at a nominal rate, often $5 per year for a quarter section, though Larkin would charge more when he thought he could get it. Other squatters simply took up a 160 acre preemption, angrily denied Larkin's rights, and refused to move.[79]

Larkin continued to buy, sell, build, and lease properties in California towns during his eastern sojourn. William J. Eames handled his affairs in and around San Francisco. He advised Larkin in February 1853 to transfer all his assets from New York to San Francisco, where he could expect a 30 percent return.[80] The following month, Eames paid the last of Larkin's liabilities on his books. Free of debt—not his usual condition—Larkin became a money lender.[81]

Larkin's interest in railroads increased in the early 1850s. Though absent from California, he was elected a member of governing bodies of a number of projected railroads, one to connect Monterey and the San Joaquin River, another to run between San Jose and San Francisco, and a third to tie Benicia and Marysville. He was eager to support all these lines, particularly the last. In fact, he had a scheme of his own in the spring of 1852 for a line connecting the two towns via Sacramento. He knew that Congress was considering granting millions of acres of land to states to support railroad construction, and he planned to try for a land grant. "[T]ake my word for it," he wrote Atherton, who was always eager for California news, "that rail roads will start from B[enicia]. in two years, and then we shall see a town of much importance there."[82]

Larkin was not often excited; it was not his nature. But in early 1853, he was excited about the discussion in the East concerning the prospects for a transcontinental railroad. To two New York leaders in the movement, he wrote: "I have a strong desire to embark in an undertaking of so much impotance to my adopted State, and beg of you such particulars of the Companys and their prospects as you can give me." He then described his place in California as a pioneer and an owner of California land. Furthermore, he said, he was at that very moment liquidating his eastern holdings to return permanently to California. This outpouring was meant to "prove to you my anxiety to see this Rail Road commenced and carried on to completion."[83] He would follow the prospect for the railroad with great interest.

Larkin had anticipated soon after arriving in the East that he would have to visit California to look after his interests there. He made two round trips, by steamship and the isthmus. He departed New York for the first time on February 14, 1851, less than a year after arriving there. He had written ahead to tell Cooper that he would visit Monterey, "where I really believe my old Paisanos will be all glad to see me, as I shall to see them."[84] At the isthmus, purely by chance he met Cooper, who was crossing by muleback.

His half-brother was going to the East to see his son, Rogerio, who was attending the same school as Oliver.[85]

Happy though he might be to see his old friends, Larkin was not at that time contemplating a permanent return to California. Just three days before leaving the East, he had written a will, directing that, in the event of his death, his California properties be sold and the proceeds invested in "any one of the old thirteen states of the United States of America" for the benefit of his wife and children.[86] During his six-month visit in California, he tended to business affairs, which were particularly troublesome after the comparatively carefree interlude in the East when he relied on his California agents. He listened to growing problems about squatters, and in May saw a disastrous fire burn some of his most valuable San Francisco properties.[87]

Larkin had kept informed on California political affairs in his absence. He had hardly arrived in New York in 1850 when he wrote to California Governor Peter H. Burnett to recommend appointments of commissioners of deeds.[88] Larkin took time now from his business affairs to attend the Whig convention in San Francisco and to write to Major Pierson B. Reading, who was farming on the upper Sacramento River, to urge him to accept the party's nomination for governor. Citing strong support in north and south, Larkin said that, for his own part, "whether you are Whigg or Democrat, I will pledge you my time, influence & money. . . . I am a moderate Whigg, claim no partisianship to any party, but am fully a Californian."[89] Larkin was not ready to cut ties with his adopted state. He was beginning to feel the tug of two regions.

Larkin returned to New York in November 1851, but he was back in California the following May. He had planned the trip before leaving California the previous November to coincide with meetings of the Land Commission.[90] Frederic and a servant accompanied him on the second trip. He placed Frederic with Cooper and Leese, now living in Larkin's former home, and other friends in Monterey where he expected the boy would enjoy himself, build up his strength, and regain his Spanish. It was a happy respite for Frederic—a return to the California of his childhood. Leese wrote Larkin in San Francisco about their two boys "a lassoing calvs and the calvs tumbled him and Jacob about so much in the dust that they looked so aughfull I cannot discribe them more nearer than monkeys."[91]

Larkin plunged into his business affairs, which now were promising indeed. Fernando Wood, the New Yorker who had agreed to the $100,000 land exchange with Larkin, had traveled on the same ship with him to San Francisco. There they put the finishing touches on the deal.[92] Larkin made a number of other lucrative land sales during the summer. The sales of the Jimeno and Punta de Piños properties have been mentioned. The news from New York suggested that the Boga sale was in the final stages.

Larkin had a particularly satisfying encounter in Sonoma with some Huichica squatters. Stopping at a Sonoma hotel, he was confronted by fifteen or twenty settlers, some of whom had fortified themselves with liquor. "[W]e had a hard & soft talk, a loud & low one," according to Larkin. He stood his ground: "You have more tongues than I have, but less tongue power." He offered everyone drinks on him—"then we shall stand about . . . equal"—and they talked. By the end of the week, he had sold 3,000 acres at $10 an acre. Only about 10 percent of the group held out.[93] The result was a tribute to the power of persuasion and free drinks.

Larkin and Frederic, with two of General Vallejo's sons, left San Francisco on September 30, 1852. Larkin felt good about California on their departure.[94]

In late 1851, Larkin began to wonder at the wisdom of the move to the East. During a stopover in Panama on the return from his first trip to California, he wrote to his closest confidant: "Atherton I do not really know what to do, or rather where to settle." Rachel preferred to live in the East, but he believed that she would go back to California if he wished. Warming to the prospect of a return, Larkin described an ambitious new venture in San Francisco, which he called "the City." With four others, he would form a limited partnership, capitalized at $200,000, including $100,000 of his own, to engage in real-estate trading and banking. The plan, which he must have only recently discussed with the four prospective partners, was "now only in our thoughts," he added.[95]

Back in New York, Larkin continued to worry about where to settle. By April 1852, as he prepared for his second trip to the west coast, he was leaning toward California, "Benicia at that," he told Atherton. The town's prospects appeared to have improved considerably lately.[96] During this second visit to the coast, Larkin probably decided on a permanent return to California. A letter written by him from San Francisco to John C. Jones, an old California hand, clearly suggests that Larkin was going back to New York to dispose of his eastern properties and to say a final farewell to the East. Larkin's letter has not survived, but Jones's reply noted his friend's intention to take his wife and children and "pitch your tent for life, amidst the golden sands of the more congenial soil of the West."[97]

In this state of mind, it is easy to understand that Larkin became increasingly disenchanted with the East. He was particularly distressed by the repeated bouts of illness that had tormented the family since their coming in 1850. Shortly after their arrival that year, while en route to Massachusetts to visit their children, Rachel had become seriously ill with dysentery. She had just begun to recover when Larkin became so sick at Baltimore with erysipelas[98] that the family despaired of his recovering. He called for newspapers every hour, read them upside down, sent telegrams to scores of friends, and repeatedly rose from his bed, dressed, and announced that he was off for New York. By the time he began to recover, Rachel, who had helped doctor him, collapsed. They both recovered, but it was two months before Larkin was himself again.[99] Newspapers, in the meantime, had announced his death. It was months before friends in California learned the truth. The experience foretold a dilemma that would grow during the next three years. "My sons keep me here," he wrote to Cooper in August 1850, "my will & wish take me back."[100]

Illness continued to plague the family. When Larkin returned to New York in October 1852 from his second voyage, he found Rachel ill. From that day to January, she or one of the two youngest children was sick constantly.[101] Larkin tried to persuade Rachel to let him take her south, to Savannah or Charleston, where he believed her health would improve, but she refused, preferring to remain in New York.[102] Larkin was irritated. "I believe this wrong, even dangerous to her," he wrote to Leese, "I disapprove of it, but she will so remain."[103]

When Caroline became ill to the point of death in late December 1852 and January 1853, Larkin, severely distressed, blamed Rachel. "[I]f your Mother had been willing to leave the House & contents to the care of others," he wrote to Frederic and Francis, "we should have been in S. Carolina ten days ago."[104] Larkin himself suffered a recurrence of his "Baltimore complaint" in January.[105] Oliver, Frederic, and Francis, away at school and living with relatives, were ill often, and the parents' letters were filled with anxiety.

Larkin finally decided, if he had not already done so, to return permanently to California. He determined to sell all his New York real estate. The eighteen rental houses, in bad condition and only half rented, had proven a poor investment. He could not sell them for his price, so he exchanged them for two new brownstone houses on posh Fifth Avenue and immediately listed them for sale. His lots were also offered. The New York speculations had not gone well. "Old folks should not try to make great trades in new & strange cities," he groaned to Cooper.[106]

The Tenth Street house sold to William H. Aspinwall for $19,000. The furniture was expected to bring $6,000. The prospect of being without a home in the city was decidedly satisfying to Larkin. The house held too many memories of serious illness in these brief three years.[107]

Larkin's disenchantment with the East was matched by his newly-found enthusiasm for California. In January 1853, he wrote Atherton, his old California paisano, still in Chile, that the new American state was "progressive under go ahead Yankees and a thousand horse power." The region gold, grainfields, free institutions, and temperate and healthy climate, he said, would make it one of the most populous and richest states in the country. "[C]an the hand of man trace out anything its equal in former days can he dream of, can he imagine any corresponding circumstance in all time to come." He urged Atherton to join him in moving back to California. "You and I were of that country. Our eyes were turned towards it in admiration and in my part in gratitude. My children were from there. They and yours will soon be."[108] He pointed out to another correspondent that his children were the first born in California to an American mother and that his brother had married into the Vallejo family.[109] Larkin was beginning to discover California anew and to see his place in its history more clearly than before.

He was eager to go back. He remembered the admonition from Leese, who had urged him to return to the coast, for "a long life in California a living on *Carne, Frejoles y Papas* [meat, beans and potatoes] . . . is much more pleasanter than a short life caused by . . . pumpkin pies, plumb puddings &c &c and then dy with the collery morbus." Come back and grow rich in the new state, he told him. "Here you wil be a lyon and there you wil hav to be as cunning as a fox."[110] Larkin would have remembered his election to the railroad boards and the planned "Larkin" post office. San Francisco and Monterey had named streets for him. California, temperate of climate and temperament, land of unlimited opportunity, also honored him. He would go home.

Rachel did not share her husband's eagerness for a permanent return, in spite of the family's repeated, debilitating illnesses. As late as mid-January 1853, when he had long since decided to make the move, Larkin did not know whether Rachel, Caroline, and Alfred would be going with him. "This is 'quien Sabe,'" he told Atherton.[111] Though she finally agreed to the move, she put off agreeing on a departure date because of her own and Caroline's illnesses and her fear of the sea—and because she did not want to leave New York. She did not want to sell the Tenth Street house, she complained to Frederic, but "your Father let me have no peace untill I did."[112] Because of the family's illnesses and Rachel's state of mind, Larkin had to change the steamer reservation more than once.[113] In the end, all was settled, and the four traveled together.

Rachel's capitulation was not unconditional. Larkin had to promise to give her six months to decide on settling permanently in California.[114] He would have remembered that Rachel had had the same sort of misgivings about New York during the first few months after their arrival there three years before.[115]

The family reached San Francisco on May 21, 1853. The three older boys remained in their eastern schools, much to the parents' dismay, for they loved their children.

Larkin now settled back into a familiar pattern of homelife and commerce. The family was much healthier, and he saw his old friends regularly. Rachel was resigned, but not completely satisfied with the move. She missed New York, though she was favorably impressed with the changes in San Francisco during their three years' absence. The Larkins rented a house, hired servants, placed their two youngest children in good local schools, and soon built a fine home. Larkin was rich and comfortable, an Episcopalian and a Whig. He was content.

This is not to say that he had come back to the golden shores to retire. He returned to his business affairs as if he had only been absent on holiday. He resumed his broker's business[116] and bought and sold lots. Within a month of his arrival, Larkin visited Monterey once and Benicia twice and talked about going to the gold regions, Los Angeles, and even New York. Rachel was not at all happy with his traveling about, and complained to Frederic that "he is away most of the time."[117] Having him at home, however, could be a mixed blessing. Sophia Larkin, who had traveled to San Francisco with her kin as governess and companion to the two younger children, grumbled to Frederic and Francis that when any of their father's associates called, they talked incessantly about "lots . . . lots, corner lots, 50 vara lots &c, &c. Your mother and myself get tired to death hearing about them."[118] In the company of his family, Larkin was an indulgent father and husband. Among his business associates and cronies, he was in another world. In that other world, he was not above a bit of profanity when the occasion warranted.[119]

Squatter problems were as troublesome as ever, but as Larkin's titles appeared more certain, settlers became more willing to lease or purchase. Now he felt sufficiently secure to threaten eviction suits against those who chose to stand against him. Some settlers, who acknowledged his title but did not wish to purchase, withdrew after he paid for their improvements. For example, he paid $1,000 for a squatter's improvements on a 160-acre fenced tract with 100 hogs, 100 pigs, and buildings.[120]

In the mid-1850s, Larkin acquired more huge properties. He bought the Ciénega del Gavilan from Antonio Chaves, who had been granted the eleven-league Monterey County rancho in 1843. José Yves Limantour, the Mexican land speculator who became notorious for his fraudulent claims, maintained that he had bought the grant from Chaves, but the Land Commission rejected the Chaves claim. Larkin later appealed in district court, and the title was confirmed after his death.[121] Also from Chaves and in Monterey County, Larkin bought Pleyto, a three-league rancho that Chaves had received by grant in 1845. The price was $2,000. Larkin bought the rancho for Oliver,[122] perhaps to make up for Oliver's not being one of the owners of the Children's Rancho. He expanded his own holdings in Colusa County in December 1857 with the purchase of two and a half leagues for $3,600 from Manuel Díaz of Monterey. The property, part of a grant that Díaz had received from Pío Pico in 1846, adjoined the Children's and Jimeno ranchos and a three-league tract that Díaz had sold to Oliver and Frederic the previous March.[123] Larkin undoubtedly initiated and financed the purchase.

In 1858, Larkin acquired an undivided half of the Cambuston grant, across the Sacramento River from the Children's Rancho and west of Larkin's Boga property. He paid Jonathan D. Stevenson $1,000 and the promise of an additional $1,500 when the title was confirmed to Cambuston. Larkin bought an additional 2,000 acres of the grant from James and Emma Crowly for $800 and pondered Stevenson's offer to sell him another 25,000 acres. In Sonoma County, he purchased from Manuel Castro one and a half leagues of the old Caslamayomi grant.[124] By this time, he was one of the largest landholders in the state, probably the largest among those who had not received grants of their own. During his lifetime, Larkin and his children had an interest in almost a quarter million acres of California land.[125]

Larkin began to push the Boga sale once more. He authorized George M. Murray to arrange for the erection of quartz works on the rancho and to pursue prospects for a sale in England. Murray reported to Larkin from London in early March 1854 that he was about to embark for California, accompanied by a mining engineer who would inspect the rancho and determine where to begin major operations. At the end of the month, he had to retract. The Crimean War had unsettled the money market in Britain and doomed an early conclusion of the Boga venture.[126]

Meanwhile, Larkin sent William Harney, with whom he had been associated on the east coast, to Boga to assess its gold potential and inventory its squatters. In July and August 1855, Harney saw considerable evidence of works—mills, tunnels, buildings, flumes, a small store—but most were abandoned. The return had been disappointing, there was little water available, and word that the property had been confirmed to Larkin had reached the camps. Harney reported that no permanent residents remained on the rancho.[127] He sent a rough sketch of the property and a map that Oliver had made during an earlier visit.[128]

Harney's conclusions were not completely correct. A number of the intruders on the Boga complained about the title confirmation and talked about contesting it or challenging the boundaries. Larkin stood firm, and no formal protests were initiated, with the possible exception of one suit.[129] With Larkin's permission, the Feather River & Table Mountain Water Company planned to reopen mining on the grant by bringing water from the North Fork of the Feather River. Larkin's only condition was that the company sell water only to those whom he had authorized to work the deposits.[130]

Larkin faced a different sort of title challenge in San Francisco. Though he had sold his Punta de Lobos claim to Bethuel Phelps, he still remained responsible for the title. His title, like many others, was in direct conflict with that of José Limantour, whose claim included most of San Francisco. Before Larkin's return in 1853 to the city, Josiah Belden took the claim seriously and offered Limantour $5,000 to release his right to 300-vara lots owned by the partnership of Belden and Larkin. Limantour asked $20,000.[131] Larkin was less impressed with Limantour's pretensions, but nevertheless assumed a leading role in fighting him.

Limantour's claim was confirmed in 1856 by the Land Commission, causing considerable alarm in the city.[132] Many property owners rushed to Limantour to secure releases on their claims. San Francisco, fearing for its municipal properties, joined private property owners in appealing the decision to the district court. All were relieved in 1858 when the district court declared the Limantour claim fraudulent.

Larkin's Punta de Lobos claim, assessed in 1856 at $500,000, suffered the same fate. It was rejected by the commission and the courts on grounds that the original title was false and antedated.[133]

Larkin's urban land business nevertheless continued profitable for the most part, but the squatter problem was vexing. In the spring of 1854, Larkin was a leader in the formation of an organization of San Francisco property holders pledged to confront squatters, who were becoming increasingly belligerent. After a thousand people joined this "Association for the Protection of Property and the Maintenance of Order," squatter encroachment declined.[134] His Sacramento lots, with titles derived largely from Sutter and Sam Brannan, were particularly troublesome. Sutter sometimes gave two or three deeds to the same lot, and squatters were unusually contentious. The Land Commission's confirmation of Sutter's New Helvetia claim in 1855 tended to assure buyers. Larkin seems to have ended speculation in Monterey by the early 1850s. He owned only a few properties there in 1858, a few lots in Los Angeles and San Jose, and one lot in Nevada City.[135]

By the mid-1850s, Benicia was declining and Larkin was beginning to withdraw, though he still owned hundreds of lots there. He was able to sell some lots, and others were sold for taxes.[136] Like San Jose and Vallejo, Benicia had proven but a way station for the state government. Named the state capital in 1853, it was abandoned by state officials the following year in favor of Sacramento. Larkin spent many weeks in Benicia in late 1853 and early 1854 trying to influence legislators, but Sacramentans, aided by much "champagne, crackers, arguments, Houses, Lots, Theatre tickets Etc. Etc.," won in the end.[137] Benicia had been designated a port of entry, but Larkin found it impossible to secure payment for the government's lease of his building for a customhouse.[138] The Benicia-Marysville Railroad had died aborning. In 1857, some town lots were being turned to pasture.

Larkin continued to invest his time and capital in any sort of venture that would return profits. In spring 1856, on hearing that a drought in the south was killing cattle, he offered to lease the Children's Rancho to Abel Stearns and his neighbors. The following year he paid José Abrego $4,900 for a herd of 508 native cattle and 15 or 20 American bulls to run on the Children's Rancho. He also revived his hog business there.[139] By spring 1858, he was harvesting barley and wheat and expected 100 tons of hay from a single cutting.[140] He pondered stocking the Boga and corresponded with men who were interested in running stock for him elsewhere on shares.[141]

Larkin acted often as agent for others, performing any number of functions. For example, he sent provisions to José Chaves at San Diego and pursued claims in Washington for others against the United States government. His fee as land broker was 10 percent, to which Henri Cambuston objected after Larkin had made a sale for him, claiming that Larkin customarily charged old Californians nothing for the service.[142] Cambuston was mistaken. Larkin often did favors for friends, but not on a regular basis if profits were concerned.

Larkin's east coast affairs receded farther into the past, and he devoted little time to them, relying on his agents to manage and liquidate his holdings there. Some of Larkin's lots on New York's Sixty-First Street were condemned by the city, but he expected a liberal award for them. In spite of the general decline in real-estate values in the mid-1850s, the prospect of some of his properties near Central Park rose. His agents advised him to keep the land for speculative purposes, but he instructed them to sell. He set a minimum price of $32,000 for fourteen adjacent lots at Broadway and Fifty-Eighth and Fifty-Ninth streets; he was pleased to see them fetch $42,000.[143]

Larkin continued to pursue his Washington claims through agents. The warrant for $6,075.06, the approved portion of Larkin's Frémont claim, was issued in October 1854, not to Larkin but to Talbot Green, who had been his agent in 1846. Green assigned the amount to Larkin, but there were still complications in collecting it. Larkin pressed for payment of the balance and must have been furious when he learned that the army board of officers investigating the Frémont claims had implied that he might have falsified a signature of one of Frémont's officers.[144] Unfortunately, Larkin's response, which must have been blistering, has not been found. He wrote a reasoned appeal to Secretary of War Jefferson Davis, asking for fairness and an explanation of the rejection. A Treasury Department auditor sent a curt reply, restating what Larkin already knew of the affair.[145]

Through Andrew Wylie, Larkin submitted to the Court of Claims the Benicia customhouse case, the rejected portion of the Frémont claim, and perhaps the naval storekeeper case.[146] In 1856, he sent a fresh appeal to the Court of Claims, once more requesting payment in full for his two navy appointments. He took the posts, he said, from patriotic motives. Having performed the duties of both, while knowing nothing of the prohibition against the same person holding two appointments, he was now being denied full compensation for either.[147] The plea fell on deaf ears. Wylie, who was handling the case, sympathized: "There is no debter who is able to pay, so difficult to deal with, as the Government of these United States."[148]

Larkin still had land claims that required attention. For a moment it appeared that Congress was going to pass a bill to confirm all titles that had been approved by the board of commissioners, but it was defeated. Larkin was a witness in at least two land cases, probably more, in the Northern California District Court.[149] He was a party to at least one United States Supreme Court case. A. H. Lawrence, one of the best land lawyers in Washington, in that case argued successfully in favor of the Jimeno title.[150] With the exception of the Punta de Lobos claim, all of Larkin's grants were eventually patented: Children's Rancho, 1857; Cotate, 1858; Huichica, 1859; Jimeno, 1862; Boga, 1865; Ciénega del Gavilan, 1867; Pleyto, 1872.[151]

After returning to San Francisco from the East, Larkin either lost interest in the Washington Monument or was negligent, as he often was, in corresponding with the society. The Washington office repeatedly wrote to ask about his progress and plead for the funds they needed to complete the monument. Then they wrote to Eames, thinking Larkin might be away.[152] It must be assumed that Larkin or Eames responded, but there are no extant letters to the society from San Francisco after 1852. The society transferred the Washington Monument to the federal government in 1877. It was finally finished in 1884 after a congressional appropriation of $200,000.[153]

A dramatic sidelight in the chaotic 1850s, when Larkin was moving between east and west and finally settling permanently in San Francisco, was the so-called Talbot Green affair. Larkin's employee, friend, and most trusted business associate, Green had come to California in 1841, a penniless immigrant who by 1850 had become one of California's leading citizens. His world fell apart in 1851 at the very moment that he was standing for mayor of San Francisco. He was recognized by an old friend from his Pennsylvania hometown as Paul Geddes, a merchant and embezzler who had fled his creditors and abandoned his family in 1841.

His California friends, numbering some of the most prominent people, were appalled at the outrageous charge. Larkin was among the first to defend him. Just before Green's departure for the East in April 1851 to clear himself, a reception was held in his honor. Larkin, returned only recently from New York, climbed upon a table and proposed a toast: "'May the most honest man among us all here assembled be as honest, and always remain as honest, as we believe Talbot H. Green to be.'" All drained their glasses, gave three cheers, and escorted Green to his steamer.[154]

Then Green dropped from sight. After his return to New York in November 1852, Larkin heard that Green had been seen in New Orleans. Larkin met Green's brother and corresponded with his mother and father.

He sent Green's picture to Philadelphia, and "all knew it." From Green/Geddes's family and friends, Larkin learned that the accusations against his old and trusted friend were true.[155]

Another year had passed when Larkin received a letter from Green. In the letter, Green acknowledged his guilt and told Larkin all about his other life. Unable to face those in the East whom he had wronged, he had gone into hiding in eastern Tennessee, where he was living in great poverty. In succeeding months, he wrote anguished letters to Larkin, asking him to keep the correspondence secret and begging for news of his California family and friends. He also asked for money. Larkin was true to Green's trust, sending him news and small amounts of money, but also castigating him for his deception.[156]

Eventually Green repented and resolved to make amends. Larkin helped him collect some sizable California debts, and Green returned to San Francisco in 1855. There Larkin and Green formally dissolved their partnership.[157] Green remained about a year, but he soon realized that he could not take up his California life again. In September 1856 he returned to Pennsylvania, where he became reconciled with the family that he had deserted fifteen years before. He wrote later to Larkin that there was an unexplainable void in this new old life. Whatever his fate, he said, he would always appreciate Larkin's kindness.[158] Larkin never saw him again.[159]

In the mid-1850s, Larkin assessed his financial condition. His land business had prospered in spite of the inflationary spiral and speculative mania since 1849. He had lost less than most in a bank crisis in 1855, perhaps because some of his money had been left in New York banks.[160] The experience led him to wonder, only briefly, whether he had made a grave mistake in not selling all his California properties and retiring permanently to New York in 1850. Childs responded to Larkin's musing, saying that he himself had felt so at the time, "& I believe got some raps on the knuckles for saying so." He assured Larkin that all works out for the best: "Having less to spend you will see more clearly the value of money & part with it less freely."[161]

Larkin clearly had overstated his suffering. This was typical of him. He often worried excessively about his financial condition. He was simply not as rich as he thought he should be. Actually, his problem was not in his worth, which was mostly in property, but in cash flow. He pressed his New York agents to push the sale of his properties and his Washington agent to get his claims settled. Rachel helped with a loan of $5,000 from a Hobson kinsman.[162] For months after returning to California, he brooded about having spent so much money in New York. He felt that he could no longer call himself rich. This lament came when he was building his San Francisco mansion, yet he could still protest: "When Alfred ask to[o] often for Rials," he told Frederic and Francis, "I tell him I require them to buy Bricks."

The brothers could also save money. In response to a question from the boys, he wrote that it would be quite appropriate for Francis to wear Frederic's clothes. There would be time for each to wear his own clothes, he told them, if the government confirmed their land.[163] In a different mood, he declared that his "'rich name'" had become a "'bore & expense'" to him.[164]

It was in this last mood that Larkin turned increasingly to non-commercial affairs. He became a social leader and civic booster. He was asked to meet with a group of men who were contemplating the publication of a newspaper in New York, devoted entirely to promoting California.[165] He donated 500 acres of Huichica land toward the founding of the "'Trinity College of Larkin,'" under the direction of the Episcopal Bishop William I. Kip.[166] Larkin was a member of the Trinity Episcopal Church of San Francisco, in Kip's diocese. Larkin also agreed to give five acres on the rancho for a schoolhouse.

Larkin's interest in railroads grew. He was among the incorporating members of the Atlantic and Pacific Railroad Company in 1853 and was active as an officer in California meetings. Influential friends in the company assured him that he would be elected a director.[167] He tried to ensure that Benicia would be its western terminus by promising to give twenty-one lots to O. M. Wozencraft if the influential San Franciscan were successful in securing the designation within two years.[168] Larkin joined Sam Brannan in 1853 in applying for a franchise to build a street railway in San Francisco from Market Street to the city limits, where it could connect with the proposed transcontinental railroad.[169] Larkin was also a leading spirit in the founding of the San Francisco and Sacramento Railroad Company, incorporated in 1856. One of five commissioners named to accept stock subscriptions, he enrolled himself for $5,000 in stock. Only one person in the initial offering subscribed for more: Theodore D. Judah.[170]

One wonders what might have been the history of California had the association with Judah not been interrupted by Larkin's death. A visionary and the father of railroad building in the state, Judah would not have had to settle in the 1860s for the financial backing of some Sacramento merchants, the avaricious Big Four—Huntington, Crocker, Stanford, and Hopkins—whose corrupting power would shape California politics and economics for a half century. He would have found an enthusiastic collaborator, rich and civic minded, in Larkin.

The welfare of his city and state stimulated Larkin's interest in politics. In early 1855, he urged old paisano, Pablo de la Guerra, a member of the state legislature, to work for bills to relieve almost-bankrupt San Francisco and to support Pierson B. Reading for senator. If you oppose him, Larkin wrote, "I will set you down as a Politician for life."[171] Jesting aside, Larkin could also be cynical about politics. He wrote to his friend Pablo in January 1856 to say that he should not fret about selecting a senator because "few of those whose names I have heard for that office are worth the sending, is any

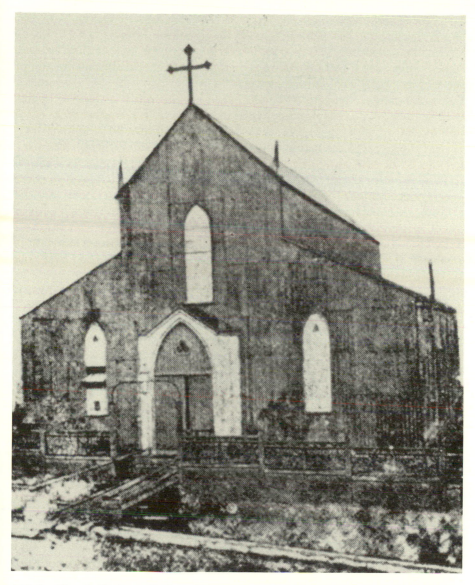

Trinity Church (Episcopal), San Francisco. Larkin worshipped here in the mid-1850s and was buried from this church. Courtesy Trinity Episcopal Church, San Francisco.

one of them[?]"[172] He went himself to Sacramento in March 1856 "to see the wire pulling for the Settlers Bill and if possible wish to have one pull at it my way."[173] The Settlers Act passed that same month over the opposition of claimants to Mexican land grants. The act required that owners whose lands had been patented must either sell occupied tracts to settlers or pay them for their improvements. Larkin was not hurt badly by the measure, and it was later struck down by the state supreme court.[174]

Larkin remained for the most part aloof from the vigilante movements of the 1850s. Vigilance committees were formed in communities throughout the state, wherever citizens believed that the authorities were unable or unwilling to enforce the law and provide adequate services. In San Francisco, the hotbed of vigilantism, the committee in 1856 forcibly removed two alleged murderers from jail and hanged them. Crowds cheered, and membership in the committee swelled to 6,000. The authorities were powerless.

It seems that Larkin took the middle ground in his comments on the events, since his correspondents expressed varying opinions. If he had taken a strong position, their responses would have revealed it. From Washington, Childs and Larkin's boys disapproved of the breakdown of law and order, but Abel Stearns believed that "the better class of citizens" in the state approved the committee's actions.[175] To Cooper, Larkin guessed that "the V. Committee will break up their outward show next week and retire to their homes, yet continue their organization for some months."[176] The repeated use of "their" seems to put Larkin outside of the membership.

Yet Larkin must have had an opinion. The San Francisco vigilance movement was widely supported by businessmen who, holding the related evils of government and taxation in equal contempt, distrusted the former and evaded the latter. Larkin was among those named by the *San Francisco Bulletin* of August 27 as tax dodgers.[177] It is no surprise then that he was one of the founding members, along with the principal leaders of the disbanded vigilance committee, of the People's Reform Party, whose principal objective was tax cuts.[178] Larkin's correspondence only hints at his subsequent involvement. In response to a letter from Larkin, Stearns wrote: "I notice all you say with regard to Vigilance, Presidential Candidates &c, &c."[179] One yearns to see that lost Larkin letter.

The comment from Stearns refers, on the other hand, to a topic that definitely interested Larkin, the election of 1856. With the decline of the Whigs, he actively supported the Republican Party and Frémont, its presidential candidate, with his time and money.[180] During the summer and autumn of the election year, Larkin corresponded frequently about politics with friends in California and the East. He pestered some of his old paisanos, who mostly favored the Democrats and James Buchanan.[181] Frederic and Francis also differed with their father. They were for Millard Fillmore, candidate of the American Party.

Larkin worked through local people to organize political meetings, perhaps even trying his hand at speaking occasionally. David Spence thought he might find an audience in Monterey, but would not likely find Spence among his listeners. "I prefer going to sleep," he told Larkin, "or ly on my bed awake and nurse my own thoughts, for I hate politics as the devil does holy water." [182] There is no evidence that Larkin tried to convert him.

Larkin's opinion of Frémont was particularly sought by Easterners. His replies to their letters are full and objective, describing Frémont as reserved and industrious, moral and persevering, and opposed to an extension of slavery. [183] His reports were circulated widely in the election campaign. Larkin apparently accepted Frémont's defeat without any considerable emotion. At least, there is no comment on the outcome of the election among his papers.

CHAPTER 12

REPOSE

On his return from New York in 1853, Larkin's pace, while still fast, was less frantic. The family had hardly settled into their rented accommodation in San Francisco when they began planning a splendid new home. Before the end of the year, Larkin had placed a number of orders with eastern suppliers. In the months following, he received grand mantle pieces, mirrors, carved marble chimney pieces, grates, hearths, all of the finest quality. Located at 282 Stockton Street, between Jackson and Pacific, the house suited one of San Francisco's foremost citizens. Three stories fronted on Stockton, and five stories in the rear overlooked a garden of 300 plants. The brick house had eighteen rooms, exclusive of storerooms, which included two parlors, ample servants' quarters, and a winding staircase that ended at an octagonal glass observatory, eleven-feet wide, on the flat roof. The Larkins moved into their new home in 1854.[1] Larkin's offices were nearby at 137 Montgomery Street, later moved to number 125. The office of the Larkin and Belden partnership was adjacent at 123 Montgomery.[2]

The family's life-style, one of opulence and gentility, reflected Larkin's success. The Larkins were conspicuously upper class. Grocer and butcher bills in April 1855 totaled $340.90. Two years later, in May 1857, the sum had risen to $377.20.[3] Sherry was purchased by the gallon. Family members were fashionably dressed and were attended by servants. On formal occasions, Rachel might wear her diamond cross, costing $700. Alfred and Caroline were placed in prestigious schools, Caroline at the Young Ladies High School in San Francisco and Alfred at Oakland High School, a private boarding school. Larkin paid pew rent at the Trinity Episcopal Church and attended regularly.[4]

Their parents now settled permanently in California, the three boys in the East began to chafe and ask their father when they might return home. Oliver was particularly anxious. He did not like his school at Cambridge or his master. Mr. Wellington in turn complained that Oliver was sometimes surly and insubordinate, setting a bad example for the other boys, who were all much younger.[5] Oliver was a shy boy and had few friends. He was hurt that his father would not place the three brothers in the same school or permit the two younger boys to vacation with him. "We all three of us must write to each other," he wrote to Frederic and Francis, "because we shall not see each other more than once a year."[6] Oliver was often ill, or imagined himself so, and he feared that he was losing his hearing.[7] Larkin would have sympathized with his son since he himself suffered from severe hearing loss.[8]

Larkin had long since realized that Oliver was no scholar, but he had hoped that his eldest would find a vocation in his schooling. Nevertheless, in May 1854, he finally gave in to Oliver's repeated entreaties and said that he could return to California. Oliver was ecstatic. He wrote a short letter to thank his parents, ending "I have no more to say to you, for my head is all full about getting ready to go home."[9] He had been away from home at school, in Oahu and the East, for almost sixteen of his twenty years.

Frederick and Francis were not so fortunate. Childs wrote regularly to Larkin to praise the brothers for their diligence and progress and manners, while also repeating his complaint that they did not appreciate the value of education and the opportunity provided by their rich father. Larkin urged the boys as often to study hard and follow Childs's guidance in all things. "Riches does not make the man," he told them, "even if I could give it to you, you must have good moral habits strict . . . conduct, and Religious principles, to carry you thro life."[10] Larkin repeatedly cautioned his boys not to rely on his uncertain "California fortune."[11]

Frederick remained at Rugby Academy until September 1855, when Childs placed him in Charles De Selding's office in Washington, where he would get experience in writing and translating. Frederick thought the work unrewarding and frequently asked his father to let him come home. Larkin finally relented—Frederick reminded his father that he was now twenty-one years old—and on February 14, 1857, Frederick arrived in San Francisco.

Francis remained with Childs and Rugby Academy after Frederick's departure. Francis was the only one of the boys that appeared to be college bound, and Larkin and Childs corresponded about alternatives. Larkin favored law study at Harvard, while Childs recommended the Virginia Military Institute or the University of Virginia. Larkin objected to the "Southern chivalry" of Virginia while Childs pointed to "the snobism of the Northern mushroom aristocracy."[12] Larkin suggested to Frederic that

The living members of the immediate Larkin family, San Francisco, 1858. From left to right: Frederick, Alfred, Mrs. Larkin, Francis, Larkin, Carolina, Thomas Oliver. Photographer (of original photograph), Chuck Bancroft. Courtesy State of California, Department

he might consider becoming a doctor, but he never followed up and soon assumed that Frederic eventually would enter his offices.

The Larkins at home were a contented family. Now that they were in their new house, the garden growing and the neighborhood more settled, Rachel was happy. Larkin doted on Alfred, a happy, active child who seemed never to be still. Sophia Larkin, still governess and companion to Alfred and Caroline, also taught in a local school. Caroline was a good student, earning mostly "A's," and an outgoing teenager. She had a holiday party in December 1856 with 120–130 guests, "including some 12 or 14 natives of California," Larkin told his brother John.[13] The elder Larkins also often entertained and had house guests. On New Year's Day 1857, Rachel welcomed over 100 visitors while Larkin and Oliver made their calls in the neighborhood.[14]

In mid-May 1858, Francis arrived in California for a two- or three-months' visit, spending most of his time on the Children's Rancho, then returned to Washington and school. He had been lonely in Washington after Frederic had left for California, but no more. Alfred accompanied him on the return voyage and was soon settled in the Childs's home and enrolled in school.[15] He was eleven years old.

Oliver was happier now, but more unsettled than ever. He traveled about San Francisco Bay for pleasure, to the Children's Rancho and between San Francisco and Monterey, where he stayed with his Uncle Cooper. He began once more to sign his letters with a flourish in imitation of his father's, something he had not done for the past year or so. He worked as a clerk in his father's office for a time and on the Children's Rancho and pondered going to sea. Larkin worried about Oliver and tried to help him find a profession. He placed him a few months with a mining and milling operation in Grass Valley so he could learn quartz mining, and he corresponded with William D. Phelps about a maritime career for Oliver.[16] Larkin eventually decided that Oliver had no business sense and had his son convey to him all his property in San Francisco.[17]

Frederick found a place for himself quickly. Even before leaving Washington, he had become quite interested in the family's land holdings, particularly the Children's Rancho, of which he was part owner.[18] He operated a store on the rancho for a few months, probably retaining an interest in it after his departure,[19] then from July 1857 worked in Larkin's San Francisco offices.

In the hard times of the mid-1850s, Larkin began more and more to reflect on his life in Mexican California and the roles that he and his old paisanos played in California affairs. To Abel Stearns, one of his dearest friends from those early days, he wrote that "I begin to yearn after the times prior to July 1846 and all their honest pleasures and the flesh pots of those days. Halcyon days they were. *We* shall not enjoy there like again."[20] To perpetuate those days and to honor kindred spirits, in 1856 he compiled for posterity a list of 285 men and women, of British or United States origins, who were living in California prior to 1840.[21] He wrote to John Gilroy, the first foreigner to settle in California, asking him to describe the early days in detail.[22] He began addressing his sons as "Frederico" and "Francisco" and included Spanish phrases in his letters. He called his daughter "Carolina" once again. Alfred Robinson was now "Don Alfredo."

He also urged the Society of California Pioneers, as its immediate past-president, to commemorate those who had a part in the Americanization of California by setting up a "First Class" of membership, open to those who had resided in the state before July 7, 1846, the date of the American landing at Monterey and thus the end of Mexican rule. "Those who contributed to bring about the events of that day," he said, "are those who are especially entitled to honor at your hands." A second class of membership would include those who lived in California before September 9, 1850, the date of California's admission as a state to the United States. As far as the honor of his own personal membership in the first class, he said with a large measure of false modesty that he neither asked for nor desired it.[23]

Larkin grieved the loss of his old paisanos. Hugo Reid died in 1852. Robert B. Semple, his contentious partner, died tragically in 1854, William E. P. Hartnell and Manuel Jimeno the same year, and W. D. M. Howard in 1856. Job F. Dye, ill and declining, moved to New England. From Monterey, David Spence wrote of his debilitating disease. Talbot Green was a perplexing memory.[24]

Larkin regretted also the passing of those halcyon days because then he was at the center of things. He was now respected and rich, but he was not among the powerful. He had received some recognition for his contribution to the Americanization of California: streets in Monterey, San Francisco, and elsewhere named for him; the presidency of the Society of California Pioneers; a new species of fish, "G. Larkinsii," named in his honor; substantial notice in the *Annals of San Francisco*, published in 1855—though he was not pleased with the account of his contribution.[25] It was scant thanks.

In January 1857, Larkin wrote to President-elect Buchanan to apply for a political appointment.[26] He would be pleased to accept any position that Buchanan might offer, but he specifically mentioned a post in Mexico and that of United States Marshall for San Francisco. He reminded Buchanan of the gratitude that he and President Polk had expressed for his services during the 1840s. Larkin explained his support for Frémont, Buchanan's Republican opponent in the recent presidential election, as a widely-supported move in California to end the control of state politics by the corrupt Democratic Party machine under David C. Broderick.

A notation on the reverse of the letter suggests the fate of the appeal: "A Fremonter begs for office."[27] Perhaps the harried President-elect never saw the application. If he did, he chose not to respond. At least, there is no evidence of a reply among Larkin's papers. One wonders how long Larkin waited, and in what state of mind. There is no further note in the record of this desire to return to public life. Perhaps he had wanted once more to join the fray, to recapture something of the excitement of the days before and during the conquest. Maybe he was bored.

The pace that Larkin had set for himself in the decade since the conquest had taken its toll. He had aged beyond his years. By the mid-1850s, his writing and particularly his signature did not show the same vigor. Perhaps it was time to slow the pace. He took the family to Monterey, but it was not the same place. "We found yr Native town dull," he wrote to Frederic and Francis, "woefully dull, but few People, and this few triste bastante [rather sad], not a ride, picknic, nor dance." The Montereños "jog on poco poco, como siempre [slowly, as always], to us appear duller than ever, because we see so much bustle here."[28] San Francisco was his town now.

He had to visit his scattered properties occasionally, but as the years passed, he increasingly disliked being away from home. He postponed a projected inspection trip to his Sacramento River holdings time and again, but finally set out, in spite of repeated warnings that many of the ranch workers were sick.[29] There Larkin fell ill with a fever, probably typhoid. He was brought home to San Francisco, where he died in less than a week on October 27, 1858. He was fifty-six years old.

In the days following Larkin's death, virtually every newspaper in northern California published articles or extended obituaries recalling his career.[30] The San Francisco *Alta California* printed a resolution adopted at a special meeting of the Society of California Pioneers, praising their past president.[31] The funeral was held at Trinity Episcopal Church on Pine Street, of which he was a member, on October 30, 1858, following which his body was interred in Lone Mountain Cemetery,[32] a new cemetery that had been dedicated on May 30, 1854. It was then beyond San Francisco's city limits and at least a mile from any residential area. By 1907, the cemetery was in the center of a densely populated residential district, and further burials were prohibited.[33] Ultimately, Larkin's body was reinterred in the Cypress Lawn Cemetery, Colma, California.[34]

Thomas O. Larkin was among the first to test what in the next century would be called the "California Dream." He had gone to that "jumping off place of the world"[35] for personal profit, that most common motive of immigrants. Like most other foreigners who had preceded him to California, he found much in the local life-style attractive and shaped a place for himself and his family that was part Hispanic and part American. Larkin combined

Rachel Larkin as a widow, wearing an ambrotype of Larkin as a brooch. Photograph of oil portrait painted in San Francisco, 1859, by Stephen William Shaw. Photographer, Chuck Bancroft. Courtesy State of California, Department of Parks and Recreation.

both patriotism and profit. Unlike his compatriots, he did not abandon his American citizenship. His patriotism found purpose in his work for an association of California with the United States.

Larkin's life serves as the best example of the transition of California from Mexican province to American state. A gentle imperialist, he favored the change at the initiation of the Californios themselves. When war interrupted the progress toward that certain event, he put his disappointment aside to serve the invaders, a role that sometimes troubled him. With the conquest completed, he became the quintessential nineteenth-century Californian, exuberently American, acquisitive, and nostalgic for a fading Hispanic past.

NOTES

Chapter 1. Introduction

1. James Buchanan to Thomas Oliver Larkin [hereinafter in correspondence citations referred to as TOL], October 17, 1845, in George P. Hammond, ed., *The Larkin Papers: Personal, Business, and Official Correspondence of Thomas Oliver Larkin, Merchant and United States Consul in California*, 10 vols. (Berkeley: University of California Press, 1951–1968), 4:44–55.

2. Ibid., pp. 45–46.

3. Archibald H. Gillespie to TOL, April 17, 1846, ibid., 4:290.

4. Zephyrin Engelhardt, *The Missions and Missionaries of California* 4 vols. (San Francisco: James H. Barry Company, 1908–1916), 4:529, 3:653.

5. Alfred Robinson, *Life in California* (New York: Wiley & Putnam, 1846; reprint, New York: Da Capo Press, 1969), 225.

6. Ibid., p. 226.

7. Thomas Jefferson Farnham, *Travels in the Californias, and Scenes in the Pacific Ocean* (New York: Saxton & Niles, 1844; reprint, *Travels in California*, Oakland: Biobooks, 1947), 148.

8. Overton Johnson and William H. Winter, *Route Across the Rocky Mountains* (Lafayette, Indiana: John B. Semans, 1846; reprint, New York: Da Capo Press, 1972), 107.

9. Bernard DeVoto, *The Year of Decision: 1846* (Boston: Little, Brown and Company, 1943), 109–10.

10. Robert Louis Stevenson, "The Old Pacific Capital (Monterey)," *Fraser's Magazine* (November 1880, reprinted in *Across the Plains, with Other Memories and Essays*, London: Chatto & Windus and New York: Charles Scribner's Sons, 1892). The essay has been included in several other reprint editions, with varying titles and inclusions, and is quoted from Robert Louis Stevenson, *From Scotland to Silverado*, ed. James D. Hart (Cambridge: Belknap Press of Harvard University Press, 1966), 159.

11. Letter of William L. Todd, April 17, 1846, quoted in DeVoto, *The Year of Decision*, 122.

12. TOL to James Buchanan, April 17, 1846, *Larkin Papers*, 4:293.

Chapter 2. Youth and Early Manhood: Massachusetts and North Carolina

1. TOL, "My Itinerary: U.S. America," ed. by Robert J. Parker, *California Historical Society Quarterly* 16 (March and June 1937): 11–29, 144–71; reprinted in Robert J. Parker, ed., *Chapters in the Early Life of Thomas Oliver Larkin* (San Francisco: California Historical Society, 1939), 9–54. The original of this commentary and travel diary for the period 1821–1826 is in the Bancroft Library, Berkeley. All quotations and factual statements not otherwise specifically cited in this chapter are taken from Larkin's "Itinerary," specifically the Parker edition published in 1939, which differs slightly in punctuation from the original. Other portions of the Parker volume will be separately cited.

2. Statement of Alfred O. Larkin [son of TOL], quoted in Rayner W. Kelsey, "The United States Consulate in California," *Publications in Pacific Coast History*, 2 vols., (Berkeley: University of California Press, 1910–1911), 1:247.

3. Dates of father's and grandfather's births are from detailed genealogies found in the Larkin House, Monterey, California. Last private possession was by Alice S. Toulmin, granddaughter of Thomas O. Larkin. Internal evidence suggests they were prepared or collected by Alfred O. Larkin, the youngest son of TOL. (Hereinafter referred to as Larkin Genealogies.) For additional and consistent genealogical references, see William E. Lincoln, *Lincoln, Pearce, Porter & Ayer & Related Families* (Pittsburgh: n.p., 1930).

4. The story is mentioned in the Larkin Genealogies.

5. Statement of Alfred O. Larkin [son of TOL] quoted in Kelsey, "The United States Consulate in California," 247. The burning of the Larkin homes during the battle of Bunker's Hill was also mentioned in a biographical sketch published while Thomas O. Larkin was still alive and therefore probably approved by him or written from information obtained from him. Frank Soulé, John H. Gihon, and James Nisbet, *The Annals of San Francisco* (New York: D. Appleton & Co., 1855, reprint, Palo Alto, Calif.: Lewis Osborne, 1966), 758.

6. Robert J. Parker, "A Sketch of Larkin's Life and an Introduction to his 'My Itinerary,'" *California Historical Society Quarterly* 16 (March 1937: 3-10; reprinted in *Chapters in the Early Life of Thomas Oliver Larkin),* 1.

7. John Woolfenden and Amelie Elkinton, *Cooper: Juan Bautista Rogers Cooper: Sea Captain, Adventurer, Ranchero and Early California Pioneer, 1791-1872* (Pacific Grove, Calif.: Boxwood Press, 1983), 9-24. The discussion in text through the next footnote is taken from this source.

8. The above material is, as indicated, drawn from ibid., 9-24. Larkin in "My Itinerary" mentions the death of his father and the move from Charleston to Lynn. The "Oliver" in Larkin's name is from his paternal grandmother's maiden name. See Larkin Genealogies.

9. Robert J. Parker, "Thomas Oliver Larkin in 1831," *California Historical Society Quarterly* 16 (September 1937: 263-70; reprinted in *Chapters in the Early Life of Thomas Oliver Larkin),* 62, n.2.

10. Robert J. Parker, "Larkin, Anglo-American Businessman in Mexican California," *Greater America: Essays in Honor of Herbert Eugene Bolton* (Berkeley: University of California Press, 1945), 415-29.

11. Ebenezer Larkin Childs to TOL, August 12, 1843, *Larkin Papers,* 2:34-35.

12. Ann Rogers Larkin Wright to TOL, April 24, 1847, ibid., 6:119 [personality]; Betsey Larkin Childs to TOL, December 5, 1846, ibid., 5:296 [appearance].

13. Ebenezer L. Childs to TOL, December 29, 1847, ibid., 7:107 [band-box order]; TOL to Isaac Childs, March 15, 1847, ibid., 6:53 [great trader].

14. TOL to Moses Y. Beach & Sons, May 19, 1846, ibid., 4:380.

15. These are contained in the *Larkin Papers.*

16. This cousin, William M. Rogers, was a frequent correspondent with Larkin during his California residence and became the minister of Franklin Street Church, Boston. William M. Rogers to TOL, January 20, 1840 and September 11, 1843, Vallejo Documents, 33:7, 358, Bancroft Library.

17. On September 11, 1791, the baptism of John B. R. Cooper, Larkin's half-brother through their common mother, was registered in the records of St. Anne's Church, the parish church of Alderney Island in the English Channel. Woolfenden and Elkinton, *Cooper,* 9. St. Anne's was a parish church of the Church of England, so it is a fair inference that Larkin's mother was an Anglican.

18. Receipts for pew rent for 1856 and 1857. Larkin, "Correspondence and Papers," C-B/105:109, Bancroft Library. A letter from Burton Weaver, Administrator of Trinity Episcopal Church, to David J. Langum, dated August 25, 1987, and in the possession of the author, confirms that membership and also that Mrs. Larkin was confirmed in that church on March 28, 1858. Since the records do not show a confirmation for Larkin himself, and since he was not attending that church simply to please his wife (because her

own membership was so recent), probably he was already a confirmed member of the Episcopal Church, perhaps from childhood. As for the burial, many of his obituaries mention Trinity Episcopal as the location of the funeral, and the records of Trinity Episcopal Church themselves confirm the funeral.

19. His children were all baptised in the Episcopal Church. Typescript found in files of Portsmouth Athenaeum and furnished to author by Jane Porter, Keeper, by letter of August 28, 1986. The material on the typescript purports to be taken from Lincoln, *Lincoln, Pearce, Porter & Ayer & Related Families.*

20. Ebenezer L. Childs to TOL, August 12, 1843, *Larkin Papers,* 2:34.

21. Soulé, et al., *The Annals of San Francisco,* 759. This biographical sketch was written during Larkin's lifetime. His "Itinerary" mentions a change of employment but does not specify that the second job was in a book and stationery store.

22. S. A. Ashe, *History of North Carolina,* 2 vols. (Raleigh: Edwards & Broughton, 1925; reprint, Spartanburg, S.C. Reprint Co., 1971), 2:275.

23. Diane C. Cashman, *Cape Fear Adventure: An Illustrated History of Wilmington* (Woodland Hills, Calif.: Windsor Publications, 1982), 47.

24. Vallejo Documents, 28:169.

25. *Larkin Papers,* 1:1.

26. Thomas G. Thurston to TOL, July 11, 1851, ibid., 9:26. ("I will be here at 3 o'clock and I wish you to loan me $500.00. With that amt. I can pay a few small bills I owe, and my passage to N. Orleans.")

27. The community has long since disappeared. As early as 1850 there was no further mercantile business there. Dempsey Harrell to TOL, January 20, 1850, in Robert J. Parker, ed., "California's Larkin Settles Old Debts: A View of North Carolina, 1847—1856," *North Carolina Historical Review* 17 (October 1940): 338. See also *Larkin Papers,* 8:281. In his "Itinerary" Larkin mentions that Rockfish was located on a creek of that name. It was almost certainly located within Rockfish Township in the extreme southwest corner of Duplin County. See generally, Leon H. Sikes, *Duplin County Places: Past and Present, A Guide to Duplin County, N.C.* (Wallace, N.C.: By the Author, 1984), 142, 147—52.

28. The date is specifically mentioned in "Itinerary." Additionally, there is a letter from William Larkin to TOL dated Wilmington, August 24, 1825. In it William gives various business information and states: "There has been 3 Deaths in town yesterday and today and a number of People sick. . . . My health is very good at present." At the bottom of the letter is a notation in TOL's hand: "W. R. Larkin was taken sick the day after he wrote this letter, and died ten days afterwards." Larkin, "Correspondence and Papers," C–B/ 105:129.

29. Dempsey Harrell to TOL, February 10, 1854, in Parker, ed., "California's Larkin Settles Old Debts," 341—42.

30. TOL to Ebenezer L. Childs, May 11, 1831, in Parker, ed., *Chapters in the Early Life of Thomas Oliver Larkin,* 56. Larkin here referred to "Dempsey Harrel my former store clerk at R. [Rockfish]," although it is entirely possible he had had other clerks at earlier times.

31. The reader is reminded that this diary is the source for all statements of fact and quotations in this chapter not otherwise specifically cited. For bibliographic information on "My Itinerary: U.S. America," see n. 1, *ante.*

32. TOL to Ebenezer L. Childs, May 11, 1831, in Parker, ed., *Chapters in the Early Life of Thomas Oliver Larkin,* 59.

33. U.S., *Fifth Census of the United States, 1830:* North Carolina, New Hanover County, 6:147A, microfilm edition of manuscript census. The entry shows that "Thomas Larkin" is the head of a household that consists of himself, two male slaves over thirty-six and under fifty-five, two female slaves over ten and under twenty-four, and two male slaves under the age of ten. No other information is given in the 1830 census except simple enumerations.

34. "C. Henry says you are rich enough . . . at one time I expect C. H. did not think you would ever be able to buy Sam back. . . . I would if I was in your place write a letter to your faithful servant. . . . I saw him last Sunday at church he came to me asking me if I had recd a letter from you he always contends that he belongs to you yet and that you will come sometime after him he is among the strongest friends you have now that is he is always speaking of you." Peyton Stringfield to TOL, May 1, 1853, Larkin, "Documents," C–B/ 44:229, Bancroft Library. (This letter was not included in the published *Larkin Papers*.) Even later, in 1856, Sam was still enthusiastic. "Sam always comes to hear us read your letter he says if you ever come back here he will go with you," letter, Susan Jane Stringfield to TOL, January 18, 1856, Larkin, "Documents," C–B/45:400. (Not included in the published *Larkin Papers*.)

35. Dempsey Harrell to TOL, January 20, 1850, in Parker, ed., "California's Larkin Settles Old Debts," 337. See also *Larkin Papers*, 8:280. ("After you left Rockfish I continued with E. Withington until he got tired of the place. He then sold out to me. I remained thare two years.")

36. TOL to Ebenezer L. Childs, May 11, 1831, in Parker, ed., *Chapters in the Early Life of Thomas Oliver Larkin*, 56. ("When I left [Rockfish] to begin the Mills.")

37. There are occasional references to Larkin's mill being located in New Hanover County, North Carolina. That is misleading since the portion of New Hanover County that contained Long Creek was part of that broken off in 1875 to form Pender County. The mill was located somewhere near the present town of Long Creek in Pender County. There was a road in this vicinity as early as pre-Revolutionary days that ran east-west from the site of the Moore's Creek Battlefield on the west toward the Cape Fear River on the east. Where that early road crossed Long Creek there was an early bridge known, appropriately enough, as the Long Creek Bridge. W. P. Cumming, *North Carolina in Maps* (Raleigh: State Department of Archives and History, 1966), plate X. Comparing historical maps with detailed modern maps, Long Creek Bridge was about 2 miles west of the fork of present state routes 210 and 133 and about 2 1/2 miles east of the intersection of state route 210 and federal route 421. In his May 11, 1831, letter to his stepbrother Childs, Larkin states that his boarding house was 1/4 mile from the Long Creek Bridge, which had become enough of a community that he was petitioning for a post office. The Mac Rae–Brazier map of 1833 shows a sawmill located about 1 1/2 miles north of Long Creek Bridge. It is probable this was the very mill that Larkin owned.

38. Ebenezer L. Childs to TOL, November 30, 1844, *Larkin Papers*, 2:296.

39. Larkin's letter of May 11, 1831, to his stepbrother Childs states that he is deeply in debt, that the mill has been turned over to another at the demands of his creditors, and that he is out of business. Parker, ed., *Chapters in the Early Life of Thomas Oliver Larkin*, 59. Also, a biographical sketch written during Larkin's lifetime confirms that the sawmill venture was a failure. Soulé et al., *The Annals of San Francisco*, 758.

40. John Larkins to TOL, October 21, 1849, in Parker, ed., "California's Larkin Settles Old Debts," 336. See also *Larkin Papers*, 8:260.

41. Larkin's brother mentioned the health of a "Withington" in his letter, William Larkin to TOL, August 24, 1825, Larkin, "Correspondence and Papers," C–B/105:129. Also, he was probably the "Witherington" who was in some way involved in Larkin's store at Rockfish, and at the end of Larkin's ownership may have had an equity interest. See comment of Dempsey Harrell quoted in n. 35 *ante*. Other correspondence with Larkin refers to Withington as a friend. David McIntire to TOL, December 19, 1850, in Parker, ed., "California's Larkin Settles Old Debts," 340. See also *Larkin Papers*, 8:359.

42. The year in the original is not entirely legible and could be read as 1826. That reading does not make sense, however, as the "Itinerary" covers that date and in it Larkin does not mention any sawmill venture. Indeed, he wrote that his duties as storekeeper, postmaster, and magistrate would be sufficient to keep him busy.

43. This bond is found in the Vallejo Documents, 30:35.

44. A detailed list of debts dated February 27, 1831 is in ibid., 30:184. It totals $3,000, but does not mention the creditors under the deed of trust, James Moore and Charles Henry. Perhaps by this time—that is, 1831—Moore and Henry had acquired an equity position in the failing mills.

45. TOL to Ebenezer L. Childs, May 11, 1831, in Parker, ed., *Chapters in the Early Life of Thomas Oliver Larkin*, 59.

46. Ibid.; TOL to Nathaniel B. March, January 29, 1850, *Larkin Papers*, 8:282. ("In 1830 to 1832 I made over property in N.C. to pay this and other debts.").

47. David McIntire to TOL, December 19, 1850, in Parker, ed., "California's Larkin Settles Old Debts," 340. See also *Larkin Papers*, 8:358.

48. TOL to Ebenezer L. Childs, May 11, 1831, in Parker, ed., *Chapters in the Early Life of Thomas Oliver Larkin*, 58–59.

49. The quotations in text until the next note are all from the May 11, 1831 letter to Childs.

50. Even to the point where Mrs. Jones referred to Larkin as "Oliver," the name by which he was known to his family. William Cameron to TOL, April 18, 1855, in Parker, ed., "California's Larkin Settles Old Debts," 344.

51. Susan Jane Stringfield to TOL, September 2, 1855, ibid., 345.

52. Susan Jane Stringfield to TOL, January 18, 1856, Larkin, "Documents," C–B/45:400.

53. His portion of the letter mentions that "Susan speaks of a lawsuit in this letter." Ibid. And indeed she did describe a lawsuit in which the Stringfields were then engaged. However, his portion of the letter is dated earlier, January 1, 1856.

54. TOL to Ebenezer L. Childs, May 11, 1831, in Parker, ed., *Chapters in the Early Life of Thomas Oliver Larkin*, 58.

55. The quotations in text until the next note are all from the May 11, 1831, letter to Childs.

56. Forceful criticisms are contained in letters to John W. Rogers to Cooper, June 7, 1831; A. B. Thompson to Cooper, March 2, 1832 ("It appears to me a singular way of transacting business and should be very glad if I could think it a mistake"); John C. Jones to Cooper, April 30, 1832 ("Such transactions as these will never answer, they were dishonorable and ungentlemanly"); James Hunnewell to Cooper, June 20, 1832, in Vallejo Documents, 30:221, 298, 307, and 31:23.

57. Woolfenden and Elkinton, *Cooper*, 44.

58. TOL to Ebenezer L. Childs, May 11, 1831, in Parker, ed., *Chapters in the Early Life of Thomas Oliver Larkin*, 57. ("I was very happy to see your copy of John's letter. . . . I have for years thought seriously on going to Mexico, and sent some letters . . . to John but have heard nothing from. I do not even see my name in his letter.")

59. The quotations in text until the next note are all from the May 11, 1831, letter to Childs.

60. Ibid., and Ebenezer L. Childs to TOL, August 27, 1831, Vallejo Documents, 30:244.

61. TOL to Ebenezer L. Childs, August 22, 1831, ibid., 30:240.

62. There is an unfootnoted manuscript biography which asserts that Larkin did propose to the cousin but that she turned him down. Robert J. Parker, "Peddler's Empire: The Life of Thomas O. Larkin" (n.d.), 72, California Historical Society Library, San Francisco. This same manuscript implies (p.82) that Larkin had kept a diary until the time he left Boston for Monterey. However, none has come to light beyond the "Itinerary," which closes in 1826.

63. Almost twenty-nine, Larkin still could strike a Byronic pose. He wrote to his stepbrother Ebenezer, that "Gold that all powerfull attraction carries us far from those we love fortune knows nothing of affections. . . . We may yet meet. I do believe we shall in at least five years from this time. I hope we shall yet come out high & yet live near each other some

day or other. . . . I do believe our family thinks . . . we shall never be much." TOL to Ebenezer L. Childs, August 22, 1831, Vallejo Documents, 30:240. Childs responded in a more sober manner: "I can with difficulty reconcile myself to this separation which I feel a presentment is to be one of *perpetual duration* . . . once more my brother may heaven bless & preserve you, may you succeed in all your plans & live long & happily." Ebenezer L. Childs to TOL, August 27, 1831, ibid., 30:244.

    64. Ann R. L. Wright to John B. R. Cooper, August 29, 1831, ibid., 30:245.

    65. TOL to Ebenezer L. Childs, August 22, 1831, ibid., 30:240.

    66. Ibid.

    67. List in "Daybook" in Larkin "Accounts," 2, C–E/6, Bancroft Library.

    68. Date is mentioned in Larkin's "Daybook," for period February 1833 through April 1837, to left of inside cover. Ibid.

Chapter 3. On to California: Business Starts and Personal Life

    1. The passport is located in Thomas Savage, *Documentos para la historia de California*, 4 vols., 2:2, Bancroft Library, quoted in John W. Pyle, "Thomas O. Larkin: California Business Man, 1832–1844" (M.A. thesis, University of California, Berkeley, 1938), 7, and Kelsey, "The United States Consulate in California," 1:247 [omitting mention of scars].

    2. Rachel Hobson Holmes Larkin to TOL, December 14, 1846, *Larkin Papers*, 5:316.

    3. An acquaintance from the late 1820s questioned in 1853, "I would ask you if you can hear any better," Peyton Stringfield to TOL, May 1, 1853, Larkin, "Documents," C–B/ 44:229. (This is one of the letters that was not printed in the Hammond compilation.)

    4. William H. Thomes, *On Land and Sea, or California in the Years 1843, '44, and '45* (Boston: Fiske & Company, 1884), 75.

    5. Soulé, et al., *The Annals of San Francisco*, 759. The biographical sketch of TOL appearing in this work was written and originally published while Larkin was still alive, and undoubtedly Larkin was consulted in connection with its preparation.

    6. "Daybook," in Larkin, "Accounts," 2, C–E/6.

    7. A. B. Thompson to John B. R. Cooper, March 2, 1832, Vallejo Documents, 30:298.

    8. John G. Toney to John B. R. Cooper, March 7, 1832, ibid., 30:299.

    9. John C. Jones to John B. R. Cooper, April 30, 1832, ibid., 30:307.

    10. Soulé, et al., *The Annals of San Francisco*, 759.

    11. Larkin noted this arrival date in his own hand on the inside cover of his "Daybook" in Larkin, "Accounts," 2, C–E 6.

    12. Mrs. F. H. Day, "Sketches of the Early Settlers of California: Mrs. Thomas O. Larkin," *The Hesperian* 2 (May 1859): 97–98.

    13. There is simply no logical place for Larkin to have stayed other than with his brother and in the large house in which the shop and office that Larkin worked in was located. That Larkin and Rachel Holmes both were with the Cooper household is asserted by Woolfenden and Elkinton, *Cooper*, 45.

    14. Letters and statements of September 21 and October 1, 1832 [two of this date], Vallejo Documents, 30:320, 321, 329.

    15. Larkin, "Accounts," 2, C–E 6 and C–E 9. He stayed on in Cooper's house, however. TOL to Abel Stearns, June 2, 1833, Box 39, Stearns Collection, Henry E. Huntington Library, San Marino.

    16. Parker, ed., *Chapters in the Early Life of Thomas Oliver Larkin*, 2. Her age is confirmed by the Mexican *padron*, or census, of 1836. Vallejo Documents, 32:14.

17. Day, "Mrs. Thomas O. Larkin," 97.

18. Ibid.

19. J. A. C. Holmes to Thomas Shaw, December 13, 1831, Vallejo Documents, 30:279 (". . . please take receipt[s] and forward them to my wife Mrs Rachel Holmes in Ipswich Mass if she should yet be there. . . . you will please to forward the remainder [of collected funds] to my aforementioned wife if yet there.").

20. Mission Register of Baptismals, 1833, entry number 971, Mission Santa Barbara, photographed and translated in John A. Hawgood, ed., *First and Last Consul: Thomas Oliver Larkin and the Americanization of California*, 2nd ed. (Palo Alto, Calif.: Pacific Books, 1970), 140–42.

21. Catherine M. Bell, "A Row of Old Houses," in Katherine B. Cheney, *Swinging the Censer: Reminiscences of Old Santa Barbara* (Santa Barbara: n.p., 1931), 120–23. This tends to be corroborated by the fact that Hill was the godfather of the child. He was then living in the Carrillo abode on East Carrillo Street.

22. Hubert H. Bancroft, *California Pioneer Register and Index, 1542–1848* (Baltimore: Regional Publishing Co., 1964, reprinted from *History of California*, 7 vols., 1884–90), 188.

23. Henry E. Virmond to Rachel H. Holmes, July 16, 1832, Vallejo Documents, 30:315.

24. TOL to Ebenezer L. Childs, May 11, 1831, in Parker, ed., *Chapters in the Early Life of Thomas Oliver Larkin*, 57.

25. Mission Register of Baptismals, 1833, entry number 971, in Hawgood, ed., *First and Last Consul*, 140–42.

26. TOL to Abel Stearns, January 7, 1833, Box 39, Stearns Collection.

27. Ibid. The letters written for Cooper, dated September 21 and October 1, 1832, indicate they were written in Monterey, Vallejo Documents, 30:320, 321, 329.

28. TOL to Abel Stearns, March 27, 1833, ("expect to start for Mont. in 4 days."), and TOL to Abel Stearns, June 2, 1833 ("am going in her [a specified ship] as far as Santa B."), Box 39, Stearns Collection. There is a romanticized reminiscence that suggests both Larkin and Rachel stayed with Daniel Hill and his wife. Larkin certainly visited there after the birth of Isabel and perhaps even during the confinement. Catherine M. Bell, "A Row of Old Houses," in Cheney, *Swinging the Censer: Reminiscences of Old Santa Barbara*, 121.

29. TOL to Francis E. Parker, Public Administrator of Massachusetts, January 29, 1850, *Larkin Papers*, 8:282.

30. TOL to John C. Calhoun, August 18, 1844, ibid., 2:206.

31. James Buchanan to TOL, July 14, 1846, ibid., 5:135.

32. William Heath Davis, Jr., *Seventy-Five Years in California* (San Francisco: John Howell, 1929; reprint, San Francisco: John Howell, 1967), 6.

33. TOL to Abel Stearns, June 26, 1833, Box 39, Stearns Collection.

34. Soulé et al., *Annals of San Francisco*, 759.

35. Day, "Mrs. Thomas O. Larkin," 98.

36. TOL to Ebenezer L. Childs, August 22, 1831, Vallejo Documents, 30:240.

37. TOL to Ebenezer L. Childs, May 11, 1831, in Parker, ed., *Chapters in the Early Life of Thomas Oliver Larkin*, 57.

38. Day, "Mrs. Thomas O. Larkin," 98.

39. California hides weighed an average of twenty-five pounds and in 1831 and 1832 Boston wholesale hide prices varied between 10 1/2 and 15 1/2 cents per pound. Sherman F. Dallas, "The Hide and Tallow Trade in Alta California, 1822–1846" (Ph.D. dissertation, Indiana University, 1955), 283, and 286n.241. Assuming a price of 12 cents for the hides in good condition and half that for the partially damaged hides, this transaction would yield a gross of $1,560. Supporting a gross of that approximate size is Holmes's instruction to Shaw to pay bills totaling $968.12 and then remit the balance to Rachel, or if she had

already left for California, to deposit the balance on interest with a bank. John A. C. Holmes to Thomas Shaw, December 13, 1831, Vallejo Documents, 30:279.

40. This is based on the United States government's statistical series, "Consumer Price Indexes—All Items 1800 to 1970, Table E-135," published in U.S. Bureau of the Census, *Historical Statistics of the United States, Colonial Times to 1970, Bicentennial Edition, Part 1*. U.S. Government Printing Office, 1975, updated by monthly periodical, U.S. Department of Commerce, Bureau of Economic Analysis, *Survey of Current Business*. A comparison for the price levels for 1831 with that of 1990 yields roughly the ratio of thirteen to one.

41. An equal partnership with Caroline Moore is shown for the ship *Franklin*, in documents that ended up in Larkin's possession. Larkin, "Accounts," C–E/1. The letter referred to from Holmes to Shaw also instructs Shaw to pay her $292.64, presumably half the profits from an earlier venture.

42. Henry E. Virmond to Rachel Holmes, July 16, 1832, Vallejo Documents, 30:315.

43. There are several small accounts, originally due Holmes, scattered throughout Larkin's early account books, and it is a fair inference that Larkin made every effort to collect them. These may be found primarily in Larkin, "Accounts," C–E Portfolio and C–E/1, and Larkin "Correspondence and Papers," C–B/105:64. He had every incentive. During the years 1833 through 1835 Larkin was starting in his retail operation and building his house in Monterey. He was hard pressed for funds, and wrote in 1836 that "on moving into the new House, I was without any funds having spent and invested every thing in Building." Larkin, "Accounts," C–E/9. Another asset valued at $1,000 in 1836, "Accounts," C–E/6, was an order on the ship *Harriet*. This was probably also an obligation due Holmes, as he had accounts with the *Harriet*, although this is not without doubt. Accounts of Holmes with the *Harriet* and other vessels are in Larkin, "Accounts," C–E/1.

44. Ibid., C–E/9. (For 1835: "The 950$ in goods this year was received for a debt due Mrs Larkin, paid by Don Frederico Becher from on Board.") This was the total amount shown in this year-end account for goods on hand.

45. Frederick G. Becher to TOL, November 16, 1835, Vallejo Documents, 31:170.

46. TOL to Ebenezer L. Childs, May 11, 1831, in Parker, ed., *Chapters in the Early Life of Thomas Oliver Larkin*, 58–59. ("I do not know a young Lady within fifty miles of W. [Wilmington] worth $3000 . . . Now with a capital of $3000, I could get clear of debts and have this Same Sum left in two years by the speculations on the part I did not pay away. Therefore could I succeed with the Lady on all other scores, She need not back out on this.")

47. Hawgood, ed., *First and Last Consul*, 142.

48. Ibid., 140.

49. Parker, "Larkin's Monterey Customers," 42.

50. Robert G. Cowan, *Ranchos of California* (Reprint ed., Los Angeles: Historical Society of Southern California, 1977), 35–36.

51. Woolfenden and Elkinton, *Cooper*, 44.

52. TOL to "Dear Brother" [John B. R. Cooper], August 5 and 6, 1834, Vallejo Documents, 31:113, 113b.

53. Larkin, "Accounts," C–E/6.

54. Ibid.

55. Soulé et al., *Annals of San Francisco*, 759. Also mention is made of the expenses of this construction in subsequent citations to his accounts.

56. Larkin, "Accounts," C–E/6.

57. TOL to Abel Stearns, November 3, 1833, February 7 and April 26, 1834, Box 39, Stearns Collection.

58. Compare TOL to Stearns, April 26, 1834, ibid., ("I think of keepng at the Auctosh near Santa Cruz two men cuting red woods (lumber Joice & rafters). what amt. do you

think you can sell at San pedro"—Larkin goes on to outline a full-scale proposition) with TOL to "Dear Brother" [John B. R. Cooper], August 5 and 6, 1834, Vallejo Documents, 31:113, 113b, which makes it clear that he had several employees cutting timber.

59. Larkin, "Accounts," C–E/6.

60. In November 1833, he noted that he had "much to pay in fixing up the house on the rancho, buying horses, mules & oxen," and in April 1834 he wrote that he had been "bringing to my notion [?], my mill, horses, mules & cattle, also preposing to raising hogs, haveing a good stock to begin with." TOL to Abel Stearns, November 3, 1833, and April 26, 1834, Box 39, Stearns Collection.

61. Larkin, "Accounts," C–E/6.

62. The month may be established from TOL to "Dear Brother" [John B. R. Cooper], August 5 and 6, 1834, Vallejo Documents, 31:113, 113b.

63. TOL to Abel Stearns, July 22, 1834, in Hawgood, ed., First and Last Consul, 7. ("I have this week taken half of the house of Mrs Hartnell.")

64. Harold Kirker, "The Larkin House Revisited," California History 65 (March 1986): 27.

65. TOL to Abel Stearns, April 26, 1834, Box 39, Stearns Collection.

66. Larkin, "Accounts," C–E/9. The "Daybook" also begins a new section for Monterey with August 1834. Larkin, "Accounts," C–E/6.

67. TOL to Andrew Johnstone, August 27, 1840, Larkin Papers, 1:50.

68. Larkin Genealogies.

69. Larkin, "Accounts," C–E/6.

70. It has been claimed that Larkin's was the first two story structure in California, but David Gebhard persuasively demonstrates that this is not so in his "Some Additional Observations on California's Monterey Tradition," Journal of the Society of Architectural Historians 46 (June 1987): 160–61. He also contends, contrary to most architectural authorities, that the source for the Monterey style was not so much New England as the American South and the Caribbean, Ibid., 168–70.

71. TOL to Andrew Johnstone, June 3, 1843, Larkin Papers, 2:19.

72. The discussion of the architectual techniques and their significance is drawn primarily from articles by Kirker, "The Larkin House Revisited," 26–33, and "The Role of Hispanic Kinships in Popularizing the Monterey Style in California, 1836–1846," Journal of the Society of Architectural Historians 43 (October 1984): 250–55. As to the history of the techniques in California, the most persuasive account is David Gebhard, "Some Additional Observations on California's Monterey Tradition," Journal of the Society of Architectural Historians 46 (June 1987): 157–70.

73. It has sometimes been asserted that Larkin's house was the basis for the spread of this style, but Gebhard convincingly establishes that A. B. Thompson's home in Santa Barbara was actually earlier by some months and that Larkin's house could not have been the model. Gebhard, "Some Additional Observations," 157, 163–64.

74. Ibid., 158, 160.

75. There are detailed itemizations of expenses in Larkin, "Accounts." This material has been collected in the fullest account of the construction process in Robert J. Parker, "Building the Larkin House," California Historical Society Quarterly 16 (December 1937): 321–35; reprinted in Chapters in the Early Life of Thomas Oliver Larkin, 63–77). The discussion concerning the construction is drawn from this piece unless otherwise noted.

76. TOL, Petition to Ayuntamiento, January 29, 1835, Vallejo Documents, 31:164.

77. TOL to Abel Stearns, April 13, 1835, Box 39, Stearns Collection.

78. TOL to Abel Stearns, May 16, 1835, ibid.

79. Parker, ed., Chapters in the Early Life of Thomas Oliver Larkin, 68 and 77n.36.

80. Larkin, "Accounts," C–E/9.

81. Kirker, "The Larkin House Revisited," 30.
82. Larkin, "Accounts," C–E/6.
83. TOL to Alfred Robinson, April 30, 1844, *Larkin Papers*, 2:113.
84. TOL to Alfred Robinson, May 27, 1845, ibid., 3:175. ("I am sorry very sorry I sent for the Furniture. . . . I think some of the articles very high. . . . I am assured if the furniture is high I must lay it to your extravegant taste.") Larkin had asked his friend Robinson to order some furniture in Boston on his behalf.
85. Petitions, TOL to *Ayuntamiento*, July 8, 1836, and April 19, 1838, Vallejo Documents, 31:164.
86. Parker, ed., *Chapters in the Early Life of Thomas Oliver Larkin*, 69.
87. Letter, TOL to Andrew Johnstone, June 3, 1843, *Larkin Papers*, 2:20.
88. From the Larkin Genealogies.
89. Cited in Bancroft's "Biographical Notes," Bancroft Library.
90. Robert G. Davis to TOL, May 27, 1842, *Larkin Papers*, 1:226. ("My brother has tried to procure a native man and woman for you, but has not succeeded; the men are willing, but it is difficult to persuade their wives; he will probably engage a good smart boy for your house.")
91. John A. Sutter to Henry D. Fitch, April 17, 1846, Fitch Documents, Document No. 391, Bancroft Library. ("At present I could spare you not young Indians as I have only these which I need for my business; but if I can get some when I make the Campagne against the horsethiefs I shall not forget you.") This was no sporadic instance. During the period 1842−1846 it was customary for Sutter to buy and sell Indian boys and girls. John Chamberlain, "Memoirs of California Since 1840," manuscript, Bancroft Library. There has not been much scholarly study of forced Indian labor during the Mexican period of California history, but there are some materials in Robert F. Heizer and Alan F. Almquist, *The Other Californians: Prejudice and Discrimination under Spain, Mexico, and the United States to 1920* (Berkeley: University of California Press, 1971); Albert L. Hurtado, *Indian Survival on the California Frontier* (New Haven: Yale University Press, 1989); and James J. Rawls, *Indians of California: The Changing Image* (Norman: University of Oklahoma Press, 1984).
92. Juan Bautista Alvarado, *Historia de California*, Chapter 38, manuscript, Bancroft Library.
93. James McKinlay to TOL, November 18, 1844, *Larkin Papers*, 2:292.
94. John A. Sutter to TOL, November 12, 1846, ibid., 5:275.
95. William Cameron to TOL, April 18, 1855, in Parker, ed., "California's Larkin Settles Old Debts," 343. ("Some two or three years ago I received a letter from you . . . and I was truly gratified to learn of your great success in business and your happiness on a domestic point of view.")
96. TOL to William Fouler, Jr., December 24, 1844, *Larkin Papers*, 2:335.
97. TOL to Rachel Larkin, December 14, 1846, ibid., 5:313 (1846 and Hawaii); and TOL to Abel Stearns, December 3, 1834, in Hawgood, ed., *First and Last Consul*, 11 (trumped-up debt).
98. TOL to Moses Y. Beach, May 31, 1845, *Larkin Papers*, 3:215.
99. TOL to Abel Stearns, August 14, 1840, Box 39, Stearns Collection; James Jackson Jarves to TOL, April 3, 1841. *Larkin Papers*, 1:82−83.
100. TOL to Moses Y. Beach, May 31, 1845, ibid., 3:215.
101. See William M. Rogers to TOL, September 1, 1845, and John H. Everett to TOL, December 12, 1845, and April 23, 1846 (enclosing sixteen novels), ibid., 3:332, 4:118, 342−43.
102. TOL to Alfred Robinson, July 12, 1845, Appleton Collection, Baker Library, Harvard Business School, Cambridge, Massachusetts.

103. J. N. Bowman, "Libraries in Provincial California," *Historical Society of Southern California Quarterly* 43 (September 1961): 426–39.

104. Thomes, *On Land and Sea*, 75.

105. William M. Rogers to TOL, July 1, 1838, Vallejo Documents, 32:144.

106. Ibid. (expressing dismay that Larkin's letters were "filled so completely with aspersions on the Missionaries").

107. TOL to Andrew Johnstone, August 27, 1840, *Larkin Papers*, 1:50–51.

108. Ibid. This letter also refers to date of departure and name of vessel.

109. Alpheus B. Thompson to TOL, September 12, 1840, ibid., 1:56.

110. Letters to TOL from Curtis Clap, October 1; Benjamin W. Parker, September 30; Henry Paty, October 14; John Paty, October 4; and Alpheus B. Thompson, October 1, 1840, ibid., 1:58, 57, 61, 60, 59.

111. Thomas O. Larkin, Jr., to TOL and Rachel Larkin, August 24, 1843, Vallejo Documents, 33:353.

112. Thomas O. Larkin, Jr. to TOL and Rachel Larkin, June 25, 1844, *Larkin Papers*, 2:146.

113. William M. Rogers to TOL, February 5, 1844, Vallejo Documents, 34:10.

114. James B. Hatch to TOL, December 13, 1844, *Larkin Papers*, 2:326.

115. Adele Ogden, *The California Sea Otter Trade, 1784–1848* (Berkeley: University of California Press, 1941; reprint ed., 1975), 181.

116. Jonathan T. Warner to TOL, December 26, 1844, *Larkin Papers*, 2:337.

117. TOL to Alfred Robinson, April 15, 1844, Appleton Collection.

118. Richard S. Den to TOL, December 23, 1844, *Larkin Papers*, 2:334 (denying Larkin's assertion of bad medical treatment).

119. TOL to Alfred Robinson, September 16, 1844, ibid., 2:232–34.

120. Alfred Robinson to TOL, January 20, May 29, 1845, January 16, 1846, ibid., 3:16–17, 204–205, 4:166.

121. Isaac Childs to TOL, March 28, 1845, ibid., 3:107, responds to these queries.

122. Ann R. L. Wright to TOL, March 22, 1845 ("When do you intend to send Thomas Oliver here."); August 31, 1845 ("I presume you will send Thomas Oliver, to the United States this Fall."); October 30, 1845 ("I suppose you will send Thomas Oliver on next year."), ibid., 3:87, 330, 4:80.

123. Receipt for $200 for January passage to Boston of the two boys dated November 28, 1845 in Larkin, "Correspondence and Papers," C–B/105:84.

124. John C. Jones to TOL, January 24, 1846, *Larkin Papers*, 4:181.

125. William D. M. Howard to TOL, December 28, 1845, and January 25, 1846, ibid., 4:133, 183.

126. James P. Arther to TOL, June 29, 1846, and March 6, 1847, ibid., 5:83, 6:39.

127. Ann R. L. Wright to TOL, July 1, 1846, ibid., 5:92.

Chapter 4. Trader and Merchant

1. The best scholarly description of the hide and tallow trade is by Dallas, "The Hide and Tallow Trade in Alta California, 1822–1846." But the most famous account is the classic written by a contemporary participant, Richard H. Dana, Jr., *Two Years Before the Mast: A Personal Narrative of Life at Sea* (New York: Harper & Brothers, 1840; reprint, 2 vols., ed. John H. Kemble, Los Angeles: Ward Ritchie Press, 1964).

2. The best biography of Stearns, rich in evocative detail, is Doris M. Wright, *A Yankee in Mexican California: Abel Stearns, 1798–1848* (Santa Barbara: Wallace Hebberd, 1977).

3. TOL to Copmann and Lomer, May 25, 1845, *Larkin Papers*, 3:196.

4. A good list of trade articles, culled from Larkin's accounts, appears in Robert J. Parker, "Larkin's Monterey Business: Articles of Trade, 1833−1839," *Historial Society of Southern California Quarterly* 24 (June 1942): 57−59.

5. The variety of his customers can be seen in *Larkin Papers*, his various accounts, and in an article by Parker, "Larkin's Monterey Customers," *Historical Society of Southern California Quarterly* 24 (June 1942): 41−53.

6. *Larkin Papers* as well as the various accounts and ledgers reflect these transactions. A biographical sketch prepared while Larkin was yet living, and presumably with his cooperation, makes the point that Larkin engaged in a far greater and wider trade than merely accepting cattle hides in payment and that he in turn traded this greater variety of local products internationally. Soulé et al., *The Annals of San Francisco*, 759−60.

7. Parker, "Larkin's Monterey Business: Articles of Trade, 1833−1839," 54.

8. A contemporary who was hostile to Larkin referred to Larkin's store as a "grog shop." Albert Ferdinand Morris, "The Journal of a 'Crazy Man': Travels and Scenes in California from the Year 1834," ed. Charles L. Camp, *California Historical Society Quarterly* 15 (June 1936): 116.

9. Larkin, "Accounts," C−E/9 (ledger).

10. Boyd Huff, *El Puerto de los Balleñeros: Annals of the Sausalito Whaling Anchorage* (Los Angeles: Glen Dawson, 1957), 36−37; Parker, "Larkin, Anglo-American Businessman in Mexican California," in Adele Ogden, ed. *Greater America: Essays in Honor of Herbert Eugene Bolton* (Berkeley: University of California Press, 1945), p. 420.

11. A "Notice to Whalers" dated August 1839, signed by Larkin, extols the advantages of the port of Monterey and his own abilities to be of aid to whalers in that port. This may be found in the Vallejo Documents, 32:294. In August 1844, Larkin prepared another advertisement addressed to whalers and designed for insertion in New England newspapers and caused the ad to be placed in the New Bedford, Massachusetts, newspaper. *Larkin Papers*, 2:189−90, 212.

12. N. and W. W. Billings to TOL, June 16, 1846, (New Bedford *Shipping List*); Moses Y. Beach & Sons to TOL, September 25, 1846, and Alfred Wilbur to TOL, December 20, 1846, ibid., 5:34, 251, 319.

13. As examples, in June 1844 the French government transport ship, *Lion*, was in Monterey and Larkin supplied it to the extent of a bill of exchange for one thousand francs [$200], which he sent for collection, together with another bill of exchange drawn by an officer of the Russian American Company for $1,000 and payable in St. Petersburg. TOL to W. W. Scarborough & Co., December 29, 1844, ibid., 2:341. In April 1844 Larkin claimed that he had for eight years supplied almost all English and French warships that had stopped in Monterey. Larkin also supplied a French whaler in March 1844. TOL to Gauden, April 21, 1844, ibid., 2:104. In the fall of 1844 Larkin acquired drafts in pounds sterling to the value of $722, drawn by officers of the British man-of-war *Modeste* and on the Accountant General of the British Navy. TOL to Uhde & Pini, December 10, 1844, ibid., 2:316−17. Undoubtedly these British drafts were for supplies.

14. TOL to Stephen Reynolds, November 18, 1842, ibid., 1:323.

15. TOL to Faxon D. Atherton, February 12, 1843, in Doyce B. Nunis, Jr., ed., "Six New Larkin Letters," *Southern California Quarterly* 49 (March 1967): 72.

16. Receipt dated December 12, 1844, *Larkin Papers*, 2:343.

17. An excellent example is letter, John A. Sutter to TOL, July 22, 1845, ibid., 3:281−84.

18. Larkin, "Accounts," C−E/9 (ledger).

19. TOL to Abel Stearns, July 20, 1845, in Hawgood, ed., *First and Last Consul*, 28.

20. Statement of TOL regarding such food dated December 6, 1840, may be found in *Larkin Papers*, 1:63. It indicates that he delivered tea, meat, bread, and beans two and at

times three times daily for the prisoners. However, one of the prisoners, who distinctly disliked Larkin, wrote later: "I am informed by Mr. Majors . . . that after his release Mr. Larkin boasted to him that the provisions that he furnished for the prisoners cost him but three reals per man, and that he made six reals profit per head." Morris, "The Journal of a 'Crazy Man,'" 225.

21. Some of these many business activities are detailed in Parker, "Larkin's Monterey Business: Articles of Trade, 1833–1839," 59–61. He was apparently proud of the flour mill. The biographical account prepared during his lifetime states that Larkin "erected the first double geared wheat-mill in that part of the country. As there were only ship carpenters ashore, he had to make models for them to work by." Soulé et al., *The Annals of San Francisco*, 759. Apparently Larkin did not personally operate the blacksmith operation, as we find a September 1845 agreement whereby he hired an operator, followed by an outright lease of the shop to this operator in January of 1846. *Larkin Papers*, 3:345–46, 4:146. The soap factory was a joint venture with José María Sánchez and located on the ranch of Sánchez. Contract between Larkin and Sánchez, April 24, 1845, ibid., 3:152–53. Larkin made estimates ($2,301) for the California government for the rebuilding of the custom-house in August 1841, ibid., 1:110–11, and Vallejo Documents, 33:254. The work was accomplished in 1842. TOL to Andrew Johnstone, June 3, 1843, *Larkin Papers*, 2:20. Still later, in 1845, Larkin built the Monterey wharf at a total expense of $8,200; Larkin was pressing the American government for the unpaid balance of $4,059 in 1847. Thomas Swords to TOL, April 23, 1847, ibid., 6:114.

22. A good analysis of Larkin's lumbering activities is in Sherwood D. Burgess, "Lumbering in Hispanic California," *California Historical Society Quarterly* 41 (September 1962): 237–48. Burgess points out that Larkin utilized both independent loggers and employees. Most interesting, however, is his conclusion that Larkin made very little profit on the lumber and timber operation, *per se*, but that he paid his contractors and employees with credits at his store, which were redeemed for merchandise that carried a high markup. He contends this is true, notwithstanding Larkin's claims to Abel Stearns, his chief customer, that he had to pay primarily cash to his employees. The claims of cash payment are clearly made in two letters from TOL to Abel Stearns, April 26, 1834: "of course I should have to pay the Sawyers and haulers mostly cash," and October 17, 1834: "The Men who Saw it take a great part in cash from me," Box 39, Stearns Collection.

23. Contract between TOL, William Trevethan, and William Brander, July 21, 1841, *Larkin Papers*, 1:99.

24. Little is known about Larkin's trip into the interior of Mexico in 1841. He was at Tepic, where he doubtless testified in connection with the foreign prisoners from California held there as a result of the Graham Affair. About the only indication that he went on to Mexico City is a draft of an agreement dated February 16, 1841, for the receipt of $8,000 of retail goods from a Hiram Teal on consignment. Vallejo Documents, 33:186. Larkin had entered into a contract with his half-brother, John B. R. Cooper, on November 30, 1840, for the carriage of Larkin and goods to and from Mazatlán and San Blas and the use of the entire schooner *California* for his purposes, unless the California government preempted half its space. Ibid., 33:160.

25. Two purchases were made from the wholesale firms of Parrott & Company and Machado & Company. TOL to John C. Jones, March 12, 1842, *Larkin Papers*, 1:172–73. There may have been smaller transactions as well. The net balances owed to these firms, $3,188.43 and $2,180.21 respectively, were paid on Larkin's account by the Honolulu firm of Peirce & Brewer. Henry A. Peirce to TOL, February 6, 1842, ibid., 1:164.

26. TOL to John C. Jones, March 12, 1842, ibid., 1:172–73.

27. Larkin, "Accounts," C–E/9.

28. An example of this was in Larkin's use of Peirce & Brewer to pay the debts he had

accumulated in Mazatlán as a result of his 1841 purchases. Larkin in this case delivered cattle hides and cash to the Hawaiian firm's agents while they were trading in California. TOL to Peirce & Brewer, December 19, 1842, *Larkin Papers*, 1:345—46.

29. For Cooper and McKinley, see Parker, "Larkin's Monterey Customers," 44, 52. Larkin prepared a chart entitled, "Wages paid Workmen from May 1833," which may be found in Larkin, "Accounts," C—E/6. It shows payments made to daily and weekly workers through June 1837. His work force was primarily comprised of foreigners, although there are several Californios and Indians as well. As for Talbot H. Green's [Paul Geddes's] beginning employment, see Bancroft, *California Pioneer Register*, 168.

30. As to Faxon's and Allen's consular employment, see ibid., 138 and 30, respectively. Allen's earlier employment as Larkin's clerk is reflected in TOL to Faxon D. Atherton, October 20—21, 1842, in Nunis, ed., "Six New Larkin Letters," 70.

31. This incident and the efforts of Larkin and Green to assure the contract's performance are described in David J. Langum, *Law and Community on the Mexican California Frontier: Anglo-American Expatriates and the Clash of Legal Traditions, 1821—1846* (Norman: University of Oklahoma Press, 1987), 200—202.

32. There is very little information on the Gilroy branch operation outside of entries in the ledgers in Larkin, "Accounts," C—E/9.

33. "I thought it best to accept of an offer made me by Mr. Larkin . . . to come to this place and take charge of a store. I had to engage for a year or nothing and at a small salary. . . . He says he will give me a share in the business next year. . . . I have my store along side of the church and am boarding with the catholic [*sic*] priest." Josiah Belden to "Dear Sister," March 21, 1842, in *Josiah Belden 1841 California Overland Pioneer: His Memoir and Early Letters*, ed., Doyce B. Nunis, Jr. (Georgetown, Calif.: The Talisman Press, 1962), 119—20.

34. Invoice of Goods, February 3, 1842, *Larkin Papers*, 1:161, totals ninety-two items for a value of $2,188.50. An additional Invoice of Goods, July 17, 1842, totaling $775.00 is in ibid., 1:249. The value of goods and lumber at the Santa Cruz store at the end of 1842 is shown in Larkin, "Accounts," C—E/9.

35. TOL to Josiah Belden, August 18, 1842, *Larkin Papers*, 1:271—72.

36. Carmichael is frequently mentioned in Belden's correspondence to Larkin during the spring of 1842 as a competitor with no indication of any other. In March 1842, Belden wrote his sister that there was only one foreigner in Santa Cruz beside himself. Josiah Belden to Mrs. Eliza M. Bowers, March 21, 1842, in Nunis, ed., *Josiah Belden*, 120. Yet in June 1843, Nicholas Dawson signed a declaration concerning that spring's fire in which he refers to himself as an employee and shopkeeper of Francis Dye and says that he had been for a year. Nicholas Dawson, "*Declaración*," June 19, 1843, *Larkin Papers*, 2:21. Evidently Dye opened a new store in late spring 1842.

37. Josiah Belden to TOL, May 15 and 29, 1842, ibid., 1:220, 227. This was a theft by a Californio, Juan Hilario. An English lumberman was also arrested for stealing lumber from the Santa Cruz operation but escaped from the local Santa Cruz jail. Josiah Belden to TOL, August 7 and 15, 1842, ibid., 1:262—63, 269.

38. A candid description by a modern Franciscan scholar is in Maynard Geiger, *Franciscan Missionaries in Hispanic California, 1769—1848* (San Marino, Calif.: Huntington Library, 1969), 247—49.

39. Josiah Belden to TOL, May 29 and December 30, 1842, *Larkin Papers*, 1:228, 350. Belden brought additional evidence to bear in his memoirs, but added, "if I had brought the charge of robbery against him, he might have made me a great deal of trouble, and have done me much injury, as he had a good deal of influence with the people. So, under the circumstances I let the matter go, and never made any complaint." Nunis, ed., *Josiah Belden*, 60—61.

40. Josiah Belden to TOL, March 28, 1842, *Larkin Papers*, 1:182–83.

41. Nunis, ed., *Josiah Belden*, 60–61.

42. Larkin, "Accounts," C–E/9.

43. Copies of the reward offer and public notice, dated June 1, 1843, are in *Larkin Papers*, 2:17–18.

44. Nicholas Dawson, "Declaración," June 19, 1843, ibid., 2:21–22.

45. Ibid.

46. The dates of closing are shown by the end of entries in Larkin, "Accounts," C–E/9.

47. Eliab Grimes to TOL, August 6, 1844, and Marshall & Johnson to TOL, May 26, 1842, ibid., 2:184, 1:223.

48. Nicholas A. Den to TOL, May 29, 1842; William D. M. Howard to TOL, January 25, 1846; and Stephen Reynolds to TOL, January 21, 1840, ibid., 1:229, 4:183, 1:33.

49. James A. Forbes to TOL, April 1, 1845, and Henry D. Fitch to TOL, September 12, 1845, ibid., 3:113, 349.

50. TOL to John Temple, July 22, 1839, ibid., 1:17–18. The entire controversy unfolds through correspondence clustered in this portion of these papers, within approximately ten pages before and twenty-five pages following this letter.

51. John Parrott to William A. Leidesdorff, August 21, 1845, Box 1, Leidesdorff Collection, Huntington Library. Later in the letter he referred to Larkin as "a petty consul, who cannot write his own language correctly." This is the only reference I have discovered as to Larkin's lack of linguistic polish.

52. TOL to Faxon D. Atherton, September 5, 1845, in Hawgood, ed., *First and Last Consul*, 130.

53. John C. Jones to TOL, September 3, 1845, *Larkin Papers*, 3:336.

54. William G. Rae to TOL, September 2, 1844, ibid., 2:214.

55. The legal knowledge of these expatriate merchants in Mexican California is analyzed generally in Langum, *Law and Community on the Mexican California Frontier*, and specifically their use of arbitration at 214–31.

56. There is considerable correspondence, between August and December 1844 on this subject, by and between TOL and the California governor, Manuel Micheltorena, subordinate Mexican officals, the American Secretary of State, and the American Minister of Legation in Mexico. *Larkin Papers*, 2:192–93, 195–96, 199–200, 207, 312–13, 321–23. Ultimately, by a decree of October 19, 1844, the Mexican governor permitted whalers to sell up to $400 dollars worth of goods in exchange for provisions. Larkin later wrote the Secretary of State that "the Departamental Government have passed a Law, allowing whalers every privilege I could ask for. My applications continued to General Micheltorena three months on the subject." Letter, TOL to James Buchanan, July 10, 1845, ibid., 3:267.

57. TOL to Henry Lindsey, December 11, 1844, ibid., 2:319–20.

58. TOL to Abel Stearns, November 9, 1836, in Hawgood, ed., *First and Last Consul*, 12.

59. For example, Henry D. Fitch to TOL, December 4, 1842; Henry A. Peirce to TOL, August 12, 1846; and William G. Rae to TOL, September 2, 1844, *Larkin Papers*, 1:331, 5:195, 2:214.

60. The profits and losses for individual years and the accumulation of capital may be seen clearly in the year end summaries found in Larkin, "Accounts," C–E/9.

61. Samuel H. Willey to Rayner W. Kelsey, January 6, 1909, "Correspondence of Samuel Hopkins Willey Concerning Larkin," C–D/5020:13, Bancroft Library.

62. For example, see TOL to Abel Stearns, August 9, 1834 ("As a few of the plank were defective tho' not to hurt, I tho' in a few."); and December 3, 1834 ("I would not

recommend you to have them [logs] haul'd to the Auctosh unless you are very sure of a Vessels going there. . . . To M. is the surest if you want them next summer") in Hawgood, ed., *First and Last Consul,* 7, 9.

63. TOL to Faxon D. Atherton, February 12, 1843, in Nunis, ed., "Six New Larkin Letters," 73–74.

64. Dana, *Two Years Before the Mast,* Kemble, ed., 1:172.

65. Agreement, TOL and Talbot H. Green, May 16, 1843, *Larkin Papers,* 2:15.

66. TOL to Talbot H. Green, May 25, 1843, ibid., 2:16.

67. TOL to Talbot H. Green, November 21, 1843, ibid., 2:57.

68. Larkin, "Accounts," C–E/9.

69. Public Notice by TOL, May 16, 1844, *Larkin Papers,* 2:121.

70. Agreement, TOL and Talbot H. Green, January 1, 1846, ibid., 4:145–46.

71. TOL to James Buchanan, April 17, 1846, ibid., 4:294.

Chapter 5. Hospitality and Associations: Associates and Profits

1. TOL to Abel Stearns, June 2, 1833, Box 39, Stearns Collection.

2. John Bidwell to TOL, April 26, 1847, *Larkin Papers,* 6:120.

3. And whose stay was not entirely personally pleasant to the Larkin family. See TOL to Parrott & Co., May 22, 1846, and Ebenezer L. Childs to TOL, June 26, 1846, ibid., 4:388–89, 5:75.

4. TOL to James Buchanan, April 17, 1846, ibid., 4:289.

5. Briton C. Busch, ed., *Alta California, 1840–1842: The Journal and Observations of William Dane Phelps* (Glendale, Calif.: Arthur H. Clark Company, 1983), 52.

6. John Paty to TOL, December 21, 1840, *Larkin Papers,* 1:66. ("I have always felt very greatfull to yourself & wife for the very kind reception I have always found at your house.")

7. TOL to Secretary of State, March 6 and 27, 1846, ibid., 4:232, 270.

8. TOL to James Buchanan, June 1, 1846, ibid., 5:4.

9. Ethan Estabrook to TOL, ibid., June 12, 1841, 1:89. ("The kindness and hospitality which I have received at your house will be long remembered.")

10. Horatio E. Hale to Ebenezer L. Childs, September 23, 1842, quoted in Henry P. Beers, ed., "The American Consulate in California: Documents Relating to Its Establishment," *California Historical Society Quarterly* 37 (March 1958): 14.

11. William M. Wood, *Wandering Sketches of People and Things* (Philadelphia: Carey and Hart, 1849), 232–33.

12. For example, he gave one ball in honor of Captain Montgomery and the officers of the ship *Portsmouth* in April 1846. TOL to Moses Y. Beach & Sons, May (n.d.) 1846, *Larkin Papers,* 4:405. Then, just weeks later, he gave a ball in honor of the special courier Gillespie, whose disguise as an invalid did not fool a perceptive female observer. Angustias de la Guerra Ord, *Occurrences in Hispanic California,* trans. and ed. Francis Price and William H. Ellison (Washington, D.C.: Academy of American Franciscan History, 1956), 58.

13. One party in October 1842 was given by Larkin "and other American residents" and was held, not at Larkin's home, but at the government house, *el cuartel.* The music, dancing, and feasting is reported to have lasted until a late hour. Davis, *Seventy-Five Years in California,* 88.

14. Ord, *Occurrences in Hispanic California,* 59.

15. Daniel D. Heustis, *A Narrative of the adventures and sufferings of Captain Daniel D. Heustis and his companions* (Boston: Redding & Co., 1847; reprint, *Remarkable Adventures: California, 1845,* Los Angeles: Glen Dawson, 1957), 5.

16. Busch, ed., *Alta California . . . The Journal and Observations of William Dane Phelps*, 307.

17. TOL to Moses Y. Beach & Sons, May 19, 1846, *Larkin Papers*, 4:379.

18. Juan Bautista Alvarado to TOL, April 30, 1847, ibid., 6:135.

19. Parker, "Larkin, Anglo-American Businessman in Mexican California," 417.

20. TOL to Faxon D. Atherton, August 14, 1847, Faxon Dean Atherton Papers, Bancroft Library.

21. Ebenezer L. Childs to TOL and John B. R. Cooper, February 25, 1833, Vallejo Documents, 31:6.

22. TOL to "Dear Brother," August 5 and 6, 1834, ibid., 31:113, 113b.

23. Ibid.

24. This record may be found in Larkin, "Accounts," C−E/6.

25. Burgess, "Lumbering in Hispanic California," 241−42. This article presents an excellent analysis of Larkin's lumber operation.

26. Biographical information from Bancroft, *California Pioneer Register*, 96.

27. John Chamberlain, "Memoirs of California Since 1840," 10−12, manuscript (1877), Bancroft Library.

28. Lawrence Carmichael to TOL, January 18, 1841, *Larkin Papers*, 1:75.

29. Morris, "The Journal of a 'Crazy Man,' " 125−26.

30. TOL, "Statement Regarding Food Provided for the Imprisoned Foreigners," December 6, 1840, *Larkin Papers*, 1:63.

31. Juan Bautista Alvarado to TOL, April 30, 1847, ibid., 6:134−35.

32. Chamberlain, "Memoirs of California Since 1840," 4.

33. Morris, "The Journal of a 'Crazy Man,' " 116.

34. Thomes, *On Land and Sea*, 75, 114, 119−20, 76.

35. Compare two accounts. Larkin himself wrote: "I have been in Mazatlan during the winter made a voyage in the Schooner California, she brought up the small pox." TOL to Alfred Robinson, April 15, 1844, Appleton Collection. John Bidwell put matters more bluntly: "On his return to Monterey the woman who washed his clothes took the small-pox. Larkin's whole family had it; it spread, and the number of deaths was fearful." John Bidwell, *In California Before the Gold Rush* (Los Angeles: Ward Ritchie Press, 1948), 73n.1.

36. William A. Streeter, "Recollections of Historical Events in California 1843−1878," 27−29, manuscript (1878), Bancroft Library.

37. TOL to Abel Stearns and John Temple, June 25, 1844, typescripts, Box 39, Stearns Collection, and in Larkin Family Collection, Huntington Library.

38. TOL to Editor of "New York Herald," June 30, 1846, *Larkin Papers*, 5:91.

39. Robert B. Semple to TOL, May 3, 1847, ibid., 6:146−47.

40. John A. Bates to Richard R. Waldron, July 4, 1840, ibid., 1:46.

41. More technical information on account collection, creation and purchase of bills of exchange, and Larkin's role in these activities may be found in the chapter, "Credit Formation and Debt Collection," in Langum, *Law and Community on the Mexican California Frontier*, 187−209.

42. TOL to William M. Rogers, November 12, 1847, *Larkin Papers*, 7:61.

43. Nathan Spear to TOL, June 1, 1844, ibid., 2:135.

44. Parrott & Co. to TOL, February 13, 1845, and Mott Talbot & Co. to TOL, May 2, 1845, ibid., 3:43, 167.

45. Davis, *Seventy-Five Years in California*, 190.

46. TOL to Salvador Vallejo, January 11, 1843, *Larkin Papers*, 2:3.

47. TOL to William S. Hinckley, October [n.d.] 1845, ibid., 4:15−16.

48. TOL to Robert T. Ridley, December 28, 1844, ibid., 2:339.

49. Mott Talbot & Co. to TOL, May 11, 1846, ibid., 4:367.

50. TOL to Thomas W. Waldron, September 1, 1841, ibid., 1:116.

51. TOL to William A. Leidesdorff, April 14, 1846, ibid., 4:285.
52. TOL to Rachel Holmes Larkin, December 14, 1846, ibid., 5:312.
53. TOL to Faxon D. Atherton, October 20-21, 1842, in Nunis, ed., "Six New Larkin Letters," 70.
54. TOL to James Buchanan, April 17, 1846, *Larkin Papers*, 4:294.
55. Certificates, March 28, 1846 [as to 1844 loan], ibid., 4:263-64; February 3, 1845, Vallejo Documents, 12:133.
56. TOL, "Description of California," April 20, 1846, *Larkin Papers*, 4:318.
57. This procedure for entry of cargo, payment of duties and the government's creditors is well described by Larkin himself in his "Description of California," April 20, 1846, ibid., 4:311-12. An example of an actual payment by bill of exchange for 130 days drawn against a vessel's supercargo is in José Abrego, "Certificate of Indebtedness," March 28, 1846 [referring to 1844 transaction], ibid., 4:263-64.
58. TOL to William E. P. Hartnell, July 10, 1840, Vallejo Documents, 33:96.
59. TOL to Charles Maria Weber, June 11, 1846, *Larkin Papers*, 5:15.
60. Such an incident is described in TOL to Alfred Robinson, July 12, 1845, Appleton Collection.
61. John H. Everett to TOL, April 26, 1846, *Larkin Papers*, 4:350.
62. For example, see Alpheus B. Thompson to Talbot H. Green, April 21, 1846, ibid., 4:335, and TOL to Abel Stearns, March 3, 1846 [misdated August 3, 1846], Box 40, Stearns Collection.
63. TOL to Abel Stearns, February 12, 1843, Box 39, Stearns Collection.
64. TOL to Abel Stearns and John Temple, July 20, 1845, in Hawgood, ed., *First and Last Consul*, 30.
65. TOL to Abel Stearns, July 20, [two letters] and August 18, 1845, ibid., 26-31, and Abel Stearns to TOL, August 3, 1845, *Larkin Papers*, 3:301.
66. TOL to Alfred Robinson, April 15, 1844, Appleton Collection.
67. TOL to Manuel Micheltorena, March 21, 1845, *Larkin Papers*, 3:74.
68. TOL to Manuel Micheltorena, June 14, 1845, ibid., 3:240.
69. Nunis, ed., *Josiah Belden*, 66.
70. See Manuel Micheltorena to TOL, ordering payment of these funds, May 24, 25, and 28, 1844, and November 19, 28, 1844, *Larkin Papers*, 2:129, 132, 293, 295.
71. TOL to Parrott & Co., December 12, 1844, ibid., 2:323-24.
72. John Parrott to TOL, April 15, 1844, quoted in Barbara D. Jostes, *John Parrott, Consul, 1811-1844: Selected Papers of a Western Pioneer* (San Francisco: Lawton and Alfred Kennedy, 1972), p. 25.
73. TOL to John Parrott, January 25, 1845, *Larkin Papers*, 3:28.
74. TOL to Manuel Micheltorena, January 20, 1845, ibid., 3:15.
75. TOL to John Parrott, January 25, 1845, ibid., 3:28.
76. Nunis, ed., *Josiah Belden*, 64.
77. TOL to Abel Stearns, March 4, 1845, in Hawgood, ed., *First and Last Consul*, 18-19.
78. TOL to Abel Stearns, March 5, 1845, Box 40, Stearns Collection.
79. Abel Stearns to TOL, May 13, 1845, *Larkin Papers*, 3:184.
80. TOL to Abel Stearns, May 21, 1845, in Hawgood, ed., *First and Last Consul*, 21-22.
81. Receipts and lists, March 23, 1845, *Larkin Papers*, 3:90-95.
82. Bancroft's "Biographical Notes" [under "Larkin" entry], citing Buelna, *Misc. Hist.*, 14-15, Doc. 25, Bancroft Library.
83. TOL to Abel Stearns, July 20, 1845, in Hawgood, ed., *First and Last Consul*, 28.
84. TOL to Abel Stearns, July 20, 1845, ibid., 29.
85. TOL to John C. Frémont, March 8, 1846, *Larkin Papers*, 4:240.

86. TOL to Secretary of State, April 2, 1846, ibid., 4:277.
87. TOL to Jacob P. Leese, Abel Stearns, and Jonathan T. Warner, April 17, 1846, ibid., 4:296.
88. TOL to Abel Stearns, April 4, 1835, Box 39, Stearns Collection.
89. TOL to Moses Y. Beach, May 31, 1845, *Larkin Papers*, 3:219.
90. John H. Everett to TOL, March 23, 1845, ibid., 3:89.
91. William M. Rogers to TOL, December 23, 1844, Vallejo Documents, 34:88.
92. Ebenezer L. Childs to TOL, November 30, 1844, *Larkin Papers*, 2:296.
93. William M. Rogers to TOL, September 11, 1843, Vallejo Documents, 33:358.
94. William M. Rogers to TOL, September 1, 1845, *Larkin Papers*, 3:331.
95. William M. Rogers to TOL, January 20, 1840, Vallejo Documents, 33:7.
96. William M. Rogers to TOL, July 1, 1838, ibid., 32:144. ("I fear the world does not go as smoothly as it might with her.")
97. Ann R. L. Wright to TOL, October 17, 1840, ibid., 33:140.
98. Ann R. L. Wright to TOL, July 16, 1841, ibid., 33:218 (emphasis in original).
99. Ann R. L. Wright to TOL, November 17, 1844, *Larkin Papers*, 2:290.
100. Ann R. L. Wright to TOL, March 22, 1845, ibid., 3:87.
101. Ann R. L. Wright to TOL, August 31, 1845, ibid., 3:330.
102. Ebenezer L. Childs to TOL, November 29, 1841, Vallejo Documents, 33:249.
103. Ebenezer L. Childs to TOL, August 12, 1843, *Larkin Papers*, 2:35—36.
104. Ann R. L. Wright to TOL, July 16, 1841, Vallejo Documents, 33:218.
105. Ruth Childs to TOL, September 14, 1843, *Larkin Papers*, 2:45.
106. Isaac Childs to TOL, March 28, 1845, ibid., 3:107.
107. Ruth Childs to TOL, March 29, 1845, ibid., 3:109.

Chapter 6. Consul and Propagandist

1. Juan Bautista Alvarado to TOL, April 30, 1847, *Larkin Papers*, 6:135.
2. Ibid.; John B. Montgomery to William A. Leidesdorff, July 3, 1846, Box 6, Halleck, Peachy & Billings Collection, Special Collections, Research Library, University of California, Los Angeles.
3. Austin J. Raines to Louis McLane, Secretary of State, October 11, 1833, in Beers, ed., "The American Consulate in California," 3.
4. Commission of Austin J. Raines as Consul at Monterey, October 17, 1833, Austin J. Raines to Louis McLane, Secretary of State, February 20, 1834, endorsement, ibid., 3, 5, and n.4.
5. Ibid., p. 16, n.4.
6. TOL to Abel Stearns, July 22 and August 9, 1834, in Hawgood, ed., *First and Last Consul*, 7—8.
7. Charles Bent to William H. Ashley, April 26, 1835; William H. Ashley to the Secretary of State, April 30, 1835, in Beers, ed., "American Consulate in California," 5—6.
8. Secretary of State to William H. Ashley, May 16, 1835, in ibid., p. 7.
9. Secretary of State to William [Jonathan] P. Gilliam, June 22, 1837, in ibid., pp. 7—8, 16, n.12,14.
10. J. T. Warren [Jonathan Trumbull Warner?] to Martin Van Buren, President, September 21, 1840, in ibid., 9—10.
11. Thomas O. Larkin, Chairman, and Henry Paty, Secretary, Resolution, July 1, 1840, an enclosure in TOL to James Buchanan, November 12, 1847, *Larkin Papers*, 7:70—71.
12. Bancroft, *History of California*, 2:792, 4:36. Estabrook was in California long

enough to be immortalized by inclusion in Larkin's list of American and British citizens resident in California in 1840. Hawgood, ed., *First and Last Consul*, 112. Estabrook wrote to Larkin in 1846, reminiscing about his year in California, thanking Larkin for his kindnesses, and asking to be remembered to "Mrs Larkin, to Thomasito, Francisquito and the other Larkinitos of your family." Ethan Estabrook to TOL, February 21, 1846, *Larkin Papers*, 4:206—08.

13. Thomas Carlile to Leverett Saltonstall, February 3, 1842; Commission of Thomas Carlile as United States Consul at San Francisco, March 10, 1842; Secretary of State to Thomas Carlile, March 17, 1842, in Beers, ed., "American Consulate in California," 10—13; Department of State to Thomas Carlile, June 9, 1843, Instructions to Consuls, June 24, 1841—May 24, 1847, 2:163, Department of State, National Archives, Washington, D.C.

14. Unless otherwise indicated, the following account of the "Affair in Monterey," as Larkin called it, is taken from TOL to Faxon D. Atherton, [undated, endorsed at end, "Affair in Monterey taking the place etc., October 20 & 21, 1842."], in Nunis, ed., "Six New Larkin Letters," 67—71. The letter is also printed in Hawgood, ed., *First and Last Consul*, 119—22.

15. Nunis, ed., "Six New Larkin Letters," 68.

16. TOL to James G. Bennett, February 10, 1843, *Larkin Papers*, 2:9.

17. John C. Jones to TOL, November 5, 1842, ibid., 1:311.

18. Nathan Spear to TOL, November 8, 1842, ibid., 1:315.

19. TOL to James G. Bennett, February 10, 1843, ibid., 2:6.

20. TOL to Faxon D. Atherton, [undated, endorsed at end, "Affair in Monterey . . . October 20—21, 1842"], in Nunis, ed., "Six New Larkin Letters," 69.

21. TOL to James G. Bennett, February 10, 1843, *Larkin Papers*, 2:7.

22. Stephen Smith to Ebenezer L. Childs, March 29, 1842, in Beers, ed., "The American Consulate in California," 13.

23. Horatio E. Hale to Ebenezer L. Childs, September 23, 1842, in ibid., 14.

24. Ebenezer L. Childs to TOL, January 25, 1843, Vallejo Documents, 33:316.

25. Ebenezer L. Childs to TOL, August 12, 1843, *Larkin Papers*, 2:33—34.

26. Ebenezer L. Childs to TOL, December 26, 1843, ibid., 2:61—62.

27. TOL to Alfred Robinson, April 15, 1844, Appleton Collection. A draft of the letter, not identical, is in *Larkin Papers*, 2:112—14.

28. Ebenezer L. Childs to TOL, December 26, 1843; John C. Calhoun to TOL, June 24; and TOL to John C. Calhoun, June 24, 1844, ibid., 2:62, 143, 145. Albert Gilliam had received a temporary appointment in August 1843. A. P. Upshur, Secretary of State, to Albert M. Gilliam, August 5, 1843, Instructions to Consuls, June 24, 1841—May 24, 1847, 2:163—64, Department of State, National Archives.

29. Richard K. Crallé to TOL, October 25, 1844, *Larkin Papers*, 2:262. Gilliam resigned on August 1, 1844. Chief Clerk to Frederick J. Teggart, October 14, 1908, C—D/5020:36, Rayner Wickersham Kelsey Correspondence, Bancroft Library.

30. TOL to William Hooper, November 4, 1844, *Larkin Papers*, 2:274.

31. TOL to Secretary of State, April 10, 1844 and April 11, 1844, ibid., 2:91, 92.

32. John Parrott to TOL, May 22, 1844, ibid., 2:125—26.

33. William Hooper to TOL, October 2, 1844, ibid., 2:250.

34. William Hooper to TOL, November 26, 1844, Box LE 28, Leidesdorff Collection, Huntington Library.

35. TOL to John C. Calhoun, December 9, 1844, *Larkin Papers*, 2:309—11.

36. TOL to Secretary of State, April 11, 1844, January 6, 1846; TOL to John C. Calhoun, August 18, 1844, ibid., 2:92—93, 4:158, and 2:206.

37. See generally, Chester L. Jones, *The Consular Service of the United States, Its History and Activities* (Philadelphia: University of Philadelphia, 1906).

38. The best general treatment of Larkin's consular activities, from which much of this discussion is drawn, is Kelsey, "The United States Consulate in California," 1:160–267. Much of the consular correspondence is contained in *Larkin Papers*.

39. Kelsey, "The United States Consulate in California," 1:177.

40. TOL to Juez de Paz, May 8, 1844, *Larkin Papers*, 2:116.

41. TOL to Pedro Narváez, September 10, 1844, ibid., 2:224. ("As . . . he has been wanting in his respects to the law its precise that he should be imprisoned but he must not be locked up without food.")

42. Kelsey, "The United States Consulate in California," 1:188–93. This was the well-known Libbey-Spear Affair.

43. TOL to James Buchanan, July 10, 1845, *Larkin Papers*, 3:267.

44. See generally, Langum, *Law and Community on the Mexican California Frontier*.

45. Kelsey, "The United States Consulate in California," 1:195–99.

46. Richard K. Crallé, Acting Secretary of State, to TOL, October 25, 1844, *Larkin Papers*, 2:262.

47. TOL to James Buchanan, James Buchanan to TOL, August 27, 1846, and January 13, 1847, ibid., 5:223 and 6:5–6.

48. Richard B. Mason to TOL, May 20, 1848, ibid., 7:268.

49. James Buchanan to TOL, June 23, 1848, ibid., 7:299.

50. TOL, "Semi-Annual Consular Returns," December 31, 1844, ibid., 2:343–56.

51. James Buchanan to TOL, October 17, 1845, ibid., 4:47.

52. TOL to James Buchanan, June 15, 1846, ibid., 5:28.

53. TOL to Rachel H. Larkin, December 14, 1846, ibid., 5:313.

54. An excellent example of which is in Stephen Pleasonton to TOL, June 12, 1845, ibid., 3:236.

55. TOL to James Buchanan, April 29, 1847, ibid., 6:129.

56. TOL to James Buchanan, August 25, 1847, ibid., 6:292.

57. William M. Rogers to TOL, June 29, 1848, ibid., 7:305.

58. TOL to William M. Rogers, August 26, 1846, ibid., 5:222. This brought an admonition from his cousin: "I do not believe you can have drawn on the Government without sending your ac/ts." William M. Rogers to TOL, November 16, 1846, ibid., 5:282.

59. TOL to James Buchanan, September 1, 1847, ibid., 6:302–303.

60. TOL to 5th auditor, Vallejo Documents, 34:219, probably written shortly after Larkin's letter of September 1, 1847 to the Secretary of State. Other copies of this letter appear in 34:231 and 34:247.

61. James Buchanan to TOL, June 23, 1848, *Larkin Papers*, 7:298–300.

62. TOL to William A. Leidesdorff, October 29, 1845, ibid., 4:75, appointing the vice consul, a position that was never officially recognized by Mexico.

63. Samuel J. Hastings to TOL, January 22, 1846, ibid., 4:177. Another version of this conversation has Polk expressing the view that Larkin was "one of the most efficient consuls the U.S. possessed." See Faxon Dean Atherton to TOL, December 3, 1846, ibid., 5:290.

64. Heustis, *Remarkable Adventures: California, 1845*, 3.

65. Bancroft's "Biographical Notes" [under "Larkin" entry], referring to manuscript statement of John Bidwell, 138–39.

66. TOL to Moses Y. Beach, May 28, 1845, *Larkin Papers*, 3:202.

67. TOL to James G. Bennett, February 10, 1843, ibid., 2:6.

68. TOL to Moses Y. Beach, May 28, 1845, ibid., 3:201–202.

69. *New York Herald*, June 12, 1845. (M.A. thesis, Auburn University, 1987), 72. Larkin mentioned in a letter to Faxon Dean Atherton that he had written a "history of the revolution" and would try to send a copy. It was a lengthy document, for he would not be

able to send the account unless he could find someone to copy it; he had no time to do it himself. TOL to Faxon Dean Atherton, June 6, 1845, Faxon Dean Atherton Papers. If the account sent to the *Herald* and published under the name, "Paisano," was not in fact Larkin's "history of the revolution," then the document remains to be discovered.

70. TOL to Moses Y. Beach, May 31, 1845, *Larkin Papers*, 3:215–18. Larkin regularly sent Oahu newspapers to eastern editors, probably in exchange for the copies of their newspapers that they sent to him.

71. TOL to Faxon Dean Atherton, June 6, 1845, Faxon Dean Atherton Papers. C–B 873, Bancroft Library, University of California, Berkeley.

72. TOL to *Journal of Commerce*, July [?] 1845, *Larkin Papers*, 3:295.

73. TOL to Faxon Dean Atherton, June 6, 1845, Atherton Papers.

74. *New York Herald*, June 12, 1845.

75. TOL to *Journal of Commerce*, July [?] 1845, *Larkin Papers*, 3:294–95. The letter was also printed in the *Charleston Mercury*, October 22, 1845, cited in Gene Allen Smith, "The Propaganda Campaign of Thomas Oliver Larkin." Master's thesis, Auburn University, 1987, 82n.43.

76. TOL to John Marsh, July 8, 1845, in Hawgood, ed., *First and Last Consul*, 25.

77. John Marsh to Lewis Cass, January 20, 1946, in "Letter of Dr. John Marsh to Hon. Lewis Cass," *California Historical Quarterly* 22 (December 1943): 315–22. In the *Picayune* letter, which he signed "Essex," Marsh noted, tongue in cheek, that he was writing because "[c]ertain wilful malicious & vile disposed neighbors" in Monterey, meaning Larkin, had forced him to write letters for publication, cutting off his supply of newspapers until he should do so. John Marsh to the Editors, *New Orleans Picayune*, February [?] 1846, John Marsh Collection, California State Library.

78. Frederick Hudson to TOL, October 14, 1845, *Larkin Papers*, 4:24.

79. Moses Y. Beach & Sons to TOL, December 24, 1845; January 12, 1846, ibid., 4:129, 159–60.

80. TOL to Moses Y. Beach & Sons, May 19, 1846, ibid., 4:379–80.

81. TOL to James G. Bennett, May 20, 1846, ibid., 4:382.

82. For example, a letter to one "Robinson," probably Alfred Robinson, was printed in the *Journal of Commerce*. Samuel J. Hastings to TOL, November 9, 1845, *Larkin Papers*, 4:93.

83. TOL to Moses Y. Beach & Sons, April [?] 1846, ibid., 4:355–56.

84. TOL to James Gordon Bennett, May 30, 1846, ibid., 4:403–404.

85. TOL to James G. Bennett, February 10, 1843, ibid., 2:8.

86. TOL to "Journal of Commerce," July [12?] 1845, ibid., 3:296. The correspondence was enclosed in a letter from Larkin to Alfred Robinson. Larkin was a subscriber to the newspaper but had never written to the editors. He asked Robinson to look the letter over and have it published if he thought it worthy. TOL to Alfred Robinson, July 12, 1845, Appleton Collection.

87. TOL to James G. Bennett, May 20, 1846, *Larkin Papers*, 4:382–84.

Chapter 7. Eden at Risk

1. James Buchanan to TOL, October 17, 1845, *Larkin Papers*, 4:46.

2. TOL to James Buchanan, July 10, 1845, ibid., 3:265–68. This was not the first letter from Larkin that showed his awareness of American national interests on the Pacific coast. In 1844, he had written to John C. Calhoun, then Secretary of State, in response to a rumor that England might purchase California from Mexico. If the rumor proved true, he wrote, the United States should approach Britain to try to arrange "an exchange of eight degrees of the country north of the Columbia for eight degrees in California [Larkin's copy

reads: for Eight degrees South of the 42° degree of Latitude] thereby taking in one of the finest countries in the world, and the best most magnificent harbours known." TOL to John C. Calhoun, August 18, 1844, ibid., 2:205–206. Larkin was suggesting that the United States give up its claim to the Oregon country north of the Columbia River in exchange for Britain's title to all of California as far south as 34 degrees latitude, just south of Los Angeles.

3. John C. Jones to TOL, June 10, 1845, ibid., 3:232.

4. TOL to John Marsh, July 8, 1845, in Hawgood, ed., *First and Last Consul*, 24.

5. TOL to James Buchanan, July 10, 1845, *Larkin Papers*, 3:267.

6. Bancroft claims that Larkin and his American correspondents completely misunderstood the situation. He suggests that Mexico City had no intention to punish the Californians for expelling Micheltorena. The Californians, he says, far from fearing the expedition, welcomed it since its purpose was to protect California from an American invasion. He suggests that Castro and Alvarado misled Larkin to conceal the preparations to defend the province against American aggressions. Hubert H. Bancroft, *History of California*, 7 vols. (San Francisco: The History Company, 1886–1890; reprint ed., 7 vols., Santa Barbara: Wallace Hebberd, 1963–1970), 4:534–35. To accept Bancroft's conclusions requires that one ignore the Californians' historical fear of any authority sent to the province by Mexico City. A Mexican general in command of troops would be in a position to exercise considerable control in California. Bancroft's argument also suggests that Larkin, who was on the closest of terms with California leaders, and his American correspondents were abysmally naïve, or that Larkin, since he reported the feared expedition as an invasion, was deceitful to an alarming degree.

7. TOL to James Buchanan, July 10, 1845, *Larkin Papers*, 3:266–67.

8. Ibid., 3:267. Larkin had not always seen the French presence as a menace. As recently as 1844, he had urged on a French correspondent at LeHavre the importance of stationing a French consul at Monterey. "This town is growing," he said, "the commerce increasing, the climate delightful the mode of living not dear nor is it otherwise than simple." TOL to (?) Gauden, April 21, 1844, ibid., 2:104.

9. Robert G. Cleland, "The Early Sentiment for the Annexation of California: An Account of the Growth of American Interest in California, 1835–1846," *The Southwestern Historical Quarterly* 18 (January 1915): 238–39.

10. James Buchanan to TOL, October 17, 1845, *Larkin Papers*, 4:44–47.

11. Ibid., 4:45.

12. Ibid., 4:44–45.

13. Ibid., 4:46–47.

14. George Bancroft to John D. Sloat, October 17, 1845, in Robert E. Cowan, ed., "Documentary," *California Historical Society Quarterly* 2 (July 1923): 167–70.

15. Harold W. Gross, "The Influence of Thomas O. Larkin Toward the Acquisition of California" (M.A. thesis, University of California, Berkeley, 1937), 111; Neal Harlow, *California Conquered: War and Peace on the Pacific, 1846–1850* (Berkeley: University of California Press, 1982), 82.

16. James Buchanan to Louis McLane, October 14, 1845, cited in Cleland, "The Early Sentiment For the Annexation of California," 243.

17. James Buchanan to James Slidell, November 10, 1845, cited in Gross, "Influence of Thomas O. Larkin," 112.

18. TOL to Faxon Dean Atherton, June 6, 1845, Atherton Papers.

19. TOL to James Buchanan, April 17, 1846, *Larkin Papers*, 4:292–93.

20. Ibid., 4:294.

21. There was perhaps some truth in this supposition. About three weeks later, during a casual conversation with Lieutenant Joseph Warren Revere, U.S.S. *Portsmouth*, General Castro asked whether the American government would offer him a brigadier-general's com-

mission if he declared himself in favor of American authority in California. Revere realized that the *comandante* spoke in jest, but believed nevertheless that "the promise of such an appointment would have had its effect." Joseph W. Revere, *Naval Duty in California* (Oakland: Biobooks, 1947), 25. Revere's book was first published as *A Tour of Duty in California* (New York: C. S. Francis & Co., 1849).

22. TOL to James Buchanan, April 17, 1846, *Larkin Papers*, 4:293-94.

23. TOL to James Buchanan, April 17, 1846, ibid., 4:289. This is the first of two letters from TOL to Buchanan on this date. Neither Larkin nor Polk could have known that British and French officialdom had never been as enthusiastic as their consuls and certain private interests in contending for California. Both British and French leaders were very interested, however, in diplomatic efforts to forestall an American takeover. For a discussion, see Norman Graebner, *Empire on the Pacific: A Study in American Continental Expansion* (New York: Ronald Press Company, 1955), chap. 4.

24. TOL to James Buchanan, April 17, 1846, *Larkin Papers*, 4:294. This is the second of two letters that Larkin wrote to Buchanan on this date.

25. TOL, Description of California, April 20, 1846, and TOL, Notes on Personal Character of the Principal Men, ibid., 4:303-22, 4:322-34. The latter document was prepared as an enclosure to the April 20 description of California.

26. José Castro "et al.," Proceedings of Military Junta, April 11, 1846, ibid., 4:282.

27. TOL to Abel Stearns, May 1, 1846, in Hawgood, ed., *First and Last Consul*, 61-62.

28. The gathering of military officers at General Castro's house mostly discussed the Paredes revolution in Mexico and the defense of California. "Since the meeting was not a harmonious one, they went to the home of T. O. Larkin, where a mixed general *junta* was opened." Mariano G. Vallejo, "Historical and Personal Memoirs Relating to Alta California," 5 vols., manuscript, Bancroft Library, C-D/21 (translation) 5 (1845-1848), pp. 58, 70.

29. Ibid., pp. 58-61, 70.

30. Revere, *Naval Duty in California*, 24.

31. Bancroft, *History of California*, 5:61.

32. Vallejo, "Historical and Personal Memoirs," 64-65. It is impossible to know how much credit to give Vallejo's recollection for Prudon's oratory.

33. Revere, *Naval Duty in California*, 23. Questions have been raised whether Vallejo indeed made this speech, but the general himself later confirmed that he had delivered it. See Josiah Royce, *California, From the Conquest in 1846 to the Second Vigilance Committee in San Francisco* (Reprint ed., Santa Barbara: Peregrine Publishers, Inc., 1970), 137; Myrtle M. McKittrick, *Vallejo, Son of California* (Portland, Ore.: Binfords & Mort, 1944), 248-49; and Vallejo's own account in Vallejo, "Historical and Personal Memoirs," 58-70. See also the following note.

34. Vallejo, "Historical and Personal Memoirs," 69; McKittrick, *Vallejo*, 249; Bancroft, *History of California*, 5:62. After giving a full account of the meetings of the Monterey junta, citing Revere, whose book, *A Tour of Duty in California*, was published in 1849, and Vallejo's memoir as his principal sources, Bancroft concludes that the meeting never took place. *History of California*, 5:63. But see the response to Bancroft in McKittrick, *Vallejo*, 248-53.

There is little doubt that the meeting was held. For evidence, see John Sutter to John Marsh, April 3, 1846, Box 240, Marsh Collection, California State Library; TOL to William A. Leidesdorff, April 13, 1846, *Larkin Papers*, 4:284; TOL to Abel Stearns, May 1, 1846, in Hawgood, ed., *First and Last Consul*, 61-62. William Heath Davis's recollections, published in 1889, three years after Bancroft's *History of California*, confirms Vallejo's account of the meeting. Davis, *Seventy-Five Years in California*, 107-108. An earlier corroboration is in the testimony of Samuel J. Hensley. See District Courts of the

United States, Northern and Southern Districts of California, "Claims For Mission Lands," San Francisco, 1859, 68, Bancroft Library.

The *course* of the meeting might still be questioned since no firsthand account exists, and Larkin did not comment further on the proceedings.

35. Larkin to John C. Calhoun, June 6, 1845, *Larkin Papers*, 3:227.

36. Ibid. See also Bancroft, *History of California*, 4:604.

37. Ibid., 5:56.

38. Cleland, "Early Sentiment for the Annexation of California," (Oct. 1914), 151, citing Juan Bautista Alvarado, "Historia de California," 2:133–34. Vallejo remembered the comment differently: "You and I both do not know how far these intruders intend to go, but I assure you that it would not surprise me to see them build ladders that would reach the sky." Vallejo, "Historical and Personal Memoirs," 59.

39. John A. Sutter to TOL, July 15, 1845, *Larkin Papers*, 3:271.

40. John A. Sutter to TOL, October 8, 1845, and TOL to James Buchanan, November 4, 1845, ibid., 4:10–11, 86.

41. John A. Sutter to TOL, November 5, 1845, ibid., 4:90.

42. TOL to James Buchanan, November 4, 1845, ibid., 4:87.

43. TOL to The Emigrants Recently Arrived at the Sacramento River, November 12, 1845, ibid., 4:97.

44. TOL to James Buchanan, November 4, 1845, ibid., 4:87.

45. Kenneth M. Johnson, *The New Almaden Quicksilver Mine* (Georgetown, Calif.: The Talisman Press, 1963), 16–17, citing *United States v. Andres Castillero, Transcript of the Record*, 4 vols. (San Francisco, 1859–60), 1:409–10.

46. Bancroft, *History of California*, 4:606–607.

47. Lansford W. Hastings to TOL, March 3, 1846, *Larkin Papers*, 4:220–21; Lansford W. Hastings to John Marsh, March 26, 1846, in Hawgood, ed., *First and Last Consul*, 51. Hastings visited Sutter in spring 1846. Hastings could be very disagreeable, and Sutter was glad to see the end of him. "[P]erhaps nobody will see him here again," Sutter wrote to Marsh, "as his life will be in danger about his book, making out California a Paradis [*sic*], even some of the Emigrants in the valley threatened his life." John Sutter to John Marsh, April 3, 1846, Box 240, Marsh Collection.

48. Thomas J. Farnham to John Marsh, July 6, 1845, in Hawgood, ed., *First and Last Consul*, 23.

49. George D. Lyman, *John Marsh, Pioneer: The Life Story of a Trail-blazer on Six Frontiers* (New York: Charles Scribner's Sons, 1931), 263–67.

50. TOL to Manuel de Jesús Castro, January 29, 1846, *Larkin Papers*, 4:186.

51. John C. Frémont, *Memoirs of My Life* (Chicago: Belford, Clarke & Co., 1887), 454.

52. TOL to Manuel de Jesús Castro, January 29, 1846, *Larkin Papers*, 4:187. Castro, in fact, notified the minister of war on March 6, 1846, that he had granted permission to secure supplies for the expedition. Bancroft, *History of California*, 5:11.

53. TOL to Secretary of State, March 6, 1846, and TOL to William M. Rogers or Joel Giles, March 6, 1846, *Larkin Papers*, 4:232–33, 233–34.

54. Frémont, *Memoirs of My Life*, 456.

55. Bancroft, *History of California*, 5:8–9; Harlow, *California Conquered*, 66.

56. However, Larkin later would claim that it was "well known in Monterey" that Frémont "was to return when he collected his men." TOL to Secretary of State, March 27, 1846, *Larkin Papers*, 4:270. We have found nothing to substantiate Larkin's claim, but he probably believed it. He had written earlier to the Secretary of State, March 6, 1846, noting that Frémont was then "in this vicinity surveying, and will be again at this Consular House during this month." Ibid., 4:232.

57. Manuel Castro to John C. Frémont, March 6 [5], 1846, and José Castro to John C. Frémont, [March 5, 1846], ibid., 4:228–29.

58. Frémont, *Memoirs of My Life*, 459. Frémont in 1884 would claim that Castro had given him permission to visit the coast. It was this promise, Frémont said, that Castro later broke. Royce, *California*, 91.

59. TOL to John C. Frémont, March 8, 1846, *Larkin Papers*, 4:240.

60. TOL to John C. Frémont, March 8, 1846, ibid., 4:240.

61. TOL to the Commander of any American Ship of War in San Blas or Mazatlán, March 9, 1846, and TOL to John Parrott, March 9, 1846, ibid., 4:243–45.

62. TOL to John C. Frémont, March 10, 1846, ibid., 4:248.

63. John C. Frémont to TOL, March 9, 1946, ibid., 4:245.

64. TOL to Secretary of State, March 6, 1846, ibid., 4:232.

65. TOL to Manuel Díaz, March 10, 1846, ibid., 4:247.

66. Kit Carson, *Kit Carson's Autobiography*, ed. by Milo M. Quaife (Reprint ed., Lincoln: University of Nebraska Press, 1966), 94.

67. Bancroft, *History of California*, 5:20.

68. Frémont, *Memoirs of My Life*, 460.

69. Bancroft, *History of California*, 5:20, n.36.

70. Frémont refers here to the promise that he claimed General Castro gave him at Monterey. Frémont, *Memoirs of My Life*, 459.

71. John C. Frémont to Jessie B. Frémont, April 1, 1846, in Mary Lee Spence and Donald Jackson, eds., *The Expeditions of John Charles Frémont*, 3 vols. (Urbana: University of Illinois Press, 1970–1984), 2:129–30.

72. Translation printed in Bancroft, *History of California*, 5:20–21, n. 35.

73. TOL to Secretary of State, April 2, 1846, *Larkin Papers*, 4:275.

74. TOL to James Buchanan, April 17, 1846, ibid., 4:289.

75. George W. Ames, Jr., "Gillespie and the Conquest of California," *California Historical Society Quarterly* 17 (June 1938): 139.

76. TOL to the Secretary of State, April 2, 1846, *Larkin Papers*, 4:275.

77. TOL to the Secretary of State, March 6, 1846, ibid., 4:232.

78. TOL to William A. Leidesdorff, March 21, 1846, LE 112, Leidesdorff Collection.

79. TOL to Abel Stearns, March 26, 1846, in Hawgood, ed. *First and Last Consul*, 53.

80. TOL to the Secretary of State, April 2, 1846, *Larkin Papers*, 4:275.

81. TOL to Abel Stearns, March 19, 1846, ibid., 4:260.

82. TOL to James Buchanan, April 17, 1846, ibid., 4:289.

83. TOL to the Secretary of State, April 2, 1846, ibid., 4:277.

84. Juan Bautista Alvarado to TOL, April 30, 1847, ibid., 6:135.

85. Frémont, *Memoirs of My Life*, p. 478.

86. John Sutter to John Marsh, April 3, 1846, Box 240, Marsh Collection. John C. Frémont to William A. Leiderdorff, April 23, 1846, Robert Ernest Cowan Collection, Bancroft Library.

87. TOL to James Buchanan, April 17, 1846, *Larkin Papers*, 4:288–89. This was the first letter that Larkin wrote to the Secretary on this date. It was finished before Gillespie's arrival.

88. Frémont, *Memoirs of My Life*, 486.

89. Harlow, *California Conquered*, 79–80; TOL to James Buchanan, June 1, 1846, *Larkin Papers*, 5:4.

90. Archibald H. Gillespie to Secretary of the Navy, April 18, 1846, in Ames, "Gillespie and the Conquest of California," 137.

91. Ibid.

92. Vallejo, "Historical and Personal Memoirs," 85−86; Bancroft, *History of California*, 5:28.

93. TOL to William A. Leidesdorff, April 19, 1846, *Larkin Papers*, 4:302−303.

94. Ibid., 4:302.

95. TOL to Archibald Gillespie, April 23, 1846, ibid., 4:340−41.

96. Ibid., 4:341.

97. Ibid.

98. TOL to William A. Leidesdorff, April 23, 1846, in Hawgood, ed., *First and Last Consul*, 56.

99. *Larkin Papers*, 4:xvii.

100. Archibald Gillespie to TOL, April 25, 1845[6!], ibid., 4:347.

101. William A. Leidesdorff to TOL, April 25, 1846, ibid., 4:348.

102. Frémont, *Memoirs of My Life*, 489−90; Royce, *California*, pp.92−93. For evidence that Senator Benton saw Buchanan's October 17, 1845 letter, see Thomas H. Benton to James Buchanan, [February 18, 1848], Spence and Jackson, eds., *Expeditions of John Charles Frémont*, 2:477−78. Benton surely talked with the Frémonts about the letter to Larkin.

103. Josiah Royce to Henry L. Oak, December 9, 1884, HM 20147, Huntington Library.

104. Royce, *California*, 112. See also Jessie B. Frémont, "Secret Affairs Relating to the Mexican War," handwritten and sent to Josiah Royce following their interview in 1884, HM 319, Huntington Library, printed in Robert J. Parker, "Secret Affairs of the Mexican War: Larkin's Californian Mission," *Quarterly of the Historical Society of Southern California* 20 (March 1938): 22−28.

105. TOL to Charles V. Gillespie, March 16, 1847 [1848], *Larkin Papers*, 7:182.

106. TOL to James Buchanan, April 19, 1848, ibid., 7:234−35.

107. Bancroft, *History of California*, 5:55.

108. Soulé et al., *The Annals of San Francisco*, 761.

109. Royce, *California*, 102−103. For an account of Gillespie's role, see John A. Hussey, "The Origin of the Gillespie Mission," *California Historical Society Quarterly* 19 (March 1940): 43−58.

110. John C. Frémont to Thomas H. Benton, May 24, 1846, in Spence and Jackson, eds., *Expeditions of John Charles Frémont*, 2:138.

111. Frémont, *Memoirs of My Life*, 534.

112. James Buchanan to TOL, October 27, 1845, *Larkin Papers*, 4:69. The word, "Cancelled," is written across the face of the letter. See also Royce, *California*, 113−16.

113. President Polk eventually would confide to his diary that Frémont had no authority to initiate military action in California. Jackson and Spence, eds., *Expeditions of John Charles Frémont*, 2:xxix.

114. TOL to Jacob P. Leese, Abel Stearns, and Jonathan T. Warner, April 17, 1846, *Larkin Papers*, 4:295−97. Stearns's copy of this letter, with minor differences from the copy in Larkin's papers, is in Hawgood, ed., *First and Last Consul*, pp. 58−60.

115. TOL to Jacob P. Leese, Abel Stearns, and Jonathan T. Warner, April 17, 1846, *Larkin Papers*, 4:296.

116. Ibid., 4:296−97.

117. Ibid., 4:296.

118. TOL, Opinion of State of Affairs in California, [April 1846], ibid., 4:297−300. The document is not dated, but since the views expressed are similar to that in Buchanan's letter of October 17, 1845, it must be assumed that it was written following April 17, 1846, probably at about the same time that he replied to Buchanan and wrote to Leese, Stearns, and Warner.

119. Ibid., 4:300.

120. TOL to William A. Leidesdorff, April 23, 1846, in Hawgood, ed., *First and Last Consul*, 56.

121. TOL to William A. Leidesdorff, April 27, 1846, ibid., 57–58.

122. Jonathan T. Warner to TOL, June 16, 1846, *Larkin Papers*, 5:33.

123. Jacob P. Leese to TOL, June 11, 1846, ibid., 5:14.

124. Abel Stearns to TOL, May 14, 1846, ibid., 4:374–75.

125. Abel Stearns to TOL, June 12, 1846, 5:19.

126. Ibid.

127. W. D. M. Howard to Abel Stearns, April 21, 1846, in Hawgood, ed., *First and Last Consul*, 54.

128. Abel Stearns to TOL, May 14, 1846, *Larkin Papers*, 4:375.

129. Bancroft, *History of California*, 5:44–45.

130. Ibid., 5:45.

131. TOL to Abel Stearns, May 24, 1846, *Larkin Papers*, 4:391.

132. TOL to Abel Stearns, May 23, 1846, ibid., 4:390.

133. TOL to Abel Stearns, May 21, 1846, ibid., 4:385–86; Bancroft, *History of California*, 5:70.

134. TOL to Abel Stearns, May 21, 1846, and TOL to Jacob P. Leese, May 21, 1846, *Larkin Papers*, 4:385–87.

135. TOL to Abel Stearns, May 24, 1846, ibid., 4:393.

136. TOL to James Buchanan, June 1, 1846, ibid., 5:3.

137. Ibid., 5:2–3.

138. TOL to William A. Leidesdorff, June 8, 1846, LE 142, Leidesdorff Collection. Apparently, Buchanan never responded to Larkin's offer to go to Mexico.

139. TOL to James Buchanan, June 18, 1846, *Larkin Papers*, 5:41. Larkin wrote Stearns that "Paredes refused to allowe any Emigrant whose native language was English." TOL to Abel Stearns, June 14, 1846, in Hawgood, ed., *First and Last Consul*, 68–69. On the other hand, it is unlikely that MacNamara would be in California pursuing his scheme if President Paredes had refused.

140. TOL to Abel Stearns, June 14, 1846, ibid., 69. Bancroft believed the whole affair was a scheme concocted by a group of London speculators, anxious to grab a large tract of California land which would increase rapidly in value after the American takeover. He admits that he has no evidence to support the claim. *History of California*, 5:220–21.

141. TOL to Abel Stearns, June 14, 1846, in Hawgood, ed., *First and Last Consul*, 69.

142. Abel Stearns to TOL, June 12, 1846, *Larkin Papers*, 5:18–19; Bancroft, *History of California*, 5:47–48.

143. Abel Stearns to TOL, June 12, 1846, *Larkin Papers*, 5:19.

144. TOL to James Buchanan, June 1, 1846, ibid., 5:5.

145. TOL to Archibald Gillespie, June 1, 1846, ibid., 5:1.

146. Bancroft, *History of California*, 5:53.

147. TOL to William A. Leidesdorff, May 29, 1846, LE 136, Leidesdorff Collection.

148. TOL to James Buchanan, June 1, 1846, *Larkin Papers*, 5:2.

149. Archibald Gillespie to TOL, June 7, 1846, ibid., 5:6–7.

Chapter 8. The Conquest

1. TOL to Manuel de Jesús Castro and José Castro, June 14, 1846, *Larkin Papers*, 5:20–21. In a letter to Atherton, Larkin gives a full account of the confused situation in California following the Bear Flag incident. TOL to Faxon D. Atherton, July 20, 1846, in Nunis, ed., "Six New Larkin Letters," 79.

2. Harlow, *California Conquered*, 95–97. Larkin later told a story that he had heard

about the incident. Arce complained about being taken by surprise. Merritt suggested that Arce and his men arm themselves, each select a good horse, "choose their distance, make their signal, and he & his men would try them again." The "trial," Larkin added, was declined. TOL to Several Americans, July 8, 1846, *Larkin Papers*, 5:120.

3. Harlow, *California Conquered*, 97–98.

4. John A. Hawgood, "John C. Frémont and the Bear Flag Revolution: A Reappraisal," *Southern California Quarterly*, 44 (June 1962): 74.

5. William A. Leidesdorff to TOL, June 17, 1846, *Larkin Papers*, 5:36–37. Leese was in Yerba Buena on June 11, en route to the South, undoubtedly to attend the Santa Barbara *consejo*, when he decided to return home. Jacob P. Leese to TOL, June 11, 1846, ibid., 5:14. He reached Sonoma just in time to be taken prisoner. If he and Vallejo had gone to Santa Barbara, as Larkin had requested, the Bear Flaggers would have had to look elsewhere for hostages.

6. TOL to James Buchanan, June 18, 1846, ibid., 5:42–44.

7. TOL to John H. Everett, June 17[18], 1846, ibid., 5:48.

8. TOL to William A. Leidesdorff, June 18, 1846, in Hawgood, ed., *First and Last Consul*, 75.

9. TOL to William A. Leidesdorff, June 18, 1846, ibid., 75; TOL to Anthony Ten Eyck and Joel Turrill, June 21, 1846, *Larkin Papers*, 5:62.

10. TOL to Abel Stearns and John Temple, June 22, 1846, in Hawgood, ed., *First and Last Consul*, 77.

11. Harlow, *California Conquered*, 101.

12. John Sutter to William Leidesdorff, July 1, 1846, in Hawgood, ed., *First and Last Consul*, 79.

13. TOL to James Buchanan, April 17, 1846, *Larkin Papers*, 4:294.

14. Francisco Guerrero y Palomares to William A. Leidesdorff, April 30, 1846, ibid., 4:354.

15. Royce, *California*, 77.

16. John C. Frémont to Thomas H. Benton, July 25, 1846, Spence and Jackson, eds., *Expeditions of John Charles Frémont*, 2:182.

17. Royce, *California*, 83–85.

18. TOL to Archibald Gillespie, June 1, 1846, *Larkin Papers*, 5:1.

19. TOL to James Buchanan, July 20, 1846, ibid., 5:144.

20. TOL to James Buchanan, July 20, 1846, ibid., 5:145. "[O]utrageous affair that Bear Party," Larkin reflected in 1847. "It took from the natives all the good American feelings which I hoped I instilled into them in /44 /45 & /46." TOL to Faxon D. Atherton, August 14, 1847, Atherton Papers. Bancroft is even more critical, holding Frémont and Gillespie "largely accountable for all the blood that was spilled throughout the war." Bancroft, *History of California*, 5:98.

21. Harlow, *California Conquered*, 121.

22. John D. Sloat to TOL, May 18, 1846, *Larkin Papers*, 4:378.

23. Ibid., 5:vii.

24. TOL to Mott Talbot & Co., June 18, 1846, ibid., 5:51.

25. TOL to John B. Montgomery, June 19, 1846, and June 20, 1846, ibid., 5:58–59.

26. John B. Montgomery to TOL, July 2, 1846, ibid., 5:94–95.

27. TOL to Anthony Ten Eyck and Joel Turrill, June 21, 1846, ibid., 5:62–63.

28. John B. Montgomery to TOL, July 2, 1846, ibid., 5:95–96.

29. TOL to the United States Commissioner and the United States Consul, Sandwich Islands, July 4, 1846, ibid., 5:102.

30. TOL to Pío Pico, July 5, 1846, ibid., 5:104.

31. John D. Sloat, Proclamation to the Inhabitants of California, July 7, 1846, ibid., 5:105–107.

32. Hawgood, ed., *First and Last Consul*, 84.

33. TOL to Faxon D. Atherton, July 20, 1846, ibid., 134.
34. John D. Sloat to TOL, July 7, 1846, *Larkin Papers*, 5:113.
35. TOL to William B. Ide, July 7, 1846, ibid., 5:110.
36. John D. Sloat to TOL, July 7, 1846, ibid., 5:113.
37. TOL to José Castro, July 8, 1846, ibid., 5:113.
38. TOL to Juan Bautista Alvarado, July 8, 1846, ibid., 5:114.
39. José Castro to TOL, July 9, 1846, and Juan Bautista Alvarado to TOL, July 9, 1846, ibid., 5:122−123.
40. TOL to John D. Sloat, July 10, 1846, and TOL, Suggested Proclamation To Be Issued By John Drake Sloat, [July ?, 1846], ibid., 5:124−25.
41. TOL to James Buchanan, July 10, 1846, ibid., 5:126−27.
42. TOL to Abel Stearns, July 14, 1846, ibid., 5:132−34. In a subsequent letter to Secretary Buchanan, Larkin added a third prospect, if the United States should withdraw: an association of California with Great Britain. Larkin did not think that the Californians would consider this alternative a change for the better. TOL to James Buchanan, July 20, 1846, ibid., 5:145.
43. TOL to William A. Leidesdorff, July 16, 1846, in Hawgood, ed., *First and Last Consul*, 86.
44. TOL to John C. Frémont, July 7, 12, 24, 1846, *Larkin Papers*, 5:112, 129−30, 158.
45. Harlow, *California Conquered*, 132.
46. Bancroft, *History of California*, 5:216.
47. TOL to Abel Stearns, June 14, 1846, in Hawgood, ed., *First and Last Consul*, 68−69; TOL to James Buchanan, June 18, 1846, *Larkin Papers*, 5:41.
48. TOL to James Buchanan, August 19, and Abel Stearns to TOL, July 8, 1846, ibid., 5:204, 117.
49. TOL to Moses Y. Beach, July 29, 1846, ibid., 5:172. Actually, Larkin's official tenure as consul would not end until 1848, when the war was ended by the signing of the Treaty of Guadalupe Hidalgo.
50. In a letter to Vice Consul Forbes, dated June 29, 1846, Governor Pico had formally requested Britain's assistance. Forbes forwarded the letter to Admiral Seymour. The admiral did not reply until July 23, the date of his departure from Monterey. Seymour's letter has not been found. Ernest A. Wiltsee, "The British Vice Consul in California and the Events of 1846," *Quarterly of the California Historical Society* 10 (June 1931): 115−17.
51. TOL to Robert F. Stockton, July 17, 1846, *Larkin Papers*, 5:138.
52. TOL to Robert F. Stockton, July 24, 1846, ibid., 5:160.
53. TOL to William M. Rogers, July 24, 1846. To John Everett, whom Larkin had recommended as supercargo for the venture, Larkin wrote that the voyage depended "on whather Presidnt Polk keap up our flag in C." TOL to John H. Everett, July 26, 1846. Later, when he was convinced that California would not be turned back to Mexico, Larkin wrote to tell Rogers to complete the transaction. TOL to William M. Rogers, August 26, 1846, ibid., 5:161, 167, 221.
54. TOL to F. M. Dimond, July 29[28], 1846, ibid., 5:171.
55. TOL to James G. Bennett, July 26, 1846, ibid., 5:169.
56. Robert F. Stockton, Address to the People of California, July 29, 1846, ibid., 5:175−77.
57. TOL to James Buchanan, July 20[29], ibid., 5:181.
58. Walter Colton, *Three Years in California* (New York: A. S. Barnes & Co., 1850; reprint, Stanford, Calif.: Stanford University Press, 1949), 17.
59. Ibid.
60. Harlow, *Conquest of California*, 144, 146.
61. TOL to Abel Stearns, August [6?], 1846, [August 6(?), 1846], [two letters], *Larkin Papers*, 5:184−86.

62. Bancroft, *History of California*, 5:264, n.10.
63. TOL to Abel Stearns, August 7, 1846, *Larkin Papers*, 5:187.
64. TOL to James Buchanan, August 23, 1846, ibid., 5:217.
65. Robert F. Stockton to TOL and James F. Schenck, August 7, 1846, ibid., 5:188; Harlow, *California Conquered*, 147–50; Bancroft, *History of California*, 5:268–70.
66. TOL to James Buchanan, August 23, 1846, [two letters], *Larkin Papers*, 5:215, 217.
67. Harlow, *California Conquered*, 151–52.
68. TOL to James Buchanan, August 23, 1846 [the second letter of this date], *Larkin Papers*, 5:216–20.
69. Ibid., 5:218.
70. TOL to William A. Leidesdorff, July 16, 1846, in Hawgood, ed., *First and Last Consul*, 85–86.
71. Robert F. Stockton to TOL, August 13, 1846, and TOL to James Buchanan, August 27, 1846, *Larkin Papers*, 5:198, 223–24.
72. TOL to William M. Rogers, August 26, 1846, and TOL to William D. M. Howard, March 1, 1847, ibid., 5:220, 6:33.
73. Harlow, *California Conquered*, 154–56.
74. Bancroft, *History of California*, 5:286; TOL to James Buchanan, September 8, 1846, *Larkin Papers*, 5:232.
75. Anthony Ten Eyck to TOL, July 20, 1846; TOL to Anthony Ten Eyck, September 19, 1846, ibid., 5:148, 240–41.
76. TOL to Rachel H. Larkin, December 14, 1846, ibid., 5:313.
77. Jacob P. Leese to TOL, August 12, 1846, ibid., 5:195.
78. Mariano G. Vallejo to TOL, September 15, 1846, ibid., 5:236–37.
79. TOL to Jacob P. Leese, September 21, 1846, ibid., 5:242–43.
80. TOL to Jacob P. Leese, September 21, 1846, ibid., 5:243; TOL to William A. Leidesdorff, September 21, 1846, in Hawgood, ed., *First and Last Consul*, 87.
81. TOL to James Buchanan, September 22, 1846, *Larkin Papers*, 5:246–47.
82. Moses Y. Beach to TOL, September 25, 1846, ibid., 5:251. With the war seemingly decided and large profits in prospect, he might also have pondered an invitation from a Mexican business associate in Mazatlán to visit him in that port. Julio Lomer to TOL, July 23, 1846, in Larkin, "Correspondence and Papers," C–B/105.
83. Harlow, *California Conquered*, 156; Robert F. Stockton to TOL, October 1, 1846, *Larkin Papers*, 5:256.
84. Harlow, *California Conquered*, 157–58.
85. Edwin Bryant, *What I Saw in California: Being the Journal of a Tour, . . . in the years 1846, 1847* (New York: D. Appleton & Co., 1848; reprint, Minneapolis: Ross & Haines, 1967), 337–38.
86. Ibid., 338–41; TOL to Rachel H. Larkin, November 9, 1846, *Larkin Papers*, 5:271.
87. Bryant, *What I Saw in California*, 340.
88. TOL to William A. Leidesdorff, November 6, 1846, Leidesdorff Collection. Leidesdorff had addressed a letter to Larkin at New Helvetia on November 2. Ibid. Apparently, Larkin had told the vice consul that he could be reached at the fort at that time.
89. Bryant, *What I Saw in California*, 346–47.
90. Joseph W. Revere to William A. Leidesdorff, October 28, 1846, Leidesdorff Collection.
91. TOL to Rachel H. Larkin, November 9, 1846, *Larkin Papers*, 5:271–72. This was not the first time that Larkin, with thin justification, had blamed Rachel.
92. TOL to Rachel H. Larkin, November 25, 1846, ibid., 5:287; "Journal of Thomas O. Larkin, Esq.," *Californian* (Monterey), February 27, 1847.
93. TOL to Rachel H. Larkin, January 17, 1847, *Larkin Papers*, 6:12.

94. TOL to Rachel H. Larkin, November 25, 1846, ibid., 5:287; Bancroft, *History of California*, 5:364.

95. TOL to William A. Leidesdorff, July 1, 1846, in Hawgood, ed., *First and Last Consul*, 81.

96. TOL to the United States Commissioner and the United States Consul, Sandwich Islands, July 4, 1846, *Larkin Papers*, 5:102.

97. TOL to William A. Leidesdorff, July 1, 1846, in Hawgood, ed., *First and Last Consul*, 81.

98. TOL to James Buchanan, January 14, 1847, *Larkin Papers*, 6:10. According to the article that he wrote, or authorized, for publication at Monterey, he told Castro, a bit more dramatically, that he could "act and threaten night by night; my life on such condition is of no value or pleasure to me. . . . make the most of me, write, I will not, shoot as you see fit." "Journal of Thomas O. Larkin, Esq." *Californian*, February 27, 1847.

99. Ibid.; TOL to Rachel H. Larkin, January 11, 1847, *Larkin Papers*, 6:2.

100. Bancroft, *History of California*, 5:366—71; "Journal of Thomas O. Larkin, Esq.," *Californian*, February 27, 1847.

101. TOL to Rachel H. Larkin, December 14, 1846, *Larkin Papers*, 5:310.

102. TOL to Rachel H. Larkin, January 11, 1847, ibid., 6:3; "Journal of Thomas O. Larkin, Esq.," *Californian*, February 27, 1847.

103. Bancroft, *History of California*, 5:695.

104. TOL to James Buchanan, January 14, 1847, *Larkin Papers*, 6:10—11.

105. TOL to Rachel H. Larkin, December 14, 1846, ibid., 5:311.

106. TOL to Faxon D. Atherton, August 14, 1847, Atherton Papers.

107. "Journal of Thomas O. Larkin, Esq.," *Californian*, March 6, 1847; Bancroft, *History of California*, 2:779; TOL to Rachel H. Larkin, December 14, 1847, *Larkin Papers*, 5:311.

108. News of his capture reached Monterey on November 16, the day after he was taken. Colton, *Three Years in California*, 97. The news arrived in San Jose on November 20. Bryant, *What I Saw in California*, 360.

109. TOL to Rachel H. Larkin, November 25, 1846, *The Larkin Papers*, 5:288.

110. TOL to Rachel H. Larkin, December 14, 1846, and January 11, 1847, ibid., 5:311, 6:3; "Journal of Thomas O. Larkin, Esq.," *Californian*, March 6, 1847.

111. Sheldon G. Jackson, *A British Ranchero in Old California: The Life and Times of Henry Dalton and the Rancho Azusa* (Glendale, Calif.: The Arthur H. Clark Company, 1987), 113.

112. TOL to Rachel H. Larkin, December 14, 1846, *Larkin Papers*, 5:311; Bancroft, *History of California*, 2:755, 773—74.

113. TOL to Faxon D. Atherton, August 14, 1847, Atherton Papers.

114. TOL to Rachel H. Larkin, December 14, 1846, *Larkin Papers*, 5:311—12.

115. Ibid., 5:313.

116. Davis, *Seventy-Five Years in California*, 212—13.

117. TOL to Rachel H. Larkin, January 11, 1847, *Larkin Papers*, 6:3.

118. TOL to Rachel H. Larkin, December 14, 1846, ibid., 5:312—15.

119. "Journal of Thomas O. Larkin, Esq.," *Californian*, March 6, 1847.

120. TOL to James Buchanan, January 14, 1847, and TOL to Rachel H. Larkin, January 17, 1847, *Larkin Papers*, 6:11—12; "Journal of Thomas O. Larkin, Esq.," *Californian*, March 6, 1847.

121. TOL to Rachel H. Larkin, January 11, 1847, *Larkin Papers*, 6:3—4.

122. TOL to James Buchanan, January 14, 1847, ibid., 6:11.

123. TOL to Rachel H. Larkin, January 11, 1847, ibid., 6:4.

124. Ibid.; "Journal of Thomas O. Larkin, Esq.," *Californian*, March 6, 1847.

125. The controversy is described in Harlow, *California Conquered*, chapters 13—15.

126. TOL to Rachel H. Larkin, January 17, 1847, *Larkin Papers*, 6:12.

127. TOL to Rachel H. Larkin, January 11, 1847, ibid., 6:5.
128. Harlow, *California Conquered*, 232.
129. Rachel H. Larkin to TOL, December 14, 1846, *Larkin Papers*, 5:316.
130. Ibid., 5:315–16.
131. TOL to James Buchanan, January 14, 1847, ibid., 6:9–10.
132. Ibid., 6:11.

Chapter 9. After the Conquest

1. TOL to Jacob P. Leese et al., April 17, 1846, *Larkin Papers*, 4:296.
2. TOL to William A. Leidesdorff, July 11, 1846, and TOL to William M. Rogers, July 24, 1846, ibid., 5:128, 161.
3. Letter, TOL to William M. Rogers, July 24, 1846, ibid., 5:162.
4. TOL to William M. Rogers, Joel Giles, Secretary of State, March 6, [two letters] and 27, 1846, ibid., 4:233–34, 236, 270.
5. Account, TOL and U.S. Navy Department, Vallejo Documents, 34:248.
6. TOL to Roussillon & Sainsevain, March 12, 1847, *Larkin Papers*, 6:48.
7. Letter, TOL to John H. Everett, February 14, 1849, ibid., 8:47.
8. Talbot H. Green to TOL, August 10, 1846, ibid., 5:193.
9. Edwin Bryant to TOL, March 31, 1847, ibid., 6:80.
10. TOL to Robert F. Stockton, May 8, 1847, ibid., 6:157.
11. TOL to Faxon D. Atherton, March 16, 1847, ibid., 6:57.
12. TOL to Robert F. Stockton, March 16, 1847, ibid., 6:61.
13. TOL to Juan Bandini, March 25, 1847, ibid., 6:72.
14. TOL to William A. Leidesdorff, April 19, 1847, ibid., 6:108, is one example.
15. TOL to William A. Leidesdorff, April 12, 1847, ibid., 6:96.
16. TOL to Robert F. Stockton, March 16, 1847, ibid., 6:61.
17. Talbot H. Green to U.S. Navy Department and U.S. War Department, June 7, 1847, ibid., 6:196–98. In form it was a settlement with Talbot H. Green. However, Larkin owned a two-thirds interest in their partnership.
18. TOL to William M. Rogers, January 18, 1849, ibid., 8:101.
19. The best treatment of the California Claims is in Bancroft, *History of California*, 5:462–68.
20. Robert F. Stockton to TOL, August 13, 1846, *Larkin Papers*, 5:198.
21. James Buchanan to TOL, January 13, 1847, ibid., 6:6–7.
22. Ebenezer L. Childs to TOL, April 24, 1847, and September 25, 1847, ibid., 6:116, 355.
23. TOL to John Y. Mason, May 3, 1847, ibid., 6:143.
24. TOL to John Y. Mason, September 17, 1847, October 28, 1847, December 30, 1847, July 1, 1848, August 16, 1848, ibid., 6:345–46, 7:44, 111, 308, 337.
25. Thomas ap Catesby Jones to TOL, January 23, 1849, ibid., 8:106–107.
26. William B. Shubrick to TOL, September 15, 1847, ibid., 6:342.
27. TOL to John Y. Mason, September 17, 1847. ibid., 6:345.
28. TOL to William M. Rogers, November 12, 1847, ibid., 7:61. The compensation for Navy Agent was actually a 1 percent commission on disbursements up to $2,000, but Larkin assumed that he could charge $2,000 in lieu of the commissions. John Y. Mason to TOL, October 5, 1848, and TOL to John Y, Mason, September 28, 1849, ibid., 8:3–4, 256.
29. TOL to Faxon D. Atherton, August 14, 1847, Atherton Papers.
30. John Y. Mason to TOL, March 27 and April 18, 1848, *Larkin Papers*, 7:209, 234.
31. TOL to John Y. Mason, August 1, 1848, ibid., 7:331.

32. TOL to Secretary of Navy, April 24, 1849, and TOL to Thomas ap Catesby Jones, June 15, 1849, ibid., 8:220, 245.

33. TOL to John Y. Mason, August 16, 1848, ibid., 7:337.

34. William B. Preston to TOL, April 10, 1849, ibid., 8:209.

35. TOL to Faxon D. Atherton, January 19, 1849, ibid., 8:104.

36. TOL to John Y. Mason, February 1, 1848, ibid., 7:132.

37. For example, see William B. Shubrick to TOL, September 25, 1847; Joseph B. Hull to TOL, September 30, 1847, ibid., 6:355—56, 359; TOL, Invoice of Provisions, September 28, 1847, Vallejo Documents, 34:307—309. The bulk of these documents are contained in the Larkin "Accounts" and "Correspondence and Papers."

38. Examples of these orders for the period July 1, 1847 through August 27, 1847, may be found in *Larkin Papers*, 6:230, 231, 251, 279, 286, 295, 296. The bulk of the documents associated with the naval agency may be found in the Larkin "Accounts" and "Correspondence and Papers."

39. Agreement, TOL and James M. Watson, Commander of U.S. *Erie*, October 3[?], 1847; Statement of Account, TOL and Navy Department, December 1847 through December 1848; bill, TOL to Navy Department, November 8, 1848, Vallejo Documents, 34:312, 324, and 35:85.

40. TOL to Secretary of the Navy, November 16, 1848, *Larkin Papers*, 8:40.

41. TOL to Thomas ap Catesby Jones, February 12, 1849, ibid., 8:140.

42. TOL to Thomas ap Catesby Jones, March 23, 1849, ibid., 8:186.

43. Rodman M. Price to TOL, March 30, 1849, ibid., 8:195.

44. William B. Preston to TOL, June 27, 1850, and L. Warrington to TOL, August 1, 1850, Naval Records Collection of the Office of Naval Records and Library, Record Group 45, Records of the Office of the Secretary of the Navy, Miscellaneous Letters sent by the Secretary of the Navy, 1798—1886, File 10-40-2, rolls 43 and 44, M 209, roll 16, pp. 12 and 439, National Archives.

45. TOL to Robert F. Stockton, October 21, 1846, *Larkin Papers*, 5:261.

46. A note appended to a letter requests that Talbot Green "will please ask Mrs. Larkin for the within amt. one hundred and sixty five dollars and pay the same to Mr. Mumm," letter, Archibald H. Gillespie to TOL, June 30, 1847, [with endorsement of TOL dated July 6, 1847], ibid., 6:228.

47. TOL to Richard M. Sherman, September 6, 1847, ibid., 6:317.

48. Lease, TOL to R.C.M. Hoyt, September 25, 1846, ibid., 5:250—51.

49. Archibald H. Gillespie to TOL, March 5, 1847, ibid., 6:37.

50. TOL to William A. Leidesdorff, April 17, 1847, ibid., 6:104—105 [requesting Leidesdorff to foreclose in Yerba Buena on a ship's mortgage that had been assigned to him by a Mazatlán firm].

51. Charles Flügge to TOL, March 26, 1846 [asking Larkin to collect claim of $1,291.63]; Jacob P. Leese to TOL, May 24, 1847 [requesting Larkin to collect claim of $5,609], ibid., 4:264 and 6:171—72.

52. Bancroft, *History of California*, 4:651—52n.

53. Memorial, TOL, Eliab Grimes, and William Heath Davis to Robert F. Stockton, October 8, 1846, *Larkin Papers*, 5:257—58.

54. See treatment of later similar requests in Bancroft, *History of California*, 5:653n.

55. TOL to Samuel J. Hastings, November 16, 1846, *Larkin Papers*, 5:279.

56. TOL to James Buchanan, August 25, 1847, ibid., 6:292.

57. TOL, List of Notes and Obligations due Thomas O. Larkin, December 31, 1849, Vallejo Documents, 35:170.

58. Annual Balance Sheet, December 31, 1847, Larkin, "Correspondence and Papers," C–B/105:118.

59. TOL to Benjamin T. Reed, June 18, 1845; TOL to William M. Rogers, May 6, 1847, *Larkin Papers*, 3:242—44, 6:155.

60. TOL to Benjamin T. Reed, March 3, 1846; Benjamin T. Reed to TOL, October 2, 1846, ibid., 4:222, 5:257.

61. William M. Rogers to TOL, September 1, 1845, ibid., 3:332.

62. TOL to William M. Rogers, June 18, 1846; TOL to John H. Everett, July 26, 1846, ibid., 5:44–47, 167.

63. TOL to John H. Everett, July 26, 1846; TOL to William M. Rogers, August 26, 1846, ibid., 5:167, 221.

64. TOL to William M. Rogers, July 24, 1846, and August 26, 1846, ibid., 5:162, 222.

65. TOL to James Buchanan, July 26, 1846, ibid., 5:168.

66. TOL to William M. Rogers, July 24, 1846, and August 26, 1846, ibid., 5:161, 222–23.

67. William M. Rogers to TOL, November 2, 1846, and December 3, 1846, ibid., 5:265, 293.

68. TOL to John H. Everett, June 17, [18] 1846, ibid., 5:48.

69. TOL to Mott Talbot & Co., June 18, 1846, ibid., 5:52.

70. TOL to John H. Everett, June 17, [18] 1846, ibid., 5:48–49.

71. TOL to Charles M. Weber, June 11, 1846, ibid., 5:15.

72. For example, TOL to James Biddle, March 6, 1847 (regarding proposed venture with John Paty to bring cargo from San Blas and Acapulco); TOL to Faxon D. Atherton, March 16, 1847 (cargo of $15,000 or $20,000 from Valparaiso), ibid., 6:39–40, 357.

73. TOL to William M. Rogers, November 12, 1847, ibid., 7:61.

74. For example, he dispatched the *Don Quixote* to Oahu in November 1846 to pick up cargo, TOL to Rachel Larkin, November 9, 1846, ibid., 5:272.

75. TOL to William D. Phelps, August 28, 1846, ibid., 5:225–26.

76. TOL to Faxon D. Atherton, March 16, 1847, ibid., 6:57.

77. W. H. Tibbey to TOL, August 15, 1848; Contract, TOL and Job Francis Dye, August 28, 1848, ibid., 7:334–35, 7:346–48.

78. Sale of Ship's Cargo, TOL & Charles L. Ross, December 2, 1848; TOL to Mott Talbot & Co., December 26, 1848; Job F. Dye to TOL, December 28, 1848; TOL to Faxon Dean Atherton, January 19, 1849, ibid., 8:53, 78, 79, 102.

79. Agreement, TOL and Job Francis Dye, January 16, 1849, ibid., 8:95–96.

80. Agreement, TOL and Albert Packard, January 17, 1849, ibid., 8:98.

81. Agreement, TOL and Cross, Hobson & Co., January 16, 1849; and Promissory Note, TOL to Cross, Hobson & Co., January 17, 1849, Vallejo Documents, 35:100, 101.

82. Contract, TOL and Jacob P. Leese, February 12, 1849, *Larkin Papers*, 8:138–39.

83. Agreement, Richard B. Mason, TOL, and Jacob P. Leese, February 14, 1849, ibid., 8:144–45.

84. Bill of Sale, Bethuel Phelps to TOL, January 16, 1849; TOL to Faxon D. Atherton, January 19, 1849, ibid., 8:96, 102.

85. Talbot H. Green to TOL, June 29, 1849, ibid., 8:247.

86. Mason sold his interest, which was half of the profits after deduction of many expenses, to James Watson on April 13, 1849, for the same price he had paid Larkin and Leese, 500 ounces of gold, or $8,000. Shortly *after* the Chinese cargo was auctioned in California, Larkin and Leese were able to buy Watson's half share of profits for only $10,000. See miscellaneous documents collected in "The Leese Scrap Book," *Society of California Pioneers Quarterly* 8 (March 1931): 26–27, 30.

87. TOL to Faxon D. Atherton, January 19, 1849, *Larkin Papers*, 8:104.

88. TOL to John B. Montgomery, May 2, 1846, ibid., 4:357.

89. TOL to "My dear Sons," July 1, 1848, *California Historical Society Quarterly* 27 (December 1948): 297.

90. TOL to Anthony Ten Eyck, June 3, 1848, *Larkin Papers*, 7:291.

91. TOL to Richard B. Mason, May 26, 1848, ibid., 7:278.

92. TOL to James Buchanan, June 1, 1848, ibid., 7:285–87.
93. TOL to James Buchanan, June 28, 1848, ibid., 7:301–305.
94. TOL to James Buchanan, July 20, 1848, ibid., 7:320–22.
95. Colton, *Three Years in California*, 248.
96. Ebenezer L. Childs to TOL, September 27, 1848, *Larkin Papers*, 7:365.
97. John S. Williams to TOL, May 27, 1848, ibid., 7:281–82.
98. TOL to John Y. Mason, August 1, 1848, ibid., 7:331.
99. Contract, TOL and Charles B. Sterling, June 19, Larkin Family Collection, Huntington Library; Charles B. Sterling to TOL, July 9, 1848, TOL to Charles B. Sterling, John S. Williams, and James Williams, July 28, 1848, TOL to James H. Gleason and Moses Schallenberger, July 29, 1848, John S. Williams to TOL, October 10, 1848, TOL to William R. Longley and M. D. Winship, December 16, 1848, *Larkin Papers*, 7:312, 323–24, 325, 8:10–11, 66.
100. Moses Schallenberger to TOL, June 8, 1848, TOL to Charles B. Sterling, John S. Williams, and James Williams, July 28, 1848, TOL to James H. Gleason and Moses Schallenberger, July 29, 1848, Moses Schallenberger to TOL, August 16, 1848, ibid., 7:296, 323, 325, 339.
101. Moses Schallenberger to TOL, August 16, 1848, ibid., 7:339.
102. Ibid., 7:338.
103. John S. Williams to TOL, September 13, 1848, ibid., 7:357.
104. Moses Schallenberger to TOL, August 16, 1848, ibid., 7:339.
105. Contract between TOL, John S. Williams, James Williams, Charles B. Sterling, William R. Longley, and M. D. Winship, September 8 (apparently never executed by the Williams brothers), Larkin Family Collection; John S. Williams to TOL, September 13, 1848, and October 10, 1848, TOL to William R. Longley and M. D. Winship, December 16, 1848, *Larkin Papers*, 7:357, 8:10–11, 66.
106. Charles B. Sterling to TOL, July 9, 1848, William R. Longley to TOL, September 4, 1848, John S. Williams to TOL, September 13, 1848, October 10 and 12, 1848, ibid., 7:314, 351, 357, 8:10, 13.
107. Charles B. Sterling to TOL, July 9, 1848, ibid., 7:312.
108. Ibid., 312–13 (emphasis in original).
109. Charles B. Sterling to TOL, August 15, 1848, John S. Williams to TOL, October 12, 1848, ibid., 7:336 and 8:13.
110. Talbot H. Green to TOL, October 15, 1848, ibid., 8:14.
111. John S. Williams to TOL, December 2, 1848, ibid., 8:53.
112. Contract, TOL, John S. Williams, James Williams, Charles B. Sterling, William R. Longley, and M. D. Winship, September 8, 1848; account between John S. Williams & Co. and TOL (undated); promissory note and order to pay, William R. Longley to TOL; William R. Longley to John S. Williams, January 11, 1848, Larkin Family Collection. Agreement, TOL and John S. Williams, January 11, 1849, *Larkin Papers*, 8:90.
113. William R. Longley to TOL, September 13, 1848, ibid., 7:358.
114. Agreement, TOL and John S. Williams, January 11, 1849, ibid., 8:90.
115. TOL to Faxon D. Atherton, January 19, 1849, ibid., 8:103–104.
116. TOL to Faxon Dean Atherton, October 21, 1848, *California Historical Society Quarterly*, 28 (June 1949): 113.
117. TOL to Mariano G. Vallejo, January 22, 1847, TOL to Rachel Larkin, January 22, 1847, and TOL to Jessie B. Frémont, March 16, 1847, *Larkin Papers*, 6:16, 15–16, 58.
118. TOL to Robert F. Stockton, April 13, 1847, ibid., 6:100.
119. TOL to Archibald H. Gillespie, April 27, 1847, ibid., 6:127.
120. For example, William B. Ide to TOL, March 8, 1847, ibid., 6:46.

121. John Bidwell to TOL, March 2, 1846, ibid., 4:219–20.

122. TOL to Jacob P. Leese, February 12, 1846, "The Leese Scrap Book," 18.

123. TOL to John D. Sloat, July 8, 1846, *Larkin Papers*, 5:118–19.

124. Mary M. Bowman, "California's First American School and Its Teacher," *Historical Society of Southern California Annual* 10, Parts 1 and 2 (1915–16): 89–90.

125. Letter, TOL to James G. Bennett, May 20, 1846, *Larkin Papers*, 4:383–84.

126. *Daily Reveille* (St. Louis, Missouri), September 13, 1846 (no title).

127. William M. Rogers to TOL, November 16, 1846, *Larkin Papers*, 5:282.

128. Ebenezer L. Childs to TOL, December 10, 1846, ibid., 5:302.

129. TOL to Archibald H. Gillespie, March 24, 1847, ibid., 6:71.

130. John Bidwell to TOL, April 26, 1847, Juan Bautista Alvarado to TOL, April 30, 1847, ibid., 6:120, 134–36.

131. Lewis Dent to TOL, April 26, 1847, ibid., 6:121.

132. TOL to Robert B. Semple, April 26, 1847, Robert B. Semple to TOL, May 3, 1847, ibid., 6:124–25, 146–47.

133. TOL to James Buchanan, April 29, 1847, ibid., 6:129.

134. William M. Rogers to TOL, September 11, 1847, Ebenezer L. Childs to TOL, September 25, 1847, ibid., 6:335–54.

135. Bancroft, *History of California*, 4:120. Larkin hired Dolores Féliz and John Armstrong to take charge of his ranch on the Sacramento River for a three-year term in the fall of 1848. TOL to John S. Williams, October 26, 1847, *Larkin Papers*, 7:41. It is difficult to believe this is the same John Armstrong, but perhaps Larkin forgave him.

136. Petition dated June 1840, contained in TOL to James Buchanan, November 12, 1847, ibid., 7:67; Bancroft, *History of California*, 4:18.

137. Henry A. Peirce to TOL, August 12, 1845, *Larkin Papers*, 5:195–98. The editor identifies this as a 1846 letter because of its archival location with other letters of late summer 1846. There was considerably more correspondence to come regarding this old dispute dating back to 1842, and it seems more reasonable that Larkin pulled the letter out of his copies of correspondence for reference and then mistakenly replaced it in the correct month and date sequence, but under the wrong year. References to other correspondence in Peirce's letter make it more probable that it was written in 1845 than in 1846.

138. Ebenezer L. Childs to TOL, December 10, 1846, ibid., 5:302.

139. James Buchanan to John C. Frémont, Spence and Jackson, eds., *Expeditions of John Charles Frémont*, 3:47.

140. Jacob R. Snyder to TOL, June 6, 1849, *Larkin Papers*, 8:241.

141. J. Ross Browne, *Report of the Debates in the Convention of California* (Washington, D.C.: John T. Towers, 1850).

142. Elisha O. Crosby, "Statement of Events in Cal.," 46–47, manuscript (1878), Bancroft Library.

143. Ibid.

Chapter 10. Land Speculation and Ranching

1. John C. Jones to TOL, December 5, 1848, *Larkin Papers*, 8:56.

2. TOL to Faxon D. Atherton, August 14, 1847, Atherton Papers.

3. TOL to Rachel Larkin, January 22, 1847, *Larkin Papers*, 6:15.

4. TOL to Abel Stearns, January 28, 1847, ibid., 6:18.

5. Colton, *Three Years in California*, 173.

6. Ebenezer L. Childs to TOL, September 25, 1847, *Larkin Papers*, 6:354.

7. TOL to Alexander McRae, March 17, 1847, ibid., 6:63; William T. Sherman, *Memoirs of General William T. Sherman*, 2 vols. (New York: A. Appleton and Company, 1875), 1:24, 26, 29, 39.

8. *Californian*, February 13, 1847.

9. Ibid., February 20, 1847.

10. Colton, *Three Years in California*, 178–79.

11. TOL to Faxon D. Atherton, August 14, 1847, Atherton Papers.

12. Ibid.

13. TOL to Archibald H. Gillespie, March 24, 1847, *Larkin Papers*, 6:70; Harlow, *California Conquered*, 243.

14. James Buchanan to TOL, January 13, 1847, *Larkin Papers*, 6:5–6.

15. TOL to James Biddle, March 5, 1847, ibid., 6:36.

16. James Biddle to TOL, March 13, 1847, ibid., 6:48–49.

17. Ibid., 6:49.

18. TOL to Robert F. Stockton, March 16, 1847, ibid., 6:61.

19. TOL to Henry F. Teschemacher, April 12, 1847, ibid., 6:98.

20. Thomas Swords to TOL, April 23, 1847, ibid., 6:114.

21. TOL to Thomas Swords, April 24, 1847, ibid., 6:117–18.

22. 36th Cong., 2d sess., 1860–1861, *Reports from the Court of Claims Submitted to the House of Representatives*, Report No. 274, Ser. 110.

23. TOL to William G. Marcy, March 16, 1848, *Larkin Papers*, 7:181.

24. After considerable correspondence, a suit was filed before the Court of Claims on October 14, 1847 (Jacob P. Leese *v.* U.S.). Larkin was questioned by the Clerk of Monterey County for use in Leese's suit. In his testimony, he estimated the original value of the wharf at $10,000. The court decided in Leese's favor on December 24, 1860. *Reports from the Court of Claims Submitted to the House of Representatives*, Report No. 274, Ser. 110.

25. TOL to Archibald H. Gillespie, March 24, 1847, *Larkin Papers*, 6:71.

26. *Reports from the Court of Claims Submitted to the House of Representatives*, Report No. 274, Ser. 110.

27. TOL to Faxon D. Atherton, [October 20–21, 1841], in Hawgood, ed., *First and Last Consul*, 122.

28. TOL to William A. Leidesdorff, March 20, 1847, LE 254, Leidesdorff Collection.

29. Paul W. Gates, "The Land Business of Thomas O. Larkin," *California Historical Quarterly* 54 (Winter 1975): 329–30; TOL to William A. Leidesdorff, September 21, 1846, in Hawgood, ed., *First and Last Consul*, 87.

30. Richard M. Sherman served as Larkin's agent after Larkin and Leidesdorff quarreled over Larkin's account. Richard M. Sherman to TOL, March 17, 1847, *Larkin Papers*, 6:65–66. Leidesdorff's argument in the affair is the more convincing. See TOL to William A. Leidesdorff, October 10, 1847, in Hawgood, ed., *First and Last Consul*, 94; William A. Leidesdorff to TOL, October 14, 1847, and TOL to William A. Leidesdorff, October 27, 1847, *Larkin Papers*, 7:21, 43.

31. TOL to Jasper O'Farrell, October 29, 1847, TOL to Richard B. Mason, June [?] 1847, ibid., 7:46, 6:229.

32. TOL to William M. Rogers, March 20, 1848, ibid., 7:192–93.

33. The original deed, signed by Pío Pico, is printed in United States District Court, Northern and Southern Districts of California, *Claims for Mission Lands* (San Francisco, 1859), 117–18, located at the Bancroft Library. Larkin's ownership is indicated in "List and Description of Real Estate in California Belonging to Thomas O. Larkin of Monterey Which is Recorded in the Archives of the Government and Alcalde Office in Said Monterey," undated, *Larkin Papers*, 6:360–61; Bancroft, *History of California*, 5:561, n.8. See also Annual Balance Sheet, December 31, 1847, Larkin "Correspondence and Papers," C–B/105:118.

34. James A. Forbes to TOL, September 13, November 4, 1844; May 12, 1845, *Larkin Papers*, 2:226, 277, 3:182.

35. Bancroft, *History of California*, 5:665−66n.

36. List and Description of Real Estate [n.d., last entry dated June, 1847] *Larkin Papers*, 6:360−61. Larkin's inventory of properties at the end of 1847 includes "two thirds of the Orchard of San Jose Mission" and indicates a cost of $1,200. Annual Balance Sheet, December 31, 1847, Larkin, "Correspondence and Papers," C−B/105:118.

37. José María Real to TOL, February 19, 1847, *Larkin Papers*, 6:26.

38. "Journal of Edward M. Kern of an Exploration of the Mary's or Humboldt River, Carson Lake, and Owens River and Lake, in 1845," in Spence and Jackson, eds., *Expeditions of John Charles Frémont*, 2:60−61.

39. On the date line, Frémont wrote "Mission of San José," and his comments describe that mission, not Santa Clara. John C. Frémont to TOL, [September [?] 1846], *Larkin Papers*, 5:255−56.

40. Ibid.

41. Gates, "The Land Business of Thomas O. Larkin," 342, n.34, citing *San Francisco Alta California*, January 16, 1848. Gates has speculated that it was a mission orchard that Frémont had in mind when he asked Larkin earlier to purchase property for him. He thinks it was more likely the orchard of Mission Santa Clara than San José. The evidence, however, points to San José. Frémont noted in a postscript to the September [?] letter: "I understand that *one* of the orchards here belongs to Alvarado." Indeed, Alvarado, with Andrés Pico, had purchased Mission San José, May 5, 1846. United States District Court, Northern and Southern Districts of California, *Claims for Mission Lands*, 108−10. Alvarado still owned one of the Mission San José orchards in 1848. TOL to Richard B. Mason, April 4, 1848, *Larkin Papers*, 7:219.

42. John C. Frémont to Pierson B. Reading, October 26, 1847, Box 286, Manuscript Collection-RC, California State Library.

43. John C. Frémont to Jacob R. Snyder, December 11, 1849, Spence and Jackson, eds., *Expeditions of John Charles Frémont*, 1:146, 2:299n.

44. James F. Reed to TOL, May 26, 1847, TOL to James F. Reed, June 7, 1847, *Larkin Papers*, 174, 6:199.

45. John A. Sutter to TOL, October 29, 1847, ibid., 7:47.

46. Andrés Pico to TOL, July 1, 1851, ibid., 9:19. Pico with Juan B. Alvarado had bought the entire mission estate in 1846 from Governor Pío Pico for $12,000, but they never took possession, and the purchase was later declared fraudulent. Bancroft, *History of California*, 5:561n., 666n.

47. TOL to Richard M. Sherman, March 13, 1847, *Larkin Papers*, 6:50.

48. Friar Ignacio Ramirez de Arellano, curate of Monterey, on September 30, 1852, issued separate statements, quoting from baptismal registers of the Monterey parish, attesting to the baptisms of Oliver, Francis, Carolina, and Sophia shortly after their births. The four documents are in the Larkin Family Collection, Huntington Library. It might be assumed that Frederic was also baptized, but documentation is lacking.

49. Larkin's request for their naturalization was held up briefly when Manuel Jimeno, Governor Micheltorena's secretary, could not find a copy of the naturalization law. Micheltorena assured Larkin that everyone was aware that the consul was a good man, that he was a great friend of the Mexican nation, and that the papers would be prepared as quickly as possible. The naturalization decrees were issued on December 13, 1844. TOL to Manuel Micheltorena, September 20, 1844; Manuel Jimeno to Manuel Micheltorena, October 1, 1844; Manuel Micheltorena to Manuel Jimeno, October 8, 1844; Manuel Micheltorena to Francis Larkin, Carolina Larkin, and Sophia Larkin, Naturalization Decrees, December 13, 1844, Larkin Family Collection.

50. Manuel Micheltorena to Francis Larkin, Carolina Ann Larkin and Sophia Adelaide Larkin, Land Grant, December 15, 1844. Ibid. It is not known why Oliver and Frederic were not included in the grant. Perhaps, since they were his two eldest, Larkin at the time

wished to retain their American purity. After Sophia's death, her share of the rancho passed to Larkin as her heir. He later deeded the share to Frederick and Alfred. Oliver was not included, probably because, by then, Larkin had decided that he was irresponsible.

51. Will S. Green, *The History of Colusa County, California and General History of the State* (Sacramento: The Sacramento Lithography Company, 1950), 35.

52. Abel Stearns to TOL, June 12, 1846, *The Larkin Papers*, 5:19.

53. TOL to Abel Stearns, December 30, 1845, Box 40, Stearns Collection.

54. Agreement, TOL and John S. Williams, October 31, 1846, Larkin Family Collection.

55. John S. Williams to TOL, January 19, 1847, *Larkin Papers*, 6:14.

56. John S. Williams to TOL, March 3, 1847, ibid., 6:34–35.

57. TOL to John S. Williams, May 15, 1848, and October 26, 1847, ibid., 7:256, 41. Williams eventually selected three Benicia lots and a strip of beach front and prepared to commence building. John S. Williams to TOL, November 22, 1847, ibid., 7:80.

58. Receipt, Henry Mellus to TOL, October 22, 1845, Larkin, "Correspondence and Papers," C–B/105:84.

59. William E. P. Hartnell to TOL, September 30, 1846; TOL to Robert B. Semple, September 8, 1847, *Larkin Papers*, 5:255, 6:325. Larkin's Annual Balance Sheet, December 31, 1847, Larkin, "Correspondence and Papers," C–B/105:118, assigns a cost of $100 to his half-interest in the Rancho Jimeno.

60. TOL to Robert B. Semple, September 8, 1847, *Larkin Papers*, 6:325.

61. TOL to John S. Missroon, October 12, 1847, ibid., 7:14–15.

62. This transaction raises an intriguing question. Was this the same John Armstrong who wrote the infamous letter printed in the (St. Louis) *Daily Reveille*, September 13, 1846, attacking Larkin? If so, Larkin would have remembered. One wonders what conversation would have ensued that led to the offer of employment?

63. TOL to John S. Missroon, October 24, 1847, *Larkin Papers*, 7:36.

64. John S. Missroon to TOL, November 23, 1847, and January 1, 1848, ibid., 7:81–82, 113.

65. TOL to John S. Missroon, March 20, 1848, ibid., 7:191.

66. Annual Balance Sheet, December 31, 1847, Larkin, "Correspondence and Papers," C:B/105:118. Elsewhere, Larkin indicated a purchase price of $2,500. TOL to Charles V. Gillespie, March 16, 1847 [1848], *Larkin Papers*, 7:182.

67. TOL to Henry A. Green, July 27, 1847, ibid., 6:238.

68. TOL to Samuel Brown, August 18, 1847, ibid., 6:281.

69. TOL and William M. West, Contract, May 12, 1847, Vallejo Documents, 34:273; Receipt, William M. West to TOL, May 12, 1847, Larkin Family Collection; TOL to Henry A. Green, July 27, 1847, *Larkin Papers*, 6:238.

70. Ibid., 6:238.

71. TOL to Faxon D. Atherton, August 14, 1847, Atherton Papers.

72. Mariano G. Vallejo to TOL, August 9, 1847, *Larkin Papers*, 6:261.

73. TOL to Mariano G. Vallejo, August 23, 1847, ibid., 6:288–89.

74. William M. West to TOL, August, 20, 1847; TOL to William M. West, September 15, 1847; William M. West to TOL, January 23, 1848, ibid., 6:284, 340, 7:125.

75. TOL to Charles V. Gillespie, March 16, 1847 [1848], ibid., 7:182.

76. Contract, TOL and Samuel Brown, July 17, 1847; TOL to Henry A. Green, August 21, 1847, ibid., 6:234, 285.

77. Samuel Brown to TOL, July 20, 1847, ibid., 6:235.

78. "List and Description of Real Estate in California Belonging to Thomas O. Larkin of Monterey Which is Recorded in the Archives of the Government and Alcalde Office in Said Monterey," *Larkin Papers*, 6:360–61; Annual Balance Sheet, December 31, 1847, Larkin, "Correspondence and Papers," C–B/105:118.

79. TOL to Charles V. Gillespie, March 16, 1847 [1848], *Larkin Papers*, 7:182. The date of transfer was January 1, according to Reuben L. Underhill, *From Cowhides to Golden Fleece: A Narrative of California, 1832–1858, Based upon the Unpublished Correspondence of Thomas Oliver Larkin, Trader, Developer, Promoter, and only American Consul* (Stanford, Calif.: Stanford University Press, 1939), 132.

80. Cowan, *Ranchos of California*, 19. Flügge arrived in California in 1841 from Oregon. He operated a store with Sutter at New Helvetia before moving to Los Angeles. Bancroft, *History of California*, 3:741–42.

81. TOL to John A. Sutter, August 11, 1847, *Larkin Papers*, 6:269.

82. TOL to Charles V. Gillespie, March 16, 1847 [1848], ibid., 7:182.

83. John Bidwell to TOL, February 28, 1848, and May 15, 1848, ibid., 7:154, 259.

84. Mariano G. Vallejo to TOL, September 15, 1846, ibid., 5:236–37.

85. Mariano G. Vallejo to TOL, September 15, 1846, ibid., 5:237.

86. Bancroft, *History of California*, 6:560n; Title, Manuel Micheltorena to Mariano G. Vallejo, June 19, 1844, Larkin Family Collection.

87. Mariano G. Vallejo to TOL, September 15, 1846, *Larkin Papers*, 5:237. Larkin was also generous with gifts, sometimes to influence events, sometimes to express his friendship. In summer 1847, he sent Vallejo a writing desk, engraved "Larkin to Vallejo 1847," and to Francisca, his wife, some engraved silverware. TOL to William A. Leidesdorff, June 19, 1847, ibid., 6:219.

88. Edwin Bryant, *What I Saw in California: Being the Journal of a Tour . . . in the Years 1846, 1847* (New York: D. Appleton & Co., 1848; reprint, Minneapolis: Ross & Haines, 1967), 342.

89. TOL to Samuel J. Hastings, November 16, 1846, *Larkin Papers*, 5:280. The date of the letter is wrong. Larkin was captured by a Californio party on November 15.

90. TOL to Mariano G. Vallejo, January 22, 1847, ibid., 6:16.

91. Bancroft, *History of California*, 5:670–71n.

92. Ibid., 671, says "for a nominal consideration of $100," but this amount is not mentioned in the transfer document. Articles of Agreement, Mariano G. Vallejo, Thomas O. Larkin, Robert B. Semple, [May 19, 1847]. Vallejo Documents, vol. 12, trans., MS 1238/1. The $100 figure is mentioned in a copy of the deed. Ibid., Pt. 4, 12:291.

93. Articles of Agreement, Mariano G. Vallejo, Thomas O. Larkin, Robert B. Semple, [May 19, 1847], Vallejo Documents, vol. 12, trans., MS 1238/1.

94. Ibid.

95. Soulé et al., *Annals of San Francisco*, 193.

96. Sherman, *Memoirs*, 1:54. In August 1847, the ferry, a thirty-six by eight-foot flat boat, was earning $100 per week. According to the original contract with Vallejo, the proceeds were destined for the support of schools. Larkin believed that the ferry's income would be sufficient to fund all the schools the town would ever want. TOL to Faxon D. Atherton, August 14, 1847, Atherton Papers.

97. Bancroft, *History of California*, 6:15, 447–48.

98. John Sutter to TOL, June 25, 1847, *Larkin Papers*, 6:223. Sutterville would grow fitfully as a competitor of Sacramento and eventually be absorbed by it.

99. Stephen Smith to William A. Leidesdorff, July 15, 1847, LE 304, Leidesdorff Collection.

100. Edward T. Bale and Ralph L. Kilburn to TOL, July 5, 1847; Contract, TOL and Henry A. Green, July 16, 1847, *Larkin Papers*, 6:231, 233.

101. Contract, TOL and Samuel Brown, July 17, 1847, ibid., 6:234.

102. TOL to Henry A. Green, July 27, 1847, ibid., 6:238.

103. TOL to Henry A. Green, August 14 [15?], 1847, ibid., 6:276.

104. TOL to Stephen Cooper, December 14, 1847, Larkin Family Collection.

105. Robert B. Semple to TOL, March 3, 1848, *Larkin Papers*, 7:164.

106. TOL to William B. Shubrick, September 13, 1847, ibid., 6:338.
107. TOL to Henry A. Green, August 14 [15?], 1847, ibid., 6:276.
108. TOL to Robert B. Semple, September 8, 1847, ibid., 6:325.
109. Deed, TOL to Rachel Larkin, July 14, 1847, Larkin Family Collection. To ensure that there would be no doubt about the identification of the heirs, Larkin later wrote a document listing the five children. Certification of Legitimate Heirs, January 8, 1850. Ibid.
110. Robert B. Semple to TOL, October 20, 1847, *Larkin Papers*, 7:31.
111. TOL to Abel Stearns, November 15, 1847, Box 40, Stearns Collection.
112. Contract, Elijah Elmer and Samuel Thompson to TOL, February 22, 1848, *Larkin Papers*, 7:149.
113. TOL to Faxon D. Atherton, August 14, 1847, Atherton Papers.
114. TOL to Charles W. Flügge, July 27, 1847, Josiah Belden to TOL, September 2, 1847, *Larkin Papers*, 6:237, 307.
115. Edward H. von Pfister to TOL, March 20, 1848, ibid., 7:199.
116. TOL to Robert B. Semple, April 24, 1848, ibid., 7:239—40.
117. Edward H. Von Pfister to TOL, May 19, 1847 [1848], ibid., 7:266—67.
118. Robert B. Semple to TOL, May 19, 1848, ibid., 7:267.
119. TOL to Mott, Talbot & Company, June 18, 1846, ibid., 5:52—53.
120. Sherman, *Memoirs*, 1:41—44.
121. Contract, TOL and others to John G. Christie, [March 7, 1848?] Larkin Family Collection.
122. TOL to John G. Christie, March 7, 1848. Ibid.
123. TOL to John Ricord et al., April 17, 1848, *Larkin Papers*, 7:232.
124. Andrew J. McDuffie to TOL, April 23, 1848, Larkin Family Collection.
125. TOL to Josiah Belden, May 18, 1848; TOL to John G. Christie, May 18, 1848; TOL to John G. Christie, May 18, 1848, *Larkin Papers*, 7:261—64.
126. TOL to John G. Christie, May 18, 1848, *ibid.*, 7:263—64.
127. Deed, John G. Christie et al., to John B. Gray, December 22, 1848, Larkin Family Collection.
128. Daingerfield Fauntleroy to TOL, October 14, 1847, George Minor to TOL, October 15, 1847; TOL to John G. Christie, May 18, 1848, *Larkin Papers*, 7:20, 23, 264.
129. The sale might have collapsed. An inventory of Larkin's properties at his death includes: "One ninth interest capital stock of Santa Clara Mining Company," valued at $100. List of Properties Owned by TOL, Deceased, Larkin, Correspondence and Papers C—B/620, Bancroft Library.
130. Contract, Elijah Elmer and Samuel Thomason to TOL, February 22, 1848, *Larkin Papers*, 7:149.
131. TOL to Dolores Féliz and John Armstrong, May 15, 1848, ibid., 7:259.
132. Charles B. Sterling to TOL, August 1, 1848, ibid., 7:332.
133. Agreement, TOL and John S. Williams, January 11, 1849, ibid., 8:90.
134. TOL to Charles B. Sterling, May 30, 1849, ibid., 8:236; Diary of Charles B. Sterling, October 31, 1849, manuscript, C—Y/224, Bancroft Library.
135. Ebenezer L. Childs to TOL, December 8, 1848, *Larkin Papers*, 8:59.
136. Property Agreement, TOL and Bethuel Phelps, December 1, 1848. The following September, Larkin bought Phelps out, paying him $75,000 for his interest in the properties. Ibid., 8:49—51. The transaction is noted in an endorsement to the property agreement.
137. TOL to Faxon D. Atherton, January 19, 1849, ibid., 8:102.
138. Robert B. Semple to TOL, July 29, 1848, and July 31, 1848, ibid., 7:325—27, 330—31.

139. Robert B. Semple to TOL, December 13, 1848, ibid., 8:63–64.

140. TOL to Robert B. Semple, December 28, 1848, ibid., 8:81–82.

141. Agreement, TOL and Bethuel Phelps, January 13, 1849. Larkin left the details of the arrangement to be worked out between Semple and Phelps. Agreement, TOL and Bethuel Phelps, February 1, 1849. The agreement was rewritten on March 16, 1849. Agreement, TOL and Bethuel Phelps, March 16, 1849, ibid., 8:91–93, 127, 176–79; Agreement, Bethuel Phelps and TOL, March 16, 1849, Larkin, "Correspondence and Papers." C–B/105:149.

Phelps did not perform as required by the contract and the following January transferred all his interests and obligations under the contract to the partnership of William M. Steuart and Henry D. Cooke. In a new contract with Steuart and Cooke, Larkin agreed to consider Phelps's obligations, now assumed by the partnership, fulfilled if the partners would complete the required survey by June 1. Agreement, William M. Steuart, Henry D. Cooke, TOL, February 22, 1850, Larkin Family Collection.

142. Robert B. Semple to TOL, January 24, 1849, *Larkin Papers*, 8:111–12.

143. Robert B. Semple to TOL, February 7, 1849, ibid., 8:132.

144. Robert B. Semple to TOL, February 18, 1849, ibid., 8:156.

145. Commodore Jones scolded the partners in June for their failure to write a strong appeal for a customhouse at Benicia for dispatch on the *Oregon*, departing for Washington on July 1. Thomas ap Catesby Jones to TOL, June 28, 1849, ibid., 8:246–47. The only explanation can be that the partners were not aware of the opportunity to send the appeal, for they all strongly favored Benicia's designation as a port of entry. Jones, who by then had a personal stake in the town's future, declared sarcastically that "Benicia *will go ahead* in spite of *its owners.*" Ibid., 247. Both Jones and Smith would eventually live in Benicia.

146. Sherman, *Memoirs*, 1:70.

147. TOL to Faxon D. Atherton, January 2, 1849, *Larkin Papers*, 8:84.

148. Thomas Douglass to TOL, March 2, 1849, ibid., 8:165–66.

149. Talbot H. Green to TOL, June 1, 1849, ibid., 8:238.

150. TOL to Faxon D. Atherton, October 21, 1848, Atherton Papers.

151. TOL to Walter Colton, April 10, 1849, *Larkin Papers*, 8:206–208. The buildings apparently were finished by autumn. Ibid., xii.

152. Persifor Frazer Smith to Robert B. Semple, Bethuel Phelps and TOL, April 9, 1849, ibid., 8:206; Bethuel Phelps to TOL, April 12, 1849, Larkin Family Collection; Agreement, TOL and Bethuel Phelps, [April 30, 1849], *Larkin Papers*, 8:222.

153. Contract, Robert B. Semple, Frances Ann Semple, TOL, Rachel Holmes Larkin, Bethuel Phelps to Albert Williams, Sylvester Woodbridge, Forest Shepherd, April 4, 1849, Larkin Family Collection.

154. Endorsement, Albert Williams to TOL, April 7, 1849, *Larkin Papers*, 8:204–205.

155. TOL, Robert B. Semple, and Bethuel Phelps to TOL, Mariano G. Vallejo, Robert B. Semple, Bethuel Phelps, Sylvester Woodbridge, Jr., Stephen Cooper et al., December [?] 1849, Larkin Family Collection.

156. TOL to Faxon D. Atherton, January 19, 1849, *Larkin Papers*, 8:102.

157. Receipt for Legal Papers, Mellus, Howard & Co. to TOL, February 20, 1850, ibid., 8:296–97. There is contrary evidence that Larkin sold but a half interest in the rancho to Phelps and Dexter Wright for $50,000 and disposed of the remainder later. Gates, "The Land Business of Thomas O. Larkin," 330.

158. Property Agreement, TOL and Bethuel Phelps, [December 1, 1848]; endorsement, September 20, 1849, *Larkin Papers*, 8:51.

159. Talbot H. Green to TOL, [January] 3, 1850, ibid., 8:273.

160. H. A. Breed & Co. to Moody & Norris, December 28, 1849. The association was stormy and short-lived. When Larkin left for the East in 1850, he abandoned the

partnership. Breed sued him for breach of contract in May 1851. Jesse B. Hart to TOL, May 8, 1851. Larkin's defense was that he had agreed to the contract on the condition that the legislature enact a limited partnership law. No such law was passed, and Breed and Larkin agreed to release each other from any claims that might have existed under the abortive partnership. Agreement, TOL and Henry A. Breed, [October 28, 1851]. Ibid., 8:270, 419, 9:59.

161. TOL and Rachel Holmes Larkin to Charles L. Ross, [December 1, 1849], ibid., 8:262—66.

162. Gillespie & Co. to TOL, August 22, 1849, ibid., 8:254.

163. Receipt for Legal Papers, Mellus, Howard & Co. to TOL, February 20, 1850, ibid., 8:296.

164. TOL to John Halls, February 10, 1849, ibid., 8:135.

165. Agreement, Jacob P. Leese, William M. Steuart and TOL, [February 6, 1850], and Jacob P. Leese to TOL, September 30, 1850, ibid., 8:284—85, 346.

166. TOL to John S. Missroon, May 1, 1849, ibid., 8:223.

167. TOL to Faxon D. Atherton, January 19, 1849, ibid., 8:104—105.

168. TOL to Talbot H. Green, February 11, 1849, ibid., 8:137.

169. Samuel H. Willey to TOL, April 25, 1849, ibid., 8:221.

170. Rachel Holmes Larkin to TOL, May 22, 1849, ibid., 8:232.

171. TOL to Jacob P. Leese, February 12, 1846, in "The Leese Scrap Book," 19.

172. Larkin offered the house completely furnished. The property included offices and other frame houses, sheds containing a carriage and wagon, saddle, harness, and horses. There were also grapevines and twenty or thirty fruit trees. *San Francisco Alta California*, November 22, 1849.

173. Ibid.

174. William M. Rogers to TOL, January 20, 1840, Vallejo Documents, 33:7.

175. Cash Account of TOL with William M. Rogers, April 30, 1847, Larkin, "Correspondence and Papers," C-B/105:179; William M. Rogers to TOL, April 26, 1847, and TOL to William M. Rogers, May 6, 1847, *Larkin Papers*, 6:123, 156. This desire for a house in Lynn, and the possibility of moving there, had been in the back of his mind since 1845. Isaac Childs to TOL, March 28, 1845, ibid., 3:107.

176. Ann Rogers (Larkin) Wright to TOL, July 18, 1841, Vallejo Documents, 33:218; W.D.M. Howard to Abel Stearns, April 21, 1846, in Hawgood, ed., *First and Last Consul*, 54—55.

177. TOL to Faxon D. Atherton, January 19, 1849, in Hawgood, ed., *First and Last Consul*, 138. The phrase, "am done trading," does not appear in Larkin's draft of the letter. *Larkin Papers*, 8:104. Perhaps the anxiety expressed in the previous paragraph—"My head whirls with speculation; my hair grows grey by the excessive working of my brain, and ambition" [Ibid.]—induced him to add the phrase which would signal relief from the turmoil of commerce.

178. TOL to Mellus, Howard & Company, February 13, 1850, ibid., 8:285.

179. Henry A. Breed to Daniel C. Baker, February 27, 1850, ibid., 8:317.

Chapter 11. California Paisano or New York Nabob?

1. George E. Childs to TOL, June 5, 1850; G. Washington Warren to TOL, February 8, 1851, *Larkin Papers*, 8:324, 385.

2. John C. Frémont to TOL et al., April 30, 1850, Spence and Jackson, eds., *The Expeditions of John Charles Frémont*, 3:146.

3. Referring to his suite at the Irving House, Larkin wrote to Leese the week following his arrival in New York: "I have a Parlor, & 3 bedrooms with my five children." TOL to Jacob P. Leese, April 13, 1850, in "The Leese Scrap Book," 35.

4. Ibid.

5. Larkin, "Correspondence and Papers," C–B/105:174.

6. TOL to Pablo de la Guerra, June 13, 1850, Guerra Family Collection, Huntington Library.

7. Ebenezer L. Childs to TOL, January 4, 1853, *Larkin Papers*, 9:190. Larkin would claim later that he had made the move to make Rachel happy. Ibid.

8. TOL to Pablo de la Guerra, June 13, 1850, Guerra Family Collection.

9. TOL to Faxon D. Atherton, September 9, 1950, Atherton Papers.

10. TOL to my Dear Sons [Frederick and Francis?], November 15, 1850, Larkin Family Collection. The fire insurance policy was assigned on November 21, 1850 to Mrs. Rachel Larkin. Larkin, "Correspondence and Papers," C–B/105:141.

11. She owned only two lots. A Full and Complete Inventory of the Separate Property and Estate of Rachel Larkin, [no date]. Ibid., 181.

12. TOL to My Dear Sons [Oliver, Frederic and Francis?], November 7, 1850, Larkin Family Collection; TOL to My Dear Sons [Frederic and Francis?] November 15, 1850, ibid.; TOL to John B. R. Cooper, January 9, 1851, Vallejo Documents, 35:268; TOL to Faxon D. Atherton, January 14, 1853, in Nunis, ed., "Six New Larkin Letters," 87.

13. Specifications for [Painting] Mrs. Larkin's House. No. 101 Tenth St. [N.Y.] [no date] José Antonio Alviso, Documentos para la historia de California. C–B/66:244, Bancroft Library.

14. John C. Jones to TOL, February 10, 1852, *Larkin Papers*, 9:82.

15. Larkin, "Correspondence and Papers," C–B/105:178.

16. Ibid., 172.

17. Ibid. The bill for the following March, 1852, was for 159 quarts of milk. Ibid.

18. TOL to Frederic Larkin, December 18, 1852, Larkin Family Collection.

19. Thomas O. Larkin, Jr., to Rachel Larkin, March 30, 1851. Ibid.

20. Thomas O. Larkin, Jr., to Frederic Larkin and Francis Larkin, February 22, 1852. Ibid. Oliver could also be devious when he thought his father overbearing. When Larkin once directed him to advise his brothers in Washington to obey the Childses, he wrote the letter and Larkin read it. When his father left the room, Oliver threw the letter in the fire and wrote another. Thomas O. Larkin, Jr., to Frederic Larkin and Francis Larkin, December 15, 1852. Ibid.

21. TOL to John B. R. Cooper, January 9, 1851, Vallejo Documents, 30:268.

22. TOL to Frederic Larkin, December 13, 1852, Larkin Family Collection.

23. TOL to Frederic Larkin, October 27, 1850. Ibid.

24. TOL to Frederic Larkin, January 18, 1851. Ibid.

25. As early as 1848, for example, he wrote in English to Andrés Pico, who apparently did not read English well, and had the letter translated into Spanish by W. E. P. Hartnell before dispatching. TOL to Andrés Pico, October [?] 1848, *Larkin Papers*, 8:28.

26. Rachel H. Larkin to TOL, August 22, 1851, Vallejo Documents, 35:336.

27. Ebenezer L. Childs to TOL, February 22, 1853, and March 25, 1853, *Larkin Papers*, 9:230, 242.

28. Ebenezer L. Childs to TOL, December 11, 1852, ibid., 9:171.

29. Larkin, "Correspondence and Papers," C–B/105:74.

30. TOL to Pablo de la Guerra, June 13, 1850, Guerra Family Collection.

31. Agreement, TOL and Fernando Wood, March 20, 1852, Larkin, "Correspondence and Papers," C–B/105:147; TOL to Faxon D. Atherton, January 14, 1853, in Nunis, ed., "Six New Larkin Letters," 85–87; W. H. Kissam to TOL, May 19, 1852, *Larkin Papers*, 9:95.

32. For cost and valuation data, see Valuations of California and New York Properties, Larkin, "Correpondence and Papers," C–B/105:145.

33. George E. Baldwin to TOL, September 4, 1852, *Larkin Papers*, 9:124.

34. Upon arriving in New York, he opened a file, titled "California Business." TOL to James Wilson, August 27, 1850, cover note, James Wilson Papers, New Hampshire Historical Society.

35. TOL to James Wilson, January 22, 1852. Ibid.

36. Ebenezer L. Childs to TOL, December 24, 1852, and January 14, 1853, *Larkin Papers*, 9:182, 207.

37. Andrew Wylie, Jr., to TOL, December 11, 1852, ibid., 9:172.

38. Henry Clay to TOL, June 10, 1850, ibid., 8:326.

39. TOL to U.S. Postmaster General and Washington National Monument Society, January 15, 1851; Washington National Monument Society to TOL, January 22, 1851, ibid., 8:368.

40. See, for example, Elisha Whittlesey to William J. Eames, March 3 and 5, 1853; William J. Eames to TOL, February 15, 1853, ibid., 9:237, 225.

41. Zachariah F. Johnston to TOL, February 7, 1851, ibid., 8:379.

42. William Steuart to TOL, August 5, 1850, ibid., 8:331–32.

43. TOL to James Wilson, August 20 and 27, 1850, James Wilson Papers. Following his departure from the Land Commission—the Senate refused to confirm his appointment—General Wilson became Larkin's attorney in some of his land claims.

44. Agreement, TOL, Bethuel Phelps and Thomas Butler King, September 24, 1850, *Larkin Papers*, 8:344.

45. Agreement, L. A. Rider and TOL, May 28, 1851, ibid., 9:7; TOL to Faxon D. Atherton, April 18, 1852, Atherton Papers.

46. TOL to V. B. Palmer, August 24, 1850, Larkin Family Collection. A young Brevet Captain Ulysses S. Grant, who in August 1852 arrived in Benicia with the Army's fourth division, would have agreed with Larkin's assessment of the town. Grant liked California and Benicia and believed that "an active, energetic person should . . . make a fortune every year." Charles G. Ellington, *The Trial of U. S. Grant: The Pacific Coast Years, 1852–1854* (Glendale, Calif.: The Arthur H. Clark Co., 1987), 76.

47. C. E. Wetmore to TOL, August 16, 1852, *Larkin Papers*, 9:120.

48. Deed, TOL to Charles M. Blake, August 2, 1853, Larkin Family Collection.

49. Promissory Note, TOL to James D. Graham, January 6, 1853. Ibid.

50. Richard Dillon, *Great Expectations: The Story of Benicia, California* (Fresno: Thomas Lithograph and Printing Co., 1980), 89–90. Eames did not trust Graham and paid him $1,250 on passage of the bill, the balance to be paid when the government had in fact moved to Benicia. William J. Eames to TOL, February 15, 1853, *Larkin Papers*, 9:223.

51. Robert B. Semple to TOL, April 24, 1851, ibid., 8:416–17.

52. List of Properties Owned by TOL, Deceased, [no date] Larkin, "Correspondence and Papers," C–B/620; Underhill, *From Cowhides to Golden Fleece*, 224–25.

53. Charles's claim for the Colus rancho, originally granted to John Bidwell in 1845, conflicted with the title of Jimeno, from whom Larkin had purchased the tract. Bancroft, *History of California*, 5:715. Charles's claim was curious, since Bidwell in 1847 had agreed with Larkin that Jimeno's grant had preceded his own. John Bidwell to TOL, August 3, 1847, *Larkin Papers*, 6:252–53.

54. Charles Sterling to TOL, October 23, 1851, Larkin Family Collection.

55. Cowan, *Ranchos of California*, 29.

56. For a summary of the surveys and the origins of the Land Commission, see W. W. Robinson, *Land in California: The Story of Mission Lands, Ranchos, Squatters, Mining Claims, Railroad Grants, Land Scrip, Homesteads* (Berkeley: University of California Press, 1948), 91–109.

57. A good review of the operation of the act, though prosquatter, is in Paul W. Gates, "The California Land Act of 1851," *California Historical Society Quarterly* 50 (December 1971): 395–430. Gates is wrong when he suggests that none of the land claims had been

surveyed before passage of the act (396). Larkin had anticipated a battle over titles, and most of his holdings were surveyed in the late 1840s. However, he had them surveyed again after passage of the Land Act of 1851.

58. TOL to John B. R. Cooper, January 9, 1851, Vallejo Documents, 30:268.

59. J. Miguel Arroyo to Alexander Juan Atocha, October 21, 1852, Larkin Family Collection.

60. Friar Ygnacio Ramirez de Arellano, Certification of Baptisms for Francis, Carolina and Sophia Larkin, September 30, 1852. Ibid.

61. TOL to John Bidwell, October 30, 1853, Box 132, Folder 5, Bidwell Collection, California State Library; TOL to Abel Stearns, June 17, 1854, Box 40, Stearns Collection.

62. John C. Jones to TOL, April 18, 1854, *Larkin Papers*, 10:57.

63. C. B. Sterling and A. C. St. John to TOL, August 5 and 30, 1851, *Larkin Papers*, 9:33, 40–41. There is a "Larkin" place-name on a map of Sacramento River gold camps, published in Weimar, Germany, in 1849. It is near the Boga rancho, not the Children's grant. Map 15.C2, H9, 1849, B, Bancroft Library. It was doubtless named for Larkin, but did not survive the end of mining.

64. Larkin and Missroon had previously sold an undivided two-thirds of the upper two leagues to Serranus C. Hastings and Major Washington Seawell. Deed, TOL and John S. Missroon to Washington Seawell and Serranus C. Hastings, September 23, 1851, "Private Record of Lots Sold by Thomas O. Larkin, California," C–E/66, Bancroft Library; A Deeds 580, Colusa County Recorder, August 17, 1854, Larkin Family Collection. To further complicate matters, John Bidwell had been granted these same two leagues by Governor Pío Pico. Bidwell then sold the property to Charles D. Semple, who lost it in a sheriff's sale to Seawell and Hastings. Bidwell, however, had long since agreed that Jimeno's grant preceeded his own and therefore Larkin's claim displaced his own. Deed, TOL and John S. Missroon to Washington Seawell and Serranus C. Hastings, September 23, 1851, "Private Record of Lots Sold by Thomas O. Larkin, California," C–E/66; John Bidwell to TOL, August 3, 1847, *Larkin Papers*, 6:252.

Larkin and Missroon joined the two purchasers briefly in offering lots in the new town of Colusa, situated on the Jimeno rancho. Power of Attorney, TOL, John S. Missroon, Serranus C. Hastings, and Washington Seawell to Augustine D. Carpenter, September 24, 1851, Larkin Family Collection. Later, Missroon gave his power of attorney to Larkin to sell their land in the Jimeno rancho and the town of Colusa. Power of Attorney, William J. Eames to Nicholas Gray, November 24, 1851. Ibid.

65. John S. Missroon to TOL, September 30, 1851, April 24, 1852; Memorandum, Adolphus C. Whitcomb to TOL, June 22, 1852, *Larkin Papers*, 9:48, 90, 111; Deed, TOL to Adolphus C. Whitcomb, July 23, 1852, "Private Record of Lots Sold by Thomas O. Larkin, California," C–E/66.

66. TOL to Jacob P. Leese and Rosalia Leese, July 7, 1853, Larkin Family Collection; TOL to Faxon D. Atherton, January 14, 1853, in Nunis, ed., "Six New Larkin Letters," 87.

67. John B. Frisbie to TOL, August 6, 1852, *Larkin Papers*, 9:119.

68. Various deeds, "Private Record of Lots Sold by Thomas O. Larkin, California," C–E/66, 1253, 1255–60.

69. Jacob P. Leese to TOL, September 30, 1851, Leese to William J. Eames, November [?] 1851, Leese to William J. Eames, December 13, 1851, *Larkin Papers*, 9:47, n.1, 64–65, 71.

70. Deed, TOL to Jacob P. Leese, July 9, 1852, "Private Record of Lots Sold by Thomas O. Larkin, California," C–E/66, 1251–52. The Land Commission eventually set aside the court's decision, thereby ruling in favor of the Larkin associates' interest, and the grant was patented in 1880. Jacob P. Leese to TOL, September 30, 1851, *Larkin Papers*, 9:47, n.1; Cowan, *Ranchos of California*, 61.

71. Instructions, Henry G. Stebbins to J. Howard Wainwright, April 28, 1852, *Larkin Papers*, 9:91. Though Frémont's Las Mariposas was a proven gold-producer, the negotiations for a sale in London became hopelessly entangled and were never consummated.

72. George E. Baldwin to TOL, June 8, 1852, ibid., 9:105.

73. Nicholas Gray to TOL, July 10, 1852, Larkin, "Correspondence and Papers," C–B/620, Bancroft Library.

74. George E. Baldwin to TOL, October 5, 1852, *Larkin Papers*, 9:143. Larkin sent Wainwright a contract which, if signed by the two parties, would have confirmed the sale agreement that had been negotiated on September 18, 1852. TOL to J. Howard Wainwright, November [?] 1852, Larkin Family Collection.

75. Henry G. Stebbins to TOL, January 14, 1853, *Larkin Papers*, 9:208.

76. TOL to Frederick Larkin and Francis Larkin, April 12, 1853, Larkin Family Collection; Charles L. Leyton to TOL, August 13, 1853, *Larkin Papers*, 9:271; J. Howard Wainwright to Henry G. Stebbins, May 3, 1853, Larkin Family Collection.

77. George E. Baldwin to TOL, September 18, 1852, *Larkin Letters*, 9:137.

78. Charles B. Sterling to TOL, April 5, 1851, ibid., 8:414.

79. In September 1852, Sterling gave Larkin a detailed description of the people who had settled on the Children's rancho. They are an interesting cross-section of the squatter/settler class of the early 1850s. Charles B. Sterling to TOL, September 6, 1852, ibid., 9:127–29.

80. William J. Eames to TOL, February 15, 1853, ibid., 9:226.

81. William J. Eames to TOL, March 15, 1853, ibid., 9:238–39.

82. TOL to Faxon D. Atherton, April 18, 1852, Atherton Papers. His prediction was wrong. The first railroad in California, a short line that ran from Sacramento northeastward along the American River, opened in 1856.

83. TOL to Simeon Draper and Peter Cooper, January 18, 1853, *Larkin Papers*, 9:211. It may be significant that this is one of the few letters following the end of his official appointments that he copied and retained.

84. TOL to John B. R. Cooper, January 9, 1851, Vallejo Documents, 35:268.

85. Woolfenden and Elkinton, *Cooper*, 82.

86. TOL, Last Will and Testament, February 11, 1851, *Larkin Papers*, 8:387.

87. He would have been distressed, but not surprised. In 1849, while making plans to build ten iron or brick houses, he observed that "San Francisco is going to burn down once and awhile." TOL to Walter Colton, April 13, 1849, ibid., 8:212.

88. C. G. Ryland to TOL, July 19, 1850, Peter H. Burnett Correspondence and Papers, C:B/345:7, Pt. I, Bancroft Library.

89. TOL to Pearson B. Reading, May 6, 1851, Box No. 289, Folder No. 11, Manuscript Collection—RC. Reading declined to seek the nomination.

90. TOL to Faxon D. Atherton, November 16, 1851, Atherton Papers.

91. Jacob P. Leese to William J. Eames, July 27, 1852, *Larkin Papers*, 9:115.

92. Deed, TOL to Fernando Wood, April 2, 1852, "Private Record of Lots Sold by Thomas O. Larkin, California;" C–E/66; Sarah M. Brooks, *Across the Isthmus to California in '52* (San Francisco: C. A Murdock & Co., 1894), 27. Brooks was charmed by a number of Californians on the voyage westward, including "Tom O. Larkin [who] told of Monterey and southern ranches. He had a famous watch-chain of black pearls, and could tell some bit of history connected with each one." Ibid., 25. A friend wrote to Larkin in 1856 to tell him that Fernando Wood, Larkin's "old and *esteemed friend*," was reelected mayor of New York, "stuffing & bullying in California style." William P. Jones to TOL, November 5, 1856, Larkin Family Collection.

93. TOL to Faxon D. Atherton, January 14, 1853, in Nunis, ed., "Six New Larkin Letters," 88.

94. During the transit of the isthmus, on October 17, 1852, Larkin paid $128 for the

hire of mules, a considerable sum in 1852. Larkin, "Correspondence and Papers," C–B/105:180.

95. TOL to Faxon D. Atherton, November 16, 1851, Atherton Papers.

96. TOL to Faxon D. Atherton, April 18, 1852. Ibid. Semple would have been pleased that Larkin had finally come to his senses, but it was too late since they had dissolved the Benicia partnership in 1851.

97. John C. Jones to TOL, November 18, 1852, *Larkin Papers*, 9:160–61.

98. A severe infectious disease of the skin accompanied by high fever and local inflammation.

99. TOL to John B. R. Cooper, August 23, 1850, ibid., 8:338–40.

100. Ibid.

101. TOL to Faxon D. Atherton, January 14, 1853, in Nunis, ed., "Six New Larkin Letters," 87.

102. TOL to Frederic Larkin, December 18, 1852, Larkin Family Collection.

103. TOL to Jacob P. Leese, December 19, 1852, Vallejo Collection, Huntington Library.

104. TOL to Frederic Larkin and Francis Larkin, December 28, 1852, Larkin Family Collection. Larkin was distressed to the point of distraction by Caroline's illness. A letter to Frederic and Francis in early January includes incomplete sentences, more misspellings than usual, and careless mistakes. For example, he speaks of sailing for "Aspinwall," meaning California. He urged the boys to study with a stronger will than ever before, relying on no one but themselves. "[R]ich fathers often die poor, and leave nothing to a child." He expected Caroline to die before the day was out. Their mother, tending her, had not undressed for five nights. The letter is heavy with his exhaustion and a father's grief. TOL to Frederic Larkin and Francis Larkin, January 3, 1853. Ibid. Larkin was soon able to write, with considerable relief, of Caroline's gradual recovery.

105. TOL to Faxon D. Atherton, January 14, 1853, in Nunis, ed., "Six New Larkin Letters," 89.

106. TOL to John B. R. Cooper, January 5, 1853, *Larkin Papers*, 9:194; Valuations of California and New York Properties, TOL, "Correspondence and Papers," C–B/105:145.

107. TOL to John B. R. Cooper, January 5, 1853, *Larkin Papers*, 9:194; TOL to Frederic Larkin and Francis Larkin, December 28, 1852, Larkin Family Collection.

108. TOL to Faxon D. Atherton, January 14, 1853, in Nunis, ed., "Six New Larkin Letters," 84. Atherton finally did move, but not until 1859, the year following Larkin's death.

109. TOL to Simeon Draper and Peter Cooper, January 18, 1853, *Larkin Papers*, 9:211.

110. Jacob P. Leese to TOL, September 30, 1850, ibid., 8:347.

111. TOL to Faxon D. Atherton, January 14, 1853, in Nunis, ed., "Six New Larkin Letters," 87. Rachel was not completely candid in 1859 when she assisted in the preparation of a biographical sketch of Larkin. In the article, she claims that she and her husband, after moving to the East, "still yearned for their adopted country." F. H. Day, "Thomas Oliver Larkin," *The Hesperian* #2 (April 1859), 52–53. In fact, she continued to complain to Frederic that she would like to have remained longer "at home," that is, the East, and "I live in hopes to visit the States once more." Rachel Hobson Larkin to Frederic Larkin, August 25, 1853, Larkin Family Collection.

112. Rachel Larkin to Frederic Larkin, January 13, 1853. Ibid. Rachel also complained to her son that his father blamed her for certain unexplained "Circumstances" arising from his speculations. Ibid. When Larkin was in the midst of settling his affairs in this eastern sojourn that had not gone well, he suggested to Childs, perhaps unkindly, that he had come east in the first place to please Rachel. Ebenezer L. Childs to TOL, January 4, 1850

[1853], *Larkin Papers*, 9:190. He thereby seemed to blame her indirectly for the unprofitable eastern investments.

113. TOL to Faxon D. Atherton, January 14, 1853, in Nunis, ed., "Six New Larkin Letters," 90.

114. TOL to Frederic Larkin and Francis Larkin, July 25, 1853, Larkin Family Collection.

115. Rachel Larkin to Frederic Larkin, November 4, 1850, ibid., William M. Rogers to "My Dear Cousin" [John B. R. Cooper?], January 1, 1850 [1851], Vallejo Documents, 35:173.

116. TOL to Faxon D. Atherton, January 14, 1853, in Nunis, ed., "Six New Larkin Letters," 89.

117. Rachel H. Larkin to Frederic Larkin, June 23, 1853, Larkin Family Collection.

118. Sophia Larkin to Frederic Larkin and Francis Larkin, September 29, 1853. Ibid. The Larkin children probably referred to their parents as "mamma" and "papa" since these are the terms used by Sophia in her letter to the boys. Ibid.

119. For example, an associate reported that Larkin told him that a certain "d———d property had cost him already more than it was worth." John Pattison to Frederic Larkin, November 5, 1859. Ibid.

120. TOL to John B. R. Cooper, July 13, 1857, Vallejo Documents, 36:242.

121. Gates, "Land Business of Thomas O. Larkin," 328–29. Larkin's executors had little faith in the claim, assigning it a value of only $10 in a listing of TOL's properties prepared shortly after his death. Estate of TOL, Deceased, [no date], Larkin, "Correspondence and Papers," C–B/620.

122. Deed, José Chaves to Thomas Oliver Larkin, Jr., March 21, 1856, Vallejo Documents, 36:213.

123. Deed, Manuel Díaz to TOL, December 1, 1857, Larkin Family Collection. Larkin's total holdings in Colusa County in 1858 are described in a somewhat garbled fashion in Larkin Properties, Colusa County, 1857, 1858. Ibid.

124. Agreement, TOL and Jonathan D. Stevenson, March 1, 1858, James F[?] Crowly and Emma A. Crowly to TOL, August 4, 1858, ibid., Estate of Thomas O. Larkin, Deceased, [no date], Larkin, "Correspondence and Papers," C–B/620; Promissory Note, TOL to Manuel Castro, May 28, 1857, Larkin Family Collection.

125. Gates, "Land Business of Thomas O. Larkin," 331.

126. George M. Murray to TOL, March 3 and 31, 1854, *Larkin Papers*, 10:31, 42–43.

127. William Harney to TOL, August 8, 1855, ibid., 10:175–78.

128. William Harney to TOL, September 11, 1855, ibid., 10:198.

129. A. Fargo to TOL, May 4, 1856, ibid., 10:270.

130. P. A. M. Rae to TOL, December 22, 1857; TOL to P. A. M. Rae, December 22, 1857, Larkin Family Collection.

131. William J. Eames to TOL, March 31, 1853, *Larkin Papers*, 9:244.

132. The clamor against Limantour is suggested by Jacob Leese's plea to a San Francisco friend: "For Gods sake do not lynch Limantour." Jacob P. Leese to Joseph P. Thompson, December 15, 1856, ibid., 10:335. He might have been jesting, but on the other hand, 1856 was the year of the vigilante.

133. Gates, "Land Business of Thomas O. Larkin," 330.

134. Soulé et al., *The Annals of San Francisco*, 541–42.

135. Estate of TOL, Deceased, [no date], Larkin, "Correspondence and Papers," C–B/620.

136. Larkin contested the sales, but the circumstances of the sales and the results of the protest are unclear. C. W. Hayden to TOL, April 22, 1854, John Currey to TOL, Decem-

ber 7, 1855, *Larkin Papers*, 10:60, 225. Larkin still owned over 600 Benicia lots in 1857. TOL, Solano County and State Tax Rolls, 1847–1858, Larkin Family Collection.

137. TOL to Frederic Larkin, December [January] 15, 1854. Ibid.

138. Andrew Wylie to TOL, January 19, 1854. Larkin pursued the claim, apparently unsuccessfully, to the Supreme Court or Court of Claims in Washington. Ebenezer L. Childs to TOL, June 3, 1856, ibid., 10:11, 276.

139. TOL to Abel Stearns, March 12, 1856, Box 40, Stearns Collection; TOL to John B. R. Cooper, October 28, 1857, *Larkin Papers*, 10:346; TOL to Samuel C. Bigelow, October 11, 1857; Promissory Note, TOL to José Abrego, October 11, 1857; George W. Van Syckle to TOL, July 17, 1857, Larkin Family Collection.

140. TOL to John B. R. Cooper, February 15, 1858, *Larkin Papers*, 10:348–49; William R. Parker to TOL, May 27, 1858, Larkin Family Collection.

141. William Welsh to TOL, July 20, 1857; C. E. Wetmore, July 27, 1857. Ibid.

142. TOL to John B. R. Cooper, January 24, 1857, *Larkin Papers*, 10:341.

143. A. D. Ditmars to TOL, April 3, 1854; Josiah Belden to TOL, January 26, 1855, ibid., 10:45, 120; TOL to T. Bailey Myers and Alfred Jones, August 19, 1856, Larkin Family Collection.

144. The board questioned whether the signature of Captain King, one of Frémont's officers, was genuine. Andrew Wylie to TOL, January 19, 1854, *Larkin Papers*, 10:11.

145. TOL to Jefferson Davis, March 28, 1855; Robert P. Morison to TOL, April 28, 1855, Larkin Family Collection.

146. Ebenezer L. Childs to TOL, June 3, 1856, *Larkin Papers*, 10:276. There are a number of letters in the Larkin Family Collection that concern the tangled customhouse claim. It was not settled at Larkin's death. The best explanation of the affair is in Andrew Wylie to Frederic Larkin, June 17, 1859, Larkin Family Collection.

147. TOL to the Judges of the Court of Claims, July 21, 1856. Ibid.

148. Andrew Wylie to TOL, September 18, 1856. Ibid.

149. Little *v.* United States, 15 F. Cas. 614, Dist. Ct., N. D. California, Hoff. Land Cas. 325 (1857); Luco et al. *v.* United States, 15 F. Cas. 1080, Dist. Ct., N. D. California, Hoff. Land Cas. 345 (1858).

150. The United States *v.* TOL and John S. Missroon, 59 U.S. 557, Sup. Ct., 15 L. Ed. 486 (1855).

151. Cowan, *Ranchos of California*, 19, 30, 37, 41, 42, 44, 62.

152. Elisha Whittlesey to William J. Eames, March 1, 1854, *Larkin Papers*, 10:27.

153. Ibid., 10:xi.

154. William F. White [William Grey, pseud.], *A Picture of Pioneer Times in California* (San Francisco: W. M. Hinton & Co., 1881), 128.

155. TOL to Faxon D. Atherton, April 18, 1852, Atherton Papers.

156. Talbot H. Green to TOL, January 22, 1854, *Larkin Papers*, 10:13–14.

157. Partnership Account Between TOL and Talbot H. Green For the years 1846, 1847 & 1848, in the Town of Monterey, November 15, 1855, Larkin Family Collection.

158. Talbot H. Green to TOL, September 19, 1856, *Larkin Papers*, 10:301. A summary of the Talbot Green affair is in ibid., 10:xv–xix. A fuller account is John A. Hussey, "New Light Upon Talbot H. Green," *California Historical Quarterly* 18 (March 1939): 32–63.

159. Green did not forget Larkin. At Larkin's death, Green claimed that the estate owed him: $2,500 which Jacob Leese in 1851 had paid to Larkin for him; one-third of an 1846 Larkin claim against the United States government of $4,780.10; and one-third of any partnership receipts since their accounts were settled in 1855. Talbot H. Green, Claim on Estate of TOL, [undated], Larkin Family Collection.

160. *Larkin Papers*, 10:xiii. Larkin and some other large San Francisco property own-

ers, trying to avoid a general panic, pondered trying to prevent a run on Page, Bacon and Company by pledging their personal property to the bank's depositors. They backed out when they realized the enormity of the risk. Dwight L. Clarke, *William Tecumseh Sherman: Gold Rush Banker* (San Francisco: California Historical Society, 1969), 108; Sherman, *Memoirs*, 1:108–12.

161. Ebenezer L. Childs to TOL, December 19, 1855, *Larkin Papers*, 10:228–29.

162. T. Bailey Myers to TOL, December 20, 1856; TOL to Andrew J. Wylie, August 4, 1857; Promissory Note, Rachel Larkin to John H. Hobson, June 18, 1856. Larkin Family Collection. See also John H. Hobson to TOL, April 22, 1857, Larkin, "Correspondence and Papers," C–B/105.

163. TOL to Frederick Larkin and Francis Larkin, October 15, 1853, November 30, 1853, Larkin Family Collection. Rachel also cautioned the brothers that their "Father is not so Rich as formley." Rachel H. Larkin to Frederic Larkin and Francis Larkin, November 15, 1853. Ibid.

164. Ebenezer L. Childs to TOL, December 19, 1855, *Larkin Papers*, 10:229.

165. Cornelius K. Garrison to TOL, October 7, [1854], ibid., 10:88.

166. Orange Clark to TOL, April 10, 1855; Ebenezer L. Childs to TOL, April 19, 1854, ibid., 10:145, 59.

167. Simeon Draper to TOL, August 23, 1853; F. M. Dimond to TOL, December 10, 1853; W. W. Leland to TOL, December 15, 1853, ibid., 9:275, 310–11. Dorothy H. Huggins, comp., *Continuation of the Annals of San Francisco* (San Francisco: California Historical Society, 1939), 27.

168. Agreement, TOL and O. M. Wozencraft, December 5, 1853, Larkin Family Collection.

169. Gates, "Land Business of Thomas O. Larkin," 339.

170. Stock Sale, San Francisco and Sacramento Railroad Company, January 21, 1856, *Larkin Papers*, 10:236; Receipt, San Francisco and Sacramento Railroad Company, December 23, 1856, Larkin Family Collection.

171. TOL to Pablo de la Guerra, January 2, 1855, Guerra Family Collection.

172. TOL to Pablo de la Guerra, January 19, 1856. Ibid.

173. TOL to Abel Stearns, March 12, 1856, Box 40, Stearns Collection.

174. Gates, "Land Business of Thomas O. Larkin," 337–38.

175. Abel Stearns to TOL, June 4, 1856, *Larkin Papers*, 10:278.

176. TOL to John B. R. Cooper, August 6, 1856, ibid., 10:293.

177. On property assessed at $124,700, Larkin was delinquent for $2,909.66 in taxes. *San Francisco Bulletin*, August 27, 1856.

178. Roger W. Lotchin, *San Francisco, 1846–1856: From Hamlet to City* (New York: Oxford University Press, 1974), 268.

179. Abel Stearns to TOL, August 5, 1856, *Larkin Papers*, 10:292.

180. Republican State Central Committee to TOL, November 6, 1856, Larkin, "Correspondence and Papers," C–B/105:94. There is a hint that Larkin himself ran for office in 1856. A receipt from Farries[?] Edwards, dated September 22, 1856, acknowledges "Fourteen dollars for one hundred copies of the Star of Empire for the campaign of T. O. Larkin." Ibid., C–B/105:74. On the other hand, the payment could have been related to Larkin's efforts on the behalf of others. A biographical sketch published in 1859, which Rachel had helped prepare, states that Larkin had never been a candidate for political office. Day, "Thomas O. Larkin," 51.

181. For example, see Pablo de la Guerra to TOL, August 16, 1856, *Larkin Papers*, 10:294–95.

182. David Spence to TOL, September 29, 1856, ibid., 10:308.

183. TOL to Alpheus Hardy, August 2, 1856, ibid., 10:290. Larkin's support of

Frémont was evidence of his objectivity. Frémont had made no attempt in the past few years to ingratiate himself to Larkin or Californians. He had declined an invitation to attend Larkin's welcoming party at the Irving House in 1850. He was too busy, he said. He declined to dine—at his convenience—with the Pioneer Society of California in April 1854. He was pressed for time. The following September, in a letter signed by Larkin and others, the Society invited him to a dinner in his honor, and he declined once more. John C. Frémont to the Pioneer Society of California, April 30, 1854, Spence, ed., *Expeditions of John Charles Frémont*, 3:478.

Chapter 12. Repose

1. A detailed description of the house is in TOL to Frederic Larkin and Francis Larkin, May 8, 1854, Larkin Family Collection.
2. *Larkin Papers*, 10:xv; Larkin, "Correspondence and Papers," C–B/105:79.
3. TOL, "Correspondence and Papers," C–B/105, contains scores of bills and receipts for household expenses. A study of them could lead to interesting conclusions about the good life in San Francisco in the 1850s.
4. Ibid., C–B/105:71, 80, 93, 109, 110; TOL to Frederic Larkin and Francis Larkin, December 31, 1854, Larkin Family Collection.
5. Ebenezer L. Childs to TOL, February 2, 1854, *Larkin Papers*, 10:15.
6. Thomas O. Larkin, Jr., to Frederic Larkin and Francis Larkin, May 19, 1853. Ibid.
7. Thomas O. Larkin, Jr., to Frederick Larkin and Francis Larkin, December 27, 1853, ibid.; Ebenezer L. Childs to TOL, February 2, 1854, *Larkin Papers*, 10:15.
8. TOL to Frederick Larkin and Francis Larkin, July 7, 1853, Larkin Family Collection.
9. TOL to Thomas O. Larkin, Jr., May 13, 1854, ibid.; Thomas O. Larkin, Jr., to TOL and Rachel H. Larkin, June 18, 1854, *Larkin Papers*, 10:74.
10. TOL to Frederic Larkin and Francis Larkin, October 25, 1853, Larkin Family Collection.
11. TOL to Frederic Larkin and Francis Larkin, October 15, 1854. Ibid.
12. Ebenezer L. Childs to TOL, June 3, 1856, *Larkin Papers*, 10:276.
13. TOL to John B. R. Cooper, December 18, 1856, ibid., 10:336.
14. TOL to Jacob P. Leese, January 3, 1857, Vallejo Collection.
15. Rachel H. Larkin to Alfred Larkin, October 4, 1858, Larkin Family Collection.
16. David Spence to TOL, December 24, 1854, Larkin, "Correspondence and Papers," C–B/105:137; *Colville's San Francisco Directory, 1856* (San Francisco: Commercial Steam Presses, 1856), 124; Melville Attwood to TOL, June 19 and November 22, 1856; William D. Phelps to TOL, May 3, 1855, *Larkin Papers*, 10:281, 330, 149; Thomas O. Larkin, Jr., to Dear Uncle [John B. R. Cooper], February 19, 1857, Vallejo Documents. 36:238.
17. Indenture, Thomas O. Larkin, Jr., to TOL, October 15, 1857, Larkin Family Collection.
18. Frederick H. Larkin to TOL, March 17, April, 2, May 2, 1856, *Larkin Papers*, 10:249–50, 254, 267; Mortimer D. Butler to TOL, [August 14, 1858], also August 30, 1858, Larkin Family Collection. Butler and Larkin were associated in a gold-mining operation in Nevada County in 1856. By early 1858, Butler was working for Larkin on the Children's rancho.
19. TOL to John B. R. Cooper, April 28, 1857, *Larkin Papers*, 10:344.
20. TOL to Abel Stearns, April, 24, 1856, in Hawgood, ed., *First and Last Consul*,

104. Stearns replied: "The days that are past never return so we must content ourselves with the future." Abel Stearns to TOL, May 7, 1856, *Larkin Papers*, 10:271. In his dark mood, Larkin likely was not reassured.

21. Hawgood, ed., *First and Last Consul*, Appendix A, 109−18. Larkin might have gotten the idea from Stearns, who had begun such a list, probably in 1839. The Stearns document shows name, country of origin, profession, and marital status. Abel Stearns, Partial List of Foreigners [in Los Angeles?], [1839?], Box 61, Stearns Collection. Larkin at first thought to restrict his list to those living in California in 1834, thereby suggesting a more exclusive roll, which would still include himself, but changed the date later to 1840. TOL to Abel Stearns, Nicholas Den, and David Spence, June 14, 1856, in Hawgood, ed., *First and Last Consul*, 107; TOL to Abel Stearns et al., July 1, 1856, ibid., 107−108. During the following two months, Larkin corresponded with many others, soliciting names and corrections to his list.

22. John Gilroy to TOL, July 28, 1856, *Larkin Papers*, 10:286.

23. TOL to The Society of California Pioneers, July 20, 1857, Larkin Family Collection. Larkin was president of the Society in 1856−1857. The Society was organized in August 1850 when he was absent in the East.

24. There is a disturbing sidelight to the suggestion here that Larkin was a sensitive, caring person. John Gilroy, aged, indigent, and unwell, wrote several times to him to ask for assistance. John Gilroy to TOL, November 21, 1851, March 27, 1855, July 28, November 25, and December 30, 1856, *Larkin Papers*, 9:62, 10:140, 287, 330−32, 338. Since Larkin made few copies of outgoing letters in the 1850s, it is perhaps unfair to draw conclusions based on the absence of letters, but the content of Gilroy's pathetic appeals suggests that Larkin did not respond.

25. William P. Gibbons to TOL, February 7, 1854; Archibald H. Gillespie to TOL, September 3, 1855, ibid., 10:17, 195.

26. TOL to James Buchanan, January 17, 1857, Letters of Application and Recommendation During the Administrations of Franklin Pierce and James Buchanan, 1853−1861, Records of the Department of State, National Archives, reprinted in Harlan Hague, "The Reluctant Retirement of Thomas O. Larkin," *California History* 62 (Spring 1983): 64−65.

27. Ibid., 65.

28. TOL to Frederic Larkin and Francis Larkin, May 8, 1854, and May 14, 1854, Larkin Family Collection.

29. Mortimor D. Butler to TOL, [September 3?], September 20, 28, October 7, 10 and 13, 1858, Larkin Family Collection.

30. In San Francisco, the following newspapers carried articles or extended obituaries: *Alta California, Chronicle, Evening Bulletin, Evening News, Herald*, and *Times*. These newspapers were joined in Sacramento by the *Daily Union*. Kelsey, "The United States Consulate in California," 1:252.

31. *San Francisco Alta California*, October 29, 1858.

32. Burial Register, Trinity Episcopal Church, San Francisco, and letter from Burton Weaver, Administrator of Trinity Episcopal Church, to David J. Langum, dated August 25, 1987, in the possession of David J. Langum.

33. The information on Lone Mountain Cemetery comes from a later lawsuit concerning its continued operation after it had become engulfed by urban development. Laurel Hill Cemetery *v.* City & County of San Francisco, 152 Cal. 464, 93 P. 70 (1907).

34. Lot 5, Section L, shown on Location Card, provided by Cypress Lawn Cemetery, Colma, California.

35. TOL to Ebenezer L. Childs, May 11, 1831, in Parker, ed., *Chapters in the Early Life of Thomas Oliver Larkin*, 57.

BIBLIOGRAPHY

Manuscript Primary Sources

Alvarado, Juan Bautista. "Historia de California." Bancroft Library, University of California, Berkeley.

Alviso, José Antonio. Documentos para la historia de California. Bancroft Library, University of California, Berkeley.

Appleton Collection. Baker Library, Harvard Business School, Cambridge, Massachusetts.

Atherton, Faxon Dean. Papers. Bancroft Library, University of California, Berkeley.

Bidwell, John. Bidwell Collection. California State Library, Sacramento.

Burial Register, Trinity Episcopal Church, 1858. San Francisco.

Burnett, Peter Hardeman. Correspondence and Papers. Bancroft Library, University of California, Berkeley.

Chamberlain, John. "Memoirs of California Since 1840." Bancroft Library, University of California, Berkeley.

Cowan, Robert Ernest. Cowan Collection. Bancroft Library, University of California, Berkeley.

Fitch, Henry D. Documents. Bancroft Library, University of California, Berkeley.

Frémont, Jessie Benton. "Secret Affairs Relating to the Mexican War." Huntington Library, San Marino, California.

Guerra Family Collection. The Huntington Library, San Marino, California.

Halleck, Peachy and Billings Collection. University Research Library, University of California, Los Angeles.

Kelsey, Rayner Wickersham. Correspondence. Bancroft Library, University of California, Berkeley.

Larkin Family Collection. The Huntington Library, San Marino, California.

Larkin Genealogies. Larkin House, Monterey, California.

Larkin, Thomas O. Accounts. Bancroft Library, University of California, Berkeley.

————. Correspondence and Papers [C–B 105, 1825–1867]. Bancroft Library, University of California, Berkeley.

————. Correspondence and Papers [C–B 620, 1831–1859]. Bancroft Library, University of California, Berkeley.

————. Documents. Bancroft Library, University of California, Berkeley.

————. Private Record of Lots Sold. Bancroft Library, University of California, Berkeley.

Leidesdorff, William A. Leidesdorff Collection. Huntington Library. San Marino, California.

Map, Sacramento River gold camps, 1849, Weimar, Germany. Map Collection, Bancroft Library, University of California, Berkeley.

287

Marsh, John. Manuscript Collection. California State Library, Sacramento.
Reading, Pierson B. Manuscript Collection. California State Library, Sacramento.
Savage, Thomas. Documentos para la historia de California. 4 vols. Bancroft Library, University of California, Berkeley.
Stearns, Abel. Stearns Collection. Huntington Library, San Marino, California.
Sterling, Charles Bolivar. Manuscript Diary. Bancroft Library, University of California, Berkeley.
Streeter, William A. "Recollections of Historical Events in California, 1843–1878." Bancroft Library, University of California. Berkeley.
United States Districts Courts, Northern and Southern Districts of California. *Claims for Mission Lands*. San Francisco, 1859.
United States *Fifth Census of the United States, 1830*. North Carolina, New Hanover County.
United States State Department. Instructions to Consuls. June 24, 1841–May 24, 1847, Vol. 2. National Archives, Washington, D.C.
Vallejo, Mariano G. Documentos para la historia de California. 37 vols. Bancroft Library, University of California, Berkeley.
———. "Historical and Personal Memoirs Relating to Alta California" (translation). 5 vols. Bancroft Library, University of California, Berkeley.
———. Vallejo Collection. Huntington Library, San Marino, California.
Willey, Samuel H. Correspondence of Samuel Hopkins Willey, Concerning Larkin. Bancroft Library, University of California, Berkeley.
Wilson, James. Papers. New Hampshire Historical Society, Concord, New Hampshire.

Printed Primary Sources

Anonymous, *Colville's San Francisco Directory, 1856*. San Francisco: Commercial Steam Presses, 1856.
Anonymous, ed. "The Leese Scrap Book." *Society of California Pioneers Quarterly* 8 (March 1931): 9–37.
Bancroft, George. "Documentary." Edited by Robert E. Cowan. *California Historical Society Quarterly* 2 (July 1923): 161–72.
Beers, Henry P., ed. "The American Consulate in California: Documents Relating to Its Establishment." *California Historical Society Quarterly* 37 (March 1958): 1–17.
Belden, Josiah. *Josiah Belden, 1841 California Overland Pioneer: His Memoir and Early Letters*. Edited by Doyce B. Nunis, Jr. Georgetown, Calif.: The Talisman Press, 1962.
Bidwell, John. *In California Before the Gold Rush*. Los Angeles: Ward Ritchie Press, 1948.
Brooks, Sarah Merriam. *Across the Isthmus to California in '52*. San Francisco: C. A. Murdock & Company, 1894.
Browne, J. Ross. *Report of the Debates in the Convention of California*. Washington, D.C.: John T. Towers, 1850.
Bryant, Edwin. *What I Saw in California: Being the Journal of a Tour, . . . in the years 1846, 1847*. 1848. Reprint. Minneapolis: Ross & Haines, 1967.

Carson, Kit. *Kit Carson's Autobiography*. 1858 [1859?]. Reprint. Edited and with
an introduction by Milo M. Quaife. Lincoln: University of Nebraska Press,
1967.

Colton, Walter. *Three Years in California*. 1850. Reprint. Stanford: Stanford University Press, 1949.

Dana, Richard H., Jr. *Two Years Before the Mast: A Personal Narrative of Life at
Sea*. 1840. Reprint. 2 vols., edited by John H. Kemble. Los Angeles: Ward
Ritchie Press, 1964.

Davis, William Heath, Jr. *Seventy-Five Years in California*. 1929. Reprint. San
Francisco: John Howell-Books, 1967.

Day, F. H. "Sketches of the Early Settlers of California. Mrs. Thomas O. Larkin." *The Hesperian* 2 (May 1859): 97–100.

————. "Sketches of the Early Settlers of California. Thomas Oliver Larkin."
The Hesperian 2 (April 1859): 49–53.

Farnham, Thomas Jefferson. *Travels in the Californias, and Scenes in the Pacific
Ocean*. 1844. Reprint. *Travels in California*, Oakland: Biobooks, 1947.

Frémont, John Charles. *The Expeditions of John Charles Frémont*. 3 vols. Urbana:
University of Illinois Press; Vol. 2, *The Bear Flag Revolt and the Court-
Martial*, edited by Mary Lee Spence and Donald Jackson, 1973; Vol. 3,
Travels from 1848 to 1854, edited by Mary Lee Spence, 1984.

————. *Memoirs of My Life*. Chicago: Belford, Clarke & Company, 1887.

Heustis, Daniel D. *A Narrative of the adventures and sufferings of Captain Daniel
D. Heustis and his companions*. Boston: Redding & Company, 1847. Reprint.
Remarkable Adventures: California, 1845. Los Angeles: Glen Dawson, 1957.

Johnson, Overton, and William H. Winter. *Route Across the Rocky Mountains*.
1846. Reprint. New York: Da Capo Press, 1972.

Larkin, Thomas O. *First and Last Consul: Thomas Oliver Larkin and the Americanization of California*. Edited by John A. Hawgood. 2d ed. Palo Alto: Pacific
Books, Publishers, 1970.

————. *The Larkin Papers: Personal, Business, and Official Correspondence of
Thomas Oliver Larkin, Merchant and United States Consul in California*. Ed-
ited by George P. Hammond. 10 vols. and index. Berkeley: University of
California Press, 1951–1968.

————. "My Itinerary: U.S. America." Edited by Robert J. Parker. *California
Historical Society Quarterly* 16 (March and June 1937): 11–29, 144–71.
Reprinted in Robert J. Parker, ed., *Chapters in the Early Life of Thomas
Oliver Larkin, Including His Experiences in the Carolinas and Building of the
Larkin House at Monterey*. San Francisco: California Historical Society,
1939.

————. "Six New Larkin Letters." Edited by Doyce B. Nunis, Jr. *Southern California Quarterly* 49 (March 1967): 65–103.

Lawsuit, Laurel Hill Cemetery *v.* City & County of San Francisco, 152 Cal. 464,
93 P. 70.

Lincoln, William E. *Lincoln, Pearce, Porter & Ayer & Related Families*. Pittsburgh, 1930.

Marsh, John. "Letter of Dr. John Marsh to Hon. Lewis Cass." *California Historical Quarterly* 22 (December 1943): 315–22.

(Monterey) *Californian*, 13 February 1847, 27 February 1847, 6 March 1847.

Morris, Albert Ferdinand. "The Journal of a 'Crazy Man': Travels and Scenes in

California from the Year 1834." Edited by Charles L. Camp. *California Historical Society Quarterly* 15 (June 1936): 103–38; (September 1936): 224–41.

New York Herald, 12 June 1845.

Ord, Angustias de la Guerra. *Occurrences in Hispanic California*. Translated and edited by Francis Price and William H. Ellison. Washington, D.C.: Academy of American Franciscan History, 1956.

Phelps, William D. *Alta California, 1840–1842: The Journal and Observations of William Dane Phelps*. Edited by Briton Cooper Busch. Glendale, Calif.: Arthur H. Clark Company, 1983.

Revere, Joseph Warren. *A Tour of Duty in California*. 1849. Reprint. *Naval Duty in California*. Oakland: Biobooks, 1947.

Robinson, Alfred. *Life in California*. 1846. Reprint. New York: Da Capo Press, 1969.

Saint Louis Daily Reveille, 13 September 1846.

San Francisco Alta California, 22 November 1849.

San Francisco Bulletin, 27 August 1856.

Sherman, William T. *Memoirs of General William T. Sherman*. 2 vols. New York: A. Appleton and Company, 1875.

Soulé, Frank, John H. Gihons, and James Nisbet. *The Annals of San Francisco*. 1855. Reprint. Palo Alto: Lewis Osborne, 1966.

Stevenson, Robert Louis, "The Old Pacific Capital (Monterey)," *Fraser's Magazine* (November 1880). Reprinted in Robert Louis Stevenson, *From Scotland to Silverado*, edited by James D. Hart. Cambridge: Belknap Press of Harvard University Press, 1966.

Thomes, William H. *On Land and Sea, or California in the Years 1843, '44, and '45*. Boston: DeWolfe, Fiske & Company, 1884.

United States Bureau of the Census. *Historical Statistics of the United States, Colonial Times to 1970, Bicentennial Edition, Part 1*. Washington, D.C.: U.S. Government Printing Office, 1975, updated by monthly periodical, U.S. Department of Commerce, Bureau of Economic Analysis, *Survey of Current Business*.

United States Congress. *Reports from the Court of Claims Submitted to the House of Representatives*. 36th Cong., 2d sess., 1860–1861. Report No. 274. Serial 110.

United States District Court, Northern California. Records. U.S. Land commission cases 325 and 345.

United States Supreme Court, The United States *v.* Thomas O. Larkin and John S. Missroon, 59 U.S. 557, Sup. Ct., 15 L. Ed. 486 (1855).

White, William F. [William Grey, pseud.]. *A Picture of Pioneer Times in California*. San Francisco: W. M. Hinton & Company, 1881.

Wood, William Maxwell. *Wandering Sketches of People and Things*. Philadelphia: Carey and Hart, 1849.

Secondary Sources

Ames, George Walcott, Jr. "Gillespie and the Conquest of California." *California Historical Society Quarterly* 17 (June 1938): 123–140; (September 1938): 271–350.

Ashe, S. A. *History of North Carolina.* 2 vols. 1925. Reprint. Spartanburg, S.C.: Reprint Co., 1971.

Bancroft, Hubert Howe. Biographical Notes. Bancroft Library, University of California, Berkeley.

———. *California Pioneer Register and Index, 1542–1848.* Baltimore: Regional Publishing Company, 1964. Extracted from Bancroft, *History of California,* 7 vols., 1884–90, vols. 2–5.

———. *History of California.* 1884–1890. Reprint. 7 vols. Santa Barbara: Wallace Hebberd, 1963–1970.

Bell, Catherine M. "A Row of Old Houses." In Katherine Bell Cheney, *Swinging the Censer: Reminiscences of Old Santa Barbara.* Santa Barbara, 1931.

Bowman, J. N. "Libraries in Provincial California." *Historical Society of Southern California Quarterly* 43 (September 1961): 426–39.

Bowman, Mary M. "California's First American School and Its Teacher." *Annual Publication, Historical Society of Southern California* 10, Parts 1 and 2 (1915–1916): 86–94.

Burgess, Sherwood D. "Lumbering in Hispanic California." *California Historical Society Quarterly* 41 (September 1962): 237–48.

Cashman, Diane Cobb. *Cape Fear Adventure: An Illustrated History of Wilmington.* Woodland Hills, Calif.: Windsor Publications, 1982.

Chorley, Lloyd K. "Thomas O. Larkin, Early California Business Man." M. A. thesis, University of California, Berkeley, 1930.

Clarke, Dwight L. *William Tecumseh Sherman: Gold Rush Banker.* San Francisco: California Historical Society, 1969.

Cleland, Robert Glass. "The Early Sentiment for the Annexation of California: An Account of the Growth of American Interest in California, 1835–1846." *The Southwestern Historical Quarterly* 18 (July 1914): 1–40; (October 1914): 121–61; (January 1915): 231–60.

Cowan, Robert G. *Ranchos of California: a list of Spanish Concessions, 1775–1822, and Mexican Grants, 1822–1846.* Los Angeles: Historical Society of Southern California, 1977.

Cumming, W. P. *North Carolina in Maps.* Raleigh: State Department of Archives and History, 1966.

Dallas, Sherman F. "The Hide and Tallow Trade in Alta California, 1822–1846." Ph.D. dissertation, Indiana University, 1955.

DeVoto, Bernard. *The Year of Decision: 1846.* Boston: Little Brown and Company, 1943.

Dillon, Richard. *Great Expectations: The Story of Benicia, California.* Fresno, Calif.: Thomas Lithograph and Printing Company, 1980.

Ellington, Charles G. *The Trial of U. S. Grant: The Pacific Coast Years, 1852–1854.* Glendale, Calif.: The Arthur H. Clark Company, 1987.

Rawls, James J. *Indians of California: The Changing Image.* Norman: University of Oklahoma Press, 1984.

Robinson, W. W. *Land in California: The Story of Mission Lands, Ranchos, Squatters, Mining Claims, Railroad Grants, Land Scrip, Homesteads.* Berkeley: University of California Press, 1948.

Royce, Josiah. *California, from the conquest in 1846 to the second vigilance committee in San Francisco, a study of American character.* 1886. Reprint, with an introduction by Earl Pomery, Santa Barbara: Peregrine Publishers, 1970.

Engelhardt, Zephyrin. *The Missions and Missionaries of California.* 4 vols. and index. San Francisco: James H. Barry Company, 1908–1916.

Gates, Paul W. "The California Land Act of 1851." *California Historical Society Quarterly* 50 (December 1971): 395–430.

————. "The Land Business of Thomas O. Larkin." *California Historical Quarterly* 54 (Winter 1975): 323–44.

Gebhard, David. "Some Additional Observations on California's Monterey Tradition." *Journal of the Society of Architectural Historians* 46 (June 1987): 157–70.

Geiger, Maynard. *Franciscan Missionaries in Hispanic California, 1769–1848.* San Marino, Calif.: The Huntington Library, 1969.

Graebner, Norman. *Empire on the Pacific: A Study in American Continental Expansion.* New York: Ronald Press Company, 1955.

Green, Will S. *The History of Colusa County, California and General History of the State.* Sacramento: The Sacramento Lighography Company, 1950.

Gross, Harold William. "The Influence of Thomas O. Larkin Toward the Acquisition of California." M.A. thesis, University of California, Berkeley, 1937.

Hague, Harlan. "The Reluctant Retirement of Thomas O. Larkin." *California History* 62 (Spring 1983): 60–66.

Harlow, Neal. *California Conquered: War and Peace on the Pacific, 1846–1850.* Berkeley: University of California Press, 1982.

Hawgood, John A. "John C. Frémont and the Bear Flag Revolution: A Reappraisal." *Southern California Quarterly* 44 (June 1962): 67–96.

Heizer, Robert F., and Alan F. Almquist. *The Other Californians: Prejudice and Discrimination under Spain, Mexico, and the United States to 1920.* Berkeley: University of California Press, 1971.

Huff, Boyd. *El Puerto de los Balleneros: Annals of the Sausalito Whaling Anchorage.* Early California Travels Series. Los Angeles: Glen Dawson, 1957.

Huggins, Dorothy H., comp. *Continuation of the Annals of San Francisco.* San Francisco: California Historical Society, 1939.

Hussey, John Adam. "New Light Upon Talbot H. Green." *California Historical Quarterly* 18 (March 1939): 32–63.

————. "The Origin of the Gillespie Mission." *California Historical Society Quarterly* 19 (March 1940): 43–58.

Jackson, Sheldon G. *A British Ranchero in Old California: The Life and Times of Henry Dalton and the Rancho Azusa.* Glendale, Calif.: The Arthur H. Clark Company, 1977.

Johnson, Kenneth M. *The New Almaden Quicksilver Mine.* Georgetown, Calif.: The Talisman Press, 1963.

Jones, Chester L. *The Consular Service of the United States, its History and Activities.* Philadelphia: University of Philadelphia, 1906.

Kelsey, Rayner W. "The United States Consulate in California." *Publications in Pacific Coast History.* 2 vols. Berkeley: University of California Press, 1910–1911.

Kirker, Harold. "The Larkin House Revisited." *California History* 65 (March 1986): 26–33.

————. "The Role of Hispanic Kinships in Popularizing the Monterey Style in

California, 1836–1846." *Journal of the Society of Architectural Historians* 43 (October 1984): 250–55.

Langum, David J. *Law and Community on the Mexican California Frontier: Anglo-American Expatriates and the Clash of Legal Traditions, 1821–1846.* Norman: University of Oklahoma Press, 1987.

Lotchin, Roger W. *San Francisco, 1846–1856: From Hamlet to City.* New York: Oxford University Press, 1974.

Lyman, George D. *John Marsh, Pioneer: The Life Story of a Trail-blazer on Six Frontiers.* New York: Charles Scribner's Sons, 1931.

McKittrick, Myrtle M. *Vallejo, Son of California.* Portland, Oregon: Binfords & Mort, 1944.

Ogden, Adele. *The California Sea Otter Trade, 1784–1848.* 1941. Reprint. Berkeley: University of California Press, 1975.

Parker, Robert J. "Building the Larkin House." *California Historical Society Quarterly* 16 (December 1937), 321–35. Reprinted in Robert J. Parker, ed., *Chapters in the Early Life of Thomas Oliver Larkin, Including His Experiences in the Carolinas and Building of the Larkin House at Monterey.* San Francisco: California Historical Society, 1939.

———. "California's Larkin Settles Old Debts: A View of North Carolina, 1846–1856." *North Carolina Historical Review* 17 (October 1940): 332–46.

———. "Larkin, Anglo-American Businessman in Mexican California." In Adele Ogden, ed., *Greater America: Essays in Honor of Herbert Eugene Bolton*, 415–29. Berkeley: University of California Press, 1945.

———. "Larkin's Monterey Business: Articles of Trade, 1833–1839." *Historical Society of Southern California Quarterly* 24 (June 1942): 54–62.

———. "Larkin's Monterey Customers." *Historical Society of Southern California Quarterly* 24 (June 1942): 41–53.

———. "Peddler's Empire: The Life of Thomas O. Larkin." Unpublished manuscript. California Historical Society. San Francisco, California.

———. "Secret Affairs of the Mexican War: Larkin's California Mission." *Historical Society of Southern California Quarterly* 20 (March 1938): 22–28.

———. "A Sketch of Larkin's Life and an Introduction to His "My Itinerary: U.S. America." *California Historical Society Quarterly* 16 (March 1937): 3–10. Reprinted in Parker, Robert J., ed., *Chapters in the Early Life of Thomas Oliver Larkin, Including His Experiences in the Carolinas and Building of the Larkin House at Monterey.* San Francisco: California Historical Society, 1939.

———. "Thomas Oliver Larkin in 1831." *California Historical Society Quarterly* 16 (September 1937): 263–70. Reprinted in Parker, Robert J., ed., *Chapters in the Early Life of Thomas Oliver Larkin, Including His Experiences in the Carolinas and Building of the Larkin House at Monterey.* San Francisco: California Historical Society, 1939.

Pulliam, James T. "Business Prelude to Conquest: Larkin and Micheltorena." M.A. thesis, Chico [California] State College, 1966.

Pyle, John William. "Thomas O. Larkin: California Business Man, 1832–1844." M.A. thesis, University of California, Berkeley, 1938.

Sikes, Leon H. *Duplin County Places: Past and Present, A Guide to Duplin County,*
   N.C. Wallace, N.C.: by the author, 1984.
Smith, Gene Allen. "The Propaganda Campaign of Thomas Oliver Larkin."
   M.A. thesis, Auburn University, 1987.
Underhill, Reuben C. *From Cowhides to Golden Fleece: A Narrative of California,*
   1832–1858, Based upon Unpublished Correspondence of THOMAS OLIVER
   LARKIN, Trader, Developer, Promoter, and only American Consul. Stanford,
   Calif.: Stanford University Press, 1939.
Wiltsee, Ernest A. "The British Vice Consul in California and the Events of 1846.
   Quarterly of the California Historical Society 10 (June 1931): 99–128.
Woolfenden, John, and Amelie Elkinton. *Cooper: Juan Bautista Rogers Cooper: Sea*
   Captain, Adventurer, Ranchero and Early California Pioneer, 1791–1872. Pa-
   cific Grove, Calif.: Boxwood Press, 1983.
Wright, Doris M. *A Yankee in Mexican California: Abel Stearns, 1798–1848.*
   Santa Barbara: Wallace Hebberd, 1977.

Index

The notes have not been separately indexed; however, many contain substantive information and should be consulted along with the parallel textual references.

295